WILEY SERIES IN MANAGERIAL ECONOMICS

Editor

Paul H Rubin, Emory University, Atlanta, USA

HIGGINS and RUBIN Deregulating Telecommunications

ECONOMIC INPUTS, LEGAL OUTPUTS

ECONOMIC INPUTS, LEGAL OUTPUTS

THE ROLE OF ECONOMISTS IN MODERN ANTITRUST

Fred McChesney, Cornell University, Ithaca, NY, USA

JOHN WILEY & SONS
Chichester • New York • Weinheim • Brisbane • Singapore • Toronto

Baffins Lane, Chichester,
West Sussex PO19 1UD, England

National 01243 779777
International (+44) 1243 779777
e-mail (for orders and customer service enquiries): cs-books@wiley.co.uk
Visit our Home Page on http://www.wiley.co.uk
or http://www.wiley.com

Other Editorial Offices
John Wiley & Sons, Inc., 605 Third Avenue,
New York, NY 10158-0012, USA

WILEY-VCH Verlag GmbH
Pappelallee 3, D-69469 Weinheim, Germany

Jacaranda Wiley Ltd, 33 Park Road, Milton,
Queensland 4064, Australia

John Wiley & Sons (Asia) Pte Ltd, Clementi Loop #02-01,
Jin Xing Distripark, Singapore 129809

John Wiley & Sons (Canada) Ltd, 22 Worcester Road,
Rexdale, Ontario M9W 1L1, Canada

British Library Cataloguing in Publication Data

A catalogue record for this book is available from the British Library

ISBN 0-471-97074-3

Typeset in 10/12pt Times from the authors' disks by Techset Composition Limited, Salisbury
Printed and bound by Antony Rowe Ltd, Eastbourne
This book is printed on acid-free paper responsibly manufactured from sustainable forestry, in which at least two trees are planted for each one used for paper production.

CONTENTS

About the Editor

Fred S. McChesney

Fred S. McChesney is Professor of Law at Cornell University. Previously, he was Robert T. Thompson Professor of Law and Professor of Economics, Emory University. He has also taught at the University of Chicago, the University of Miami, Northwestern University and the Université d'Aix-Marseille (France). His law degree is from the University of Miami, and his PhD (economics) from the University of Virginia. Following law school, he clerked in the United States Court of Appeals for the Ninth Circuit, practiced law with the Washington, DC, firm of Steptoe & Johnson, and served as associate director of the Federal Trade Commission's Bureau of Consumer Protection. Professor McChesney has written dozens of articles for economics and law journals. He is the co-author of *Causes and Consequences of Antitrust: The Public Choice Perspective* (University of Chicago Press, 1995) and a casebook, *Antitrust Law: Interpretation and Implementation* (Michie/Lexis, 1998). His book, *Money for Nothing: Politicians, Rent Extraction and Political Extortion* (Harvard University Press) appeared in 1997.

About the Contributors

Roger Blair

Roger Blair is the Huber Hurst Professor of Business and Legal Studies in the Department of Economics at the University of Florida. He is the co-author of *Antitrust Economics, Law and Economics of Vertical Integration and Control*, and *Monopsony: Antitrust Law and Economics*. He has published extensively in economics journals and law reviews. He has served as an antitrust economics consultant to the Federal Trade Commission, the Antitrust Division of the Department of Justice, and the Attorneys-General of Arizona, California, Florida, Missouri, Oregon, and Washington. Professor Blair is on the editorial boards of *The Antitrust Bulletin* and the *Review of Industrial Organization*.

Duncan J. Cameron

Duncan J. Cameron is a Senior Vice President of Capital Economics and Director of the Los Angeles and Silicon Valley offices. Dr Cameron specializes in antitrust economics, damage assessment, vertical restraints, securities, and regulatory matters. His experience in the antitrust area includes analysis of a number of mergers as well as monopolization, price fixing, vertical restraints, tying and price discrimination matters. Dr Cameron also has experience in the calculation of damages in cases involving breach of contract, securities fraud, patent infringement and other commercial litigation.

Dr. Cameron's analyses of mergers and joint ventures have covered a wide variety of industries, including basic manufacturing, high-tech manufacturing, and services and he has testified before Federal agencies in a number of these matters.

Dr. Cameron has also written, published and presented papers in the areas of medical care cost containment, the significance of 'captive' production in merger analysis, antitrust market definition, economic analysis of mergers in differentiated products industries, hospital mergers, financial trading rules and pricing of spot radio advertising. He is currently Adjunct Professor at the University of Utah and also taught at UCLA, George Mason University, California State University, Los Angeles, and California State University, Long Beach.

Dr Cameron holds a PhD in Economics from UCLA. He is a member of the American and Western Economic Associations and the American Bar Association.

Andrew Dick

Andrew Dick is an economist with the Antitrust Division, US Department of Justice. Before joining the division in 1996, he was a Assistant Professor of Economics at UCLA for seven years. Andrew has published twenty articles on antitrust economics, international trade theory, and industrial organization. He is the author of *Industrial Policy and Semiconductors: Missing the Target*. Currently, Andrew is working on an extended research project assessing the competitive dynamics of industry cartels. His chapter was written while he was on the UCLA faculty.

Luke Froeb

Luke Froeb (AB Stanford; PhD Wisconsin) is an Associate Professor of Management at the Owen Graduate School of Management at Vanderbilt University. Professor Froeb previously worked at the Antitrust Division on merger, price-fixing, bid rigging, sentencing, and discrimination cases. Professor Froeb credits his experience at Justice with exposing him to a wide range of problems that continue to shape his research agenda.

During his time at Justice, Professor Froeb became especially interested in empirical analysis of mergers, publishing a series of articles critical of 'structural' merger policy. Professor Froeb's dissatisfaction with merger policy lead him and colleague Gregory Werden to develop an alternative methodology to 'simulate' or compute the effects of mergers. Recently both the Justice Department and FTC have begun using this computational approach with Froeb's software, Sim Merger™. Froeb has also developed computational models for analyzing mergers in auction markets and maintains an antitrust web site ⟨www.antitrust.org⟩.

Mark A. Glick

Mark A. Glick is a Special Consultant to Capital Economics. Dr Glick's fields of expertise include antitrust industrial organization matters, intellectual property damages and tort damage matters. He has published very many articles.

Dr Glick has consulted in a wide variety of industries including: oil, industrial chemicals, waste management, computer software, steel, retail food, aerospace, explosives, electrical equipment, hospitals, telecommunications, electric generation and transmission.

Dr Glick is a professor of economics at the University of Utah where he teaches industrial organization and law and economics. He is also an adjunct professor at the University of Utah College of Law where he has taught law and economics and regulated industries. Dr Glick has also taught at UCLA, NYU, Barnard College, and California State University–Los Angeles. Dr. Glick was formerly a member of the antitrust department of Skadden, Arps, Slate, Meagher & Florn.

Mark Glick holds a PhD in economics from the New School for Social Research and a JD from Columbia University. He is a member of the American Economics Association, the economics committee of the antitrust section of the American Bar Association and the Industrial Organization Society.

Mark J. Glueck

Mark J. Glueck is a Principal Associate in the litigation and regulatory practice of Nathan Associates Inc., an economic and management consulting firm located in Arlington, Virginia. Mr Glueck's research and consulting involves matters concerning antitrust, intellectual property, international trade and other commercial disputes. He has provided testimony and acted as a consultant in matters before the Federal Trade Commission, Department of Justice, International Trade Commission and federal and state courts. His antitrust consulting has involved questions of market definition, assessment of market power, the impact on competition from select business practices and the measurement of damages. Mr Glueck holds a BA in economics from The American University and is a PhD candidate in economics and public finance at the University of Maryland.

Richard S. Higgins

Richard Higgins, Senior Vice President of Capital Economics, supervises the economics component of both merger and other antitrust investigations. He received a PhD in economics from the University of Virginia in 1969 and was a postdoctoral fellow at the University of Chicago in 1975. He was on the faculties of the University of Georgia and Auburn University before joining the US Federal Trade Commission in 1980. Dr. Higgins joined Capital Economics after seven years at the US Federal Trade Commission (FTC) as Deputy Director of the Bureau of Economics.

Dr Higgins is the author of many papers published in professional journals, including the *American Economic Review*, the *Journal of Law and Economics* and the *Journal of Legal Studies*. Several of his papers were first published or reprinted in books on political economy, including *Public Choice and Regulation: A View from Inside the Federal Trade Commission*, edited by Robert Mackay, James C. Miller III and Bruce Yandle. His most recent book, co-edited with Paul Rubin, is a collection of essays by prominent economists on telecommunications, *Deregulating Telecommunications: The Baby Bells Case for Competition*.

Keith N. Hylton

Keith N. Hylton is Professor of Law at Boston University, where he has been teaching since 1995. Professor Hylton, a graduate of Harvard College, holds a JD from Harvard Law School and a PhD in economics from the Massachusetts Institute of Technology. His research is in the area of law and economics, focusing on torts, antitrust, labor law, and the economics of litigation. Professor Hylton has published articles in several economics journals that emphasize law and economics research (such as the *Rand Journal of Economics* and the *Journal of Legal Studies*) and in several law reviews.

David P. Kaplan

David P. Kaplan is President of Capital Economics and specializes in, among other areas, industrial organization and antitrust economics. Mr Kaplan has authored a number of papers concerning antitrust and competition issues, including a book he co-authored entitled *Competition and Concentration: The Economics of the Carbonated Soft Drink Industry*. Mr. Kaplan is a Lecturer in Economics at George Mason University where he teaches microeconomics and an Adjunct Professor of Economics at the University of Utah where he teaches, in junction with others, an antitrust seminar. He has also served as a guest lecturer at the George Washington School of Law and as a consultant to the Federal Trade Commission (Bureau of Economics), the United States Department of Justice, and the Senate Judiciary Committee (on issues related to antitrust). Mr Kaplan has submitted testimony as an expert in the courts, before arbitration panels, before Congress, and before state and federal agencies, including the Department of Justice, the Federal Trade Commission, and the International Trade Commission. Mr Kaplan has a BA and MA in economics from the George Washington University and a JD from the George Washington University National Law Center.

Benjamin Klein

Benjamin Klein is a Professor of Economics at UCLA and President of Economic Analysis Corporation, an economics consulting firm located in Los Angeles. Professor Klein's research is concentrated primarily in the areas of antitrust economics and on questions of efficient contractual arrangements and business organizations. His articles on law and economics have appeared in numerous academic journals, including the *Journal of Law and Economics*, the *American Economic Review* and the *Supreme Court Economic Review*.

Professor Klein has served as a consultant to numerous law firms, corporations and governmental agencies, including the US Federal Reserve Board of Governors, the New Zealand Treasury, the US Federal Trade Commission, Bureaus of Competition and Consumer Protection, and the Antitrust Division of the US Department of Justice. He has testified over the past decade on antitrust, contract, intellectual property and damage issues.

Mark L. Lasser

Mark L. Lasser currently is an Associate in the litigation department of the law firm McCutchen Doyle Brown & Enersen in San Francisco, California. He specializes in antitrust law. Mr. Lasser received his AB, *cum laude*, with distinction in economics, from Duke University in 1992. He received his JD from Northwestern University in 1996.

Michael J. McDonald

Michael J. McDonald is an economist at Capital Economics specializing in economic analysis for the purpose of addressing antitrust issues raised by mergers, price fixing, predatory pricing and vertical restraints. He received his BS from Western Oregon State College, MA from George Mason University and PhD from George Mason University.

Dr McDonald is the author of papers published in *Economic Inquiry* and *Emperica*. His papers have also been published in books addressing antitrust issues, including *The Causes and Consequences of Antitrust: A Public Choice Perspective* and *Deregulating Telecommunications: The Baby Bells Case For Competition*.

William H. Page

William H. Page received a BA in 1973 from Tulane University and a JD *summa cum laude* in 1975 from the University of New Mexico. For three years, he was a trial attorney in the Antitrust Division of the US Department of Justice. In 1979, he received an LLM from the University of Chicago.

He was taught at Boston University School of Law from 1979–81 and 1987–88. Since 1981, he has been on the faculty of Mississippi College School of Law, where he was named J. Will Young Professor of Law in 1991.

He has published numerous articles in, among others, the University of Chicago, Stanford, Michigan, Vanderbilt, and Virginia *Law Reviews*, the *Duke Law Journal*, the *Antitrust Bulletin*, the *Supreme Court Economic Review*, and *Managerial & Decision Economics*. He edited and co-authored *Proving Antitrust Damages: Legal and Economic Issues*, published by the ABA's section on antitrust law.

Eileen C. Reed

Eileen C. Reed is a partner with De Greve & Partners in Washington, DC (the US office of a Dutch management consulting firm). She has a BA in economics from William & Mary and an MA in economics from Georgetown University. Ms Reed has been a consulting economist for over 15 years, engaged in applied microeconomics and financial analysis both at the Federal Trade Commission and in private consulting practice in general business issues, including antitrust and other regulatory areas. Specific industry experience includes competition and market studies in pharmaceuticals; consumer food and household products; cement and other building materials; hospital and physician services; insurance and health care financing. Her focus has been on the evaluation of competitive impact and measurement of potential injury resulting from mergers and acquisitions, vertical restraints, price-fixing, and price discrimination, and other trade restraints frequently in the context of large antitrust court cases in federal and state courts. At De Greve & Partners, Ms Reed is helping European clients participate and expand in US markets and is advising European clients in the area of antitrust policy and compliance.

Richard E. Romano

Richard E. Romano is Gerald L. Gunter Professor of Economics at the University of Florida. He is author of numerous articles on policy issues, with papers appearing in the *American Economic Review*, the *Journal of Political Economy*, and the *Quarterly Journal of Economics*. His present research focus is on education policy with support from the National Science Foundation. He is currently on the editorial board of the *American Economic Review*. He teaches managerial economics, industrial organization, and game theory.

Professor Scheffman

Professor Scheffman is the Justin Potter Professor of American Competitive Enterprise at the Owen Graduate School of Management at Vanderbilt University, where he teaches graduate and Executive Education courses on business strategy, marketing, distribution, pricing, and the valuation and management of intellectual assets. Professor Scheffman is also a Principal in LECG, Inc., a national economics and litigation consulting company. Prior to joining the faculty at Vanderbilt, he held several senior positions at the Federal Trade Commission, including Director of the Bureau of Economics from 1985–88. He received a BA in mathematics and economics, *magna cum laude* from the University of Minnesota and a PhD in economics from MIT.

Professor Scheffman's research has been broad, concentrating currently on antitrust and regulatory economics, business strategy, marketing and pricing, intellectual assets and brand equity. He has lectured widely on antitrust and regulatory issues, business strategy, and marketing.

Scheffman has consulted with a number of companies on a variety of business, marketing, and strategy issues. He has also consulted with numerous attorneys on investigations and matters in litigation, been an expert witness in a number of cases, and has made a number of presentations at the FTC and DOJ.

William F. Shughart II
William F. Shughart II is Professor of Economics and holder of the P. M. B. Self, William King Self, and Henry C. Self Free Enterprise Chair at the University of Mississippi. He received his PhD in economics from Texas A&M University in 1978, and has taught at Clemson University and at George Mason University, where he was also a senior research associate at the Center for Study of Public Choice. Dr Shughart, who served as Special Assistant to the Director of the Federal Trade Commission's Bureau of Economics during the Reagan administration, is a research fellow of the Independent Institute, associate editor of the *Southern Economic Journal*, the book review editor for *Public Choice* and *Managerial and Decision Economics*, and a member of the Southern Economic Association's Board of Trustees.

Dr Shughart has published more than 100 scholarly articles, book chapters, and reviews. His books include *The Organization of Industry* (Irwin 1990; 2nd edn, Dame Publications 1997); *Antitrust Policy and Interest-Group Politics* (Quorum 1990); and *Modern Managerial Economics: Economic Theory for Business Decisions* (South-Western Publishing 1994), co-authored with William F. Chappell and Rex L. Cottle. He is the co-author (with Fred S. McChesney) of *The Causes and Consequences of Antitrust: The Public Choice Perspective* (University of Chicago Press, 1995), and the editor of the Independent Institute book, *Taxing Choice: The Predatory Politics of Fiscal Discrimination* (Transaction Publishers, 1997).

Pablo T. Spiller
Pablo T. Spiller is the Joe Shoong Professor of International Business and Professor of Business and Public Policy at the Haas School of Business of the University of California, Berkeley, a Senior Research Fellow at the Institute for Policy Reform, Washington DC and a Principal at the Law & Economics Consulting Group, Inc. Prior to 1994, he was the W.B. McKinley Professor of Economics and Public Utilities and Professor of Government and Public Affairs at the University of Illinois, Urbana-Champaign. Since 1980, he has been a principal investigator on four National Science Foundation Grants, and has received grants from the National Center for Supercomputer Applications and from the Pittsburgh Supercomputer Center to undertake high powered econometric research. He currently is a Co-Editor of the *Journal of Law, Economics and Organization*, a Co-Editor of the *Journal of Economics and Management Strategy*, and Associate Editor of the *Journal of Industrial Economics* and of the *Journal of Policy Reform*. Much of his academic research has been in the area of antitrust, telecommunications, and regulatory policy in developing countries. He has published over 60 articles in journals and has published three books in the area of antitrust and regulation. He has served as consultant for several telecommunications and utility companies in the United States and overseas, the Federal Trade Commission, the US Department of Transportation, the World Bank and other international organizations.

Timothy J. Tardiff
Timothy J. Tardiff is a Vice President with National Economic Research Associates (NERA). He received a BS with honors in mathematics from the California Institute of Technology and a PhD in social science from the University of California, Irvine. At NERA since 1984, he has conducted research and participated in regulatory proceedings on pricing policies for competitive telecommunications markets, including pricing access services to competitors; actual and potential competition for telecommunications services, including new rate structures; the market potential for mobile telephony: and the terms and conditions for interconnection and unbundled elements, including evaluations of cost models.

Robert D. Tollison
Dr Robert D. Tollison is Duncan Black Professor of Economics and General Director of the Center for Study of Public Choice at George Mason University in Fairfax, Virginia. He has previously held academic appointments at Cornell University, Texas A&M University, Virginia Tech, and Clemson University. Dr Tollison has also served in government twice, once as a senior staff economist on the President's Council of Economic Advisers and again as Director of the Bureau of Economics at the Federal Trade Commission. His academic specialities are in the areas of public choice and industrial organization, where he has published numerous books and articles over the years. He is also the author of a best-selling economic principles textbook for the first college course in economics. Dr Tollison is a past president of the Southern Economic Association and the Public Choice Society. He is also a joint editor of the scientific journal, *Public Choice*. Dr. Tollison has served as a consultant to a wide variety of government agencies and corporations.

Gregory J. Werden
Gregory J. Werden is Director of Research, Economic Analysis Group, Antitrust Division, US Department of Justice. He has worked in the Antitrust Division since receiving a PhD in economics from the University of Wisconsin in 1977. He has been involved with a wide range of antitrust enforcement and competition policy issues. He was a principal author of the 1982 and 1984 Merger Guidelines, the 1997 Merger Guidelines revision on efficiencies, and the 1994 Antitrust Guidelines for Licensing of Intellectual Property. He participated in the preparation of numerous amicus briefs filed with the Supreme Court and the courts of appeals. He has published more than fifty articles on antitrust policy and related issues. His principal areas of research have been market delineation and merger policy.

Introduction: The demand for and supply of economics in modern antitrust

Fred S. McChesney

Cornell University, Ithaca, NY, USA

This book began as a special issue of the journal *Management and Decision Economics*, published in 1996 on the role of economists in modern antitrust. The subject is an interesting one in itself, but also has wider ramifications for the economics profession. Most persons unversed in economics hear about it only in its macro-economic manifestations, when stories about inflation, unemployment and the like make the news. Meanwhile, the large majority of the profession, the microeconomists, toil in relative obscurity.

One exception is the industrial-organization economists involved in antitrust law. Highly publicized legal cases involving corporations like Microsoft, General Electric, Eastman Kodak, and Toys 'R' Us expose to a general audience the fact that economists are key players in antitrust law enforcement. Whether there is general understanding of those players' roles is another matter, one that this book is partly designed to address.

The earlier journal issue could consider only some of the many ways in which economics has come to dominate the law (including enforcement) of antitrust. Thus, a more detailed, book-length treatment of the subject seemed superior. Although complete coverage of all the work that economists do in antitrust would be impossible, the present volume illustrates most of the major tasks that economists are now called upon to perform. The focus is on American antitrust law and the role that economists have played therein.

BACKGROUND

Economists have long studied the subject now known as industrial organization, although its early students, from Smith to Marshall, did not know it by that name. But the modern variant of industrial organization found in courtrooms—antitrust—is of much more recent vintage. As perhaps befits a New World society weaned on capitalism but increasingly raised on law, antitrust was a nineteenth-century American concoction. It was aimed at economic phenomena but derived from mixed political and legal origins (DiLorenzo, 1985; Boudreaux *et al.*, 1995; Ekelund *et al.*, 1995). Produced originally for home consumption, antitrust has been successfully exported from the New World to the Old, even to the Third. The export has found buyers abroad among both economists and lawyers.

That is not to say, however, that economists and lawyers were equally responsible for the birth of antitrust. Indeed, as has been noted elsewhere, economists were largely bystanders as legal and political events coalesced to produce the first antitrust law (Stigler, 1982; McChesney, 1995). Apparently, most economists were not even paying much attention. It was the legal–political establishment—Congress (and earlier, a majority of state legislatures)—that was responsible for antitrust.

Gradually, however, antitrust developed a devoted following among economists. Today, surveys repeatedly show that economists think antitrust a 'good thing'. Whether that is true as a normative proposition, no one would deny as a positive proposition that antitrust has thrust economists into a different realm, the domain of law enforcement.

Such is the subject of this volume: the role of economists in the enforcement of antitrust law (including the reverse effect on economists of their involvement with antitrust). The authors of the chapters that follow are particularly qualified to present the various ways economists function in the world of antitrust. Collectively, they bring great experience to bear on the subject, including not just academic analysis of industrial organization but also work in many dozens of antitrust legal proceedings. In that latter capacity, they have worked for government, private plaintiffs, and private defendants.

Economists involved in antitrust proceedings function in different capacities. One function they typically undertake is not represented in any detail in the chapters that follow: calculation of antitrust damages (treble damages, in most cases).[1] That subject was omitted intentionally here, for two reasons. There already exist many articles on the economically optimal calculation of damages in antitrust cases (e.g. Landes, 1983) and (although there are exceptions) most courtroom exercises in antitrust damage estimation involve as much the use of accounting information and the manipulation of spreadsheet data as they do any application of real economics. American antitrust law has not made the subject any more precise economically by declaring that the showing of damages can be less rigorous, once liability has been found.[2]

ECONOMISTS AND ANTITRUST LIABILITY

Thus, the collection here begins with the role of economists in deciding issues of antitrust liability itself. The work of economists in this domain has expanded exponentially in the past 25 years, largely as a result of three developments, the first in economics and the latter two in law.[3]

a. Identifying Conspiracy

The economic development concerns economists' increasing empirical ability to measure the effects of collusion and (at least some claim) to identify industries in which collusion occurs. In the typical antitrust case, the existence of collusion is a threshold issue. American antitrust law distinguishes broadly between concerted and single-firm behavior.[4] For most of antitrust's history, however, enforcement has concentrated on concerted behavior.

The first chapter of this book, by Richard Higgins, Mark Glueck, David Kaplan and Michael McDonald, illustrates empirically the fundamental economic case against collusion. Higgins *et al.* study the effect of the international aluminum cartel created in 1994. As one would expect, the impact of cartelization on aluminum prices was enormous, amounting to well over a $1 billion transfer from consumers to producers annually. The chapter goes on to estimate, using the event-study methodology developed in financial economics, what the transfer meant for participating firms' wealth. Corroborating the estimates of large consumer losses, the positive stock-price effects for cartel participants were sizable and significant.

International contracts, combinations and conspiracies are not uncommon. (Perhaps the best-known international cartel in recent times was the uranium cartel of the early 1970s.) But, as the chapter by Higgins *et al.* points out, although the antitrust authorities may not like an international cartel agreement orchestrated by various governments, it is not clear what national antitrust law can do about it. However, when the alleged infraction is a domestic collusive agreement in restraint of trade, such as price-fixing, no impediment to antitrust enforcement arises. Successful pursuit of the alleged conspirators, of course, requires a showing that there was indeed collusion.

In many instances, the existence of a contract or conspiracy is undisputed, or can be proven from direct testimony (such as that from a conspirator). However, the allegation of collusion sometimes rests more on circumstantial economic evidence, rather than any direct testimony, that firms have conspired. Especially following an exploratory article by one economically minded antitrust lawyer (Posner, 1969), many economists have tried to use structural variables (things like the number of sellers and product homogeneity) to predict the industries in which anticompetitive activity would be more likely.

The results heretofore have not been promising.[5] The problems are legion, not the least of which is separating the higher prices and reduced quantities that may result from true collusion (conspiracy) from the higher prices and reduced quantities that reflect unilateral behavior in markets that admittedly are not mirrors of textbook-perfect competition. Firms' behavior in duopolies or oligopolies may well be interdependent, but fall short of outright collusion. Economists' predilection for calling interdependent but nonetheless unilateral behavior 'tacit' collusion has confused the issues even further, since collusion under the Sherman Act requires an actual 'contract, combination or conspiracy', not just some 'tacit' understanding.

Inquiries into the determinants of true collusion have been bedeviled also by sample problems. Previous studies have largely concerned themselves with identifying the industry characteristics of *illegal* cartels that have been discovered and brought into the courtroom (e.g. Hay and Kelley, 1974). This sample raises obvious selection problems, as Andrew Dick discusses in the second chapter of this book. Dick analyzes the determinants of collusion in a different way, building on earlier work of his own by looking at *legal* industry cartels formed under the Webb–Pomerene Export Act of 1918.

His findings are interesting, indicating that many factors that economists have fervently believed furthered cartelization—with little empirical evidence to back up their beliefs—in fact do not. In particular, cartelization is found to be a significant but *negative* function of industry concentration. Economists have traditionally thought (with little convincing empirical evidence) that concentration is perhaps the single most important variable in predicting the presence of collusion. (As noted below, Dick's finding has interesting implications for the Cameron–Glick chapter in this book, which also discusses concentration.)

Dick's contribution to this issue raises yet another point. As discussed below, the law of antitrust now recognizes that even horizontal collusion (such as price-fixing) may sometimes have beneficial effects.[6] If so, economists' tests for conspiracy would be more useful if they could separate 'bad' from 'good' conspiracies. This is not an area that has interested economists nearly as much as merely locating conspiracies.[7] Dick's results show that it is not easy to discriminate empirically between good and bad conspiracies—a result that should give economists some pause. Dick concludes that it is easier to identify firms with greater incentives to cartelize (particularly when it is legal) than to decide whether the cartelization would be economically desirable or harmful.

As the chapter by Roger Blair and Richard Romano demonstrates, however, even if economists could solve the problem of identifying industries in which *collusion* exists, the question of who the *colluders* were remains. Successful collusion does not require that all members of an industry join the conspiracy. (In the government's successful price-fixing cases that Hay and Kelley, 1974, studied, only some industry participants were inculpated in most of the cases.) Indeed, as more firms agree not to compete, the incentive increases for firms not yet in the conspiracy to stay out of it. Nonparticipants in the cartel benefit from the higher industry prices due to collusion by participants, without exposing themselves to antitrust liability.

Blair and Romano propose a simple test that would identify a firm that is *not* colluding, even if others are. The test cannot be price-based. Higher industry prices may follow from collusion (as Higgins *et al.* demonstrate), but both colluders and non-colluders will charge higher prices. The relevant inquiry, Blair and Romano show, should focus on the quantity axis. Non-colluders can expand output to take advantage of the output restriction colluders must place on themselves to raise prices. Firms in a colluding industry that increase output, *ceteris paribus*, should thus be adjudged nonparticipants in the cartel.

The Blair and Romano chapter teaches an important message. Economics is better able to show who is not colluding than who is. Price-based tests, as noted, are inconclusive, because all firms predictably will raise prices when collusion by only some occurs. The Blair–Romano quantity-based test can show who was not colluding: firms that expand output with the onset of price-fixing. But it does not follow that a firm that failed to expand output was a colluder, since a non-colluding firm might decide unilaterally (in an oligopolistic industry characterized by interdependent yet unilateral decision making) not to increase its output.

b. Economic Analysis in Rule-of-reason Cases

As noted, most antitrust cases following passage of the Sherman Act involved allegedly concerted conduct under section 1. Further, plaintiffs (both governmental and private) could expect to win those cases just by showing that firms had acted collusively rather than independently, regardless of actual competitive impact or any other consideration. The very act of contracting, combining or conspiring, that is, sufficed for a finding of liability.

In legal parlance, most concerted actions were *per se* illegal. Under a *per se* test, there was little role for economists' input, as long as the fact of contracting between or among firms had been established. Such conduct (including, naturally, horizontal price fixing) was under all circumstances illegal, regardless whether it actually was welfare-enhancing or not.

In the past twenty years, however, the demand for economists in antitrust proceedings has risen as the result of two important legal developments diminishing the scope of the traditional *per se* rule. The first legal development was courts' progressive shift from *per se* of illegality to the so-called 'rule of reason'. Culminating a trend in lower courts, the Supreme Court announced in 1977 that *per se* rules should be the exception in antitrust law (*Continental TV v. GTE Sylvania, Inc.*, 433 US 36 (1977)). A 'rule-of-reason' approach ordinarily should guide antitrust review of challenged business conduct.

This ruling was a watershed in American antitrust jurisprudence. Henceforth, it seemed, even horizontal price-fixing arrangements might qualify for rule-of-reason treatment, and therefore might even be legal.[8] Two years later, indeed, the Supreme Court so held

(*Broadcast Music, Inc. v. Columbia Broadcasting System, Inc.*, 441 US 1 (1979)).

But what exactly did 'rule of reason' mean? As the cases developed, it became clear that legality turned on the relative competitive costs and benefits of the conduct, something economists were specifically trained to analyze. The role of economists in such determinations is all the greater, given that businessmen are constantly evolving new contractual means of conducting their affairs. Thus, new sorts of practices are constantly coming to courts' attention, brought into the courtroom by either government enforcers or private plaintiffs. Common-law courts, basing their current decisions on precedent (previous holdings in cases entailing similar facts), find little help in prior-decision rules when presented with new business practices.

In the next two chapters here, William Shughart and Benjamin Klein analyze one such business practice—tying—in the context of two different legal matters. Traditionally treated as *per se* illegal, tying was in 1984 finally included among practices that could be legal under the rule-of-reason (*Jefferson Parish Hospital District No. 2 v. Hyde*, 466 US 2 (1984)). Thus was the way opened for practice of the economist's art in explaining what might be economically benign or malign about tying.

The *per se* rule against tying was a based in considerable part on the theory that it was a device whereby a seller with market power could 'foreclose' rivals from the market for complementary goods. A firm with market power in the market for product A could require, as a condition of purchasing A, that the buyer also purchase the firm's product B, supposedly foreclosing other sellers of product B. But as both Shughart and Klein illustrate, tying often occurs for reasons having nothing to do with foreclosure. And as Shugart explains in his discussion of the FTC's investigation of Boeing's tying policies, depending on the particular conditions of the case, tying may be a good or a bad thing.

Economic and legal interest in tying has intensified with the Supreme Court's recent decision in *Eastman Kodak Co. v. Image Technical Services, Inc.*, 504 US 451 (1992). The *Kodak* case was a legal lightning-bolt, seeming to say that a firm could have market power (and thus be subject to antitrust liability and treble damages) solely in sales of one's own products in 'aftermarkets'. Eastman Kodak had been sued because of conduct concerning service and replacement parts for its own copiers. Relative to other copier manufacturers (Xerox, etc.), Kodak was a relatively small player in the copier market. But Kodak naturally had a very dominant share of the 'aftermarket' for service and parts on just its own machines. The Supreme Court agreed that Kodak had no market power in the copier market, but held nonetheless that power in the 'aftermarket' for one's own service and parts *could* constitute market power relevant for antitrust purposes, and remanded the case for trial.

At that point, the economist's role begins. Since the Supreme Court held that market power in one's own service and products could confer market power, the issues become (1) whether Kodak in fact had market power and, if so, (2) whether it acts on net enhanced or retarded economic efficiency (wealth). Those are the issues addressed by Ben Klein.

Shughart's and Klein's analyses are insightful in several respects. Each applies general microeconomics to a specific practice or type of contract not previously addressed by economists, advancing both an economic understanding of specific contracts and an antitrust appreciation of how those same contracts are not competitively worrisome. Indeed, Klein's fundamental point is that even exclusionary contract terms may have no real implications for competition law, a point that courts have begun, slowly, to appreciate. A contract may as a practical matter foreclose certain competitors from a market, but without appreciable influence on prices or quantities (and therefore on economic welfare) in that market.

Were Boeing and Kodak using tying to 'foreclose' rivals in the market for the tied good? There were important differences in the two cases. For one, Kodak accounted for only about 20% of photocopying machine sales, whereas Boeing was (and is) the dominant manufacturer of commercial aircraft. Equally important, many of Kodak's customers relied on Kodak service personnel to maintain their machines, while all of Boeing's customers performed their own maintenance. Despite these differences, both Klein and Shughart conclude that, rather than being used anticompetitively to exclude rivals, the tie-in sales adopted by Kodak and Boeing served to tailor more closely to individual customer demands the price of a 'bundle' of goods: the original durable good (aircraft, copiers) plus the parts and service necessary to ensure satisfactory performance.[9]

In both instances, then, tie-in sales represented a form of price discrimination between high- and low-intensity users. But such price discrimination does not suggest problems of the sort antitrust is supposed to prevent: higher prices and restricted outputs. Both contributors stress recognition of the fact that any 'overpricing' of parts and service implies corresponding 'underpricing' of the equipment itself, with no necessary overpayment for the complete bundle. Klein also considers (and rejects) the possibility that Kodak opportunistically took advantage of customers who, because of high switching costs, were locked into Kodak's photocopying machines.

c. Antitrust Injury

The second legal development of particular importance in raising the demand for economics was the Supreme Court's announcement of the 'antitrust injury' doctrine in *Brunswick Corp. v. Pueblo Bowl-O-Mat, Inc.*, 429 US 477 (1977). In that case, the Court held that a private antitrust plaintiff must show not only (1) that an antitrust violation had occurred and (2) that he had sustained injury as a result thereof—ordinary legal requirements of causation—but also (3) that the injury sustained was of the sort that the antitrust laws were designed to prevent. Already, the Court was increasingly swinging over to the position that the antitrust laws were designed to further economic (allocative and productive) efficiency and wealth-maximization, not some more populist notion of 'small is beautiful'. Thus, following the *Brunswick* decision, the courts awaited instruction from economists on how the myriad practices on which private plaintiffs bring suit furthered or retarded the stated antitrust goal of economic efficiency. (The fact that some 90% of all antitrust cases are private actions made the economist's role even greater overall.)

That is the setting for Chapter 6 here, by Roger Blair and William Page. They first explain how the *Brunswick* doctrine arose, in the context of a merger/acquisition case. They then sketch out the implications of the antitrust-injury requirement for other types of business practices. Their analyses are particularly noteworthy, because the courts themselves have not yet applied the *Brunswick* doctrine in many case-law areas. The Blair–Page chapter thus provides a guide to how a court applying the antitrust-injury requirement might approach new types of business practices as they come under a court's scrutiny.

Perhaps the most provocative point in their analysis is the Blair–Page notion of efficient *violations* of the antitrust laws. Much conduct that is almost certainly efficient (e.g. maximum price fixing, either horizontally or vertically) remains illegal *per se* under the antitrust laws (*Arizona v. Maricopa County Medical Society*, 457 US 332 (1982); *Albrecht v. Herald Co.*, 390 US 145 (1968)). This means that the government, if it chooses to pursue such cases, should win them with little trouble, once the existence of the conduct is shown. But the same conduct will not likely result in liability if challenged in a private action, because—being efficient—the conduct has caused no injury of the sort the antitrust laws were designed to prevent (*Atlanta Richfield Co. v. USA Petroleum Co.*, 495 US 328 (1990)).

Not surprisingly, the *Brunswick* requirement of antitrust injury has been a boon to economists who hire on as experts in antitrust litigation. If there has ever been a case for which no economist could be found to testify whether the practice challenged was efficient, or whether the harm suffered was the sort of thing that the antitrust laws were designed to guard against, I have not heard of it. As economists hired for the task argue for one side or the other over the efficiency of various business practices, judges have been transformed into arbitrators of what is and is not economically desirable. It is unclear to what extent courts can be counted on to reach the right conclusion. Nor is it clear that holding themselves out for hire as experts has been beneficial for economists as professionals, either, the point of William Shughart's final chapter in this book.

MARKET DEFINITION

Once rule-of-reason analysis has been defined as the norm in antitrust, economic models are required in order to determine whether the societal benefits or costs of a particular practice dominate. The benefits often require economists to undergo on-the-job training about conditions (including relevant transaction costs) that might explain why firms use the challenged practices. As Ben Klein says in his chapter here, 'it is important not to rely solely on formal economics, but to get one's hands dirty and examine the facts of the situation'. In antitrust cases, therefore, economists often—even must—become experts in the details of particular industries, in order to understand whether or not the conduct at issue makes procompetitive, economic sense.

On the social cost side of the ledger, the inquiry focuses on market power, specifically on firms' ability to use the challenged conduct either to create power or to exploit it. Exercise of market power translates directly into welfare losses, the primary evil against which an antitrust policy is supposed to guard. Market power alone is not sufficient in a rule-of-reason context to condemn a practice, since even practices advancing market power may have countervailing benefits (Williamson, 1968). Market power, that is, is a necessary but not sufficient condition for a practice or contract to be deemed anticompetitive on net.

Because market power is a necessary condition, rule-of-reason cases early begin to inquire into its existence. But whether market power exists cannot be determined until the market itself is defined, along with both its product and geographic margins. These market-definition exercises often reduce to computation of rule-of-thumb statistics like market shares, from which in turn inferences about the extent of market power are made.

To many, the entire chore of defining relevant antitrust markets seems to force a separation of antitrust from basic microeconomics. Market definition in antitrust means drawing bright lines to separate substitute products competing with one another from those that do not, and drawing bright lines geographically to separate areas in which substitute products do and do not compete with one another. Market definition in that rigid antitrust sense is a notion unknown in economics more generally. True, microeconomics works routinely with notions of markets, in both the product and geographic senses. Outside the antitrust world, however, not even the least Austrian of economists would pretend to be able to define the product or geographic boundaries of markets with any useful precision.

But inside that antitrust world, market definition is required by the legal dictates of measuring market power—and so routinely performed. The lawyers demand, and the antitrust economists respond, with considerable econometric precision and skill. As David Scheffman and Pablo Spiller write in their chapter here, 'it has become increasingly common in antitrust analysis to use econometric methods in market delineation. The FTC [Federal Trade Commission] and DOJ Antitrust Division have generated a demand for such analyses, with agency economists pioneering econometric analyses in connection with the review of mergers.'

The demand for highly quantified market definitions is all the greater, given that a court's (or jury's) finding as to market definition frequently determines the outcome of the entire case. As William Shughart, Robert Tollison and Eileen Reed write in Chapter 7, 'Defining the relevant market is the first and in many respects the most important question in antitrust analysis. In most antitrust cases, the outcome falls neatly from the resolution of the market-definition issue.'[10] Finding that a particular product sold in a particular place has many substitutes in the same area, or that producers geographically nearby would enter the market and compete away any attempt to increase price anticompetitively, effectively ends many a plaintiff's antitrust challenge. Wide product- and geographic-market definitions translate into an absence of meaningful market power, a necessary condition of antitrust liability. In many cases, therefore, the percentage of resources involved in defining markets, relative to the total resources consumed by the litigation altogether, is high.

Even economists uneasy with the concept of delineating antitrust markets presumably would agree that good techniques in defining markets are preferable to bad ones. Economists don't make the law that demands rigid, bright-line market delineations; they supply services only in response to the demand. Some of the chapters here offer improvements in that all-important antitrust area of market definition.

The chapter by Shughart, Tollison and Reed focuses on the first part of market definition, the relevant product (although, as they note, their technique extends to definition of relevant geographic markets as well). The chapter provides a useful summary of both theory and empirical technique concerning market definition, in the context of the highly publicized Federal Trade Commission case against the major American breakfast-cereal producers. The authors' results indicate that cereal itself should not be deemed a relevant market. Moreover, given the own-price elasticity of demand for breakfast cereals, the likelihood that cereal manufacturers would adopt a monopolizing strategy is even less.

Addressing the second aspect of market definition, the geographic market, Scheffman and Spiller provide an excellent overview of the state of geographic market delineation, and suggest improvements. They are well qualified to do so. Both have written extensively on the subject.[11] Readers of Scheffman and Spiller will discover not only a workable approach (given existing data) to estimating market contours but also considerable sensitivity as to what estimation techniques do and do not capture the underlying economics.

They also suggest that economists would do well to start reconciling their estimation techniques with those employed by market researchers. This suggestion is provocative. Economists estimate demand elasticities *ad hoc* and episodically, incident to litigation. Market researchers do so routinely and repeatedly, fine-tuning their models as they go. Even more impressive, those paying for market research (unlike economists) put their money where their models are. There is more work to be done here, surely.

Several other authors, antitrust-litigation veterans all, tackle other issues on the market-definition front. Developing the data from which to circumscribe product and geographic markets is a task in itself, David Kaplan notes in Chapter 9, although market definition is only one area in which economists function as developers of facts. Guiding fact development requires an economist working in antitrust to 'sensitize' the lawyer for whom he works, and (even more) to sensitize the client, as to what is germane to the case. Things that seem innocuous to the businessman, or of no probative importance to the lawyer, may speak volumes to the forensic economist, or at least indicate a line of further inquiry that otherwise would not occur to anyone in the case.

In that sense, Kaplan forcefully seconds Klein's motion for the expert to get down in the trenches and get his hands dirty digging for the facts. As Sherlock Holmes demanded impatiently in *The Adventure of the Copper Beeches*—'Data! data! data! I can't make bricks without clay!'—so it is with the good economist working in antitrust. The economist's data inputs and statistical outputs—the clay and the bricks—are nicely demonstrated in the examples Kaplan provides concerning estimates of demand and demand elasticities.

Like Scheffman and Spiller, Kaplan underscores the value of comparing the results of applying economic science with what other disciplines, notably marketing, generate by way of data. Unbeknownst to many economists, marketing as practised by many marketers has become more like economics, a highly theoretical discipline with a wealth of sophisticated empirical studies. Although the two disciplines seemingly go out of their way to walk on opposite sides of the street, marketing's theory and empirics often complement the economic approach.[12] From my own experience, presenting economic arguments using the lingo and empirical results from marketing (e.g. 'consumer resistance to higher prices') is often more persuasive in court than relying on more rarefied economic jargon ('demand elasticity').

MARKET POWER

Duncan Cameron and Mark Glick extend the discussion of market definition and market power by reconsidering what is doubtless the single most persuasive number in all merger and monopoly cases, and many other antitrust actions as well: market share. Once a market has been defined, structural economists (and most courts) instinctively turn next to the question of market share as an indication of market power. In the old days of the Department of Justice's 1968 Merger Guidelines, market share was usually measured by 4-firm concentration ratios. Officially at least, potentially merging parties had some inkling whether their merger was likely to be challenged by consulting the threshold levels of DOJ concern expressed in terms of those ratios. (Of course, the parties could not be sure how DOJ and its economists would define the markets in the first place.)

More recent versions of the Merger Guidelines have refined concentration, using the Herfindahl–Hirschman Index (HHI) instead of simple concentration ratios. More important, as the influence of the structuralists in economics has faded, subsequent versions of the Merger Guidelines have abandoned the virtually exclusive reliance on concentration, however measured. But HHI-type concentration remains one of several factors that at the margin matter in government enforcers' decision whether to challenge a merger.[13]

For all that, one would think that the theoretical case for use of market shares as indicating worrisome market power would be relatively ironclad, and that courtroom use of market shares in antitrust was well deserved. As the Cameron–Glick chapter shows, however, neither proposition is true. Their chapter argues that market-share data are used in oversimplified ways that fail to discriminate among numerous situations with different efficiency implications.

Like good economists, Cameron and Glick focus on the theory behind using market share data as indications of market power. In fact, they say, the problem begins precisely with the *lack* of useful theory.

> Market share enters into all [the] standard models in such a way that, *ceteris paribus*, greater concentration will generally be associated with reduced market performance. This is a basis for the courts' inferences about market performance

derived from market structure. But in real situations in which courts must make decisions, the assumptions underlying these models are generally not applicable.

Indeed, as emphasized by Andrew Dick's empirics in Chapter 2, the empirical case for the importance of market shares and concentration ratios remains remarkably slim as well. One can at least hope, if not expect, that the more nuanced treatment of market-share information proposed by Cameron and Glick will begin to percolate through the antitrust enforcement and adjudication system.

The extent to which economists' rule-of-thumb measures adequately capture market power concerns Keith Hylton and Mark Lasser as well. Aside from market share, the classic measure of market power is the 'Lerner index', which measures the extent to which prices diverge from marginal cost. In Chapter 11, Hylton and Lasser focus on measuring market power in a particular situation, when a firm has market power at two vertical levels. Recomputing the Lerner index, they find that the extent of competition in both markets matters in evaluating the extent of market power at any one level: 'Society should not be indifferent to the manner in which a monopolist exploits its monopoly.'

The Hylton–Lasser analysis of bi-level monopoly generates broad conclusions, most fundamentally that the simple Lerner index is an inaccurate measure of market power in many familiar antitrust settings. The recomputed index also leads to a number of interesting implications, among them the utility of the Herfindahl–Hirschman Index to measure market power in merger cases. Hylton and Lasser find that when firms have market power at more than one vertical level 'a simple comparison of pre- and post-merger [HHIs] overstates the increase in market power that results from a merger of rival firms'.

The point of departure for Luke Froeb, Timothy Tardiff and Gregory Werden in Chapter 12 is similar to that of Hylton and Lasser. Froeb and his co-authors are interested in how particular industry characteristics should alter analysis of welfare losses and gains from mergers. Their specific focus is a phenomenon little studied in economics, how mergers cause shifts in production among firms in the industry in which the merger takes place. The shifts in production patterns result from asymmetric price effects caused by the merger among firms in an industry. The changes in production considered are of different sorts, including shifts between the merging parties themselves and especially shifts from merging to non-merging firms.

So viewed, mergers may have several effects not included as part of economists' standard analysis. For example, since larger firms are assumed to be more efficient (the 'Demsetz Postulate' referred to in their title), even a merger between two smaller firms that would lessen competition among them (as evaluated under the government's merger guidelines) might nonetheless be procompetitive overall. The otherwise anticompetitive merger would raise the merging firms' prices, thus causing buyers to shift to the larger, more efficient firm. The efficiency gains of shifting production to the larger firm could outweigh any anticompetitive losses from the merger itself.

In other words, the world modeled by Froeb and his co-authors is an economically realistic one in which firms have varying levels of efficiency and mergers have not only implications for the merging parties but also ripple effects on non-merging firms. Mergers that are anticompetitive in themselves may be procompetitive in the end, once a new equilibrium is established. Indeed, the simulations of Japanese mergers run by Froeb, Tardiff and Werden indicate that efficiency gains overall are precisely what they expect in this situation, when firms operate at varying levels of efficiency. They conclude, 'To the extent that merger policy remains essentially structural, it should recognize that high market concentration may not merit greater restraints on the mergers of smaller firms'.

THE EFFECT OF ECONOMISTS ON ANTITRUST, AND VICE VERSA

One of the more fascinating papers on economists and antitrust was published in the 1970s by Ronald Coase (1972, reprinted 1988). In it, Coase discussed the interplay between standard microeconomics (price theory) of the firm and antitrust. He pointed out ruefully that with the advent of the Sherman Act, 'the antitrust aspects of industrial organization came to dominate the subject' (1988, p. 66).

Coase admitted that the domination of industrial organization by antitrust concerns had its benefits. Antitrust focused economists' attention on practices—ones being attacked in courts—that economics had not considered before.[14] The Shughart and Klein chapters here (on parts and service 'aftermarkets' for durable machinery) represent exactly the sort of antitrust-motivated inquiry to which Coase was referring.[15]

But the focus on antitrust has had its costs as well. Since the antitrust establishment (lawyers, judges) demand answers that economists are better qualified to answer than anyone else, antitrust has deflected economists to tasks of greater litigation than economic interest (such as defining relevant antitrust markets). Worse, it has sometimes turned economists into special pleaders for litigating parties. Disinterested scientific inquiry then gives way to result-driven application of the economist's art.

The practices being scrutinized legally are frequently ones that economists themselves have not investigated rigorously outside the courtroom. Thus, an economist risks becoming a special pleader providing answers that have not been vetted and are not necessarily accepted (substantively or methodologically) by others in the profession. To quote Coase, antitrust

> has therefore encouraged men to become economic statesmen—men, that is, who provide answers even when there are no answers. This tendency has discouraged a critical questioning of the data and of the worth of the analysis, leading the many able scholars in this field to tolerate standards of evidence and analysis which, I believe, they would otherwise have rejected. This association with policy—and antitrust policy in particular—gave a direction to the study of industrial organization which prevented certain questions from being raised or, at any rate, made it more difficult for them to be raised. (Coase, 1988, p. 66)

In short, Coase points out, economists have altered antitrust by their claimed ability to answer antitrust-type questions. On the other hand, antitrust has altered economists, by compensating them for providing answers, even when the ordinary process of economic learning has not determined what the correct answers are. Coase was extraordinarily prescient. The problem that he identified for economists in 1972 now afflicts many other disciplines, and problems of 'junk science' and 'liability science' are now routine when law intersects with science (including social science) in the courtroom (Huber, 1993).

In the final chapter of the book, William Shughart examines this darker side of the Coasean street, the way that antitrust turns economists into special pleaders ('economic statesmen'). As long as the legal and political demand for economic punditry remains, so predictably will there be a supply of pundits. Shughart returns to Coase's 1972 point, and asks whether the fabled 'Chicago Revolution' in antitrust thinking since the early 1970s should allay fears of what antitrust is doing to the economics profession. Despite courts' admitted embrace of a more Chicagoan approach to their economics, Shughart finds the role of the economics profession still compromised by its complicity with antitrust enforcers.

But Shughart's concern springs from a source different from that of Coase. Coase believed that antitrust had caused economists to make an unfortunate detour away from 'true' industrial organization, and then, lost in the *terra incognita* of the new antitrust, to offer opinions and conclusions that were hasty or unfounded. Shughart says the problem is not one of economists' errors, but of their resolute refusal to treat antitrust as just another form of economic regulation. Economists see nothing untoward about 'helping the Justice Department's Antitrust Division and the Federal Trade Commission identify and attack sources of allocative inefficiency in the economy so as to enhance consumer welfare. Yet many of these same economists would not be caught dead making similar recommendations to the Interstate Commerce Commission or to the now-defunct Civil Aeronautics Board.' That is, the same economists who are naturally suspicious, even scornful, of government regulation generally believe that antitrust is different.

On what basis do they set antitrust apart from other economic regulation? None, Shughart says. Indeed, research since Coase's cautionary article 'has produced fairly strong evidence that politics shapes antitrust processes in much the same way it does more traditional forms of regulation'. In the end, the profession's continued support for antitrust cannot be explained away as error—Coase's detour. The continued acceptance of antitrust, Shughart says, reflects economists' plumping for what is in their own interests. As analysts *par excellence* of rent seeking in other industries, economists should have learned a trick or two about how the process might work closer to home, to their own benefit.

CONCLUSION

The chapters to follow illustrate the numerous roles—normative as well as positive—that we economists play on the modern antitrust stage. In our economic roles, depending on the situation, we may prescribe, or describe, or decry. Whether the world is better for our involvement, and whether we economists have advanced the profession by our involvement, are matters worth further investigation. The chapters here furnish excellent discussions of those matters and outlines for subsequent analyses of the issues.

Most of the chapters in this volume were published as a special issue of *Managerial and Decision Economics*, March–April 1996, Volume 17, Number 2. *Managerial and Decision Economics* is published by John Wiley & Sons, Ltd, Baffins Lane, Chichester, West Sussex, UK.

Acknowledgement

I thank William Shughart for his comments on several of the points discussed here.

NOTES

1. The third chapter, by Blair and Romano, does extend its discussion of liability for collusion to consider the implications of their model for damages calculation.
2. Perhaps the most oft-quoted statement of the rule comes from *Story Parchment Co. v. Paterson Parchment Paper Co.*, 282 US 555, 562 (1931): 'There is a clear distinction between the measure of proof necessary to establish the fact that petitioner has sustained some damage and the measure of proof necessary to enable the jury to fix the amount.'
3. This is not necessarily to say that economic-theoretic developments did not precede the legal changes. The work of Bork (1978) in particular is frequently cited as having influenced courts. Some would dispute that claim, however, as the final contribution from William Shughart to this volume indicates. For another dissent from quite a different perspective, see Kaplow (1987).
4. Section 1 of the Sherman Act outlaws 'contracts, combinations ... and conspiracies' that are 'in restraint of trade', while section 2 of the Act forbids conduct to 'monopolize' (or attempt to monopolize).
5. For example, the Posner approach to identifying collusion has been tried in the real world, at the Federal Trade Commission. As the then-Director of the FTC's Bureau of Economics afterwards wrote, 'The kindest thing I can say about the effort is that it was a resounding flop' Scherer, 1977, p. 983).
6. Empirically, previous researchers have questioned whether government trust-busters are capable of separating anticompetitive behavior from benign business practices that entail collusion (e.g. Asch and Seneca, 1976; Marvel *et al.*, 1988).
7. But see Bittlingmayer (1995), who investigates the effects of the relatively brief suspension of the antitrust laws under the National Industrial Recovery Act of 1935. Bittlingmayer concludes that there is no reason to think that government's allowing (even requiring) cartelization had economically deleterious price–quantity effects overall.
8. Recall that Dick, in Chapter 2 of this volume, discusses the possible social benefits of price fixing.
9. See also Eisenach, Higgins and Shughart (1984), who show how tying sales of repair parts and the purchase of original equipment can be used to charge actuarially fair prices for warranties.
10. As the Supreme Court has said, 'market definition generally determines the result of the case' (*Eastman Kodak Co. v. Image Technical Services, Inc.*, 504 US 451, 469 n.15 (1992)).
11. In addition, Dave Scheffman is a former Director of the Bureau of Economics at the Federal Trade Commission, where he was responsible for applying the FTC/DOJ Merger Guidelines, the wellspring of attempts to introduce greater science to issues of market definition.
12. For further discussion of this point, see Scheffman (1996). As he notes (p. 240), 'Most economists, to the extent they think about it at all, turn up their nose at marketing'.
13. It appears that greater concentration than that designated in the Guidelines has been required before a merger is challenged. See Coate and McChesney (1992). This is an interesting reversal. Under the 1968 Guidelines, mergers entailing *lower* concentration than that claimed necessary to elicit a challenge nonetheless were challenged (Rogowsky, 1984).
14. "In referring to contracts 'in restraint of trade', or to arrangements whose effects 'may be substantially to lessen competition or to tend to create a monopoly', the principal antitrust statutes are relatively vague. Little statutory guidance is provided for distinguishing benign from malign practices. Thus, judges have been left to decide for themselves which practices run afoul of the antitrust laws...To answer such questions, judges sometimes have turned to economists for guidance. In the early years of antitrust, though, economists were of little help. They had not extensively analyzed arrangements like tying, information sharing, resale price maintenance, and other commercial practices challenged in antitrust suits. But as the cases exposed areas of economic ignorance or confusion about different commercial arrangements, economists turned to solving the various puzzles" (McChesney, 1993, p. 386).
15. For a very interesting collection of articles concerning specific antitrust cases, written by economists who worked as experts for one party in each case, see Kwoka and White (1989).

REFERENCES

P. Asch and J. J. Seneca (1976). Is collusion profitable? *Review of Economics and Statistics*, **58**, 1–12.

G. Bittlingmayer (1995). Output and stock prices when antitrust is suspended. In *The Causes and Consequences of Antitrust: The Public–Choice Perspective* (edited by F. S. McChesney and W. F. Shughart II), Chicago: University of Chicago Press.

R. Bork (1978). *The Antitrust Paradox: A Policy at War with Itself*, New York: Basic Books.

D. J. Boudreaux, T. J. DiLorenzo and S. Parker (1995). Antitrust before the Sherman Act. In *The Causes and Consequences of Antitrust: The Public Choice Perspective* (edited by F. S. McChesney and W. F. Shughart II), Chicago: University of Chicago Press , pp. 255–70.

R. H. Coase (1972, reprinted 1988). Industrial organization: a proposal for research. In *The Firm, the Market and the Law*, Chicago: University of Chicago Press.

M. B. Coate and A. N. Kleit (eds) (1996). *The Economics of the Antitrust Process*. Boston: Kluwer Academic Publishers.

M. B. Coate and F. S. McChesney (1992). Empirical evidence on FTC enforcement of the Merger Guidelines. *Economic Inquiry*, **30**, 277–93.

T. J. DiLorenzo (1985). The origins of antitrust: an interest-group perspective. *International Review of Law and Economics*, **5**, 73–90.

J. A. Eisenach, R. S. Higgins and W. F. Shughart II (1984). Warranties, tie-ins, and efficient insurance contracts: a theory and three case studies. *Research in Law and Economics*, **6**, 167–85.

R. B. Ekelund, Jr, M. J. McDonald and R. D. Tollison (1995). Business restraints and the Clayton Act of 1914. In *The Causes and Consequences of Antitrust: The Public Choice Perspective* (edited by F. S. McChesney and W. F. Shughart II), Chicago: University of Chicago Press, pp. 271–86.

G. A. Hay and D. Kelley (1974). An empirical survey of price-fixing conspiracies. *Journal of Law and Economics*, **17**, 13–38.

P. Huber (rev. edn 1993). *Galileo's Revenge: Junk Science in the Courtroom*, New York: Basic Books.

L. Kaplow (1987). Antitrust, law and economics, and the courts. *Law and Contemporary Problems*, **50**, 181–216.

J. E. Kwoka, Jr and L. J. White (eds) (1989). *The Antitrust Revolution*, New York: HarperCollins.

W. M. Landes (1983). Optimal sanctions for antitrust violations. *University of Chicago Law Review*, **50**, 652–78.

F. S. McChesney (1993). Antitrust. In *The Fortune Encyclopedia of Economics* (edited by D. R. Henderson), New York: Time-Warner Books, pp. 385–89.

F. S. McChesney (1995). In search of the public-interest model of antitrust. In *The Causes and Consequences of Antitrust: The Public-Choice Perspective* (edited by F. S. McChesney and W. F. Shughart II), Chicago: University of Chicago Press , pp. 25–32.

H. P. Marvel, J. M. Netter and A. M. Robinson (1988). Price fixing and civil damages: an economic analysis. *Stanford Law Review*, **40**, 561–78.

R. A Posner (1969). Oligopoly and the antitrust laws: a suggested approach. *Stanford Law Review*, **21**, 1562–1606.

R. A. Rogowsky (1984). The Justice Department's Merger Guidelines: a study in the application of the rule. *Research in Law and Economics*, **6**, 135–66.

D. T. Sheffman (1996). Antitrust, economics, and 'reality'. In *The Economics of the Antitrust Process* (edited by M. B. Coate and A. N. Kleit), Boston: Kluwer Academic Publishers, pp. 239–52.

F. M. Scherer (1977). The Posnerian harvest: separating wheat from chaff. *Yale Law Journal*, **86**, 974–88.

G. J. Stigler (1982). The economists and the problem of monopoly. In *The Economist as Preacher and Other Essays*, Chicago: University of Chicago Press.

O. E. Williamson (1968). Economies as an antitrust defense: the welfare tradeoffs. *American Economic Review*, **58**, 18–36.

1
The Causes and Consequences of the Aluminum MOU

Richard S. Higgins, Mark Glueck, David P. Kaplan and Michael McDonald

Capital Economics, Washington, DC, USA

Aluminum is an important basic input for myriad commodities consumed in the United States, including beverage cans and automobile transmissions, among many other products. Domestic consumption of fabricated aluminum products was $18.6 billion in 1993.[1] The market value of the primary and secondary aluminum ingot used in their production was $8.8 billion.[2] Imports of aluminum into the United States are significant. Approximately 30% of US consumption of aluminum was imported during 1993. An increasing amount of these imports came from Russia, following the collapse of the Soviet Union.

In the last week of January 1994, a Memorandum of Understanding (MOU) was signed by representatives of the major aluminum-producing countries which effectively reduced the supply of aluminum inputs. Between January and November 1994, the real price of primary aluminum ingot rose by 58%. An increase of 58% in the price of aluminum inputs translates into $5.1 billion extra that US consumers would pay for products made from aluminum. This paper evaluates the impact of the MOU on the market price of primary aluminum ingot.

An econometric supply and demand analysis was conducted to measure the impact of the MOU on the price of primary aluminum ingot. Based on this analysis, we estimated that 26–38% of the (58%) ingot price increase between January and November 1994 was attributable to the MOU. This translates into an aluminum product price increase of 15–22%, or about $1.3–1.9 billion in extra annual expense for consumers of aluminum-containing products.

We also conducted an 'event analysis' of daily stock-market data to further examine the impact of the MOU on company values. To the extent that the realized price increase in 1994 for aluminum ingot was caused by the MOU instead of normal supply and demand factors, event analysis may show a positive effect of the MOU's announcement on equity values for primary aluminum producers. We found that on the day the MOU was announced, the equity value of a portfolio composed of Alcoa, Reynolds, and Alcan rose 3% more than the overall market. Moreover, during the week in July when Alcoa, Kaiser, and Alcan each announced a new can-stock pricing policy which would tie sheet prices to ingot prices the value of this same portfolio rose nearly 6% more than the market.[3]

THE ALUMINUM INDUSTRY

Aluminum is used to make numerous products, including window and door frames, siding, gutters, beverage cans, electrical transmission lines, chain-link fence material, transmission housings, pistons, engine parts, panels for automobile bodies, and storage tanks. These end uses typically incorporate intermediate aluminum inputs such as sheet, plate and foil; extruded shapes; and rod, bar and wire.

The aluminum that goes into making these products comes from either 'primary' or 'secondary' ingot. *Primary*, or 'virgin', aluminum is made from bauxite. The bauxite is ground to a uniform size and heated to remove as much of the free water as possible before it is shipped to an alumina refinery. At an alumina refinery, bauxite is refined to produce alumina, which is a fine white powder. Alumina from the refinery is shipped to a reduction plant or smelter where the refined alumina is converted to molten aluminum. Molten aluminum is then cast to produce alloy ingot, sheet ingot, and extrusion billet. *Secondary* ingot is made from recycled aluminum, a segment which grew from 29% of total US aluminum consumption in 1983 to 38% in 1993.[4]

The largest consumer of aluminum in the United States is the container and packaging industry, which uses rolled aluminum sheet as stock for beer and soft-drink cans. For 1993, such containers and packaging represented 30% of total US aluminum consumption, while transportation products represented 26%, building and construction 17%, and the remainder was divided between electrical (8%), consumer durables (8%), machinery (6%), and other miscellaneous uses (3%).[5]

An increasing portion of the aluminum used in the United States is imported, including both primary ingot and more refined aluminum stock. Imports of primary ingot and fabricated aluminum stock as a percent of total US consumption increased from approximately 20% in 1989 to 30% in 1993.[6] During 1993, the major exporters of aluminum to the United States were Canada and Russia. Canada represented almost 64% of US imports and Russia represented over 17%.[7] Canada and Russia are also two of the world's three largest primary aluminum-producing countries, with Canada representing 12% of world primary aluminum production in 1993 and Russia representing 15% (the United States was the largest producer with almost 19% of world production).[8]

The United States has approximately 13 producers of primary aluminum. Their market shares in 1983 and in 1993 are given in Table 1. Despite merger and acquisition activity over the last decade, levels of market concentration were stable. For example, the Herfindahl–Hirschman Index (HHI), a measure of market concentration routinely examined by US antitrust authorities, was at approximately the same level in 1993 as it was in 1983. It should also be noted that many of the domestic producers of primary aluminum are vertically integrated. Several own bauxite mines or are integrated backwards into alumina production; also, many of the domestic primary producers are integrated forward into intermediate aluminum production.

Based on the estimated value of shipments for intermediary aluminum products (sheet, plate, and foil; extruded products; and rolling and drawing), the total value of fabricated aluminum products consumed domestically in 1993 was $18.6 billion.[9] Based on the average London Metals Exchange (LME) cash market prices for primary and secondary

Table 1. US Primary Aluminum Producers: Industry Concentration 1983 and 1993

Company	1983 Capacity[a] metric tons (000)	1983 Share of capacity (%)	1983 HHI	1993 Capacity[a] metric tons (000)	1993 Share of capacity (%)	1993 HHI
Aluminum Company of America	1429.7	28.6	818	1285.0	30.9	955
Alumax, Inc.[c]	595.1	11.9	142	629.0	15.1	228
Reynolds Metals Co.	884.5	17.7	313	448.0	10.8	117
Kaiser Aluminum & Chemical Co.	656.8	13.1	172	273.1	6.6	44
Ormet Corp.[e]	–	0.0	0	245.0	5.9	35
Noranda, Inc.	204.1	4.1	17	215.0	5.2	27
Southwire Co.[i]	86.2	1.7	3	186.0	4.5	20
Alcan Aluminum Corp.[d]	–	0.0	0	180.0	4.3	18
Columbia Falls Aluminum[d]	–	0.0	0	168.0	4.0	16
Ravenswood Aluminum[h]	–	0.0	0	168.0	4.0	16
Columbia Aluminum[f]	–	0.0	0	167.8	4.0	16
Vanalco	–	0.0	0	115.9	2.8	8
Northwest Aluminum[g]	–	0.0	0	82.0	2.0	4
National Aluminum Inc.	86.2	1.7	3	–	0.0	0
Consolidated Aluminum Co.	294.1	5.9	35	–	0.0	0
Revere Copper & Brass Inc.	184.9	3.7	14	–	0.0	0
Martin Marietta Aluminum Co.	249.5	5.0	25	–	0.0	0
ARCO Aluminum[b,d]	326.6	6.5	42	–	0.0	0
Howmet[c]	–	0.0	0	–	0.0	0
Total	4997.7	100	1584	4162.8	100	1504

[a]Capacities shown are as reported as of 31 December. They include nominal ownership of plants owned by more than one company.
[b]Formerly the Anaconda Company, Aluminum Division.
[c]Alumax acquired Howmet in 1983.
[d]Alcan and Columbia Falls acquired 50% each of ARCO's aluminum in 1985.
[e]Formerly included with Consolidated and Revere.
[f]Formerly Commonwealth's Goldendale plant.
[g]Formerly Martin Marietta's The Dalles plant.
[h]Formerly included with Kaiser Aluminum and Chemical Corp.
[i]100% interest in National–Southwire purchased by Southwire in 1990.
Source: The Aluminum Association, Inc., *Aluminum Statistical Review for 1993*.

aluminum ingot, the value of the 5.1 million metric tons of primary aluminum and the 2.9 million metric tons of secondary aluminum consumed in the United States in 1993 is approximately \$5.9 and \$2.9 billion, respectively.[10]

THE MOU

The collapse of the Soviet Union resulted in a substantial decline in the Eastern bloc's demand for primary metals.[11] As a consequence, Eastern bloc producers of primary metals suddenly looked to the West for customers. Metals such as nickel, titanium, molybdenum, and aluminum were increasingly exported to the West after 1989. For example, in 1989 the Russian Republic exported a mere 250 000 metric tons of aluminum to the West, but in 1993 exported nearly 1.7 million metric tons.[12]

The redistribution of Eastern bloc output to the West was equivalent to an increase in Western primary aluminum capacity of nearly 15% (Sfiligoj, 1994). As a result, the Western world price of aluminum ingot fell from \$0.94 per pound (\$2067 per metric ton) in September 1990 to \$0.47 per pound (\$1040 per metric ton) in November 1993.[13] Other factors, such as a recession in the United States and the rest of the world and increased recycling, also likely contributed to the decline in the price of aluminum ingot.

In response to the decline in the price of aluminum ingot, US primary aluminum producers reduced output by 8.7% over the same period, some 354 000 metric tons. In addition, smelter capacity was shut down or 'shuttered' during this period. Some 1.1 million metric tons or 27% of US capacity in 1990 was closed at least temporarily.[14] Such ouput reductions are consistent with falling demand. Production lines or plants may be shut down whenever price over the near term is expected to fall below the average variable cost.[15]

Primary producers of aluminum in the United States also sought relief from the federal government in reducing supply. Specifically, the primary aluminum producers apparently petitioned Congress and the Administration to obtain an agreement from the Russians to restrict production, at least temporarily (*Metals Week*, 1993a). A common argument was that the Russians were displacing American jobs by exporting to the United States inferior-quality aluminum produced in low-wage, high-pollution smelters. One proposed solution was for the US government to subsidize the refurbishing of the outmoded Russian plants in the interest of 'international cooperation'. Of course, one side effect of this proposed reconstruction was that the Russian smelters would be incapacitated for several years.

Efforts by the US primary producers of aluminum ingot to obtain relief finally led to a round of discussions among government officials representing several of the West's major aluminum producers and Russia. In October and November of 1993, representatives of the United States, Australia, Canada, Norway, the European Economic Community (EEC), and Russia met to discuss prospects for ending the world 'glut' of primary aluminum (*Metals Week*, 1993b,c). No final agreement was reached, but the same countries' representatives met again in January in Brussels apparently to hammer out an agreement (*Metals Week*, 1993d). The result, the Memorandum of Understanding, called for the Russians to curtail ouput by 500 000 metric tons per year for approximately two years in return for investment subsidies. It has also been suggested that, although not memorialized in the language of the MOU, Western countries agreed to restrict their own output of primary aluminum by two to three times the cutback in Russian production.[16]

To monitor compliance with the MOU, 'a Working Group' was established to meet periodically and to exchange output, capacity, and import/export data through the auspices of the International Primary Aluminum Institute (IPAC). This group met approximately six times.

SUPPLY AND DEMAND ANALYSIS

From January 1994 to November 1994 the real price of aluminum ingot rose from \$1198 per metric ton to \$1893 per metric ton, a 58% increase.[17] The price of aluminum ingot, of course, may be affected by a number of demand and supply factors, in addition to the MOU. A standard technique employed by economists for separating out the effects of individual influences is multivariate regression. Our statistical supply and demand analysis measures what the average monthly price of aluminum ingot would have been after January 1994 in the absence of the MOU, and any systematic difference between this but-for price and the actual price represents an estimate of the effect of the MOU.

The multivariate regression analysis permits one to estimate the contribution of the MOU to the 1994 price increase holding constant the effect of individual demand and supply factors. The demand for primary aluminum is dependent on the demand for aluminum products in end-use sectors such as packages and containers, automobiles, and building construction. The supply of primary aluminum is dependent on the prices of inputs in aluminum production (for example, workers' wages, electricity, alumina, and bauxite) and on primary aluminum capacity.

The primary aluminum price series examined in the regression analysis was the real monthly average London Metals Exchange (LME) daily cash price from January 1980 to September 1994. The demand for primary aluminum was accounted for by including the following three variables in the regression model: (1) the industrial production index for the G7 countries (*LG7PROD*); (2) US automobile production (*LCARIND*); and (3) US aluminum can production (*LCANPRD*).[18] The supply of primary aluminum was accounted for by including the following variables: (1) world primary aluminum capacity (*LWLDCAP*); (2) the average real exchange rate for the major primary aluminum exporting countries of Australia, Canada and Norway (*LRXR*) based on primary aluminum production weights; and (3) a binary variable which assumes the value of 1 after 1989 to capture the effect of Russian exports to the West (*RUSSIA*). To measure the MOU's contribution to the 1994 price increase a binary variable (*MOU*), which assumes the value of 1 after the signing of the MOU in January of 1994 and zero otherwise, was included in the specification.

Our results are reported in Table 2. The estimated coefficients on the variables have the predicted signs, and most are statistically significant. All three demand-side variables are positive and statistically significant. The production-weighted exchange rate for the major exporting countries is also positive and statistically significant. Both the world primary aluminum capacity variable and the Russian export binary variable are negative.

Finally, the *MOU* coefficient is positive and statistically significant. The magnitude of the coefficient on the *MOU* binary variable measures the percentage price increase caused by the *MOU*, and the statistical significance of the *MOU* variable indicates whether the measured *MOU* effect is real or the result of sampling error. Since the coefficient on the *MOU* variable is positive and statistically significant we can be confident that the *MOU* caused an increase in the aluminum price.

Table 2. Real LME Daily Cash Price Regression

Variable	Estimated coefficient
C	41.19 (4.48)[a]
LG7PROD	2.18 (6.22)[a]
LCARIND	0.48 (4.24)[a]
LCANPRD	0.26 (1.85)[b]
LWLDCAP	−3.05 (−5.71)[a]
RUSSIA	−0.08 (−1.32)
MOU	0.20 (4.42)[a]
LRXR	1.71 (11.20)[a]
N	177
R^2	0.73

t-statistics in parentheses.
[a]Statistically significant at the 1% level.
[b]Statistically significant at the 10% level.

In order to account for the possibility of omitted variables causing serial correlation, we also estimated the coefficients using feasible generalized least squares.[19] These results are contained in Table 3. We find that all the variables have the theoretically predicted signs and all variables, except for the *WRUSSIA* binary variable, are statistically signifi-

Table 3. Real LME Daily Cash Price Regression

Variable	Estimated coefficient
WCONST	14.91 (1.46)
LWG7PROD	1.95 (5.09)[a]
LWCARIND	0.27 (3.05)[a]
LWCANPRD	0.22 (3.72)[a]
LWWLDCAP	−1.28 (−2.03)[b]
WRUSSIA	−0.04 (−0.55)
WMOU	0.14 (1.98)[b]
LWRXR	1.83 (10.25)[b]
N	176
R^2	0.99

t-statistics in parentheses.
[a]Statistically significant at the 1% level.

cant. In particular, the *MOU* coefficient is positive and statistically significant. The size of the coefficient is somewhat less than reported in Table 2 based on OLS estimation. Specifically, the *MOU* coefficient in Table 3 implies an MOU effect of 15%.

Summary

Applying this methodology, we estimate that the MOU caused a 15–22% increase in the real LME daily cash price holding other demand and supply factors constant. Thus, since the real daily cash price increased 58% between January and November, the MOU accounted for 26–38% of the increase in the LME daily cash price. We also estimate that demand-side factors caused the daily cash price to increase by 20–22%. Demand-side factors accounted for an additional 34–38% of the increase in the daily cash price. In other words, the MOU's contribution to the price increase for aluminum ingot is roughly equal in magnitude to the contribution of demand increases.

Based on the estimated MOU effect, one can compute the cost that the MOU imposed on US customers. Given the market value of primary and secondary aluminum ingot consumed in the United States in 1993—$8.8 billion—an increase in the ingot price of 15–22% translates into an additional annual expense of $1.3–1.9 billion for US consumers for at least the duration of the MOU.[20]

EVENT ANALYSIS

Event analysis is a technique used in financial economics. It measures stock market reaction to announcements of changed conditions that affect the equity value of publicly traded firms. Because securities prices reflect relevant information about firms' future cash flows, changes in securities prices can be used in certain circumstances to analyze the impact of changed future circumstances on individual firms' operations (see Sharpe, 1985, or Fama, 1991). By examining the rate of return associated with holding a portfolio of equities for primary aluminum producers, we can review the causes of the 1994 aluminum ingot price increases. Also, the relationship of value changes to the timing of particular events or announcements can provide another means of deducing the source and significance of structural change.

The first step in an event analysis is to identify the timing of each relevant event. A 'window' is defined as a time period that brackets the event in question. Specifically, since we use daily holding-period returns to measure firm performance, a window will typically include the day of the event and possibly the days immediately before and after the event—thus, a three-day window. Second, we measure the impact of the event on the holding-period rates of return for the portfolio in question and for the market portfolio. In the third step, we subtract out the market rate of return to convert gross returns to net returns (after adjusting for broad market changes). The last step is important so that we do not wrongly attribute to the event movement in the target portfolio's value that merely reflects market movement for the duration of the window.

There are a number of producing and consuming groups of interest that would arguably be impacted by an agreement to restrict world-wide aluminum output. The group of firms that could be expected to benefit most would be aluminum ingot producers. In the United States there were 13 firms with installed primary aluminum capacity in 1993. Three of these firms—Alcoa, Reynolds Metals, and Alcan Aluminum—are publicly traded and actively followed by investment analysts and the popular financial press. As a group, they may reflect the general profit potential for primary US aluminum producers at any point in time.[21] Collectively, these three producers held 46% of installed US capacity in 1993. These three firms were combined into a portfolio for purposes of measuring the impact on their expected future cash flows from (1) events surrounding the formal agreement to reduce world-wide aluminum output and (2) the means by which such an agreement would be monitored.

Results

The first window evaluated related to the announcement of a formal agreement to restrict aluminum output and is detailed in Table 4. Individual firm and portfolio returns to equity for the trading days directly preceding (27 January 1994) and following (3 February 1994) the announcement of the MOU are displayed. Table 4 reports that gross returns for each of the individual producer's common stocks ranged from 3.6% to 5.4%. The value weighted aluminum portfolio appreciated by 3.9% during the period.[22]

The returns in Table 4 have been expressed as the increase in the overall equity value of the firms and

Table 4. Movement in the Price of Primary US Aluminum Stocks in the Period Surrounding the Announcement of the Memorandum of Understanding Concerning World-wide Aluminum Output

Firm	Price on 1/27/94	Price on 1/31/94	% Change	Change in firms' equity value ($mil)	Change in firms' equity value adjusted for change in the S&P 500 ($mil)
Alcan Aluminum	23 1/4	24 1/2	5.4	280.5	234.8
Alcoa	76 1/2	79 1/4	3.6	244.7	183.8
Reynolds Metal	51 1/4	53 3/8	4.2	131.7	104.8
Aluminum Portfolio	40 1/2	42 1/4	3.9	656.9	523.4
S&P 500	477.05	481.06	0.9		

Events surrounding the International Aluminum MOU

1/16–1/21/94	Multilateral Aluminum Conference—Brussels
1/28/94	Conference Imposed deadline
1/30/94	Chairman's press statement announcing MOU
1/31/94	Confirmation of Russian agreement to reduce production by 500 000 tons/yr.

the overall portfolio. The gross return for the window surrounding the announcement of the MOU represented a $656.9 million increase in the equity value of the portfolio. The table also indicates that the two-day return to the Standard & Poor's 500 Index was 0.9%. The far right-hand column indicates the market adjusted change in the equity value of the portfolio by netting out the appreciation in the broader Standard & Poor's Index. This measure indicates that the announcement of the Memorandum of Understanding increased the equity value of the aluminum portfolio by $523 million, or by 3%.

A regression model was also used as a basis for estimating market adjusted rates of return for a series of windows surrounding the negotiations, announcement, and implementation of the MOU. Returns were estimated for one-, two-, seven- and ten-day windows surrounding the MOU conference and announcement in Brussels, the 42-day period representing initial consultations held in Washington which culminated in the MOU announcement on 28 January in Brussels, and a two-day period at the beginning of March where other international producers, most notably Pechiney, announced plans to reduce capacity in advance of an MOU status meeting held in Ottawa.[23] The returns for these windows, which are summarized in Table 5, range from $557 million valuation for the one-day window formally announcing the MOU to the $1.6 billion return representing appreciation accrued over the longer negotiating period beginning in mid-December.

During July 1994, a number of significant US aluminum producers also announced changes in their pricing practices which greatly reduced the lagged adjustment between changes in world cash prices and product contract prices. These announcements, which took place during the first two weeks in July, were examined to estimate their separate effect on expected producer cash flows. The results were shown to be highly significant. Adjusting for performance of the S&P 500 produced a 5.8% return to the aluminum portfolio ($838 million) during the period in which the revised pricing policy was announced, while adjusting for performance of a basic material index resulted in a 5.3% excess return ($766 million). In both cases, this pricing adjustment window resulted in a greater revaluation in expected producer cash flows than the announcement of the MOU itself.

Finally, in late August, it was revealed that the United States Justice Department (DOJ) had initiated a formal investigation of the MOU and US producer participation in its implementation. While the announcement did not specify that a formal antitrust complaint would be issued against any individual or group of domestic producers, the announcement should have conveyed a measure of uncertainty as to the ultimate effectiveness of the MOU and under what terms future capacity restraints could be maintained. The window around the 29 August public announcement of the DOJ investigation was tested to analyze investor reaction to potential changes in the MOU. Estimated excess returns for the period incorporating announcement of the investigation indicate that, based on the statistical insignificance of the test period variable, the DOJ

Table 5. Return on US Aluminum Portfolio Resulting From Enactment of the International Memorandum of Understanding on Primary Aluminum Output

Period	Return over the S&P 500 (%)	Market adjusted return[a] ($ mil)	Return over basic material index (%)	Market adjusted return[a] ($ mil)
1 day—1/31/94 First trading day after announcement of the MOU; including the terms and Russian acceptance	3.7	557	3.2	482
2 days 1/28, 31/94 Announcement of the MOU and the first trading day	3.6	541	3.0	451
7 days 1/25–2/2/94 4 days prior and 3 days following the announcement of the MOU	4.0[c]	591	3.8[c]	562
10 days 1/18–31/94 Period encompassing MOU conference in Brussels and announcement of MOU terms	6.0[b]	874	4.7[b]	685
42 days 12/1/93–1/31/94 Period including multilateral conference in Washington to discuss world-wide supply conditions, MOU conference in Brussels, announcement of the MOU	12.2[b]	1653	4.7[c]	632
2 days 3/1–2/94 Pechiney (French aluminum producer) agrees to capacity cut-back as part of MOU obligation, announcement made prior to MOU status conference in Ottawa	1.7[c]	255	2.5[b]	375
8 days 7/1–13/94 Period during which Alcoa, Kaiser Aluminum and Alcan announced price increases and adoption of a commodity price-based formula based on the LME	5.8	838	5.3	766
1 day—8/29/94 Public announcement of DOJ investigation of MOU, CIDs served on aluminum producers	0.5[c]	80	−0.5[c]	−80

Unless noted, values are statistically significant at the 95% level.
[a]Market adjustment based on the change in the equity value of the US aluminum portfolio from the trading day preceding each event.
[b]Statistically significant at the 90% level.
[c]Statistically significant at less than 90%.

announcement apparently had no significant impact on the perceived future cash flows of aluminum producers. It is unclear whether the prevailing market information in effect overrode the announcement or that investors determined that it was overly speculative to conclude that any actions taken by DOJ would negatively impact producers before the two-year agreement would expire on its own.

CONCLUSION

A multilateral Memorandum of Understanding was agreed upon in January 1994 by the major aluminum-producing countries of the world. Based on an econometric analysis of supply and demand, we estimate that this agreement accounted for 26–38% of the January/November price increase for aluminum ingot (a total of 58%). We also estimate that a price increase of this magnitude translates into $1.3–1.9 billion a year in additional expense for US consumers of aluminum products for the period of MOU compliance. Our conclusions from this supply and demand analysis are bolstered by the results of our study of aluminum stock prices, using a separate 'event analysis' methodology. That is, we estimated the impact of several important MOU-related events on the equity values of three principal domestic producers of primary aluminum. We found that the value of these firms' equities increased significantly in excess of market-wide revaluations on the first trading day after the MOU agreement was reached and during the first two weeks in July when the three principal producers of primary ingot and can stock announced new pricing policies. These value increases support our finding that the MOU contributed substantially to the increased price of primary aluminum during 1994.

NOTES

1. Arsen J. Darney, *Manufacturing USA*, 1994 ('Darney'), pp. 1245, 1250 and 1256.
2. The Aluminum Association, Inc., *Aluminum Statistical Review for 1993*, ('Aluminum Association'), pp. 31 and 61 and *Platt's Metals Week Price Handbook*, 1994, pp. 22 and 34.
3. It should be noted that our analysis was prepared without access to the files and records of aluminum producers and other possibly relevant documents and materials.
4. Aluminum Association.
5. Statistical and Market Research Committee of the Aluminum Association, Inc.
6. Aluminum Association.
7. *Id.*
8. *Id.*
9. Darney, pp. 1245, 1250 and 1256.
10. Aluminum Association.
11. Much of this discussion relies on the lengthy *Wall Street Journal* article, 'Foiled competition', June 1994.
12. Aluminum Association, Inc., CIS Aluminum Fact Sheet, p. 2 and American Metal Market, *Metal Statistics 1994*, 1994, p. 14.
13. *Platt's Metals Week Price Handbook*, 1991 and 1994.
14. US Bureau of Mines, 'US primary aluminum smelter closures'.
15. It is estimated that average variable cost is roughly 52 cents per pound for US smelters and that average total cost is roughly 82 cents per pound. These costs are US averages. Across the United States, average costs likely differ by location. The major inputs in making aluminum are alumina, power, and labor. Among these, power and labor are the inputs whose prices vary most across the United States, with the Pacific Northwest enjoying lower hydroelectric power rates, and the South enjoying differentially lower labor costs. See Norton (1993) and US Bureau of Mines (1994, p. 19).
16. The official language of the MOU does not include a reciprocal agreement on the part of the West to cutback output. However, it has been argued that there was an implicit agreement involving cutbacks by all signatories. See Commodity Metals Management Company (1994a,b).
17. *Metals Week*, February 1994 and December 1994.
18. The G7 countries are Canada, France, Germany, Italy, Japan, the United Kingdom, and the United States.
19. We first estimated least squares estimators and tested for the statistical significance of autocorrelation. Finding significant serial correlation, we then tested for the presence of omitted variables. We found that relevant independent variables may be omitted from the regression model. We corrected for omitted variables in this analysis using a weighted least squares procedure recommended by Maddala (1988, pp. 208–9).
20. This estimate is conservative for the following reasons. One, it is likely that primary aluminum consumption in the US was greater in 1994 than in 1993 because of the increase in demand. Two, the market value of primary aluminum consumption from which this estimate derived was based on 1993 prices which are less than 1994 price levels.
21. The other major publicly held aluminum producer, Kaiser Aluminum and Chemical Co., is a more broadly diversified firm with less of its total cash flow directly affected by changes in world-wide primary aluminum prices than the three firms chosen.
22. The variation in the individual firm returns appears to be related to the relative concentration of firm assets dedicated to the production of primary and fabricated aluminum products and to alumina and bauxite production. Alcoa's alumina production is significantly greater than either of the other two firms. A world-wide agreement to restrict aluminum output could be expected to negatively impact alumina producers and as such would mitigate expected returns from Alcoa's aluminum production activities.
23. In addition to employing the features of the capital asset pricing model to adjust for returns to the S&P 500, returns to the aluminum portfolio were adjusted for a more narrow portfolio of basic material producers whose products more closely reflect the prevailing outlook for markets related to the production and use of primary and fabricated aluminum. The Basic Material Index is a composite of 52 firms producing aluminum, non-ferrous metal, chemical, forest, mining, paper, precious metal, and steel products. The index is compiled and reported daily in the *Wall Street Journal* and the Dow Jones News retrieval service.

REFERENCES

Commodity Metals Management Company (1994a). FAX-Update from Aluminum Insight. 26 January, Pittsburgh, PA.

Commodity Metals Management Company (1994b). Regional impact of aluminum curtailments. 10 February, Pittsburgh, PA.

E. Fama (1991). Efficient capital markets II. *Journal of Finance*, **46**(5), December.

G. S. Maddala (1988). *Introduction to Econometrics*, New York, Macmillan, 208–9.

Metals Week (1993a). Aluminum Assn. sends resolution to USTR, 27 September.

Metals Week (1993b). Russia extends invite to discuss aluminum. 18 October.

Metals Week (1993c). Aluminum prices crumble as talks progress slowly. 1 November.

Metals Week (1993d). Aluminum roadshow heads for Brussels. 6 December.

E. Norton (1993). Alcoa will cut output by 25%, trim US force. *Wall Street Journal*, 28 June.

E. Sfiligoj (1994). Demand for materials makes itself felt in beverage packaging prices. *Periscope*, 30 November, 3.

W. F. Sharpe (1985). *Investments*, Englewood Cliffs, NJ: Prentice Hall.

US Bureau of Mines (1994). Impact of former Soviet Union aluminum exports on world producers: a network flow model analysis. 19 January.

2
Identifying Contracts, Combinations and Conspiracies in Restraint of Trade

Andrew R. Dick

University of California, Los Angeles, CA, USA

Antitrust guidelines rely on structural screens to review horizontal merger proposals for possible anti-competitive effects. This paper extends this screening approach to forecast where industry cartels will form, and where cartel agreements are more likely to raise price. I test the screen's reliability for a unique data set of legal, privately enforced industry cartels that formed under the Webb–Pomerene Export Trade Act. Consistent with screening assumptions, I find that cartels formed more frequently in industries with significant potential market power, high barriers to entry, and conditions facilitating the enforcement of agreements. However, these characteristics generally perform less well at distinguishing when cartels are likely to raise price without generating offsetting cost-savings, suggesting that screening is reliable only as a preliminary check for possible anti-competitive behavior.

INTRODUCTION

Section 1 of the Sherman Act declares illegal "every contract, combination... or conspiracy in restraint of trade." In his 1969 article, 'Oligopoly and the Antitrust Laws: A Suggested Approach', Richard Posner suggested how a simple review screen that combined economic theory with data might guide enforcement of the Sherman Act.[1] Posner divided the screening process into two stages. First, to concentrate investigative resources where they would be most productive, the screen would identify industries whose structure might encourage and ultimately sustain explicit cartel activity. Second, acknowledging that cooperation among competitors can both raise price and lower cost, the screen would attempt to distinguish anti-competitive conspiracies from efficient cost-saving agreements. A variant of two-stage screening is used currently to review horizontal mergers. For example, both the Department of Justice (DOJ) and the Federal Trade Commission (FTC) consider industry concentration levels as an indicator of firms' potential market power in preliminary merger investigations. Before deciding whether to challenge a merger, however, the agencies review other structural evidence on entry conditions, the ease of enforcing collusion and whether the industry has a history of anti-competitive behavior.[2]

This paper consider whether an analogous antitrust screen could reliably forecast the initiation of cartel agreements among rivals. I answer this question using a unique data set on legal, privately enforced industry cartel agreements established under the Webb–Pomerene Export Trade Act of 1918. The Act granted US exporters blanket antitrust immunity for form cartel associations, and allowed exporting firms to fix prices, allocate markets, exchange price and sales information, and coordinate all facets of marketing. While these cartel agreements were fully legal, however, they were not court-enforceable and therefore members were responsible for policing and discipline. Following Posner, I divide the screening analysis into two parts. First, in a data set where we can verifiably observe which industries exported under cartel agreements, I ask whether key structural characteristics can accurately forecast cartel formation. Next, using disclosure information on cartels' reported objectives, I ask whether these same characteristics can forecast which cartels sought primarily to raise prices versus cartels that may have generated offsetting efficiencies through cost savings.

I find that a concise structural screen forecasts with approximately 75% accuracy industries in which export cartels formed. Consistent with antitrust screening assumptions, cartels formed more frequently in industries with significant potential market power (reflected in a large export market share and the absence of secondary markets), high barriers to entry (reflected in large fixed capital requirements), and with conditions facilitating the enforcement of agreements (reflected in product standardization and growing demand). However, contrary to expectations, the existence of agreements was unrelated to business cycle timing, the variability of demand conditions, concentration among buyers, and whether the industry had a history of cartelization. Moreover, cartels were actually *more* likely to form in industries that had many small producers.

One explanation for this last finding, which is supported by micro-econometric evidence reported in Dick (1992), is that some Webb–Pomerene cartels formed instead to enable groups of small producers to economize on selling costs by coordinating their export marketing. To investigate further, I incorporate direct information on cartels' apparent primary objective. I find that simple price-fixing agreements were confined to industries where firms had a large export market share, buyers were small and dispersed, and entry was slowed by large fixed capital requirements. However, this screen misses approximately 30% of price-fixing cartels, and incorrectly attributes price-fixing to 25% of cartels that may actually have been efficient cost-saving agreements. Both types of errors impose potentially large welfare costs. Together, the empirical findings suggest that screening may be reliable only as a preliminary check for possible anti-competitive behavior. Further caution is warranted in light of the fact that Webb–Pomerene cartels were legal agreements. When price fixing instead is illegal, cartels face the additional burden of concealing their activities from antitrust authorities. Structural characteristics that assist cartel members in detecting cheating may at the same time raise cartels' visibility to antitrust authorities. Cartels that form under these conditions therefore may differ substantially from those analyzed here.

After a brief review of prior cartel research, the next section explains the Webb–Pomerene antitrust exemption and summarizes the extent of cartel formation. The third section develops and applies a structural screen for predicting where Webb–Pomerene cartels formed. The fourth section gauges the screen's ability to discriminate between price-raising and cost-lowering cartels. The final section summarizes and concludes.

EXISTING RESEARCH AND WEBB–POMERENE CARTELS

Prior Cartel Research

There is surprisingly little direct econometric evidence on the factors leading to cartels' formation. To paraphrase George Stigler (1968, p. v), the ratio of theory and anecdotes to actual data remains distressingly high. A small number of studies sketch the following 'stylized facts'. Price-fixed conspiracies are more common in industries with slow sales growth (Asch and Seneca, 1975), in industries selling homogeneous producer goods rather than differentiated consumer goods (Hay and Kellye, 1974; Asch and Seneca, 1975), in highly concentrated industries (Hay and Kelley, 1974; Fraas and Greer, 1977; but cf. Asch and Seneca, 1975), and in industries with comparatively stable technologies and cost conditions (Fraas and Greer, 1977).

These early studies reviewed case histories of prosecuted price-fixing agreements to infer the economic conditions supporting collusion. By selecting cases based on their prosecution status, however, these studies failed to separate cleanly the determinants of cartel formation from those guiding successful antitrust enforcement. The result was biased sampling that led to misleading interpretations of the evidence. As an example, because low industry concentration and large memberships can raise cartels' visibility to antitrust enforcement agencies, cartels with these characteristics appeared more numerous in some studies (Posner, 1970). Oligopoly theory predicts, however, that both characteristics should make cartels less viable. Biased sampling could explain several anomalous empirical findings, including Asch and Seneca's (1976) conclusion that on average, colluding industries displayed *lower* profit rates than non-colluding industries.

More recent empirical studies of cartels have sought to explain their longevity. Jacquemin *et al.* (1981) analyzed lifespans of Japanese export cartels, while Suslow (1988) and Marquez (1992) analyzed the duration of international commodity cartel agreements. These studies avoided biases from antitrust prosecution because both sets of cartels were unregulated by national antitrust laws. But the samples introduced an opposite bias, tending to inflate firms' incentive to enter into (and to continue) cartel agreements. Japanese export cartels typically were mandated by government decrees to extend to all firms in an industry, sharply lowering free-riding obstacles to cartel formation. International commodity cartels often were enforced by member country governments, making them quasi-state trading associations rather than private agreements. By failing to control for what amounts to state subsidization, Dick (1996) found that these studies over-estimated the longevity of industry cartels, the probability that they would re-form following a break-up, and the propensity of cartels to learn from past failures.

The Webb–Pomerene Antitrust Exemption

This paper avoids sampling biases that limited earlier cartel research by constructing a unique empirical experiment. The cartels analyzed in this paper formed under the Webb-Pomerene Export Trade Act of 1918, which authorized US exporters to enter into joint selling agreements for overseas markets. The Act explicitly exempted export cartels from Section 1 of the Sherman Act, which forbids conspiracies in restraint of trade, and from Section 7 of the Clayton Act, which prohibits mergers that reduce competition. Webb–Pomerene cartels operated virtually unfettered by antitrust oversight and restrictions. A cartel automatically received immunity from antitrust prosecution when it filed with the FTC a list of members and a copy of its articles of agreement. Failure to register within 30 days exposed the cartel to standard antitrust oversight and penalties. To remain immune from prosecution, cartels were required simply to file a brief annual report with the FTC, updating their membership list and summarizing their primary activities and volume of export sales during the past year.

Congress and the FTC nominally restricted cartels' activities in three areas but, in practice, undermined each restriction through narrow interpretations and lax enforcement. First, Congress indicated that export cartels should not 'adversely or intentionally' affect domestic prices. In 1924, however, the FTC determined that an export contract which 'incidentally or indirectly restricts' domestic pricing did not violate the Act.[3] Second, while the Act prohibited 'restraints of the export trade of any domestic competitor', Webb–Pomerene cartels were permitted to negotiate exclusive dealing agreements that could impede non-cartel firms' access to particular foreign markets. Finally, in a change of policy in 1955, the FTC began prohibiting side-agreements between Webb–Pomerene cartels and foreign producers. During the time span that I study, however, the FTC investigated just twelve agreements and ultimately prosecuted only two cartels for entering into side-agreements.[4]

While Webb–Pomerene cartels were immune from antitrust prosecution, the agreements were only privately enforceable. Neither the government nor the courts intervened to enforce agreements or to adjudicate disputes among members. Cartels instead relied upon contractual incentives and internal monitoring with sanctions to enforce agreements. Cartels structured their contracts to limit firms' short-run profit from defection, under the threat of expulsion. Contractual incentives were supplemented by internal mechanisms to investigate alleged infractions and resolve disputes. In most cases, the cartel created a governing body that was empowered to audit members' shipping records and financial statements. Members that failed to provide regular reports or that exceeded their quotas were sanctioned with fines or quota reductions. Because internal sanctions were not court-enforceable, however, ultimately cartels were forced to rely upon contractual incentives to ensure self-enforcement.

The Webb–Pomerene Act's minimal compliance obligations, together with its requirement that cartels register to receive antitrust immunity, raise two issues. First, the data set of registered Webb–Pomerene cartels should provide a complete listing of export agreements that would have been illegal without the antitrust exemption. Cartels apparently were not dissuaded from registering out of a fear that registration would invite antitrust scrutiny of their members' domestic activities (Larson, 1970, p. 499). There is no evidence that the FTC targeted Webb–Pomerene members for additional domestic antitrust oversight. Firms also were unlikely to shun registration in favor of maintaining tacit collusion. This is supported by the fact that Webb–Pomerene cartels formed in industries such as phosphates, abrasives, carbon black and crude sulphur where four-firm concentration ratios above 70% and world market shares between 45% and 90% should have made collusion sustainable even without a formal agreement.[5] While exporters were likely already to have been colluding tacitly in these industries, each formed a Webb–Pomerene cartel shortly after the antitrust exemption was enacted. The opportunity to formalize their agreement in a Webb–Pomerene contract offered tacitly colluding firms the advantages of adopting more efficient monitoring and punishment mechanisms that previously had been rejected because of their visibility to antitrust enforcers. Moreover, in at least two of these cartels, post-agreement export prices were higher than prices under tacit collusion, providing further evidence of the formal agreement's value to members (Dick (1992)).[6]

Second, there is the possibility that some firms might have registered as a cartel, so as to immunize themselves from antitrust scrutiny, yet never became active in any meaningful sense. To exclude these cases, I distinguish between 'registered' and 'active' cartels. I define a cartel to have been active if either (1) it operated as a common sales agency, to centralize order-taking, billing and shipping on behalf of members, or (2) the cartel set export price guidelines for the industry while leaving the logistics of shipping of member firms. When active cartels are defined using these criteria, approximately three-quarters of all registered cartels were active in an average year.

Cartel Motives and Effects

Table 1 summarizes Webb–Pomerene cartel formations between 1920 and 1965. Most noteworthy is the fact that very few industries availed themselves of the antitrust exemption. In a typical year, between 30 and 35 cartels were active, and collectively these cartels accounted for just 5% of total manufactured exports. However, these aggregate statistics obscure the fact that Webb–Pomerene cartels tended to concentrate in specific sectors. Approximately 30% of the cartels exported raw or semi-finished industrial materials (such as lumber, sulphur and copper), another 30% exported agricultural products (such as rice, flour and dried fruit), and a further 10% exported simple manufactures (such as pencils, buttons and clothespins). In total, approximately 70% of Webb–Pomerene exports consisted of standardized, relatively less processed commodities.[7] The remaining cartels exported a diverse range of manufactured products, including electrical machinery and automobile tires.

Table 1. Webb–Pomerene Cartels' Frequency and Export Share

Time period	Number of active cartels	Share of total US exports (%)
1920-24	30	2.9
1925-9	39	7.9
1930-34	35	12.2
1935-9	31	6.2
1940-44	30	2.1
1945-9	33	4.9
1950-54	30	4.5
1955-9	31	5.1
1960-64	27	4.6
1920-65	130	4.8

Source: United States Federal Trade Commission (1967, p. 23).

Researchers typically have emphasized price fixing as the primary motive for export cartels' formation. Several observations lend support to this emphasis in the case of Webb–Pomerene cartels. First, among cartelized industries, the US share of the world export market averaged 26%, suggesting the potential for firms to exercise collective market power. In many industries, the US export market share was significantly higher, such as in the earlier cited examples of crude sulphur (90%), carbon black (80%) and phosphates (45%). Second, Table 2 indicates that approximately four in five Webb–Pomerene cartels directly fixed prices and allocated foreign markets among sellers. While in some cases these competitive restraints were ancillary to other primary cartel objectives, they nonetheless provided a mechanism by which to exploit collective market power. Third, the distribution of firm sizes among cartel participants suggests that price-fixing may have been more important than reaping scale economies in many cartels. One-third of cartel members were at least as large as a *Fortune 500* firm in their era, and collectively these firms accounted for 90% of total Webb–Pomerene exports.[8] Finally, there is direct econometric evidence of successful price fixing by Webb–Pomerene cartels. Dick (1992) found that cartels exporting carbon black and crude sulphur successfully exploited overseas market power to restrict sales by an average 14.6% and raise price by an average of 6.5% when they were active.

However, other evidence indicates that many cartels did seek to share costs in common marketing activities. Dick (1992) found that cartels in canned milk, dried fruit, metal laths, milled rice and paperboard significantly expanded United States exports by exploiting economies of scale in joint marketing. Specifically, these cartels on average expanded export sales by 59.5% when they were active, and achieved cost savings reflected in an 11.5% average price reduction. Historical accounts of Webb–Pomerene cartels' activities confirm firms' cost savings from export cooperation in joint distribution, warehousing and marketing services. Scudder (1955, p. 45) found that one cartel reduced its members' selling costs by pooling advertising expenditures and other administrative overhead. According to Scudder, the cartel's activities also allowed more efficient

Table 2. Functions Performed by 23 Active Webb–Pomerene Cartels in 1962

Function	No. of associations
Price setting and market allocation	19
Foreign sales offices and/or agents	13
Market research and information	9
Sales to US government agencies	9
Freight and insurance	8
Negotiating with foreign governments and agencies	7
Promotional activities	6
Publications	6
Representing members before US agencies	5
Statistical services	4
Engineering and related services	4
Distributing and licensing activities	4
Market development	3
Foreign storage facilities	2
Financing	2
Credit information	1

Source: United States Federal Trade Commission (1967, p. 48).
Note: Data are based on 23 (out of 26) Webb–Pomerence cartels that were active in 1962. Each association performed two or more of the functions listed.

placing of orders and the development of new export markets.

FORECASTING WHERE CARTELS WILL FORM

Developing a Screen

Posner (1976, p. 47) argued that a 'firm's decision to collude ... is presumably made by balancing the potential gains of collusion ... against the costs of collusion. By examining the factors that bear on the private benefits and costs of colluding, we can identify the kinds of market settings in which collusion is likely to be attempted'. In this section, I develop a structural screen to predict where the net private benefits to cartelization will be greatest. Consistent with Posner's search for a concise screen, I use two criteria in developing the screen. First, I include industry characteristics that traditional price theory and previous empirical studies have suggested should be relevant to explaining cartels' formation. Second, I include industry characteristics that resemble those currently relied upon by the FTC and Department of Justice in their own horizontal review guidelines. Following those guidelines, I group industry characteristics into four categories: potential market power, entry conditions, the ease of enforcing collusion, and whether there is a history of cartel activity in the industry.

Potential Market Power

The maximum profit that firms may earn under a price-fixing agreement is limited by their potential market power. Webb–Pomerene cartels' potential market power rose with their industry's share of the world export market. Cartel agreements also will tend to be less costly to monitor when a large fraction of world sales is sourced from cartel members. However, the potential cost savings from pooling common marketing activities will tend to be smaller when firms already have established a substantial presence in overseas markets. Thus, depending upon a cartel's primary objectives, a larger industry market share might raise or lower the frequency of cartelization. I denote the United States' share of total world exports as *MKTSHR*. *MKTSHR* should positively affect price-fixing cartels' formation, but may discourage formation of cartels with cost-reducing objectives.

A cartel's potential market power also will depend upon whether there is a secondary market for its product. Product durability reduces the cartel's pricing discretion by introducing competition from the secondary market. Secondary markets further raise the cartel's enforcement costs by removing sales from its purview and effective control. At the same time, potential cost savings from joint marketing may tend to be smaller for durables. Durables may require partially customized marketing, which will reduce order size and narrow the economies of scale and scope that the cartel can capture. A dummy variable *DURABLE* will distinguish goods whose services are consumed over a period of three or more years, and it is expected to correlate negatively with cartel formation.

Entry Conditions

The ease with which entry can occur in an industry directly constrains cartels' potential profitability. Entry tends to be slower in industries with large economies of scale and sunk costs. By slowing entry, these characteristics lengthen the time during which the cartel can sustain supracompetitive profits. Cartel enforcement costs also tend to be lower when firms must sink specific investments to enter the industry. If a cheating firm is punished by forfeiting the future cartel return on its sunk assets, its short-run incentive to behave opportunistically by under cutting the cartel price is attenuated. Finally, when production is characterized by scale economies or large sunk costs, firms are more likely to specialize at the production stage so as to economize on the fixed managerial input. It follows that these firms are more likely to assign marketing functions to a cartel body than to perform them in-house. I will include a variable *CAPITAL* to measure industries' ratio of fixed capital stock to output, and I expect cartel frequency to depend positively on *CAPITAL*.

The Ease of Collusion

Beginning with George Stigler's (1964) seminal analysis, oligopoly theory has suggested a wide range of economic factors that may facilitate enforcement of cartel agreements. These include product standardization, high industry concentration, unconcentrated buyers, price stability and growing demand. Dick (1996) found that many of these factors helped to sustain Webb–Pomerene cartels after they formed. Here, I investigate their influence on an industry's decision of whether to form a cartel.

Cartels should form less frequently for differentiated products. Differentiation may raise the cost of enforcing cartel agreements because product quality and style differences must be identified and monitored to deter cheating along non-price dimensions. Differentiation also may be associated with differences in firms' production technologies, and this will tend to raise cartel costs further by requiring periodic quota reallocations whenever input prices change. Finally, differentiation may limit a cartel's opportunities to capture economies of scale and scope in export marketing. I will use a dummy variable *DIFFERENTIATED* to distinguish differentiated consumer products from relatively more standardized producer commodities, and expect it to enter negatively.

Next, if cartels are motivated solely by price fixing, they should be more common in industries with just a few, large domestic producers. High industry concentration should reduce the cost of initially reaching an agreement among firms, and should lower enforcement costs by improving the cartel's ability to detect less extreme instances of price cutting. If cost sharing were an important motive, however, this prediction could be reversed. In unconcentrated industries, economies of scale are more likely to remain unexploited if firms export individually. This implies larger potential benefits from coordinated marketing. If these greater cost savings outweigh the cartel's higher organizational costs, then cartels might form in unconcentrated industries. I include the standard four-firm industry concentration measure, CR4, to test between these hypotheses.

Cartels also should tend to form in markets with low buyer concentration. Identifying potential customers and tracking variation in local demand conditions are subject to economies of scale and scope. When buyers are numerous and spread geographically, it will be more cost effective to pool information about local demand across multiple firms. Working in the same direction, cartel enforcement costs should be lower when buyers are numerous and dispersed. Cartels will have access to a larger number of transaction prices which they can analyze to identify cheating and free-riding.[9] A variable *BUYSIZE* will measure the percentage of US exports in an industry that were purchased by the four largest importing countries. Because Webb–Pomerene cartels generally exported to a single purchasing agent in each foreign country, *BUYSIZE* will be directly correlated with average buyer size, and it is expected to affect cartel formation negatively.

Cartels also should find it more profitable to form in industries with price stability. When prices are not highly variable, the cartel will find it easier to distinguish random pricing deviations from deviations caused by unauthorized price cutting. Price stability also will reduce the occasions that the cartel must renegotiate firms' quotas. By reducing contracting and enforcement costs, therefore, price stability should tend to promote cartelization. As a measure of price volatility, I use the coefficient of variation in quarterly export prices during the year preceding the event date, *PRICEVAR*, and expect it to enter negatively.[10]

Finally, the industry's demand conditions should affect the ease of enforcing collusion. Stronger demand growth extends the cartel's expected horizon, and raises the maximum punishment that the cartel can impose by expelling a cheating firm and denying it the cartel return on future sales (Klein and Leffler, 1981). I use *EXGROWTH* to measure the rate of growth in US exports in the sector three years prior to the event date, and expect it to be positively associated with cartel frequency.[11] Cartel activity also may be linked to the industry's position in the business cycle. Green and Porter (1984) predict that collusion will cease, as part of an equilibrium enforcement strategy, whenever an unanticipated downturn in industry demand causes price to fall below a trigger level. Anticipated business cycles also could influence cartel formation. If some cartel members are likely to have exited from the industry by the end of the next downturn because of bankruptcy constraints, then the cartel's expected horizon again is shortened, which raises its enforcement costs. Dick (1996) found that anticipated (but not unanticipated) industry downturns precipitated cartel dissolutions. I define *EXCYCLE* as a dummy variable that equals one if the sector was in a downturn in the event year, and equals zero if the sector was in an upturn.[12] *EXCYCLE* is expected to enter negatively.

It is possible also that firms might have used legal Webb–Pomerene agreements to help enforce illegal collusion domestically. As noted above, during most of the Act's history, the FTC and the courts failed to scrutinize possible spillovers between export cartelization and the domestic market. Export cartels might have been used as an escape valve for excess supply that otherwise would have destabilized a tacit collusive agreement in the domestic market. Thus, when the domestic market entered a downturn, firms could have sustained their collusive domestic price by diverting sales to the export market through the cartel.[13] I construct a dummy variable *USCYCLE* equal to one if the domestic sector was in a downturn in the event year, and expect it to enter positively under this hypothesis.[14]

A History of Cartel Activity

If particular industries are structurally predisposed to cartelization, their past behavior should be a reliable predictor of their current (and future) behavior. Some earlier research offers support for this assumption. Suslow (1988) and Mar-

Table 3. Summary of Variables
(250 Observations, except as noted)

Variable	Definition[a]	Mean	Std dev.	Data source
BUYSIZE	Percent of U.S. export sold to four largest importing countries (−)	53.36	18.62	(10)
CAPITAL	Ratio of fixed capital stock to output (+)	0.410	0.339	(6)
CARTEL	1 if product is exported by a cartel	0.500	0.501	(1)
CR4	four-firm industry concentration ratio (+/−)	42.88	25.68	(7)
DIFFERENTIATED	1 for consumer goods (−)	0.360	0.481	(5)
DURABLE	1 for goods consumed over 3 or more years (−)	0.408	0.492	(5)
EXMKTSHR	US share of total world exports (+/−)	20.27	18.76	(8)
EXGROWTH	Growth in sector's exports for 3 years before event year (+)[b,c]	0.098	0.363	(9)
EXCYCLE	1 if export sector was in a downturn in event year[b,c] (−)	0.504	0.501	(4)
PRICE-FIX	1 if cartel acted primarily to fix price or allocate markets[d]	0.469	0.502	(5, 13, 14)
PRICEVAR	Coefficient of variation in quarterly export prices in year before event date[b,c] (−)	0.162	0.101	(2, 3, 4, 11)

Variable	Definition[a]	Mean	Std dev.	Data source
PRIOR-CARTEL	1 if product was previously exported by a cartel (+)	0.188	0.392	(1)
USCYCLE	1 if domestic sector was in a downturn in event year[b,e] (+)	0.252	0.428	(12)

[a]Predicted sign appears in parentheses for independent variables. Variables are measured as closely as possible to the event date.
[b]Event year is defined as either the year of cartel formation or, for control industries, the randomly selected year in the (industry, year) pair.
[c]Products were classified into one of four sectors: fooodstuffs, crude materials, semi-finished manufactures, or finished manufactures.
[d]Data available for 99 observations.
[e]Products were classified into one of three sectors: mining, non-durable manufactures, or durable manufactures.

Legend for data sources:
(1) US Federal Trade Commission (1967)
(2) Lipsey (1963)
(3) US Statistical Abstract (1940-1945)
(4) Mintz (1967)
(5) Temporary National Economic Committee (1941)
(6) Creamer, Dobrovolsky and Borenstein (1960)
(7) National Resources Committee (1939)
(8) US Department of Commerce (1969)
(9) US Department of Commerce (1975)
(10) United Nations (1952)
(11) US Department of Commerce (1972)
(12) US Board of Governors of the Federal Reserve System (1972)
(13) US Senate (1946)
(14) US Senate (1967)

quez (1992) found that between 36% and 64% of international commodity cartels made multiple attempts at fixing price. However, these studies' conclusions were biased by the fact that host countries were nearly five times as likely to aid enforcement after an international cartel's initial episode, thus inflating the private return to cartels in later episodes.[15] In contrast, only 19 out of the 125 privately enforced Webb–Pomerene cartels made repeated attempts to organize a cartel agreement. This suggests either that most breakdowns in cartel discipline stemmed from fatal enforcement problems that could not be corrected or that cartels dissolved permanently after they outlived their initial purpose. A complementary hypothesis is that, with time, buyers may learn to destabilize a cartel agreement or cartel members may learn how to conceal their cheating. In these cases, cartels could actually be *less* likely to re-form in industries with a history of cartelization. To investigate the impact of an industry's history on its current behavior, I include a dummy variable *PRIOR-CARTEL* that equals one if the industry had previously formed a Webb–Pomerene cartel.

Applying the Screen

To predict where cartels formed, I constructed a sample of 250 exporting industries that was divided evenly between cartelized and non-cartelized (control) products.[16] The sample includes all 125 Webb–Pomerene cartels that first registered between 1918 and 1965 and which remained active for longer than one year. I defined a cartel as active if either (1) it operated a common sales agency to centralize order taking, shipping and billing on behalf of members, or (2) the cartel set an export price target for the industry (but left shipping logistics to member firms). Recalling that firms were required to register at little cost to receive antitrust immunity, the population of registered cartels should provide a complete listing of export agreements that formed during the sample period. I chose to limit the sample to agreements that were active for longer than one year so as to exclude cartels that registered in error, that formed solely to market a temporary surplus in production, or that quickly dissolved for other reasons.[17] Data were matched as closely as possible to cartels' initial year of operation.[18]

The remaining 125 sampled industries were chosen randomly from among all exporting industries that did not organize into a cartel any-time during the study period.[19] These 125 industries comprised the control group. The control industries corresponded to the same level of product disaggregation as the Webb–Pomerene cartels, and they were restricted to industries that exported during the study period. Each control industry was paired with a randomly selected year between 1918 and 1965 to create (industry, event date) observation pairs to mimic the identifier for cartelized industries. Definitions, summary statistics and data sources for each of the variables used in the regression analysis are reported in Table 3.

Table 4 reports the regression results, based on logit estimation. The screen correctly predicts which industries formed cartel associations approximately 75% of the time. Since a naive prediction would have yielded a 50% accuracy rate, the screen's pseudo-R^2 is approximately 0.50. The model's prediction errors are fairly evenly

Table 4. Predicting Cartels' Formation

Dependent variable *CARTEL* = 1 for cartelized industries
Logit estimation
250 observations
(t-statistics in parentheses)

Variable	(1)	(2)	(3)	(4)
Constant	−1.244	−1.332[a]	−1.352	−0.703
	(−1.78)	(−1.95)	(−1.84)	(−1.49)
DIFFERENTIATED	−1.397[b]	−1.360[b]	−1.355[b]	−1.412
	(−4.01)	(−3.90)	(−3.68)	(−4.06)
DURABLE	−0.664[a]	−0.686[a]	−0.771[a]	−0.708[a]
	(−2.06)	(−2.13)	(−2.27)	(−2.22)
CAPITAL	2.468[b]	2.244[b]	2.849[b]	2.574[b]
	(3.44)	(3.37)	(3.78)	(3.61)
CR4	−0.013[a]	−0.013[a]	−0.015[a]	−0.014[a]
	(−2.02)	(−1.99)	(−2.20)	(−2.18)
EXMKTSHR	0.047[b]	0.047[b]	0.046[b]	0.048[b]
	(4.43)	(4.47)	(4.21)	(4.56)
EXGROWTH	1.712[b]	1.709[b]	1.813[b]	1.774[b]
	(3.12)	(3.22)	(3.23)	(3.43)
PRICEVAR	1.252	1.017	1.695	...
	(0.77)	(0.62)	(1.00)	
EXCYCLE	0.072	...	0.133	...
	(0.22)		(0.38)	
USCYCLE	...	0.436	...	...
		(1.19)		
BUYSIZE	0.58 E-2	0.67 E-2	0.20 E-2	...
	(0.70)	(0.79)	(0.23)	
PRIOR-CARTEL	...	...	13.700	...
			(0.08)	
% correct predictions	73.5%	72.7%	77.4%	75.8%
Log-likelihood	−129.21	−128.52	−116.15	−129.82
Chi-squared	88.15[b]	89.53[b]	114.28[b]	86.94[b]

[a] 5% significance.
[b] 1% significance.

balanced between false positives and false negatives. Individually, six characteristics enter significantly at customary statistical levels. Webb–Pomerence cartels were more likely to ship non-durable, capital-intensive, standardized products, to form in industries with low seller concentration, and to form in growing export markets where the United States had a large market share. While these six variables had a statistically significant impact on cartel frequency, their economic impact usually was small. For example, using column (4)'s specification, differentiated products were 7.8% less likely to be exported through a cartel, and durable products were 3.9% less likely to be cartelized. A doubling in capital intensity led to a 5.8% rise in the probability of cartel formation. Raising industry concentration by 20 points lowered the probability of cartelization by just over 1.5%. Doubling the industry's world export market share made cartel formation just 5.4% more likely, while doubling the rate of growth of export demand raised this probability by just 1%. Finally, cartel formation was consistently unrelated to business cycle timing (in either the export or domestic market), the industry's cartel history, concentration among buyers, and price volatility.

The screening results are each consistent with traditional theories of price fixing, with the noteworthy exception that Webb–Pomerene cartels formed more frequently in unconcentrated industries. This finding is consistent, however, with the hypothesis that some cartel may have sought to exploit economies of scale through collective marketing. The potential cost savings from coordinating firms' investments in overseas marketing would have been greater the smaller were individual manufacturers. Under a role of reason standard, cartels that sought to share common costs should be subject to a weaker level of antitrust scrutiny than simple price-fixing agreements. To develop a refined screen, therefore, the next section seeks to isolate cartels with the greatest potential to raise price.

ISOLATING PRICE-FIXING CONSPIRACIES

Posner's second purpose in developing an antitrust screen was to distinguish between pro- and anti-competitive cartel behavior. In general, a cartel will seek both to lower marketing costs, by capturing specialization efficiencies, and to exploit collective pricing power, by restricting output. If firms may cite efficiencies as an antitrust defense, then the relevant standard for review is whether, on balance, a cartel raises or lowers total welfare (Williamson, 1968). Clearly, a sufficient condition for total welfare to rise is that the cartel raise industry output and lower price. A weaker, necessary and sufficient condition is that the cost savings from cartel efficiencies exceed the deadweight loss cause by exercising market power. Williamson (1968) demonstrated that even very small cost savings can more than offset market power effects. This suggests that the initial antitrust screen should be refined to classify cartels according to the likelihood that they will generate non-trivial cost savings.

Because Webb–Pomerene cartels did not face the threat of antitrust prosecution, registration documents and annual filing reports should provide reliable information about cartels' declared objectives and, in turn, the likelihood that cartels might have generated offsetting efficiencies. Approximately 45% of Webb–Pomerene cartels reported setting a common price and/or allocating markets as their primary or sole objectives. Examples of these cartels include the Phosphate Export Association, which sought primarily to achieve 'stable export prices at profitable levels', and the US Alkali Export Association, which sought to 'eliminate unnecessary competition in export sales by members' and to 'insure an equitable distribution of the export business' across firms.[20] These cartels were unlikely to have generated significant cost savings for members.

The remaining 55% of cartels reported primary functions that could have enabled firms to lower their selling costs by capturing economies of scale from specialization. These functions included combining advertising, collaborating on market research, and pooling warehousing and shipping facilities. As earlier cited, Scudder (1955, p. 45) estimated the savings to one Webb–Pomerene cartel from consolidated marketing to equal approximately 50% of its total selling costs. These cartels could have generated cost savings large enough to offset any deadweight losses imposed by their exercise of market power.

Table 5 estimates logit regressions where the dependent variable *PRICE-FIX* equals one for Webb–Pomerene cartels whose primary function

Table 5. Identifying Price-fixing Cartels

Dependent variable *PRICE FIX* = 1 for price-fixing cartels
Logit estimation
96 observations
(*t*-statistics in parentheses)

Variable	(1)	(2)	(3)
Constant	0.507	0.548	0.159
	(0.47)	(0.51)	(0.14)
DIFFERENTIATED	1.286	1.334	1.319
	(1.71)	(1.76)	(1.70)
DURABLE	−0.455	−0.485	−0.597
	(−0.73)	(−0.78)	(−0.94)
CAPITAL	2.310[a]	2.310[a]	2.728[a]
	(1.90)	(1.93)	(2.12)
CR4	0.013	0.011	0.013
	(1.23)	(1.08)	(1.20)
EXMKTSHR	0.028[a]	0.028[a]	0.027[a]
	(2.18)	(2.22)	(2.06)
EXGROWTH	−0.278	−0.245	−0.258
	(−0.40)	(−0.36)	(−0.37)
PRICEVAR	2.207	2.164	2.862
	(0.72)	(0.69)	(0.90)
EXCYCLE	0.395	...	0.507
	(0.78)		(0.95)
USCYCLE	...	0.401	...
		(0.60)	
BUYSIZE	−0.067[b]	−0.064[b]	−0.070[b]
	(−3.59)	(−3.52)	(−3.70)
PRIOR-CARTEL	...	...	1.333
			(0.05)
% price-fixing cartels wrongly identified	33.3%	28.9%	28.9%
% cost-saving cartels wrongly identified	27.4%	25.5%	21.6%
Log-likelihood	−51.87	−52.00	−49.79
Chi-squared	28.96[b]	28.71[b]	33.13[b]

[a] 5% significance
[b] 1% significance.

was to fix prices or allocate markets among member firms.[21] The screen correctly identifies cartels' primary function in approximately 70% to 75% of industries. However, only three screening characteristics have individually significant influences on price fixing. Specifically, price fixing was more common where the industry had a large export market share, buyers were unconcentrated, and entry was slow. Because we are focusing on the much smaller sample of cartelized industries, however, the economic significance of these characteristics is now much larger. For example, doubling a cartel's world export market share raises by 37.0% the likelihood that it concentrated its efforts on price fixing. Reducing the *BUYERSIZE* variable in half nearly doubles the probability that a cartel sought primarily to fix prices. And doubling the industry's capital intensity, which should slow entry in response to cartel profits, makes it 63.0% more likely that a cartel will seek primarily to fix price. The remaining structural characteristics fail to distinguish between price-raising and cost-lowering agreements, rendering them unreliable predictors for an antitrust screen.

Additional concern arises from the screen's error rate in distinguishing between cartels that are likely to be price-raising or cost-lowering. The screen misidentifies price-fixing cartels between 29% and 33% of the time, concluding instead that these cartels were likely to have generated offsetting cost savings. These industries would be subjected erroneously to weaker antitrust scrutiny, imposing the cost of not investigating instances where cartels were likely to raise price. At the same time, the screen incorrectly identifies 22% to 27% of cartels as having sought only to fix price, in spite of their actual objectives that may have generated cost savings. These industries would be subjected erroneously to heightened antitrust scrutiny, imposing the cost of discouraging cooperation that may be relatively harmless or actually efficient.

CONCLUSIONS

This paper extended antitrust screening procedures to forecast where industry cartels will form, and where cartel agreements were more likely to raise price on balance. It found that cartels formed more frequently in industries with significant potential market power, high barriers to entry, and conditions facilitating the enforcement of agreements. However, these structural characteristics performed much less well at distinguishing when cartels were likely to raise price without generating offsetting cost savings. Together, these findings suggest that Posner's screening process could reliably forecast industries where cartelization is more likely to occur, but that attempt to screen cartels more finely would both erroneously target cost-saving agreements and neglect some anticompetitive conspiracies.

Acknowledgements

I thank UCLA's Business Organization and Regulation workshop participants, Doug Allen, Benjamin Klein, Jean Laurent Rosenthal and Michael Sproul for comments, and Ken Serwin for research assistance.

NOTES

1. Posner (1976, Ch. 4) elaborates on the original screening discussion.
2. Coate and McChesney (1992) provide direct empirical evidence on this two-stage review process for FTC merger investigations.
3. US Federal Trade Commission (1967, pp. 102-6).
4. US Federal Trade Commission (1967, p. 109).
5. US Senate (1946), Table B, Part I.
6. Thus, the raw data offer no apparent support for Fraas and Greer's (1977, p. 43) assertion that 'formal cartels arise most often where the structural conditions are not particularly favorable to collusion'.
7. United States Federal Trade Commission (1967, Appendix C2).
8. United States Federal Trade Commission (1967, p 44) and Larson (1970, pp. 476-7).
9. Noting that '[n]o one has yet invented a way to advertise price reductions which brings them to the attention of numerous customers but not to that of any rival', Stigler (1964, p. 47) predicted that 'oligopolistic collusion will often be effective against small buyers even when it is ineffective against large buyers'.
10. To avoid endogeneity, *PRICEVAR* is measured at a sectoral level of aggregation, as explained in Table 3.
11. To avoid endogeneity, *EXGROWTH* is measured at a sectoral level of aggregation, as explained in Table 3.
12. As with *EXGROWTH, EXCYCLE* is derived using a sectoral series to avoid endogeneity. See Table 3 for details.
13. Consistent with this hypothesis, Dick (1996) found that Webb–Pomerene cartels tended to be longer lived when the domestic market was depressed.
14. As with *EXCYCLE, USCYCLE* is derived using a sectoral series to avoid endogeneity. See Table 3 for details.
15. Dick (1996) discusses this bias at greater length.
16. Following the methodology outlined in Palepu (1986), where necessary I made the appropriate corrections in statistical calculations to reflect the fact that the equally weighted, state-based sample is not a random sampling across industries. These corrections affect the model's error rate and, in turn, estimates of marginal effects for individual regressors.
17. This eliminated five observations from the population.
18. As the data analyzed in Dick (1996) indicate, Webb–Pomerene cartel formations were spread widely across the sample period (1918-65), so that there is unlikely to be a period-specific effect explaining cartel formation patterns.
19. The product universe was defined by the National Resource Committee's (1939) listing of industries. Removing industries that did not export, and removing industries that organized a Webb–Pomerene cartel anytime between 1918 and 1965, I randomly selected 125 industries to constitute the control group.
20. Temporary National Economic Committee (1940, p. 210) and US Senate (1946, p. 43).
21. The sample size is reduced to 96 observations, because for some cartels it was not possible to verify their primary function from FTC documents.

REFERENCES

P. Asch and J. J. Seneca (1975). Characteristics of collusive firms. *Journal of Industrial Economics*, **23**, No. 3, March, 223–37.

P. Asch and J. J. Seneca (1976). Is collusion profitable? *Review of Economics and Statistics*, **68**, No. 1, February, 1–12.

M. B. Coate and F. S. McChesney (1992). Empirical evidence on FTC enforcement of the Merger Guidelines. *Economic Inquiry*, **30**, No. 2, April, 277–93.

D. Creamer, P. Dobrovolsky and I. Borenstein (1960). *Capital in Manufacturing and Mining: Its Formation and Financing*, Princeton: Princeton University Press.

A. R. Dick (1992). Are export cartels efficiency-enhancing or monopoly-promoting? *Research in Law and Economics*, **15**, 89–127.

A. R. Dick (1996). When are cartels stable contracts? *Journal of Law and Economics*, **39**, No. 1, April, forthcoming.

A. G. Fraas and D. F. Greer (1977). Market structure and price collusion: An empirical analysis. *Journal of Industrial Economics*, **26**, No. 1 September, 21–44.

E. J. Green and R. H. Porter (1984). Noncooperative collusion under imperfect price information. *Econometrica*, **52**, No. 1, January, 87–100.

G. A. Hay and D. Kelley (1974). An empirical survey of price fixing conspiracies. *Journal of Law and Economics*, **17**, No. 1, April, 13–38.

A. Jacquemin, T. Nambu and I. Dewez (1981). A dynamic analysis of export cartels: the Japanese case. *Economic Journal*, **91**, 685–96.

B. Klein and K. B. Leffler (1981). The role of market forces in assuring contractual performance. *Journal of Political Economy*, **89**, No. 4, 615–41.

D. A. Larson (1970). An economic analysis of the Webb–Pomerene Act. *Journal of Law and Economics*, **13**, No. 1. April, 461–500.

R. E. Lipsey (1963). *Price and Quantity Trends in the Foreign Trade of the United States*, Princeton: Princeton University Press.

J. Marquez (1992). Life expectancy of international cartels: an empirical analysis. Board of Governors of the Federal Reserve System, Discussion Paper No. 439.

I. Mintz (1967). *Cyclical Fluctuations in the Exports of the United States Since 1879*, New York: National Bureau of Economic Research.

National Resources Committee (1939). *The Structure of the American Economy*, Washington, DC: US Government Printing Office.

K. G. Palepu (1986). Predicting takeover targets: a methodological and empirical analysis. *Journal of Accounting and Economics*, **8**, 3–35.

R. A. Posner (1969). Oligopoly and the antitrust laws: a suggested approach. *Stanford Law Review*, **21**, No. 6, June, 1562–1606.

R. A. Posner (1970). A statistical study of antitrust enforcement. *Journal of Law and Economics*, **13**, 365–419.

R. A. Posner (1976). *Antitrust Law: An Economic Perspective*, Chicago: University of Chicago Press.

R. A. Scudder (1955). *The History and Operations of Webb–Pomerene Export Associations*, unpublished dissertation, University of California at Berkeley.

G. J. Stigler (1964). A theory of oligopoly. *Journal of Political Economy*, **72**, No. 1 February, 44–61.

G. J. Stigler (1968). *The Organization of Industry*, Homewood, IL: Richard D. Irwin.

V. Y. Suslow (1988). Stability in international cartels: an empirical survey. Hoover Institution Domestic Studies Program Working Paper No. E-88-7.

Temporary National Economic Committee (1940). *Export Prices and Export Cartels*, Investigation of Concentration of Economic Power, Monograph No. 6, Washington, DC: Government Printing Office.

Temporary National Economic Committee (1941). *The Structure of Industry*, Investigation of Concentration of Economic Power. Monograph No. 27, Washington, DC: Government Printing Office.

United Nations (1952). *Commodity Trade Statistics, Series D, No. 10*, New York: United Nations.

United States Board of Governors of the Federal Reserve System (1972). *Industrial Production — 1971 Edition*, Washington, DC: Board of Governors of the Federal Reserve System.

United States Department of Commerce (1940-45). *Statistical Abstract of the United States*, 1939 to 1944 editions, Washington, DC: Government Printing Office.

United States Department of Commerce (1969). *The Position of the United States in World Commodity Exports in 1968*, Technical paper No. 23, Washington, DC: Government Printing Office.

United States Department of Commerce (1972). *Indexes of U.S. Exports and Imports by Economic Class: 1919 to 1971*, Washington, DC: Government Printing Office.

United States Department of Commerce (1975). *Historical Statistics of the United States: Colonial Times to 1970*, Washington, DC: Government Printing Office.

United States Federal Trade Commission (1967). *Webb–Pomerene Associations: A 50-Year Review*, Washington, DC: Government Printing Office.

United States Senate (1946). *Small Business and the Webb–Pomerene Act*, Report of the Foreign Trade Subcommittee of the Special Committee to Study Problems of American Small Business, Washington, DC: Government Printing Office.

United States Senate (1967). International aspects of antitrust, 1967. Hearings before the Subcommittee on Antitrust and Monopoly of the Committee of the Judiciary, United States Senate, 19th Cong., 1st session, Washington, DC: Government Printing Office.

O. E. Williamson (1968). Economies as an antitrust defense: the welfare tradeoffs. *American Economic Review*. **58**, March, 18–36.

3

Distinguishing Participants from Nonparticipants in a Price-fixing Conspiracy: liability and damages

Roger D. Blair and Richard E. Romano

College of Business Administration, University of Florida, USA

INTRODUCTION

The cast iron widget industry has had a stable and concentrated market structure for many years: there has been little change in its production technology, and the producers face identical input prices because they are all located in the Birmingham area. Consequently, the firms have the same cost curves. Brand preferences are unimportant inasmuch as cast iron widgets must meet exacting industry specifications. All indications are that prices and outputs have been determined independently in the past. For the industry, 1987 was a year of stability in costs as well as demand. As a result, price and output were also stable.

The industry held its annual trade show in early January 1988. Although the focus of the show was the promotion of new uses for cast iron widgets, there was a good deal of grumbling among the producers that prices and profits were too low. Following the meeting, prices rose dramatically to a record peacetime high. As a result, quantities sold fell and excess capacity developed. Distressed customers attempted to shop around, but none of the five manufacturers would budge on price. As one would expect, the customers' dismay turned to outrage as their costs rose and their first-quarter profits fell. Several customers complained openly about gouging and a perceptive few observed that the price rise had been uniform across all firms and had followed closely on the heels of the annual trade show. It occurred to one customer that this apparently inexplicable pricing behavior might be collusive. A group of disgruntled customers contacted an antitrust attorney who filed suit alleging that the five manufacturers of cast iron widgets had violated section 1 of the Sherman Act by engaging in a price-fixing conspiracy.

The plaintiffs sued all five members of the industry and offered a mixture of circumstantial and 'smoking gun' evidence. First, they pointed to the price evidence. Shortly after a trade association meeting, they noted that prices rose for no obvious reason. In particular, neither costs nor demand had increased appreciably. Second, in the past, the presence of excess capacity had led to severe price wars as each firm attempted to expand its share of a diminished market at the expense of its rivals. In this instance, however, excess capacity led to no price cutting at all; in fact, prices rose substantially. Third, no increase in any other form of competition was evident. For example, there had been no increase in favorable credit terms, free delivery, or the like. Without hard evidence of conspiracy, these otherwise inexplicable bits of data would have remained merely circumstantial evidence of collusion.

The plaintiffs, however, did not have to rely solely on circumstantial evidence, for there was some weak 'smoking gun' evidence as well. First, the firms had exchanged price lists.[1] In addition, they all sold on a delivered price basis.[2] Finally, each firm offered precisely the same discount for prompt payment.

On the basis of the above evidence, a jury could easily find that price fixing had occurred and that all five sellers were responsible. But one of the producers, American Cast Iron Widget, insists that it is innocent. Although spokesmen for American have been somewhat guarded about what may have led to the price rise, they have been adamant in proclaiming their firm's innocence of any wrongdoing. American contends that while the other four producers may have met and decided upon a price above the competitive level, its own people did not participate. Convinced of their client's innocence, American's attorneys have retained the economic consulting firm of B&R Associates to provide litigation support. What can these economists do to help American's lawyers?

In the next section, we attempt to answer this question by proposing a fairly simple output test that will provide economic evidence of a firm's participation or nonparticipation in a price-fixing conspiracy. We then apply this test in a dominant firm context to demonstrate the usefulness of the test. Drawing upon experience in an actual case, we provide an example of how our test was applied in practice. After analyzing the liability issue, we turn our attention to the interesting damages question posed by the presence of nonparticipants.

A SIMPLE OUTPUT TEST

As the preceding discussion suggests, the problem is to find a practical test for distinguishing participation in a price-fixing agreement from nonparticipation in such an agreement. Any economic test should be based firmly upon economic theory. Widely accepted economic theory predicts that *all* firms in an industry will increase price following a price-fixing agreement among a *subset* of the firms in that industry. Hence, even though data on industry prices can easily be misinterpreted to indicate that a particular firm is guilty of price fixing, such data actually are inconclusive on the question. But economic theory also predicts that the observable behavior of participants in a price-fixing agreement will differ fundamentally from that of a nonparticipant. In particular, participants will limit their outputs following such an agreement, while nonparticipants will do the opposite. Because data on output patterns are likely to be readily available through the discovery process, participants and nonparticipants can be identified easily. Thus, B&R Associates proposes a simple output test to draw the distinction.[3]

To demonstrate the usefulness of this test, we will describe how all the firms behaved prior to the formation of a cartel by a subset of the firms. Then we will examine how the participants and the nonparticipant behave following the formation of the cartel. In this description and examination, we will employ a collusive variant of the dominant firm model.

DOMINANT FIRM (CARTEL) MODEL

Suppose that prior to any price-fixing activity, the five widget producers competed on price.[4] This would result in prices equal to marginal cost. For the cast iron widget industry, then, price and output will be determined by the equality of supply and demand. Here, the industry supply function is the horizontal sum of the marginal cost curves of the five producers. In Fig. 1, we can see that S, which is the horizontal sum of the firms' marginal cost curves, intersects industry demand D at a price of $5000 and an output of 5000 cast iron widgets.

A Partial Conspiracy Model

If we assume that American Cast Iron Widget is telling the truth about its noninvolvement, then the other producers have embarked on a price-fixing conspiracy while American has continued to pursue an independent and competitive pricing policy. When the cartel was formed, the four cartel members set the price so as to maximize their joint profits, taking into account that American would continue to produce that level of output at which its marginal cost equals whatever price the cartel selected. Although it may seem odd that an equal-sized firm in a five-firm oligopoly would behave passively as a price taker, this is a natural consequence of the initial price competition. Moreover, this passive behavior is quite profitable. As we shall see, the passive nonparticipant enjoys the benefits of the higher price without a corresponding obligation to restrict output in order to make the price rise stick.

In order to see the outcome of our model graphically, we must first find the conspirators' residual demand curve, which equals the market quantity demanded minus American's output at all prices. Next, we find the residual demand's associated marginal revenue curve in order to identify the profit-maximizing price and joint output of the cartel. These curves are shown in Fig. 1 as d and mr, respectively. The cartel maximizes its joint profits by producing the output where the residual marginal revenue (mr) equals the cartel's joint marginal cost (the horizontal sum of their four marginal cost curves), which is shown as S′. Associated with this, the colluding firms adopt the new price of $5600, *which the competitive nonparticipant also adopts.* At this point, it is important to note that the nonparticipant's price will be bid up to $5600. If American Cast Iron Widget originally did not increase its price, new customers would place orders at the old price. But reference to Fig. 1 makes clear that the nonparticipant will not wish to sell *additional* output at the old price because doing so would reduce its profits. Because American's disappointed customers face the rigid alternative price of $5600, they have an incentive to offer a higher price to the nonparticipant. Competition among the customers will bid up the

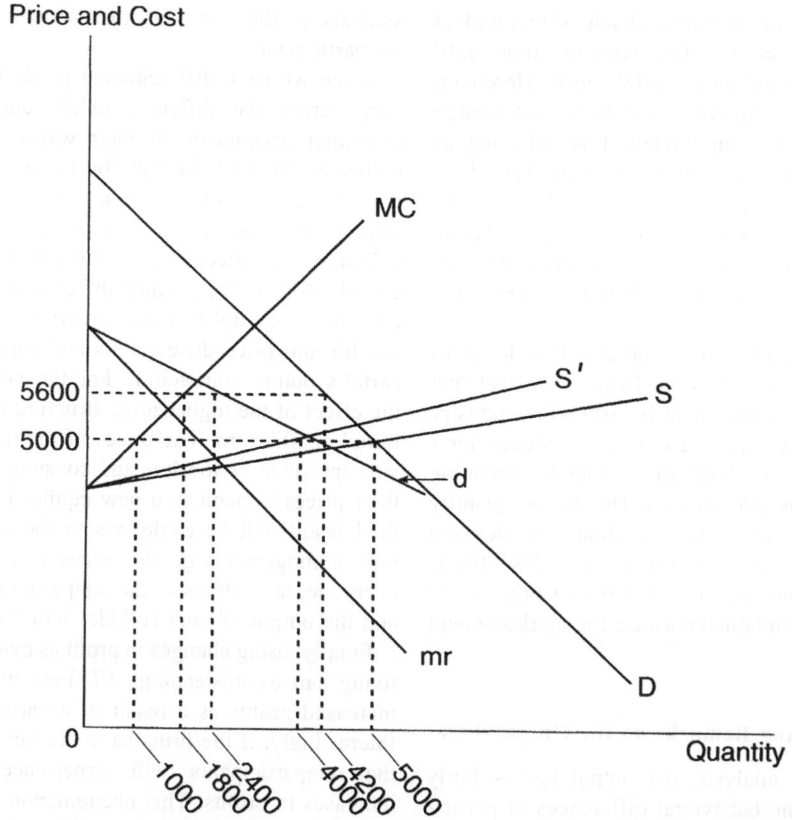

Figure 1.

nonparticipant's price until it is in line with the market—that is, until it equals \$5600. One should also note that prior to the formation of the cartel, American produced 1000 units while the price fixers collectively produced 4000 units. Of course, industry output (5000 units) equals the sum of American's output (1000 units) and that of the other firms (4000 units). If American behaved as it claims to have behaved, its output would have risen from 1000 units to 1800 units following the formation of the price conspiracy because its marginal cost (mc) equals the collusive price of \$5600 at an output of 1800 cast iron widgets.

Economic Results

The economic results of the partial conspiracy model are not complicated. First, each of the *participants* will produce less than before the collusion started, and therefore the aggregate output of these firms will decline. To see this, note that the colluding parties initially produced an output of 4000 units where S′ crosses d. As a result of the collusion, their output fell to 2400 cast iron widgets. The economic logic driving this result is that marginal revenue (mr) lies below the residual demand (d), and that price fixing led these firms to produce where mr crosses S′. That each cartel member reduces its output follows from the facts that marginal cost is equal across all firms both before and after formation of the cartel and that collective output has declined.[5] Specifically, each of the colluders reduces output from 1000 to 600 units.

Second, American—the nonparticipant—produced more output after the formation of the cartel than before: 1800 units versus 1000 units. The reason that American expands its production following the price rise is straightforward. Prior to the price conspiracy, American produced 1000 units where its marginal cost equalled the price of \$5000. When the price fixers set the market price at \$5600, additional production became profitable for American. Because the price (\$5600) exceeded American's marginal cost (\$5000), an additional widget would increase sales revenue more than it would increase cost and therefore production and sale of that widget would increase profit. This remains true until American hits an output of 1800 units. Moreover, as discussed above, American eventually will charge the collusive price even though it is behaving as competitively as a firm can behave. In the case where there are multiple nonparticipants, it is also true that each nonparticipant will expand its output. Again, positively sloped marginal cost curves and an increased price assure that each firm's output will increase.

Finally, it is clear that total output will be lower as a result of the price collusion. Despite the fact that American increased its output by 800 units, industry output declines because the colluders reduced their collective output by 1600 units, thereby reducing industry output by 800 widgets. Due to the quantity reduction, the industry moves along the demand curve from a price of \$5000 to a price of \$5600. If total output had not declined, the higher price could not have been maintained because the market would not have cleared.

Some Concluding Remarks on the Output Test

From the above analysis, the output test is fairly obvious due to the behavioral differences of participants and nonparticipants. Every cartel participant will decrease its output while the opposite is true for a nonparticipant. Thus, economists providing litigation support for American's lawyers should gather output data to determine whether American expanded while the other industry members reduced output. These data are easily obtainable during the discovery process. This test is somewhat more complicated when costs and/or demand are changing, but the principle is the same. Here the observed outputs should be compared to the output pattern that would result under noncooperation following the cost and/or demand changes. We do not mean to minimize the complexities of controlling for these factors.

The output test is not confined to the model we have presented. It can be extended to other models of oligopolistic behavior.[6] In addition, it can be used in situations where there are multiple nonparticipants and/or differentiated products (see Appendix). Intuitively, what occurs with multiple nonparticipants is that each behaves as American did in the analysis presented above (Blair and Maurer, 1982). The residual demand facing the colluders is the market demand minus the sum of the competitive supply responses of the nonparticipants. The rest of the analysis is the same as that shown for a single nonparticipant.

When we have differentiated products, price may vary across the different sellers due to varying consumer acceptance of their wares. Prior to any collusion, there will be equilibrium price differentials that reflect consumers' valuations of the array of imperfectly substitutable products. If a group of firms colludes on price, the optimization problem is complicated by the product differentiation, but what emerges is a higher price structure complete with equilibrium price differentials and supported by the cartel's output contraction. For the nonparticipants, the effect of the higher price structure is to upset the initial equilibrium. The prices of the nonparticipants will appear to be too low and consumers will bid up their prices to achieve a new equilibrium. Thus, the final result will be analogous to the case involving only homogeneous goods: prices will be higher for everyone, the outputs of the nonparticipants will rise, and the output of each colluder will contract.

Finally, using changes in profit as evidence of price fixing can be misleading. *All* firms will experience increased profits as a result of a partial conspiracy. Interestingly, if the firms have the same cost curves, the nonparticipants will experience the largest increases in profits. This phenomenon should not be misconstrued as an indictment of the nonparticipants. On the contrary, these firms enjoy the largest increases in profits precisely because they expand output—a choice that is socially desirable. Although these remarks would seem to suggest a profits test to identify nonparticipants—a nonparticipant should experience a greater increase in profits than the participants in a partial conspiracy—there are good reasons to prefer an output test. Our central point here is to caution against the misinterpretation of profit data. In most instances, output can be measured unambiguously. This is not true of economic (as opposed to accounting) profit. There are a host of difficulties in properly imputing capital costs and the opportunity costs of owned resources. Moreover, a profits test fails when cost curves vary significantly across the firms. For some useful insights, see Fisher and McGowan (1983).

AN EXAMPLE

Economic analysis of the facts and circumstances in *E.W. French & Sons, Inc. v. General Portland, Inc.* provides a real illustration of the output test's usefulness. French sold ready-mix concrete, which is made from sand, water, aggregates, and cement. General Portland produced and sold cement to French and French's rivals. Among other things, French alleged that General Portland and five rivals had conspired to fix cement prices at artificially higher levels in Southern California. A version of the output test was presented to the court and proved persuasive for the defendant General Portland.[7]

The cement industry in Southern California undeniably was (and still is) concentrated. In Table 1 the shares of productive capacity, measured in tons per year, are displayed. Based upon the data in Table 1, we can see that the four-firm concentration ratio is 82.6. The Herfindahl Index is 2075, which falls in the highly concentrated range according to the Department of Justice's Merger Guidelines. Of course, one of the major concerns surrounding a highly concentrated industry is the ease of collusion among its component firms.

Much of our opening hypothetical was applicable to the Southern California cement industry. Technological change in the production of cement had been fairly slow. The industry was fairly localized due to the shipping costs of cement relative to the value of the product. Because the plants are of varying ages and locations, it is probably not true that the producers have identical cost curves. Nonetheless, the output test permits variation in costs. The firms did face similar input prices. Moreover, cement is a homogenous product, and for that reason it is physically fungible across brands. Finally, there appears to be long-run excess capacity in the industry. Over the 1970–80 period, capacity utilization varied from a low of 64.5% in 1975 to a high of 89.8% in 1978. At a time when excess capacity was expanding, French alleged that cement prices rose dramatically. Thus, French inferred that General Portland and its rivals had fixed cement prices.

Interestingly, General Portland was the only cement producer sued by French.[8] Consequently, there was very little evidence regarding the other cement producers. Fortunately, though, the evidence was sufficient for use of the output test. The evidence indicated that General Portland did not participate in a price-fixing conspiracy, if indeed one even existed.

Table 2 contains the evidence regarding General Portland's activity over time. General Portland's production shows the usual sorts of ups and downs that a cement producer is likely to experience. The demand for cement is derived from the demand for construction activity, which is somewhat unstable. Moreover, each cement producer's fortunes will depend to some extent on how its customers fare in their bids for new construction contracts. Nonetheless, it is evident that General Portland's production levels were fairly high. Over the crucial period of 1973–6 we see that General Portland was expanding its output. In addition, General Portland's capacity utilization was increasing over time.[9] Finally, General Portland's market share always exceeded its share of capacity. Moreover, its share was expanding during the 1973–6 period. In fact, during 1976 General Portland's share of industry production (11.1%) was 40% higher than its share of capacity (7.9%). This pattern of activity is inconsistent with active participation in a price-fixing

Table 1. Shares of Productive Capacity: 1976

Firm[a]	Capacity[b]	Share[c] (%)
California Portland[d]	2 360 000	30.2
Amcord[d]	1 992 000	25.5
Southwestern	1 128 000	14.4
Kaiser	980 000	12.5
Monolith	730 000	9.3
General Portland	620 000	7.9

[a]Amcord's capacity was inferred from industry totals. For all other firms, Bureau of Mines reports were used.
[b]Capacity was measured in short tons of grinding capacity.
[c]Shares do not total 100.0 due to rounding.
[d]California Portland and Amcord each have two plants; the remaining firms each have one.

Table 2. General Portland: Output, Capacity Utilization, and Market Share 1968–76

Year	Output[a]	Capacity Utilization[b] (%)	Market Share[c] (%)
1968	497	80.2	9.2
1969	500	80.6	8.5
1970	509	82.1	8.2
1971	521	84.0	8.4
1972	584	94.2	8.8
1973	570	91.9	8.5
1974	497	80.2	9.1
1975	527	85.0	10.5
1976	612	98.7	11.1

[a]Output is measured in thousands of short tons.
[b]The percentage capacity utilization rate is calculated as production divided by capacity. Based upon Bureau of Mines reports and Bureau of Mines, *Mineral Yearbooks*, various years.
[c]General Portland's market share is calculated as General Portland production divided by industry production as reported in the *Mineral Yearbooks*.

conspiracy. Presumably for these reasons, the district judge directed a verdict in favor of General Portland on the price-fixing allegation.

DAMAGES AND STANDING

The Basic Damages Rule

Private plaintiffs generally sue for injuries suffered to their business or property. Section 4 of the Clayton Act provides in relevant part:

> That any person who shall be injured in his business or property by reason of anything forbidden in the antitrust laws may sue therefor in any district court of the United States in the district in which the defendant resides or is found or has an agent, without respect to the amount in controversy, and shall recover threefold the damages by him sustained, and the cost of suit, including a reasonable attorney's fee. (15 USC §15).

This apparently plain language would seem to confer a property right on any person who has suffered any economic injury due to an antitrust violation. This, however, is not the case, because the courts have restricted the pool of plaintiffs permitted to seek treble damages.

General Standing Criteria

In principle, a single antitrust violation could affect the entire economy. As a result, the courts have attempted to deal with the enormous numbers of potential plaintiffs by restricting access through standing requirements. In general, the courts have demanded the following:

(1) That the plaintiff be injured in fact
(2) That the injury be to his 'business or property'
(3) That the injury be of the type the antitrust laws were intended to prevent
(4) That there be a significant causal connection between the defendant's violation and the plaintiff's injury, and
(5) That the injury flow from that which makes the defendant's act unlawful (Areeda and Turner, 1978, at ¶334).

Returning to our original hypothetical, let us assume that American Cast Iron Widget did not conspire with anyone, but that the other four producers fixed prices among themselves. This raises two questions. First, do American's customers have standing? Second, if they do have standing, who should compensate them for their injury?

The Antitrust Standing of American's Customers

It is clear from Fig. 1 that American's customers pay \$5600 instead of \$5000 solely because of the price-fixing conspiracy.[10] It is equally clear that they have suffered injury to their property due to the \$600 increase in price. Thus, American's customers can easily make it over the first two hurdles. Similarly, the third requirement is easily met because the antitrust laws were intended to prevent monopoly pricing (Bork, 1966; Lande, 1982).

The fifth requirement, which involves a demonstration of antitrust injury, is straightforward in this case.[11] The Supreme Court's *Brunswick* decision ushered in the modern era of antitrust injury. Brunswick, a manufacturer of bowling equipment, had extended credit to several bowling alleys that were headed for bankruptcy. Rather than foreclose on the alleys and have a warehouse full of used equipment, Brunswick acquired them as going concerns and operated them in competition with the plaintiff, a competitor of the acquired alleys. The plaintiff complained that Brunswick's acquisition violated section 7 of the Clayton Act, which prohibits mergers that substantially lessen competition or tend to create a monopoly. The plaintiff's substantive theory was that the presence of Brunswick, a large manufacturing firm, in the bowling alley market could 'substantially lessen competition' as the smaller competitors were driven out of the market. The damages sought by the plaintiff were calculated as the profit that Pueblo would have earned had the failing bowling center been closed.

Instead of addressing the substantive question of whether Brunswick's acquisitions violated section 7, the Supreme Court attacked the remedial issue. For the Court, the question was not whether the plaintiff had suffered some sort of injury as a result of Brunswick's entry. Rather, the question was whether the injury claimed was '"by reason of" that which made the acquisition unlawful' (*Brunswick*, 1977, p. 488).

Pueblo's claim for lost profit was not due to injuries incurred 'by reason of' a forbidden act. The loss, the Court noted, would have been the same regardless of the size or power of a new entrant into the market. More generally, Pueblo's injury was due to an *increase* in competition that kept it from acquiring market power itself. According to the Court, Pueblo had failed to demonstrate that it had suffered 'antitrust injury' which it defined as 'the type the antitrust laws were intended to prevent and that flows from that which makes the defendant's acts unlawful' (*Brunswick*, 1977 p. 489). Pueblo's alleged loss was linked to increased competition in the bowling alley market, but not to any predatory conduct. Accordingly, Pueblo had not alleged an antitrust injury as a result of Brunswick's acquisitions. The same, however, cannot be said of American's customers in our hypothetical.

From Fig. 1, it is clear that the preconspiracy price was $5000. When the four colluders raised their prices to $5600, they did so in the knowledge that customers would bid American's price up to $5600 as well. Every customer who purchases at the collusive price of $5600 is injured by $600 per unit irrespective of the seller's identity. The fact that one customer buys from one of the colluders while another buys from American is simply irrelevant. Each and every customer is paying exactly the same overcharge as an immediate result of the conspiracy. All of American's customers unequivocally have been injured due to the antitrust violation, which in our view clearly constitutes 'antitrust injury'.

The final consideration is whether there is a significant causal connection between the defendants' violation and the injury suffered by American's customers. One would certainly think that this requirement is met in our hypothetical. The judicial test is the target area test: 'In order to state a cause of action under the antitrust laws a plaintiff must show ... that he is within the area of the economy which is endangered by a breakdown of competitive conditions in a particular industry' (*Loew's*, 1951, pp. 54–55). Areeda and Turner have pointed out that victims can satisfy the target area test without showing that the colluders were aiming at them. In our hypothetical, the price fixers restrained competition in the cast iron widget industry. There was clearly a breakdown in the competitive conditions in this market, and American's customers obviously participated in this area of the economy even though they did not purchase from the price fixers.

In circumstances like those we have described, a court may deny standing to customers of a nonconspirator by misusing the *Illinois Brick* rule. *Illinois Brick* was among the judicial progeny of *Hanover Shoe* (1968), a case in which the Court ruled that a defendant may not reduce the damages due to price fixing by demonstrating that the plaintiff had passed on part of the overcharge to subsequent purchasers.

Illinois Brick addressed the analogous question of whether a plaintiff could use the pass-on theory in order to collect damages from a seller from which it had not made a direct purchase. The Court first noted that consistency required it to deny such an action unless *Hanover Shoe* were overruled. The rationale was that permitting the pass-on theory for offensive purposes, but not for defensive purposes, would create the possibility of multiple liability and duplicative damage awards. Thus, the Court worked from the premise that the rules regarding passed-on overcharges should be the same for plaintiffs and defendants.

The more general issue, therefore, was whether to change the judicial approach and make the pass-on theory available for *both* offensive and defensive use. The Court ruled against use of the theory and denied standing to indirect purchasers. It is important to understand that the issue was not whether indirect purchasers had suffered an 'antitrust injury'. Certainly they had, inasmuch as the overcharge is the logical and direct consequence of a price fixing arrangement. Instead, the concern is less substantive and more policy oriented in that it asks whether there are good reasons for construing section 4 as excluding indirect purchasers from the pool of potential plaintiffs.

The primary rationale offered by the Court for excluding indirect purchasers was the complexity likely to result from apportioning an overcharge among various levels of direct and indirect purchasers. The Court noted that although economic theory offers methods of making the apportionment, these methods depend upon numerous simplifying assumptions that are unlikely to mirror reality. Moreover, such efforts at apportionment are not judicially manageable.[12] Thus, *Illinois Brick* stands for the proposition that the injuries to indirect victims are to be borne by the victims. The Court's implied theory is that, even though the attenuated ripple effects of price fixing are caused in fact by the colluders, they are not *proximately* caused by this behavior.

The majority argued that its decision furthered the interest of using the treble damage action as a deterrent. It reasoned that an attenuated process of apportioning damages would lower the stakes for any potential 'private attorney general' while increasing litigation expenses and thereby decreasing the incentive to sue. The Court acknowledged that to some extent its decision subordinated the compensatory function of section 4 to the goal of deterrence.

In any event, the Court's *Illinois Brick* concerns are not relevant to the problem at hand. First, American's customers are *not* indirect purchasers; they are direct purchasers. They buy cast iron widgets at the same point in the chain of distribution as do the customers of the colluders. Second, granting standing to American's customers does not raise the specter of multiple liability and duplicative damages. The damages are limited to the actual injury (overcharges) caused by the price fixing conspiracy; there can be no double counting. Finally, the claims of American's customers are no more complicated to prove than any other buyer's claims. One merely measures the overcharge for all customers, including American's customers who were injured directly by the collusive activity of the other sellers.[13]

Source of Compensation

Assuming that American's customers are deemed to have standing, they should be compensated by the colluders. When the four colluders agreed to raise their prices from $5000 to $5600, they imposed antitrust injury on all purchasers. They should be held accountable for all of the damages that their actions caused, and therefore should be liable for all of the overcharges. The colluders collected $1 440 000 in overcharges. In contrast, American collected $1 080 000; thus, the total overcharges amounted to $2 520 000. One could argue that the colluders should not have to pay the $1,080000 overcharge collected by American because they did not receive any direct benefit from these overcharges. This, however, is spurious because the economic analysis shows clearly that the overcharges suffered by American's customers were due entirely to the price fixing activity. Moreover, it would be wholly inappropriate to require American to compensate its customers. First, American expanded its output and thereby incurred higher costs because its price was bid up to the level dictated by the conspirators. Second, one cannot presume that American even knew that the $5600 price was an illegal price. Finally, it would be manifestly unfair and inconsistent with the spirit of the antitrust laws to punish American for behaving competitively. Such a precedent would leave law abiders in a quandary and might even tend to encourage their participation in price-fixing conspiracies.

PROBLEMS IN PRACTICE

There are two related problems in implementing the output test. First, shifts in demand for the product may complicate matters. Second, it may be difficult to identify a competitive preconspiracy period following a change in demand. We shall examine these two issues in turn.

Shifts in Demand

Suppose that there is a shift in the demand curve to the right during the collusive period. Because this means that more will be sold at all prices, everyone may actually expand output while some (or all) of the sellers are fixing prices. If one examines the output change of a single firm without reference to the other firms, a conspiracy participant might be incorrectly pardoned.

There are two approaches to dealing with this problem. First, if one can obtain reasonable empirical estimates of demand for cast iron widgets, econometric tools can be employed to control for shifts in demand. Using the estimated demand function, one would determine whether the total output was smaller than it would have been absent the suspected conspiracy. A nonparticipant's output would be larger than it would have been absent a conspiracy. Thus, the output test works in principle. In practice, however, reliable estimates of demand may be difficult to obtain. Fortunately, there is a much simpler alternative: we can recast the output test as a market share test.

Beginning with the preconspiracy market shares of the industry members, one can examine changes in market shares. In our static example, each firm accounted for twenty percent of the total output of cast iron widgets. Following the implementation of the price fixing conspiracy, total output fell from 5000 units to 4200 units. American's share rose from 20% to about 43%. Each of the colluders saw its market share fall from 20% to about 14%. Thus, the alternative market share test provides the same information.

Now, suppose that there is some circumstantial evidence of a price-fixing conspiracy, but that demand has shifted to the right. A nonparticipant should be able to show that its share of the expanded market is larger while the shares of the price fixers have gone down. Thus, even though everyone's output may have increased, the change in *relative* performance, as measured by market share, will reveal who participated and who did not. The same is true for contractions in demand. Even though each producer's output may fall, the output of the nonparticipant will not decline as much as that of a participant and therefore the market share of the nonparticipant will rise.

Identifying a Competitive Benchmark

Shifts in demand also complicate the estimation of damages. Following an increase in demand that occurs during a conspiratorial period, it will be difficult to identify the price 'but for' the conspiracy, i.e. the competitive benchmark price. Ordinarily, an increase in demand would cause the price to rise without any collusion. The collusion exacerbates the price increase. For purposes of damages estimation, the influence of the collusion must be isolated. If one looks only at the price differential, the overcharge will be overestimated.

In our example and in our proposed liability tests, we compare behavior in a conspiracy period with corresponding behavior in a clearly identified non-conspiratorial period. In some instances, it will be difficult to identify a preconspiracy period that will establish a nonconspiratorial benchmark that can be compared to outputs (or market shares) of individual firms. For example, there may be clear evidence of a price-fixing conspiracy, but data limitations may prevent an unambiguous identification of the cartel's inception and a preconspiracy output pattern. In these instances, it will be difficult to employ the output (or market share) test to distinguish between participants and nonparticipants. In order to determine how important this problem is, one would have to do some empirical research on the relative frequency of cases with indeterminate dates of cartel formation. In instances where the date is determinate, however, the output (or market share) test remains quite useful.

This problem is not unique to the determination of liability; it also plagues damage estimation, as in the case of shifting demand. Nearly all damage models depend upon finding a competitive benchmark for inferring 'but-for' prices. If such benchmarks cannot be found, damages are extremely difficult to estimate. Generally, however, the courts require a much lower standard of proof for determining the quantum of damages than for establishing the fact of damages. The Supreme Court has allocated the burden of potentially imprecise damage calculations on the defendants. For example, in *Bigelow* (1946; p. 264), the Court noted that the defendant 'by his own wrong has prevented a more precise computation'. This seems to be reasonable inasmuch as the problem would not have arisen without the antitrust violation.

CONCLUSIONS

Circumstantial evidence of collusion can persuade a jury that an entire industry is guilty of price fixing. To identify those who were not active participants in the collusive activity, we have proposed a simple output test and a market share variant. If the output or market share of the firm that claims to be innocent rises in response to the price increase, that firm's claim should be accepted as true. The most important culprit who escapes under these tests is the firm that agrees to participate and then fails to do so. Although this hole in the net may be somewhat troubling, it creates added incentives for cartel members to cheat or defect, thus undermining the cartel. Moreover, these tests do not indict innocent firms.

Interestingly, the output test also identifies as colluders any tacit members of the cartel. In our example of a five-firm oligopoly, we assumed that four were *active* participants. If instead those four firms reached an understanding through wholly tacit means,[14] our economic test will identify them as colluders.[15]

APPENDIX: DIFFERENTIATED PRODUCTS AND MULTIPLE NONPARTICIPANTS

Here we show that our results generalize to the case of differentiated products and to multiple nonparticipants. We employ a simple model of differentiated products, with the key features that the ith of N producers faces inverse demand

$$P_i = a - q_i - \frac{1}{2}\sum_{\substack{j=1\\ j\neq i}}^{N} q_j \text{ for } (P_i, q_i) > (0, 0), \qquad i = 1, \ldots, N \quad \text{(A1)}$$

and has total cost

$$C_i = cq_i, \qquad i = 1, \ldots, N \qquad \text{(A2)}$$

Note that $\partial P_i/\partial q_i < \partial P_i/\partial q_j < 0$ for $i \neq j$, indicating that goods (q_i, q_j) are imperfect substitutes. The model has some symmetry properties (e.g. $C_i = C_j$) which allows a much easier solution. In particular, it resolves existence-of-equilibrium and multiple equilibrium problems.

Consider first the equilibrium without any collusion. The Nash equilibrium in quantities is the simultaneous solution to the N maximization problems

$$\max_{q_i \geq 0} \Pi_i \equiv \left(a - c - q_i - \frac{1}{2}\sum_{j \neq i}^{N} q_j\right) q_i \qquad i = 1, \ldots, N \tag{A3}$$

In Eqn (A3) and henceforth, the notation $j \neq i$ means $j = 1, \ldots, N$ and $j \neq i$. There exists an equilibrium (in pure strategies) since Π_i is concave in q_i and continuous in q_j (see Friedman, 1986, Theorem 2.4, p. 39). The first-order conditions accompanying Eqn (A3) are

$$a - c - \frac{1}{2}\sum_{j \neq i} q_j - 2q_i = 0 \quad \text{for} \quad q_i > 0 \tag{A4}$$

It is not difficult to demonstrate that the *only* equilibrium is symmetric, i.e. has $q_i = q_j$ for all (i, j). Specifically, it has

$$q_i \equiv q^N = \frac{a - c}{2 + (N-1)/2} \quad \text{for all } i \tag{A5}$$

Now consider the problem where there is a partial conspiracy. Without loss of generality, suppose that the first K firms collude where $1 < K < N$. Hence, there are N–K nonparticipants who continue to act as Nash-output competitors. The K conspirators maximize their joint profits with Nash output conjectures regarding the set of nonparticipants. The problem is

$$\max_{q_1, q_2, \ldots, q_k \geq 0} \sum_{i=1}^{K} \left(a - c - q_i - \frac{1}{2}\sum_{j \neq i} q_j\right) q_i \tag{A6}$$

Analogously to the Nash equilibrium before the conspiracy, the nonparticipants will produce symmetrically, i.e. $q_i = q_j$ for $i, j = K+1, \ldots, N$. Let q^{NP} denote each nonparticipant's output.

Then, the set of first-order conditions corresponding to problem (A6) is

$$a - c - (N-K)q^{NP}/2 - \sum_{\substack{j=1 \\ j \neq i}}^{K} q_j - 2q_i = 0 \text{ for } q_i > 0 \qquad i = 1, \ldots, K \tag{A7}$$

It is not hard to show that it is optimal for each conspirator to produce the same output level. Let q^c denote the output level of each conspirator. Using Eqn (A7) we then obtain:

$$q^c = \frac{a - c}{K+1} - \frac{\frac{1}{2}(N-K)}{K+1} q^{NP} \tag{A8}$$

which is the pro rata best-reply function for each conspirator.

Using Eqn (A4) and the symmetry properties of equilibrium we have noted, one obtains the analogous best reply function for nonparticipants:

$$q^{NP} = \frac{a - c}{2 + \frac{1}{2}(N-K-1)} - \frac{\frac{1}{2}K}{2 + \frac{1}{2}(N-K-1)} q^c \tag{A9}$$

The equilibrium values in the presence of a partial conspiracy then solve Eqns (A8) and (A9), and we denote these values by (q^{c*}, q^{NP*}). It is straightforward to obtain:

$$q^{c*} = \frac{a - c}{f(K)} \tag{A10a}$$

where

$$f(K) = K + 1 + (N-K)\left(\frac{1}{3} + \frac{1}{6}K\right) \tag{A10b}$$

and

$$q^{NP*} = \frac{a - c}{2 + \frac{1}{2}(N-K-1)} \times \left[\frac{K + 2 + (N-K)(2+K)/3}{2K + 2 + (N-K)(2+K)/3}\right] \tag{A11}$$

Confirming the validity of the output test corresponds to showing that

$$q^{c*} < q^N < q^{NP*} \tag{A12}$$

Consider the first inequality in Eqn (A12). Using Eqns (A5), (A10a), and (A10b), this result follows if

$$f(K) > 2 + (N-1)/2 \quad \text{for} \quad K = 2, \ldots, N \tag{A13}$$

We have

(i) $f(1) = 2 + (N-1)/2$
(ii) f is continuous in K

(iii) $f'(1) = \frac{1}{3} + \frac{1}{6}N > 0$
(iv) $f''(K) = -\frac{1}{3}$ so f is concave
(v) $f(N) = N + 1 > 2 + (N - 1)/2$ (for $N > 1$)

Note that (i) simply confirms we have made no errors as it implies $q^{c*} = q^N$ if the 'conspiracy' has only one firm. Then (ii)–(v) imply Eqn (A13) and the result.

Now consider the second inequality in Eqn (A12). It is a little more tedious to show this. Using Eqns (A5) and (A11), this result requires that (for $K > 1$):

$$\frac{K + 2 + (N - K)(2 + K)/3}{[2 + \frac{1}{2}(N - K - 1)][2K + 2 + (N - K)(2 + K)/3]}$$
$$> \frac{2}{N+3} \leftrightarrow (N + 3)[K + 2 + (N - K)(2 + K)/3]$$
$$> [4 + (N - K - 1)][2K + 2 + (N - K)(2 + K)/3]$$
$$\leftrightarrow (N + 3)[K + 2 + (N - K)(2 + K/3]$$
$$> [(N + 3) - K][K + \{K + 2 + (N - K)(2 + K)/3\}]$$
$$\leftrightarrow 0 > (N + 3)K - K[2K + 2 + (N - K)(2 + K)/3]$$
$$\leftrightarrow 2K^2 + 2K + K(N - K)(2 + K)/3 - NK - 3K$$
$$> 0 \leftrightarrow h(K) > 0 \qquad \text{(A14a)}$$

where

$$h(K) \equiv 2K - 1 + (N - K)(2 + K)/3 - N \qquad \text{(A14b)}$$

We have:

(i) $h(1) = 0$
(ii) h is continuous in K
(iii) $h'(1) = 1 + (N - 1)/3 > 0$
(iv) $h'(K) = -\frac{1}{3}$ so h is concave
(v) $h(N) = N - 1 > 0$

Analogously to the above, (i) only confirms that there has been no error in the calculations since the case of $K = 1$ corresponds to the Nash equilibrium without a conspiracy. Eqn (A14a) and the result are implied by (ii) – (v).

Hence, the output test is robust. It is also useful to show that a price test fails. This gets very messy in this model, so, rather than prove it generally, we just present an example. Suppose that $N = 6$ and $K = 4$ so that there are two nonparticipants. The following calculations are all straightforward to make. The pre-conspiracy Nash equilibrium has:

$$q^N = \frac{2}{9}(a - c) \qquad \text{(A15)}$$

and

$$P^N = \frac{2}{9}a + \frac{7}{2}c \qquad \text{(A16)}$$

where P^N is the price adopted by each firm. Under the conspiracy, the values are

$$q^{c*} = \frac{1}{7}(a - c) \qquad \text{(A17)}$$

$$q^{NP*} = \frac{2}{7}(a - c) \qquad \text{(A18)}$$

and

$$P^{c*} = P^{NP*} = \frac{2}{7}a + \frac{5}{7}c \qquad \text{(A19)}$$

where P^{c*} and P^{NP*} are, respectively, the conspirators' and nonconspirators' prices. Keeping in mind that $a > c$, note that $q^{c*} < q^N < q^{NP*}$ and $P^{c*} = P^{NP*} > P^N$. Hence, both conspirators and nonconspirators charge a higher price than in the initial Nash equilibrium, and, in this example, they charge the *same* price. This last result is, no doubt, an artifact of this particular model, but illustrates well the problem with price tests.

Acknowledgments

The authors appreciate the financial support of the Public Policy Research Center and the College of Business Administration at the University of Florida. Although the helpful suggestions and encouragement of Jordan Leibman and Charles Mueller were most useful, they must not be blamed for the above. We also wish to inform readers that the firm of B & R Associates referred to above is purely imaginary, as is the cast iron widget industry. Note: This article with minor revision is reprinted with permission from *American Business Law Journal* **33**, 28 (1990).

NOTES

1. Under section 1, information exchanges are suspect under some circumstances. See Blair and Kaserman (1985, pp. 181–8). For the judicial concerns, see *Container Corp.* (1969) and *United States Gypsum Co.* (1978). These cases related to transaction prices, not list prices.

2. Delivered pricing occurs when all sellers quote prices on the basis of the lowest combination of mill price plus transportation cost. Such pricing can be a collusive oligopolistic practice. See Blair and Kaserman (1985, pp. 210–16) and Scherer (1980, pp. 325–34). Delivered pricing violates the antitrust laws only when it is collusive.
3. Areeda (1986), ¶1503(b) points out that '... output is a sound general measure of anticompetitive effect.... An increase in output is procompetitive.'
4. Technically, the oligopoly's behavior is characterized as Bertrand—i.e. each firm selects its price assuming that the rival firms will not change their prices. As a result, prices will be bid down to the competitive level. The application in our case presumes any higher priced sellers capture no market share whether or not the lower priced sellers stock out, e.g. unsatisfied demanders postpone purchases.
5. Although we have assumed identical cost curves for all firms, this is not necessary to our argument. The qualitative results are the same.
6. We have examined two scenarios where industry members are Nash–Cournot output competitors prior to the partial conspiracy. In the first case, the participants jointly play a Nash output game against the nonparticipant following the formation of the cartel. In the second case, the participants jointly behave as a Stackelberg leader *vis-à-vis* the nonparticipant following formation of the cartel. Our output test remains valid for these models as well.
7. One of the authors (Blair) was retained by the lawyers representing General Portland. This example of industry analysis is drawn from the extensive litigation support provided in that case.
8. Due to the imposition of joint and several liability on horizontal price fixers, it is not necessary to sue all of the co-conspirators. In this case, however, the original complaint primarily involved Robinson–Patman allegations. The price-fixing allegation came much later, and joining additional defendants at that point would have prolonged discovery.
9. Capacity utilization data are somewhat difficult to interpret. First, many firms overstate their ability to produce through unrealistic estimates of down time for maintenance and repairs. Second, in most plants there is residual production capacity that can be used only at very high start-up and operating costs.
10. Other factors may change as well, but that is a complication in any case. Controlling for other influences can be accomplished. We abstract from these complications for ease of exposition here, but return to this issue in the next section.
11. Antitrust injury is not a simple matter in all instances. See Areeda (1976), and Blair and Harrison (1989), and Page (1980), (1985).
12. For a debate on these issues, see Harris and Sullivan (1979), Landes and Posner (1980), and Snyder (1985).
13. After reviewing the post-*Illinois Brick* decisions, Areeda and Hovenkamp (1988, ¶334.1b) conclude generally that (American's) customers 'must show (1) that the alleged violation tends to reduce competition in some market and (2) that the plaintiff's injury would result from a decrease in that competition...' Areeda and Hovenkamp (1988 ¶337.3) also specifically address the standing of umbrella plaintiffs: 'At least in the case of homogeneous products, umbrella plaintiffs should generally be granted standing. They are injured in fact, the injury results from that which makes the cartel illegal, and their injury is the type that the antitrust laws are designed to prevent.'
14. For skeptical views of the viability of tacit collusion, see Elzinga (1984) and Spence (1978).
15. Judge Posner (1969) has argued that unilateral and (presumably silent) agreements to restrict output should be deemed a violation of the antitrust laws. His view is predicated on the idea that a voluntary sacrifice of short-run profit that makes sense only if the other firms in the industry do the same thing constitutes a unilateral agreement that is just as much a restraint as overt agreements. Our output test and its market share equivalent are consistent with Posner's view. In contrast, Turner (1962) does not share this view. Turner feels that firms in concentrated industries must pursue profits while recognizing the mutual interdependence that exists among all firms in such industries. To the extent that this demands that a firm restrain itself in order to avoid an outbreak of price competition, it is unreasonable to suppose that firms will behave otherwise. Public policy cannot require that firms ignore the economic environment in which they live. Given the complexity of the economic analysis of oligopolistic markets, this is not the place to resolve the Posner–Turner dispute.

REFERENCES

P. Areeda (1976). Antitrust violations without damage recoveries. *Harvard Law Review* **89**, 1127–39.

P. Areeda (1986). *Antitrust Law*, Vol. 7, Boston: Little, Brown and Company.

P. Areeda and H. Hovenkamp (1988). *Antitrust Law (Supplement)*, Boston: Little, Brown and Company.

P. Areeda and D. Turner (1978). *Antitrust Law*, New York: Little, Brown and Company.

Bigelow v. RKO Radio Pictures, 327 US 251 (1946).

R. D. Blair and J. L. Harrison (1989). Rethinking antitrust injury. *Vanderbilt Law Review*, **42**, November, 1539–73.

R. D. Blair and D. L. Kaserman (1985). *Antitrust Economics*, Homewood, IL: Richard D. Irwin.

R. D. Blair and V. G. Maurer (1982). Umbrella pricing and antitrust standing: an economic analysis. *Utah Law Review*, 763–96.

R. Bork (1966). Legislative intent and the policy of the Sherman Act. *Journal of Law and Economics*, **9**, October, 7–48.

Brunswick Corp. v. Pueblo Bowl-O-Mat, Inc., 429 US 477 (1977).

Conference of Studio Unions v. Loew's, 193 F. 2d 51 (9th Cir. 1951).

K. Elzinga (1984). New developments on the cartel front. *Antitrust Bulletin*, **29**, Spring, 3–26.

F. Fisher and J. McGowan (1983). On the misuse of accounting rates of return to infer monopoly profits. *American Economic Review*, **73**, March, 82–97.

E. W. French and Sons v. General Portland Cement Company. Civil Action No. 78-1928-TJH (Tx) (CD Cal. Oct. 2, 1985).

J. W. Friedman (1986) *Game Theory With Applications to Economics*, New York: Oxford University Press.

Hanover Shoe Company v. United Shoe Machinery Corporation, 392 US 481 (1968).

R. Harris and L. Sullivan (1979). Passing on the monopoly overcharge: a comprehensive policy analysis. *University of Pennsylvania Law Review*, **128**, December, 269–360.

Illinois Brick Co. v. Illinois, 431 US 720 (1977).

R. Lande (1982). Wealth transfers as the original and primary concern of antitrust: the efficiency interpretation challenged. *Hastings Law Journal*, **34**, September, 61–151.

W. Landes and R. Posner (1980). The economics of passing on: a reply to Harris and Sullivan. *University of Pennsylvania Law Review*, **128**, 1274–90.

W. Page (1980). Antitrust damages and economic efficiency: an approach to antitrust injury. *University of Chicago Law Review*, **47**, Spring, 467–504.

W. Page (1985). The scope of liability for antitrust violations. *Stanford Law Review*, **37**, July, 1445–1512.

R. Posner (1969). Oligopoly and the antitrust laws: a suggested approach. *Stanford Law Review*, **21**, June, 1562–1606.

F. M. Scherer (1980). *Industrial Market Structure and Economic Performance* (2nd edition), Chicago: Rand McNally College Publishing Company.

E. Snyder (1985). Efficient assignment of rights to sue for antitrust damages. *Journal of Law and Economics*, **28**, May, 469–82.

A. M. Spence (1978). Tacit coordination and imperfect information. *Canadian Journal of Economics*, **11**, August, 490–505.

D. Turner (1962). The definition of agreement under the Sherman Act: conscious parallelism and refusals to deal. *Harvard Law Review*, **75**, February 655–706.

United States v. Container Corporation of America, 393 US 333 (1969).

United States v. United States Gypsum Co., 438 US 422 (1978).

4

Durable Goods, Maintenance, and Tying Arrangements

William F. Shughart II

University of Mississippi, University, MS, USA

In early April 1980, the Federal Trade Commission voted to grant a request by its Seattle Regional Office for subpoena power ('compulsory process') to pursue an investigation of Boeing Aircraft Company. The SRO wanted 'to determine whether Boeing Company and others may be engaged in unfair methods of competition . . . , including but not limited to tying arrangements, boycotts and related practices in connection with the manufacture, sale, distribution and maintenance of commercial airplanes and replacement parts for commercial airplanes.' The FTC's Seattle attorneys listed three specific practices which they hoped to challenge. These were (1) the duty imposed on purchasers of Boeing's commercial aircraft to buy their spare parts only from Boeing; (2) foreclosure of aircraft repair facilities not authorized by Boeing from access to a source of spare parts, and (3) Boeing's refusal to deal with certain independent aircraft repair facilities.

It was subsequently learned that the repair parts tying provision, though included in Boeing's standard form sales contract, was flagrantly breached by many of the largest commercial airlines. Boeing's verbal threats to void aircraft warranties by reason of the airlines' use of non-Boeing parts had evidently never been carried out. Failure to enforce the tying arrangement, along with the prospect of protracted antitrust litigation, led Boeing to eliminate the relevant contract language in December 1979.

As a result of Boeing's action, SRO shifted the focus of its investigation toward restrictions imposed on smaller firms that manufactured spare parts under Boeing subcontracts. Examples of these restrictions were Boeing's requirement that its subcontractors destroy any production overruns of spare parts; Boeing's assertion of the right to audit its subcontractors' records; admonitions that its subcontractors not disclose drawings, tools, or other parts manufacturing specifications to third parties; and prohibitions which forbade Boeing's subcontractors from producing non-proprietary parts for third parties. In addition, Boeing adopted a policy of designating 'authorized' aircraft repair facilities and began refusing to sell parts to other such customers which Boeing suspected of dealing in bogus parts.

The question addressed by SRO's investigation was whether these practices were sufficient in and of themselves for Boeing to perpetuate a *de facto* tie-in sale in the absence of explicit contract language requiring its customers to buy their spare parts only from Boeing. In other words, by taking steps to eliminate all replacement parts not authorized by Boeing could the aircraft manufacturer achieve a result equivalent to an unlawful tying arrangement?

This paper explores the use of tie-in sales as a method of vertical control. It integrates certain aspects of the price discriminatory 'metering' hypothesis with results taken from the literature on durable good quality. By incorporating both durability and maintenance considerations, the model offers a somewhat novel explanation for Boeing's repair parts tying policy, which does not seem to fit alternative theories of tie-in sales. In particular, the analysis suggests that Boeing reduced the prices of its aircraft and increased the prices of its replacement parts in order to prevent its customers from opportunistically extending the useful lives of Boeing aircraft and, hence, buying fewer of them, than would be consistent with the firm's profit maximizing objectives.

The development of the present theory proceeds as follows. The next section considers the profit opportunities of a competitive industry which employs a durable good as one input in its production process. Unintegrated downstream firms choose rates of utilization and levels of maintenance effort to minimize the per period cost of the services withdrawn from the durable good. In the third section, the behaviour of an upstream monopolist durable good seller is analyzed in light of the constraints imposed by the downstream industry's profit-maximization objectives. The model contrasts the behavioral implications that emerge when the durable good producer can and cannot control the sale of repair parts used in downstream maintenance activities. An important finding is that a repair parts tying arrangement entails opposing welfare effects. In particular, the tie-in sale induces the upstream monopolist to supply a larger output of higher-quality durable goods. On the other hand, the output of repair parts is restricted below the competitive level and, consequently, the prices of replacement parts are higher than they would be in the absence of the tie-in sale. Conclusions are contained in the final section.

UTILIZATION INTENSITY AND MAINTENANCE EFFORT IN A DOWNSTREAM COMPETITIVE INDUSTRY

A tying arrangement is said to exist when the sale of one good (the tying good) is contingent on the purchase of some other good (the tied good). The extant literature identifies a variety of hypotheses about this widely used business practice,[1] the most prominent of which is price discriminatory 'metering'. Hansen and Roberts (1980) took exception to this view, however. Moreover, in demonstrating the equivalence of tie-in sales with vertical ownership integration, lump-sum entry fees, and franchise contracts, Blair and Kaserman (1978, 1980) and Inaba (1980) have raised doubts that metering always serves to extract consumer surplus.

In his seminal work, Burstein (1960a,b) observed that the most prevalent kind of tying arrangement is one which involves a low-valued good such as salt, rivets, shoe buttons, or computer punch card tied to the sale or lease of a durable good. The question of durability has been addressed in the studies of Epple and Zelenitz (1977), Parks (1974), Ramm (1974), and Su (1975). These contributions extended Swan's (1970, 1971) pioneering analysis of the relationship between market structure and durable good quality. In addition, Parks (1979) and Schmalensee (1974, 1979) have explored the impact of maintenance effort in durable good models.

The model developed by Epple and Zelentiz (1977) provides an important point of departure for the present analysis. Their work compared durable input quality under sale of good, lease of good, and sale of service policies. This chapter extends their analysis by incorporating the effect of durable good maintenance.

Assume that the production process in some competitive industry requires two inputs: the services of a durable good plus quantities of a second factor which, for convenience, will be referred to as labor, L. The total per period flow of services from the stock of durables is represented by S and denominated in units such as operating hours per months. If the inventory of durables is given by Q, then the utilization rate (intensity of use), s, of each durable good becomes

$$s = S/Q \tag{1}$$

Each durable is assumed to be endowed with a built-in deterioration rate, γ, which is established at the time of manufacture. The durable decays at an exponential rate during its lifetime and has no scrap value. The durable's actual deterioration rate, δ, rises with its intensity of use, but the purchaser may lower the decay rate by performing appropriate maintenance. For simplicity, maintenance possibilities are limited to the replacement of parts so that an increase in repair activities can be represented by larger purchases of spare components, m. These relations are given by[2]

$$\delta = \delta(s, \gamma, m) \qquad \text{with } \delta_s > 0, \delta_\gamma > 0, \delta_m < 0 \tag{2}$$

In utilizing the services of the durable good, the downstream purchaser confronts a per-period opportunity cost associated with having funds committed to holding the stock. The inventory holding cost is of the form rPQ, where P is the durable's purchase price and r a discount rate. In addition, δPQ represents the per-period depreciation costs. Finally, the per-period expenditures on maintenance are given by mp_m, where p_m is the unit price of parts. Thus, the per period price of durable good services, P_S, is

$$P_S = mp_m + P(r + \delta)/s \tag{3}$$

The variable m is denominated in units of parts per hour of durable operation so that the per-period price of services is in terms of dollars per hour. Total expenditures on durable services are given by $P_S S$, where (\$/hour) times (hours/month) yields units of dollars per month. The downstream firms are assumed to be price takers with respect to both parts and units of the durable good.

Minimization of P_S by choice of utilization rate and parts purchases requires

$$\partial P_S/\partial s = (P/s^2)[s\delta_s - (r+\delta)] = 0 \quad (4a)$$

$$\partial P_S/\partial m = p_m + P\delta_m/s = 0 \quad (4b)$$

The first-order conditions in Eqn (4) have their usual interpretations. The downstream firm selects an intensity of durable utilization such that the value of the reduction in opportunity cost, $P\,(r+\delta)/s^2$, is just offset by the rise in deterioration expenses, $P\delta_s/s$. Furthermore, the firm chooses maintenance up to the point where the value of the marginal reduction in deterioration, $P\delta_m/s$, is equal to the additional per unit expenditure on parts, p_m.[3]

The objective of a representative downstream firm is to maximize a profit function of the form

$$\pi = R(S, L) - wL - P_S S \quad (5)$$

by choice of service flow (S), quantity of labor (L), intensity of durable utilization (s), and level of parts purchases, m.[4]

The firm's revenue is assumed to be a function of its rate of use of the two inputs, $R = R(S, L)$; labor is assumed to be in infinitely elastic supply at a (constant) unit wage rate, w. Assuming an interior solution, the first-order conditions for profit maximization are given by

$$\partial\pi/\partial S = R_S - mp_m - P(r+\delta)/s = 0 \quad (6a)$$

$$\partial\pi/\partial L = R_L - w = 0 \quad (6b)$$

$$\partial\pi/\partial s = -(PS/s^2)[s\delta_s - (r+\delta)] = 0 \quad (6c)$$

$$\partial\pi/\partial m = -S[p_m + (P\delta_m/s)] = 0 \quad (6d)$$

Total differentiation of the relations in Eqn (6) permits investigation of the comparative static properties of the model. Some of the most interesting results are contained in the following three propositions. Table 1 presents a summary of the signs of the relevant partial derivatives.

Table 1. Comparative static results for downstream firms

	Exogenous variables				
Choice variables	p_m	P	r	γ	w
S	–	–	–	–	?
L	?	?	?	?	–
s	+	?	+	?	0
m	–	+	?	?	0

Note: '?' indicates indeterminant sign.

Proposition 1. Other things equal, an increase in the unit price of parts leads the downstream firm to reduce its consumption of durable input services:[5]

$$\partial S/\partial P_m = m(s/PS)^2[R_{LL}/(R_{SS}R_{LL} - R_{SL}^2)] < 0 \quad (7)$$

All terms in equation (7) except for R_{LL} are positive, therefore the derivative is unambiguously negative.

In addition, it can be shown that $(\partial s/\partial p_m) > 0$; that is, if the durable becomes more costly to maintain, the downstream industry 'uses up' the durable stock at a more rapid rate. This rise in utilization intensity increases the durable's actual decay rate ($\delta_s > 0$), so that the firm moves to the lower level of input services in the long run by operating fewer units of the durable, with each unit employed more intensely. On balance, a smaller number of the durable goods are purchased per time period, but the rise in s leads to a more rapid turnover of the durable stock; the firm replaces its smaller inventory more often (the average age of the durable inventory falls). In the short run, however, for a constant durable stock, the decline in S must be accomplished via a *lower* intensity of use.

Proposition 2. *Ceteris paribus*, a rise in the purchase price of the durable input results in a lower utilization rate. This interpretation depends upon the sign of δ_{ms} being positive:

$$\partial s/\partial P = (\delta_m/P)(\delta_{ms} - \delta_m/s)[\delta_{mm}\delta_{ss} - (\delta_{ms} - \delta_m/s)^2] < 0 \text{ if } \delta_{ms} > 0 \quad (8)$$

The term $\delta_{ms} > 0$ if rising utilization rates increase the productivity of maintenance in lowering deterioration. This proposition implies that if the cost of replacing the durable stock rises relative to operation costs, the downstream firms will reduce the utilization rate of their current inventory. The decline in intensity of use lowers the durable's actual decay rate; the average age of inventories rise as the durable stock is replaced less often. In the short run, per period service flow and intensity of use decline in equal proportions to maintain a constant durable stock.

Proposition 3. Other things equal, purchases of repair parts fall with an increase in their own price; a rise in the durable's purchase price leads to greater levels of maintenance activity:

$$\partial m/\partial p_m = -|H|^{-1}(PS^2\delta_{ss}/s)(R_{SS}R_{LL} - R_{SL}^2) < 0 \tag{9a}$$

$$\partial m/\partial P = -|H|^{-1}(PS^2\delta_m\delta_{ss}/s)(R_{SS}R_{LL} - R_{SL}^2) > 0 \tag{9b}$$

These effects reinforce those of Propositions 1 and 2. The decline in maintenance resulting from a rise in the unit price of parts contributes to an increase in the durable's actual decay rate ($\delta_m < 0$) and further raises inventory turnover. In contrast, as the durable's purchase price increases, greater levels of repair activity extend the expected lifetime during which a unit of the durable can remain in service. The latter effect lowers the rate of inventory replacement. Note that for a given built-in deterioration rate, the optimal actual decay rate for the downstream firms falls with an increase in the durable's price and rises as parts costs increase; that is,

$$\delta_P = \delta_s(\partial s/\partial P) + \delta_m(\partial m/\partial P) < 0$$

and

$$\delta_{p_m} = \delta_s(\partial s/\partial p_m) + \delta_m(\partial m/\partial p_m) > 0$$

The results in this section, though interesting, are hardly surprising. Where the services of a durable good are one input utilized in the production process of a competitive industry, we expect the firms in that industry to combine maintenance levels and utilization intensity in such a way that the cost of the durable's services is minimized. If the factors which affect the cost of replacing the stock are relatively great, then the firm will be induced to employ fewer units of the durable and to lower the rate of inventory turnover by using each good less intensively. On the other hand, if the price of repair parts or deterioration costs loom large, the firm can be expected to reduce maintenance activity and raise the rate of inventory replacement by engaging in more intensive utilization of each durable input.

The substitution possibilities for the downstream industry set the stage for an analysis of the profit opportunities faced by the upstream durable good producer. The cost minimization adjustments described in this section impose a constraint on the level of profits obtainable through durable sales. This topic is taken up next.

PROFIT RELATIONS FOR THE PRODUCER OF AN INTERMEDIATE DURABLE GOOD

Taking cognizance of the stock-flow relation in Eqn (1), we see that the choice of per period service flow, S, and intensity of durable utilization, s, completely specify the downstream demand for units of the durable good, Q. In this section we investigate the profitability of durable good sales under such a marketing constraint. Initially, the upstream firm is assumed only to sell units of the durable good. The downstream industry may forestall deterioration by performing maintenance, but repair parts are assumed to be available competitively from firms which are independent of the durable good producer. This assumption is then relaxed and the upstream firm is permitted to require that the downstream industry buy repair parts as a condition of purchase of the durable good.

Solution of the downstream first-order conditions in Eqns (6a-d) yields implicit demand functions for utilization intensity and parts of the following form:

$$s^* = s^*[P, p_m, r, \delta(s, m, \gamma)]$$

and

$$m^* = m^*[P, p_m, r, \delta(s, m, \gamma)]$$

In addition, the demand for durable services is a function of the price of services, i.e. $S^* = S^*(P_S)$.

Furthermore, suppose that the marginal cost of durable production is given by $C = C(\gamma)$, with $C_\gamma < 0$. That is, production of a durable of lower 'quality' (a higher built-in decay rate) reduces marginal cost. The upstream firm maximizes discounted profits by choice of durable price and quality:

$$\pi = (P - C)Q + \int_0^\infty (P - C)Q\delta e^{-rt}dt \tag{10}$$

which becomes

$$\pi = (P - C)Q[(r + \delta)/r] \quad (10')$$

First-order conditions for maximization of Eqn (10′) are:

$$\partial\pi/\partial P = (Q/r)[(r + \delta)(C/P) + (P - C)\delta_m m_P] = 0 \quad (11a)$$

and

$$\partial\pi/\partial\gamma = (Q/r)[(P - C)\delta_m m_\gamma - C_\gamma(r + \delta)] + (Q/r)(P - C)s_\gamma[\delta_s - (r + \delta)/s] + (Q/r)\delta_\gamma[P/(r + \delta)][(r + \delta)(C/P) + (P - C)\delta_m m_P] = 0 \quad (11b)$$

Referring to Eqn (11b), it is seen that the second term is zero by the downstream choice of intensity of use and the third term vanishes by Eqn (11a).[6] Thus, the first-order conditions simplify to

$$\partial\pi/\partial P = (Q/r)[(r + \delta)(C/P) + (P - C)\delta_m m_P] = 0 \quad (11a')$$

and

$$\partial\pi/\partial\gamma = (Q/r)[(P - C)\delta_m m_\gamma - C_\gamma(r + \delta)] = 0 \quad (11b')$$

The upstream firm's profit-maximizing durable price occurs at the level where the loss in net revenue resulting from downstream maintenance—given by the second term in brackets in Eqn (11a′)—is equal to the discounted value of marginal cost expressed as a percentage of price. The built-in deterioration rate is raised until the discounted value of the cost savings from producing a durable of lower quality, $C_\gamma(r+\delta)/r$, is just offset by the reduction in discounted net revenue due to the change in downstream maintenance activity, $(P - C)\delta_m m_\gamma$.[7]

Now suppose that the upstream firm also sells the parts used in durable good maintenance. Let parts be produced at a constant marginal cost, ϕ. Alternatively, the durable good producer can purchase the repair components from a competitive parts industry and resell them to the downstream firms. In either case, it is assumed that the parts sales are effectively conditioned on the purchase of the durable good. Costs associated with enforcement of the tie-in sale are assumed to be negligible. No fixed relation between parts purchases and durable good utilization is imposed; downstream firms may employ durable good services and maintenance in variable proportions.

The upstream firm now maximizes a profit function of the following firm:

$$\pi_t = (p_m - \phi)m + (P - C)Q + \int_0^\infty (P - C)Q\delta e^{-rt}dt \quad (12)$$

where the subscript t denotes profits under the tying arrangement. Upon performing the integration, Eqn (12) becomes

$$\pi_t = (p_m - \phi)m + (P - C)Q(r + \delta)/r \quad (12')$$

Choice variables are durable good price, P, built-in deterioration rate, γ, and unit price of parts, p_m. The first-order necessary conditions for maximization of Eqn (12′) are:[8]

$$\partial\pi_t/\partial P = (Q/r)[(r + \delta)(C/P) + (P - C)\delta_m m_p] + (p_m - \phi)m_P = 0 \quad (13a)$$

$$\partial\pi_t/\partial\gamma = (Q/r)[(P - C)\delta_m m_\gamma - C_\gamma(r + \delta)] + (p_m - \phi)m_\gamma = 0 \quad (13b)$$

$$\partial\pi/\partial p_m = [(Q/r)(P - C)\delta_m + p_m](1 - \eta_m) + \phi\eta_m = 0 \quad (13c)$$

where $\eta_m = -(\partial m/\partial p_m)(p_m/m) > 0$ is the own-price demand elasticity for parts.

Comparison of the first-order conditions in Eqns (13a-c) with those in (11a′-b′) yields the following:

Proposition 4. In the absence of the tying arrangement, an increase in downstream maintenance activity lowers the profits of the durable good producer. From Eqn (10′), we have

$$\partial\pi/\partial m = (Q/r)(P - C)\delta_m < 0 \quad (14)$$

since $\delta_m < 0$. The decline in profits is due to fewer replacement sales as the increase in maintenance lowers the durable's actual decay rate.

Proposition 5. The imposition of a parts tie-in by a seller of an intermediate durable good leads to a decline in the input's selling price. Inspection of Eqns (11a′) and (13a) reveals that the two profit-maximization conditions differ by the term $(p_m - \phi)m_P$, which represents the addition to net revenue from parts sales when the durable's purchase price is raised. Since the upstream firm's marginal revenue is larger under the tying arrangement, the durable producer expands output of the tying good. Given a downward-sloping demand curve, the upstream firm must reduce the durable's price in order to sell more units of the good.[9]

Proposition 6. The imposition of a parts tie-in leads the durable good seller to lower the good's built-in deterioration rate. Under the tying arrangement, the marginal cost of raising the decay rate is the same as it was in the absence of the tie, i.e. $(Q/r)(P - C)\delta_m m_\gamma$. That is, when the durable producer increases γ, the downstream firms are induced to perform more repairs in order to forestall the increase in the actual decay rate. In the absence of the tying arrangement, greater maintenance efforts must be entirely offset by the cost savings from producing a durable good of lower quality. When vertical control of repair parts is exercised, the upstream firm realizes a gain in net revenue from selling more spare components, $(p_m - \phi)m_\gamma$. Thus, the required reduction in marginal production cost is smaller under the tying arrangement than when the upstream firm cannot sell parts. If parts are sold at marginal cost $(p_m = \phi)$, however, the tying arrangement will not lead to an increase in durable good quality.

Why does the upstream producer choose to engage in parts tying rather than simply reduce the quality of the durable good? Obviously, a change in the built-in decay rate only affects the profitability of future durable sales and does not directly influence the actual deterioration rate of current downstream inventories. Vertical control of parts prices gives a more flexible means of influencing durable maintenance. In addition, Proposition 6 accords with Coase's (1972) argument that a monopoly seller of an infinitely lived durable good can only charge a monopoly price if he somehow guarantees that supply will not be increased (and price lowered) in the future. Coase (1972, p.147) concludes that 'lessened durability reduces the gain from an increase in supply and thus reduces the likelihood that it will occur'. In the absence of a repair parts tying arrangement where the upstream firm extracts all monopoly rents from the sale of the durable alone, a higher built-in decay rate is consistent with Coase's observation.

Proposition 7. In equilibrium, the profit-maximizing unit price of parts for the upstream firm is independent of the own-price elasticity of demand for the durable good.[10] From this result, the repair parts tying arrangement could not form the basis for price discrimination wherein the upstream firm charged higher parts prices to those input buyers with more inelastic demands for units of the durable good.

The 'metering' explanation for price discriminatory tie-ins is not consistent with our model because repair parts are not required to be used in fixed proportion with durable good utilization. In fact, it would be counterproductive for the upstream firm to 'load' an additional utilization charge onto the unit price of parts since an increase in repair costs would lead to a long-run rise in intensity of durable use and correspondingly smaller input inventories (see Proposition 1). Moreover, charging different parts prices to different customers would place additional burdens on the durable producer in preventing resale of spare components.

SUMMARY AND CONCLUSIONS

Once an intermediate durable good is sold, control of its rate of utilization passes to the downstream purchaser. Given that output in the industry depends upon the flow of durable input services, the analysis in this chapter led to some important behavioral implications. It was found that an increase in either unit maintenance costs or durable price would lead to a reduction in the per period service flow. In the short run, the downstream firms would respond to higher parts prices by lowering the intensity of durable use. Utilization rates would fall if the downstream industry were faced with a higher durable price. The more expensive the durable, the more repair parts the firm would be willing to purchase. Finally, the greater (lower) the durable utilization rate, the greater (lower) will be the rate of inventory replacement.

The substitution possibilities in the downstream industry impose a constraint on the profit opportunities of the monopolized upstream durable good producer. Our analysis compared the upstream firm's profits when all revenue was due to durable good sales with an alternative which involved a repair parts tying arrangement. It was found that forcing the downstream firms to purchase all of their parts supplies from the durable producer led to a lowering of the durable good's selling price. In the absence of the tie-in sale, the upstream firm would produce a durable of lower quality (higher built-in decay rate). Since profit maximization under the tying arrangement requires that the upstream firm raise the price of parts and lower the price of the durable input, the net welfare effects of tying are ambiguous: a larger output of higher-quality durable good is produced, but the output of repair parts is restricted below the competitive level.

In assessing vertical marketing strategies where a relatively low-valued commodity is tied to the sale of a durable good, policy-makers must weigh these opposing welfare effects. In cases where the benefits of tying exceed the costs, society would gain from a policy which allowed the tie-in sale to continue. The conclusion that metering tie-ins are everywhere a price discrimination device is not justified. The present model indicates that a repair parts tie may be effectively employed as a method of vertical control.

ACKNOWLEDGEMENTS

I wish to thank Richard Zerbe as well as former FTC colleagues James Langenfeld and Perry Brown for helpful comments. As is customary, however, I accept full responsibility for any remaining errors.

NOTES

1. For example, Scherer (1980, pp. 582–3) lists leverage, coordinated pricing, price discrimination, quality control, distribution economies, and evasion of price controls as 'reasons for attempting to tie the sale of one product to that of another'.
2. With the exception of the variables P_s and p_m (defined below), subscripts denote partial differentiation. For example,

$$\delta_m = \partial\delta/\partial m, \delta_{mm} = \partial^2\delta/\partial m^2,$$

and so on.

3. The second-order sufficient conditions, which ensure minimization of the per-period price of durable services, are:

$$\partial^2 P_s/\partial s^2 = (P/s)\delta_{ss} > 0$$
$$\partial^2 P_S/\partial m^2 = (P/s)\delta_{mm} > 0$$
$$(P/s)^2[\delta_{ss}\delta_{mm} - (1/s^2)(s\delta_{sm} - \delta_m)^2] > 0$$

As usual, the second-order conditions require diminishing marginal productivity of maintenance in lowering the actual decay rate ($\delta_{mm} > 0$) and that increases in intensity have a diminishing effect on actual deterioration, i.e. $\delta_{ss} > 0$.
4. Choice of s and S jointly determine the stock of durables, Q, via the relation in Eqn (1).
5. The determinant of the fourth-order Hessian is equal to the following

$$\det \mathrm{H} = (PS/s)^2[\delta_{ss}\delta_{mm} - (\delta_{ms} - \delta_m/s)^2] (R_{SS}R_{LL} - R_{SL}^2)$$

Second-order sufficient conditions for profit maximization require negative definiteness of H so that

$$R_{SS}, R_{LL} < 0 \qquad (R_{SS}R_{LL} - R_{SL}^2) > 0 \qquad \det \mathrm{H} > 0$$

6. See Eqn (4).
7. Though it was not possible to sign $\partial m/\partial\gamma$ in the earlier downstream comparative statics, $\pi_\gamma = 0$ implies $m_\gamma > 0$.
8. Equations (13b) and (13c) contain terms which vanish from downstream choice of utilization intensity.
9. From Eqn (11), the profit-maximizing durable price without the tying arrangement is

$$P^* = -Cm_\gamma/C_\gamma m_P > 0$$

Similarly,

$$P^{**} = \frac{Q(1-\eta_m)[C_\gamma{}^2 m_P(r+\delta) - C\delta_m m_\gamma^2] + r\phi m_\gamma C_\gamma m_P}{Q(1-\eta_m)\delta_m m_\gamma C_\gamma m_P} > 0$$

is the optimal durable price under the tie-in sale. The difference between these two prices has the form

$$P^* - P^{**} = \frac{-[Q(1-\eta_m)C_\gamma(r+\delta) + r\phi m_\gamma]}{Q(1-\eta_m)\delta_m m_\gamma}$$

which is positive so long as $\eta_m < \{1 + r\phi m_\gamma/[QC_\gamma(r+\delta)]\}$. Thus, $P^* > P^{**}$, which demonstrates Proposition 5.
10. The optimal parts price is

$$p_m^* = \frac{QC\delta_m(m_\gamma + C_\gamma m_P)(1-\eta_m) - r\phi C_\gamma m_P \eta_m}{rC_\gamma m_P(1-\eta_m)}$$

REFERENCES

R. D. Blair and D. L. Kaserman (1978). Vertical integration, tying, and antitrust policy. *Amer. Econ. Rev.*, **68**, June, 397–402.

R. D. Blair and D. L. Kaserman (1980). Vertical control with variable proportions: ownership integration and contractual equivalents. *Southern Econ. J.*, **46**, April, 1118–28.

M. L. Burstein (1960a). The economics of tie-in sales. *Rev. Econ. Statist.*, **42**, February, 68–73.

M. L. Burnstein (1960b). A theory of full-line forcing. *Northwestern U. Law Rev.*, **55**, March-April, 62–95

R. Coase (1972). Durability and monopoly. *J. Law Econ.*, **25**, April, 143–9.

D. Epple and A. Zelenitz (1977). Consumer durables: product characteristics and marketing policies. *Southern Econ. J.*, **44**, October, 277–87.

R. S. Hansen and R. B. Roberts (1980). Metered tying arrangements, allocative efficiency, and price discrimination. *Southern Econ. J.*, **47**, July, 73–83.

F. S. Inaba (1980). Franchising: monopoly by contract. *Southern Econ. J.*, **47**, July, 65–72.

R. W. Parks (1974). The demand and supply of durable goods and durability. *Amer. Econ. Rev.*, **64**, March, 37–55.

R. W. Parks (1979). Durability, maintenance and the price of used assets. *Econ. Inquiry*, **17**, April 197–217.

W. Ramm (1974). On the durability of capital goods under imperfect market conditions. *Amer. Econ. Rev.*, **64**, September, 787–96.

F. M. Scherer (1980). *Industrial Market Structure and Economic Performance* (2nd edition), Boston: Houghton Mifflin.

R. Schmalensee (1974). Market structure, durability, and maintenance effort. *Rev. Econ. Studies*, **41**, April, 277–87.

R. Schmalensee (1979). Market structure, durability and quality: a selective survey. *Econ. Inquiry*, April, 177–96.

T. T. Su (1975). Durability of consumption goods reconsidered. *Amer. Econ. Rev.*, **65**, March, 148–57.

P. L. Swan (1970). Durability of consumer goods. *Amer. Econ. Rev.*, **60**, December, 884–94.

P. L. Swan (1971). The durability of goods and the regulation of monopoly. *Bell J. Econ.*, Spring, 347–57.

5
Market Power in Aftermarkets

Benjamin Klein*

University of California, Los Angeles

Many recent antitrust cases involve aftermarkets — the provision of spare parts or service for use with a previously purchased durable good. These cases rely on the Supreme Court's decision in *Eastman Kodak Co. v. Image Technical Services, Inc.*[1] to argue that imperfectly informed consumers may find themselves 'locked-in' to a particular brand of equipment after they make their initial equipment purchase. As a result, even if intensive competition exists when consumers make their equipment purchase, a manufacturer may possess significant market power, if not a monopoly, in the aftermarket and may use this power to increase aftermarket prices.

This paper explains why aftermarket prices often are high and examines the implications of such high aftermarket prices for antitrust. Contrary to the 'lock-in' analysis of the Supreme Court's decision, the many instances of systematically high aftermarket prices we observe in the marketplace are unlikely due to manufacturers taking advantage of imperfectly informed consumers to charge supracompetitive package prices. We show that even if consumers are totally uninformed about aftermarket conditions when they purchase their equipment, they pay a competitive package price because competition forces manufacturers to offset later aftermarket price increases with initial equipment price decreases.

The Supreme Court's example of an aftermarket hold-up, where consumers do pay a higher than competitive package price, requires a market 'surprise' and, therefore, is an unlikely explanation for the systematically high aftermarket prices we observe in the marketplace.

Rather than uninformed consumers or hold-ups, high aftermarket prices are explained as a form of price discrimination. Manufacturers selling differentiated products use the aftermarket as a way to meter intensity of individual consumer demand and thereby to discriminate between consumers in terms of the package prices they pay. While such discriminatory pricing could not exist in a perfectly competitive world, it is not indicative of antitrust market power. In fact, such pricing is a ubiquitous and important element of the competitive process. Economists that advocate antitrust regulation of such 'market imperfections' illustrate the danger of using deviations from the abstract economic model of perfect competition as a policy standard.

I. THE KODAK CASE

The most noteworthy aftermarket antitrust case concerns the policies adopted by Eastman Kodak in providing service for its high-volume photocopier and micrographics equipment. In the early 1980s independent service organizations (ISOs) began servicing this equipment in competition with Kodak, often at prices substantially lower than Kodak's service prices. There was no systematic evidence that the service supplied by ISOs was of a lower quality than Kodak's service; in fact, some customers testified that ISO service was of a higher quality than Kodak's service. In spite of this, in late 1985 and 1986 Kodak adopted policies to limit the availability to ISOs of replacement parts for Kodak equipment. Kodak had previously sold its replacement parts in three ways: a) to customers as part of a Kodak service call; b) to customers who did not use Kodak service and either serviced their machines themselves or made the parts available for use by ISOs; and c) to ISOs directly. After the change in policy, Kodak sold replacement parts for its high-volume copying and micrographic machines only

---

*This paper extends the analysis in Klein (1993). I thank Kevin Murphy and Michael Smith for helpful discussions.

to customers who used Kodak service or who repaired their own machines, eliminating sales to ISOs and customers who made the parts available for ISOs. Unable to obtain parts, many ISOs were forced out of business and their customers were forced to switch to Kodak service. In 1987 eighteen of these ISOs brought suit against Kodak, claiming an illegal tie of the sale of service to the sale of Kodak replacement parts and the monopolization of the aftermarket of service for Kodak machines.

At the time of the litigation, Kodak had a 23 percent share of the high-volume copier market and less than a 20 percent share of the micrographic equipment market. The ISOs conceded that Kodak did not have market power in either original equipment market. However, the ISOs claimed that the tying product was not Kodak equipment but Kodak replacement parts, of which Kodak controlled essentially 100 percent. Kodak was alleged to have used its monopoly power in the Kodak parts aftermarket to gain control of the Kodak service aftermarket by means of an illegal tie of its service to its parts. The primary issue before the Court was whether Kodak's absence of market power in the equipment market necessarily precluded as a matter of law an absence of market power in the aftermarkets for replacement parts and service.

The district court granted summary judgment for Kodak, accepting Kodak's argument that competition in the equipment market made it impossible for Kodak to harm purchasers in the service aftermarket.[2] Kodak's theoretical argument, accepted by the district court, was that any increase in prices of aftermarket parts or service would be viewed as tantamount to a price increase for equipment and, therefore, given that there is competition in the equipment market, Kodak would have to offset any aftermarket price increase with a decrease in equipment prices or else would experience a dramatic loss of equipment sales. Consumers would demand on offsetting equipment price decrease because they can be thought of as demanding an equipment-service-parts package and Kodak can be assumed to face a highly elastic demand for this package.

The Ninth Circuit reversed the district court's grant of summary judgment, stating that the question of whether competition in the equipment market prevented Kodak from exercising market power in the Kodak parts aftermarket was an issue of material fact and noting that 'market imperfections' may keep economic theories about how consumers act in the marketplace from mirroring reality.[3] Justice Blackmun, writing for the Supreme Court majority in affirming the reversal, endorsed this 'market imperfections' argument, stating that the correctness of an economic theory is an empirical issue that must be determined by an examination of 'actual market realities', not solely by resort to theoretical arguments.[4]

The actual market realities considered by the Court were buyer information costs and switching costs. The Court noted that, contrary to Kodak's theory of package price competition, buyers are unlikely to be fully informed at the time they make their equipment purchases about the prices of parts and service they will later have to purchase.[5] In addition, the Court noted that when buyers do become aware of higher aftermarket prices, they may find it costly to switch to an alternative equipment supplier. Switching costs are present because the market for used equipment is likely to be imperfect and because buyers make investments that lock themselves in to the Kodak equipment, such as the development of manuals and the training of employees in the use of the particular Kodak machines and software.

Because of this lock-in, Kodak can take advantage of their existing customers by increasing aftermarket prices. In particular, Kodak can use a parts tie to increase aftermarket service prices without fear of competition from ISO service competitors and thus force consumers to pay supracompetitive package prices. Whether a firm such as Kodak could profitably hold up its existing locked-in customers in this way, the Court emphasized, is an empirical question that involves a company trading off the increased short-run profit received from existing locked-in customers with the reduced long-run profit received from sales to new customers. Such a trade-off is more likely to be profitable, the Court claimed, when switching costs are high relative to the increase in service prices and when the number of locked-in customers is high relative to the number of new customers.

Kodak has been recognized as standing for the proposition that economic theory should be rejected in favor of an examination of 'the facts' of a case. However, what the Court actually did in *Kodak* was not reject all economic theory for the facts but, rather, reject a particular economic theory that appeared to be inconsistent with the facts and accept an alternative economic theory which it found more plausible, or at least plausible enough to survive Kodak's summary judgment motion. In particular, the Court rejected the defendant's economic theory of fully informed consumers that consider full package prices before making purchases and accepted the plaintiffs' economic theory of an aftermarket hold-up of imperfectly informed consumers locked in due to high switching costs.

II. THE ROLE OF CONSUMER INFORMATION IN AFTERMARKET HOLD-UPS

To analyze the role of imperfect consumer information that underlies the Court's alternative economic theory, I initially consider two cases. In the first case I assume consumers are fully informed about the aftermarket at the time they make their equipment purchases; in the second case I assume consumers are completely uninformed about aftermarket conditions at the time of their equipment purchases. In both cases I assume a lock-in which forces consumers to deal solely with their chosen equipment manufacturer in the aftermarket. In both cases, whether consumers are fully informed or uninformed, consumers will pay a competitive package price as long as sufficient competition exists among sellers in the equipment market.

case 1: when customers are fully informed about aftermarket prices, a hold-up is not possible.

If consumers know at the time they make their equipment purchases that later they will have to purchase aftermarkets parts and services from the same manufacturer and if consumers also know the prices they will be charged for these parts and services, then manufacturers do not have the ability to hold up consumers.[6] Consumers can take account of known aftermarket conditions before they make their initial equipment purchase and become locked in to a particular brand in either of two ways. Informed consumers may attempt to control aftermarket prices contractually, for example, by negotiating long-term aftermarket prices as part of the initial equipment purchase. This could take the form of a parts and services warranty. Or, when contractual control of aftermarket prices is not possible, informed consumers will demand an offsetting decrease in equipment prices for the higher aftermarket prices they know they will pay after they become locked in. As a result, informed consumers will pay a competitive price for the total package of equipment, parts and service. This is the essential economic analysis underlying the argument presented by Kodak at trial.

The fact that consumers pay a competitive package price does not mean that some elements of the package may not be supracompetitively priced. For example, consider the case of 'overpricing' of popcorn in a movie theater. Moviegoers can be thought of as facing a sole supplier of an important complementary input, popcorn, after they purchase a theater ticket, similar to the case in which consumers face a sole supplier of aftermarket parts and service after they purchase a durable good.[7] Theater owners can be assumed to be engaging in a type of 'tie in' sale by preventing consumers from bringing into the theater their own popcorn or popcorn purchased from competing suppliers. If consumers wish to buy the movie ticket, the popcorn they buy must be supplied by the theater owner.

While popcorn may not be essential to viewing a movie in the way a replacement part can be essential for using a machine, even if buying popcorn were a requirement for movie viewing, we would not consider high popcorn prices to be an aftermarket hold-up. This is because consumers purchasing movie tickets presumably know in advance that popcorn prices in the theater are high. The theater owner is not unexpectedly increasing popcorn prices after consumers purchase their movie tickets. Perhaps when I buy a movie ticket for the very first time I may be surprised to find out that the theater's popcorn prices are very high, but I soon learn about and anticipate high popcorn prices. High popcorn prices are not the result of poorly informed, locked-in buyers, but are merely a part of the total package price informed buyers pay in the competitive movie theater marketplace. That some elements of the competitive package price may be priced high (and other elements correspondingly priced low) is not a concern of the antitrust laws. In fact, the Supreme Court explicitly concludes in *Kodak* that there is not an antitrust problem in cases of high aftermarket prices as long as the overall package price is competitive.[8]

Why competitive popcorn prices are high in spite of the fact that consumers are fully informed ex ante about the popcorn aftermarket is a separate, interesting question. It seems that knowledgeable customers would demand (and theaters supply) lower popcorn prices in return for a willingness to pay higher ticket prices. One possible reason high aftermarket overpricing may survive in a competitive environment where consumers are fully informed is because of the inability to write complete aftermarket contracts. As a result manufacturers cannot commit contractually to charge low aftermarket prices and informed consumers must demand offsetting equipment price decreases up front.

While it is obviously correct that contracts are not complete, incomplete contracts are an unlikely explanation for the existence of high aftermarket prices. At least partial contractual control of aftermarket prices is a fairly easy thing to accomplish in many cases and, as we shall see, established manufacturers can and do use their reputations as a way to commit on elements of their performance that are not controlled contractually. However, in many of the cases of high aftermarket prices we do not see transactors even attempting to control aftermarket prices and the companies do not experience a loss of reputation as would be evidenced by declining sales. I discuss later a more reasonable explanation for high aftermarket prices. What we know now is that if consumers are fully informed at the initial point of purchase and manufacturer competition is present at this point, high aftermarket pricing cannot be explained by a consumer aftermarket hold-up that results in a supracompetitive package price.

A fundamental legal implication of this economic analysis is that when consumers are fully aware of the existence of an aftermarket tie and of increased aftermarket prices, the level of competition should be measured at the point in time before the buyer makes any specific investments and before any lock-in occurs. If the market at this point in time is competitive, then the tie is merely the form in which a company is collecting the total competitive price. This economic reasoning is, in fact, consistent with much of the established law on tying. For example, in *Mozart v. Mercedes*,[9] where Mercedes dealers were required to purchase replacement parts from Mercedes, the Court correctly emphasized that Mercedes had no market power at the point in time when individuals were deciding whether to become Mercedes dealers.[10] Presumably, the individuals who decided to become Mercedes dealers accepted the parts tie as an element of a freely negotiated, competitive contractual arrangement.[11]

This economic reasoning, that when a tie pre-exists and buyers are aware of it, competition should be determined at the point in time before buyers make any specific investments, is not disturbed by *Kodak*. The Court in *Kodak* was not concerned about the legality of a pre-existing tie that fully informed consumers were aware of when they purchased their equipment, but about the legality of an unanticipated *change* Kodak made in its marketing policy in 1985, after consumers were locked in and established ISOs were servicing Kodak equipment. Indeed, Steven Salop, the economic expert for the plaintiff ISOs, recognized that pre-existing ties in a competitive equipment market are not anti-competitive, stating that 'if Kodak had announced its policy in advance and applied it prospectively only to new purchasers, then the installed base opportunism theory [what he calls a hold-up] would not apply. Its policy would have been simple bundling of service and equipment by a firm without market power.'[12]

The Court in *Kodak* correctly emphasized, citing *Jefferson Parish*, that relevant antitrust product markets should be determined by the choices available to consumers.[13] However, the key unstated economic question that must be answered in all aftermarket cases is: choices available to consumers at what point in time? We have seen that when consumers are fully informed, one should consider choices available to consumers before they have made any specific investments and have become locked in to particular suppliers. However, when consumers are not fully informed, *Kodak* cannot be read for the contrary proposition that one must consider the choices available to buyers after they have made specific investments and are locked in to particular suppliers. It certainly would make no sense to claim that at the point in time a patient is being wheeled into an operating room at Jefferson Parish Hospital the patient has no choice regarding an anesthesiologist and, therefore, the hospital has market power. Although consumers may not have been fully informed about aftermarket conditions and, in particular, may not have been fully aware of the fact that the hospital had chosen to contract exclusively with a particular group of anesthesiologists, the Court in *Jefferson Parish* believed that the relevant product market should be defined at the earlier point in time when consumers were choosing their hospitals. Why the Court was correct to focus on competition before a lock-in occurs even when consumers are imperfectly informed is now analyzed by considering the extreme case where consumers are totally uninformed about aftermarket conditions when they make their foremarket purchasing decisions.

case 2: when customers are totally uninformed about aftermarket conditions, a hold-up is not possible as long as competition exists among informed sellers in the primary market.

The level of consumer information that actually exists in the real world deviates substantially from the assumption of full consumer information that permits us to ignore aftermarket 'monopolies' and to focus solely on the equipment market. For example, even in a case such as *Kodak*, where consumers were generally sophisticated and highly knowledgeable and considered complete life-cycle pricing, consumers were far from omniscient about aftermarket conditions at the time they made their initial equipment purchase. However, the existence of fully informed consumers is a sufficient condition, but not a necessary condition for focusing solely on the primary equipment market and ignoring the aftermarket. If consumers are not fully informed about aftermarket conditions but equipment sellers are informed, it remains appropriate to consider the level of competition in the equipment market and to ignore the aftermarket.

For example, consider a case in which equipment purchases are made by consumers that are much less sophisticated and informed than the customers in *Kodak*, such as individuals purchasing small copiers or printers intended for home use. Rather than assuming consumers are omniscient about the aftermarket, and therefore are fully aware of the package price they will pay over time, let us now make the opposite assumption that these unsophisticated consumers are totally uninformed about aftermarket conditions. In particular, assume that these consumers are totally unaware at the time they purchase their machines that later they also will have to purchase toner cartridges for use with the machines. Therefore, rather than demanding fully offsetting equipment price decreases whenever aftermarket prices are increased, in this case consumers are assumed not to consider aftermarket prices at all when making their equipment purchases.

Sellers of copiers and printers in this environment know that consumers will become locked in after they make their equipment purchase. Hence, sellers know they will be able to increase aftermarket cartridge prices up to the amount of the consumer's switching costs. (The present discounted value of aftermarket prices cannot be increased by more than switching costs because consumers would, by definition, switch sellers after they learn about the high cartridge prices.) As a result, sellers competing with one another for sales in the equipment market are forced by competition to reduce equipment prices by the same amount by which they will later increase aftermarket cartridge prices. Any supplier that does not lower equipment prices by this amount will lose sales to competing suppliers because consumers, even though they are totally unaware of aftermarket prices, will not purchase equipment from such higher priced suppliers in a competitive market. As informed suppliers of equipment actively compete with one another to make initial equipment sales by lowering initial equipment prices, any supracompetitive profit being earned in the industry will be competed away. Therefore, even in this extreme case where consumers are totally ignorant about aftermarkets, consumers will pay a competitive package price, with equipment prices lower and aftermarket service prices higher by the magnitude of consumer switching costs. In spite of consumer ignorance, competition is taking place when consumers are choosing among alternative equipment suppliers and, therefore, once again, the relevant antitrust market should be defined at this point in time.

However, the examples in which aftermarket prices are high, such as Kodak copier service, popcorn prices and printer toner cartridges, are unlikely to be explained on the basis of firms competing to take advantage of ignorant consumers in the aftermarket by charging low offsetting equipment prices initially. Although initial equipment prices are generally low in these cases, it is not realistic to assume that this is because consumers are totally uninformed about the aftermarket. We would expect ignorant consumers to learn about the aftermarket over time and for competing sellers to serve as one channel of information, instructing consumers about why other firms' initial equipment prices may be low and of the importance of aftermarket prices in making equipment purchase decisions. High aftermarket pricing due to consumer ignorance will not survive because, once again, we would see attempts in the market to control the phenomenon.

The one example which may fit the assumptions of totally uninformed consumers is government purchasers of equipment. The Court in *Kodak* notes that these buyers, such as the U.S. General Services Administration, are required by their purchasing systems to consider only equipment prices and to ignore aftermarket prices when making their purchase decisions.[14] However, even in this case buyers will get the full benefits of the competitive process and not pay a supracompetitive package price. The buyers may be unhappy when they later pay high aftermarket prices, but they are getting the full benefit of competition in the form of lower negotiated equipment prices and competitive package prices at the original point of their decision. These are the buyers ISOs would be expected to concentrate their sales efforts on. However, if sellers were forced from the start to charge lower aftermarket prices (e.g., if they were required to make parts available and thereby permit competing sellers of lower priced service), then competition would result in higher initial equipment prices. Sellers would not be able to charge lower initial equipment prices because they would not be able to make it up in the aftermarket.

The fact that competition exists in the equipment market does not imply that a hold-up in the sense of a supracompetitive package price can never occur. What a hold-up requires, in addition to consumers having imperfect information, is that sellers also possess imperfect information of future market conditions, the case we now turn to.

III. WHY AFTERMARKET HOLD-UPS OCCUR

To analyze the conditions under which an aftermarket hold-up in the sense of a supracompetitive package price is likely to occur, we first make more realistic assumptions regarding consumer information. We do not assume that when consumers make their equipment purchases they are perfectly informed about aftermarket conditions (case 1) or that they are totally ignorant about aftermarket conditions (case 2). Under either of these assumptions a hold-up would not be possible. As we have seen, fully informed consumers either control aftermarket prices or demand an offsetting initial equipment price decrease that corresponds to the known maximum aftermarket price increase (determined by consumer switching costs); and totally uninformed consumers will receive an offsetting initial equipment price decrease from competing suppliers that similarly corresponds to the maximum aftermarket price increase. Instead, we assume that consumers are generally informed enough to recognize at the time they make their equipment purchases that they are making investments that will place them in a position where they will become locked in and, therefore, where aftermarket prices can later be increased. Because consumers presumably know the magnitude of switching costs, they also know the maximum amount by which aftermarket prices can be raised in the future. However, rather than accepting this maximum aftermarket price increase and demanding an offsetting initial equipment price decrease, consumers generally decide it is more efficient to pay higher equipment prices and take precautions to protect themselves against the possibility of an aftermarket hold-up.

There are two general ways in which consumers aware of the possibility of an aftermarket hold-up attempt to protect themselves. First of all, consumers may attempt to control aftermarket prices or otherwise limit contractually what the seller may do in the future.[15] Consumers are aware that there are costs associated with specifying future performance contractually and, therefore, that such aftermarket control will not be perfect.[16] Therefore, consumers may attempt to control aftermarket prices in a second way, by deciding to deal with a seller that possesses a sufficiently strong reputation for fair dealing. Because reputable sellers are collecting a premium on their sales (which may be thought of as a return on their brand name or reputational capital), such sellers have more to lose than less reputable sellers if their future sales decline. Therefore, reputable sellers can be expected to honor non-contractually specified constraints regarding future aftermarket prices.

Consumers and sellers jointly will decide to use both contractual and reputational mechanisms in designing their contractual relationships. However, because contracts are imperfect and seller reputational capital is limited, the contractual and reputational protections chosen by transactors will only reduce but not eliminate the possibility of an aftermarket hold-up. As a result, conditions may develop where sellers will find it profitable to hold up their customers in the aftermarket.

case 3: a hold-up occurs when a marketplace surprise impacts the contractual relationship chosen by imperfectly informed buyers and sellers.

We implicitly assumed in case 2, when analyzing the competitive actions undertaken by sellers in the equipment market in response to the prospect that they can charge high aftermarket prices, that sellers were aware of the level of prices they would be charging in the aftermarket. While this is a reasonable general assumption, sellers in fact are not fully informed about all future changes in market conditions and, therefore, of the level of aftermarket prices they will charge under all circumstances. This has important consequences for hold-ups.

As I have analyzed in detail elsewhere,[17] it is unanticipated changes in market conditions that determine whether a manufacturer will find it profitable to engage in an aftermarket hold-up. At every point in time a seller considering an increase in aftermarket prices to locked-in customers can be thought of as comparing the short-run gain of such a change in terms of the increased profit on existing sales with the long-run cost of such a change in terms of the loss profit on future sales.[18] If the long-run cost to the seller of engaging in a hold-up exceeds the short-run hold-up gain, the contractual understanding (that the seller will not engage in a hold-up) will be 'self-enforcing'.

Consumers enter contractual relationships with sellers generally believing that it will not be in the sellers' interest to engage in a hold-up, that is, consumers believe the seller has more to lose in terms of long-run costs than it has to gain in terms of engaging in a hold-up. However, an unanticipated change in market conditions may move the contractual relationship outside 'the self-enforcing range' (defined by the contractual terms chosen by the parties and by the parties' reputational capital) so that it would become profit-maximizing for the seller to engage in a hold-up by increasing aftermarket prices. That is, a change in market conditions can make the seller's reputational capital inadequate to prevent the seller from engaging in a hold-up.[19]

For example, a seller may find it in its interest to engage in an aftermarket hold-up when there is an unexpectedly large increase in the demand for aftermarket services by locked-in customers. Such an increase in demand raises the seller's short-run gain from violating the intent of the contractual understanding by engaging in a hold-up. If the demand increase is large enough, the short-run gain from engaging in a hold-up may become greater than the long-run reputational cost and a hold-up will take place. This is, for example, what occurred in the now infamous General Motors-Fisher Body case, where General Motors' demand for Fisher's bodies increased dramatically, making it profitable for Fisher Body to hold up General Motors.[20]

Another situation where a seller may find it in its interest to engage in a hold-up is when there is an unexpectedly large decrease in the future likely demand for equipment by new (non-locked-in) customers. This decreases the seller's long-run reputational cost from engaging in a hold-up. If the future demand decrease is large enough, the long-run cost of engaging in a hold-up may become less than the short-run gain of such an action and a hold-up will occur. This is, for example, what is likely to have occurred in the aftermarket case of *Systemcare v. Wang*.[21] When Wang raised aftermarket prices its sales had begun to decline dramatically and Wang may have believed that it was going out of business in the near future. In such a 'last period' situation, the brand name cost associated with the lost premium on future sales becomes an unimportant constraint on seller behavior and it becomes wealth maximizing for the seller to hold up its existing locked-in customers.

Transactors enter their contractual arrangements knowing that contractual and reputational protections are limited and, therefore, that there is a probability of an aftermarket hold-up occurring if market conditions change sufficiently.

Transactors entering contractual arrangements have decided to assume this residual risk that they know they cannot protect themselves against and presumably have been compensated for this risk up-front. In particular, the expected value of a hold-up occurring will be in the initial equipment price, either because consumers demand such an initial offsetting price decrease (case 1) or because sellers supply such an offsetting price decrease (case 2). Therefore, in an expected value sense, package prices are competitive. However, ex post when a change in market conditions leads to an aftermarket hold-up, the package price actually paid by consumers will turn out to be exceptionally high.

This analytical framework may be consistent with the hold-up alleged to have occurred in *Kodak*. The change instituted by Kodak in its policy regarding parts availability to ISOs can be thought of as an unanticipated change in its contract with its existing locked-in customers. One could argue that these customers did not demand explicit contract protections regarding aftermarket service prices and did not demand offsetting lower initial equipment prices before they became locked-in because they believed ISO service was available as a competitive alternative. This is why the fact that successful ISOs were forced out of business by Kodak's policy change is economically important — it is evidence that customers may have anticipated the availability of competing lower-priced suppliers of service when they made their initial equipment purchase decision and, therefore, were willing to pay higher initial equipment prices than otherwise. If this is the case, it implies that Kodak's parts availability policy change resulted in supracompetitive package prices.[22]

However, this does not appear to be what happened in *Kodak*. First of all, no obvious change occurred in the marketplace to push Kodak's relationship with its customers outside the self-enforcing range. Rather than Kodak's customers purchasing their equipment with the expectation of the availability of low priced ISO-supplied aftermarket service, when Kodak entered the market in 1975 it was the sole supplier of aftermarket parts and service for its machines.[23] In fact, one can argue that intially, when Kodak was the only one familiar with its machines, it was necessary for them to supply aftermarket service in order to effectively compete against Xerox. Similar to the other competing manufacturers, Kodak charged relatively high prices for service, and correspondingly low competitive prices for its equipment. (Why competitive package pricing took this form is discussed later.)

When the ISOs, established by ex-Kodak employees who had access to Kodak manuals, tools, testing equipment and knowledge of Kodak's customers,[24] entered in 1982, this was an unexpected windfall gain to the existing locked-in customers. The customers that switched their service from Kodak to these ISOs were paying a lower than competitive package price. (If Kodak had known ex ante that it would not be making the service sales, it would have charged these customers a higher equipment price.)[25] This customer switching led Kodak in 1985 to formalize in writing and to enforce vigorously what previously it had considered to be its long-established policy, namely that it would sell parts only to customers who used Kodak's service or serviced their own machines.[26]

If Kodak equipment customers were implicitly relying on low priced service supplied by ISOs when they made their equipment purchases, we would expect customers to demand offsetting lower equipment prices after Kodak's parts policy change in 1985. On the contrary, the evidence indicates that new equipment prices were not adjusted downward by Kodak, and that Kodak's sales did not decline after the policy change. The Court used this failure of Kodak's demand to decline as evidence against Kodak's theory of perfect competition.[27] However, even if Kodak faced a less than perfectly elastic demand, we would expect some decrease in its demand if its effective package prices had increased as a result of the policy change. The fact that Kodak's demand did not decline can only be confirming evidence for the fact that there was not any increase in the effective package price caused by the policy change, i.e., that a hold-up did not take place for any significant number of customers.

Further evidence that a hold-up in the sense of supracompetitive package prices did not occur after the Kodak parts policy change in 1985 is the fact Kodak's contract terms with its customers did not change. If Kodak equipment customers were implicitly relying on low priced service supplied by ISOs when they made their equipment purchases and were held up with the policy change, we would expect customers to insist upon aftermarket contract protections. Instead, there is no evidence that contract terms are significantly different in terms of aftermarket protections after 1985 than the contract terms buyers agreed to before 1985.

Finally, and perhaps most significantly, additional evidence that Kodak was not engaging in a hold-up is the fact that Kodak made every effort to make the change in its parts supply policy prospective. In particular, Kodak instituted its restrictive parts policy only for purchases of new (post-1985) models of micrographic equipment and continued to supply parts to ISOs to service pre-1985 models. If Kodak had wanted to hold up its customers, it would have maximized its gain by making the restrictive policy change on all parts sales, especially targeting existing locked-in customers who had purchased the old models. Limiting the marketing change to new models and continuing to supply parts to ISOs on old models is clear evidence that Kodak was concerned about taking any actions that could be interpreted as a hold-up.

IV. AFTERMARKET HOLD-UPS ARE NOT EVIDENCE OF ANTITRUST MARKET POWER

Even if a hold-up were occurring in *Kodak*, it would not be an exercise of market power. Identifying hold-ups with the exercise of market power would imply that market power was present in most contract disputes, including cases which everyone would agree do not involve market power. To illustrate, in Klein (1993) I used the hypothetical example of a tenant leasing office space from a landlord in a competitive office rental market. After the tenant signs a competitive lease agreement and makes nonsalvageable investments in the space, an unanticipated change occurs in market conditions so that it becomes wealth maximizing for the landlord to take advantage of the incompleteness of the lease contract (and the fact that his reputational capital is limited) to raise parking rates in the building. The tenant's disagreement with the landlord in this case clearly is a business dispute that should be handled by contract law. The fact that reliance investments have been made which locks the tenant in to the particular space may be a relevant legal consideration in contract disputes, but that does not make the landlord a monopolist or the disagreement between the landlord and tenant an antitrust case. In particular, it does not make economic sense to define the relevant office rental market so narrowly as to encompass solely the particular office space of the individual tenant. The landlord's decision to engage in a hold-up in the parking aftermarket may be a violation of an implicit contractual understanding, but it has nothing to do with the exercise of market or monopoly power.

A hold-up problem such as a landlord-tenant disagreement is economically distinct from a monopoly problem in a number of ways. A hold-up requires a) that specific investments be made by transactors, b) that there are gaps in the contractual arrangement covering the transactors' relationship, and, as we have seen above, c) that there is an unanticipated event that places the relationship outside the self-enforcing range given by the transactor's reputational capital and the agreed-upon contract terms. On the other hand, none of these three conditions is necessary for the existence of a monopoly. For example, if there is only one potential landlord of office space in a city, then that landlord will be able to charge a monopoly price for office space even if tenants do not make specific investments, even if lease contracts are fully specified, and even if nothing unanticipated occurs after the lease agreement is signed. The monopoly landlord will not be able to hold up the tenant under these conditions, but the landlord will still be able to exercise its monopoly power in the setting of rental terms. In addition, a hold-up problem is necessarily a one-time phenomenon, dependent upon the existence of unique ex-post market conditions not anticipated when the original contractual agreement was reached. Transactors will not make any new specific investments unless these conditions are controlled (with sufficient contractual/reputational protections) so that such a hold-up is prevented from occurring in the future. A monopoly, on the other hand, need not be a one-time phenomenon, but can continue to exist over the long term.

Contract law is superior to antitrust law in hold-up cases because it explicitly takes account of the contractual environment. In particular, contract law generally recognizes the pervasiveness of transactor-specific investments and the imperfect nature of written contracts, and that transactors generally are aware that they cannot eliminate entirely the hold-up risks associated with exchange that are implied by these two facts. In particular, contract law recognizes that transactors, by adopting contractual arrangements that they understand protect against but do not eliminate hold-up risks, may voluntarily place themselves in a position where they know they can be held up. Therefore, in return for accepting such hold-up risks, transactors are compensated in the terms set at the initial point of contractual agreement. Moreover, even in cases where consumers are not aware ex ante of the hold-up risk, if suppliers are aware ex ante of the hold-up risk, competition will lead to initial compensation. As a result contract law deals with hold-up problems in a subtle way by not attempting to eliminate (and certainly by not imposing treble damages against) every perceived hold-up that may arise in a continuing contractual relationship. Instead, contract law deals with hold-ups on a case-by-case basis, recognizing the importance to commerce of a legal system that generally enforces agreements, however 'imperfect' or 'unfair' they may appear to be at times.[28]

Antitrust law should not interfere with the competitive contracting process even though that process sometimes results in a hold-up. In particular, transactors should not be prevented from voluntarily making specific investments that lock themselves in to another transactor and from using incomplete contracts where they knowingly put themselves in a position where they may face a hold-up in the future. As long as sufficient competition exists at the point in time before transactors make their specific investments and become locked-in, any resulting hold-up is part of the competitive bargain. This is a fundamental difference between alleged aftermarket and foremarket market power. Although supracompetitive package prices are paid when a hold-up caused by unanticipated changes in market conditions leads to an ex-post increase in aftermarket prices, this is very different from the case when foremarket power imposes a high aftermarket price or perhaps an aftermarket tie ex ante. While consumers in both cases appear to face reduced choices at the point in time aftermarket prices are increased, in the former case of alleged aftermarket market power the consumer being held up in the aftermarket has assumed the hold-up risk at the initial point of contracting in a competitive market and, therefore, has been compensated for the risk of paying a supracompetitive package price. In the latter case of foremarket market power, on the other hand, the high package price is imposed upon the consumer initially when the consumer faces a less than competitive situation and, therefore, there is no way for the consumer to avoid or to demand compensation for the supracompetitive package price.

For example, consider the case discussed above of the fully anticipated and freely negotiated contractual tying arrangement in *Mozart v. Mercedes*. It is reasonable to assume that when Mercedes dealers negotiated their initial parts contract with Mercedes, Mercedes had no market power. However, Mercedes dealers knew by accepting the tie-in terms they were placing themselves at risk of a hold-up. For example, if market conditions changed dramatically so that the future expected demand for Mercedes automobiles was reduced significantly, it could pay Mercedes to hold up existing dealers and consumers by increasing parts prices. An extreme example of this phenomenon would arise if market conditions shifted so dramatically that Mercedes anticipated going out of business in the near future, as may have occurred in the Wang and Prime Computer cases.[29]

Mercedes dealers (and consumers) presumably assured themselves that the reputational capital of Mercedes and the other terms contained in their contracts minimized this hold-up risk. But they knew they were not omniscient and that unanticipated changes in market conditions could occur so that it could become profitable for Mercedes to engage in such a hold-up. Because Mercedes offered and dealers accepted their contract terms in a competitive market where Mercedes was competing for dealers with other automobile companies and perhaps with all franchisors, the contractual arrangement offered by Mercedes and accepted by dealers must have adequately compensated the dealers for the residual risk they voluntarily assumed. (Presumably companies with less of a history of success and more of a likelihood of going out of business in the future would have to compensate their dealers even more for this added risk in the initial competitive contracting market.) However, if market conditions changed unanticipatedly so that it became profitable for Mercedes to take advantage of their locked-in dealers, would we now assert that the relevant product market has changed and, in particular, that Mercedes had become a monopolist in a single firm market? This would not be a useful definition of monopoly. Such an ex-post monopoly is quite different from the case where Mercedes was the only automobile franchisor, or, perhaps, the only company offering franchise contracts for any product and, therefore, where ex-ante contract terms are set in a monopolistic way.

Kodak does not claim that all hold-ups are exercises of market power, but appears to extend the protection of the antitrust laws to one particular type of hold-up — a hold-up of uninformed consumers with the use of a tie to accomplish the unexpected increase in aftermarket prices. When consumers are uninformed, it can be argued that they have not knowingly assumed any hold-up risk. (But they may still have received the benefits of competition, including some compensation for hold-up risks, in the initial equipment prices charged by competing sellers.) When the hold-up does not occur via a tie, for example, if Kodak had merely increased replacement parts prices to its locked-in customers without imposing a tie and continued to sell parts to ISOs, it is unlikely the Court would consider such a hold-up as constituting an exercise of market power.[30] Antitrust law, and in particular *Kodak*, does not require the courts to microregulate the reasonableness of all aftermarket prices.

However, what is the fundamental difference between these two cases if the aftermarket price increase is unanticipated and results in supracompetitive package prices? The only difference is that in one case the hold-up has been accomplished with the use of a tie and in the other case without a tie. Although a tie is a per se offense, an illegal tie requires market power in the tying good. And market power is present in both types of hold-up cases only in the misleading sense that a consumer lock-in can be claimed to create market power in the aftermarket for an individual company's product — power that exists independent of the size of a company and is present merely because of the nature of the product under consideration.[31] However, by this consumer lock-in standard of market power, a replacement parts price increase or, for example, an unanticipated increase in tenant parking rates would represent exercises of market power, a result that is counter to common sense and accepted legal doctrine.

V. HIGH AFTERMARKET PRICES AS DISCRIMINATORY MARKETING

Whether or not one wishes to label a hold-up as an exercise of market power, it is unlikely that our examples of high aftermarket prices, such as the pricing of Kodak copier service or computer printer toner cartridges or movie theater popcorn, can be explained on the basis of a hold-up. These examples of high aftermarket prices clearly are not one-time surprises, but survive as long-run phenomena. As we have seen, it also is unlikely that high aftermarket prices can be explained by the inability of fully informed consumers to make contractual arrangements that protect against high aftermarket prices at the time they make their initial equipment purchases, with informed consumers accepting high aftermarket prices but demanding offsetting decreases in equipment prices (case 1). In addition, it is also unlikely that high aftermarket prices can be explained by an assumption that consumers are totally uninformed about aftermarket conditions, with uninformed consumers charged high aftermarket prices but receiving offsetting decreases in equipment prices from firms competing for the privilege to charge the high aftermarket prices (case 2).

Instead of imperfect contracts, uninformed consumers, or unexpected hold-ups, high aftermarket prices primarily exist because they serve as a way to meter intensity of consumer demand. In particular, high aftermarket prices is a way to charge more intensive users higher package prices and low intensive users lower package prices. The price discrimination I am referring to here is not price discrimination in the sense prohibited under the Robinson-Patman Act, where competing buyers are charged different prices for the same commodity. It is price discrimination purely in a technical economic sense, where a company uses a marketing arrangement to induce buyers to voluntarily separate themselves into classes on the basis of some particular variant of the good they decide to buy, in this case the intensity of aftermarket demand, so that the company can indirectly set different package prices (and earn different profit margins) on sales to the different classes of customers.[32]

The marketing arrangement generally recognized as an example of this phenomenon is the sale of razors at relatively low prices (in fact, razors are sometimes given away free of charge) while razor blades are sold at relatively high prices. By placing an 'upcharge' on the price of blades in the aftermarket in this way the company can, in effect, charge different consumers different prices for its shaving system based upon how intensively they use blades. This will be profitable if consumers that use more blades per unit time place a greater value on the company's shaving system (either because they have heavier beards or because they have a greater demand for a closer shave).

Numerous examples of similar discriminatory marketing arrangements exist in the marketplace. For example, a company may separate customers on the basis of their willingness to forego particular product features and price 'deluxe' models of a product (which include these features) at a higher level (relative to marginal cost) than 'standard' models. Another example is a restaurant's 'over-pricing' of after-dinner coffee and dessert so that customers willing to forego these elements of a meal end up paying a lower price relative to marginal cost than customers that consume coffee and dessert with their meal. This is also the likely rationale for the tie and over-pricing of popcorn in movie theaters. Presumably those customers that have a greater demand for the movie viewing package also are more likely to demand popcorn. Therefore, by tying and over-pricing popcorn the theater can separate out and earn a greater profit margin on those customers that have a higher reservation demand. Other marketing arrangements may involve a company separating customers on the basis of their willingness to delay consumption of a product, with the company pricing earlier versions of the product at a higher level than later versions. Examples include pricing of first-run versus later-run movies, or hardback versus paperback books. Other marketing arrangements may involve separating customers on the basis of their willingness to expend time and effort searching for a price discount, with a company using, for example, coupons to give a subset of customers a price discount. Since it is costly for customers to collect and redeem coupons because of the extra time and effort involved, this is a way for the company to charge customers with lower time values lower prices.[33]

Kodak's tie may facilitate a similar type of price discrimination because it is likely that the value different buyers place on Kodak equipment is correlated with their demand for service, i.e., those buyers that demand more parts and service have a greater value for the equipment. This metering explanation for the Kodak service tie makes sense presumably because those consumers who use the Kodak equipment more intensively and, therefore, demand more aftermarket service presumably place a greater value on the particular Kodak package.

However, if metering of the intensity of consumer demand is the explanation for Kodak's equipment-service tie, an obvious question is why Kodak did not merely use replacement parts as the meter. Since some of Kodak's replacement parts were proprietary, Kodak could have placed an extra upcharge over marginal cost on these replacement parts and thereby discriminated among buyers on the basis of intensity of use without resorting to a service tie.

As I noted in Klein (1993), the problem with Kodak using its proprietary replacement parts as the sole metering device is that parts and service are not demanded in fixed proportions.[34] Parts and service are to some extent substitutes for one another. In particular, parts will need to be replaced less frequently if customers maintain their equipment more carefully. Therefore, an increase only in the price of parts would lead customers to economize on parts by servicing their equipment more often. (And, similarly, an increase only in the price of service would lead customers to reduce maintenance service by replacing parts more often.) Moreover, if Kodak had placed its entire aftermarket metering surcharge solely on parts, the substitution effect between parts and service would likely have been large. This is because the cost of Kodak proprietary parts is a relatively small share of total aftermarket expense. As a consequence, Kodak would have had to increase the price of parts substantially if they wished to meter intensity of demand and collect differential equipment profit solely with their pricing of parts. This would have created a very large incentive to substitute competitively supplied (ISO) service for Kodak parts and have resulted in a significant reduction in Kodak's profit.[35]

In addition, Kodak may not have used its proprietary replacement parts as the sole metering device because parts demand is not as good a meter of consumer value as service demand. In particular, some buyers, such as individuals who service their own equipment, may demand a relatively large quantity of Kodak parts per unit time but have a relatively low reservation demand for the Kodak package. As a result, if replacement parts were used by Kodak as the sole metering device, replacement parts would be priced above the profit maximizing level and Kodak would lose a significant share of sales in the self-service segment of the market.[36]

Finally, Kodak's service tie, as opposed to solely a parts upcharge, may have facilitated another form of profitable price discrimination. Kodak buyers are likely to differ in the value they place on the Kodak package based upon not only the quantity but also the type of service they demand. In particular, buyers that demand more immediate service (e.g., one-hour response, the availability of weekend and evening calls, etc.) are likely to have a higher reservation demand for the Kodak package than buyers that require less immediate attention (e.g., next day response). Therefore, those buyers who demand more immediate service can be charged a higher price relative to marginal cost than buyers who demand less immediate service. This form of price discrimination can be accomplished only if the equipment manufacturer controls the provision of service. Otherwise, competition in service would cause the manufacturer to lose a significant number of immediate-service customers.

VI. DISCRIMINATORY MARKETING IS NOT EVIDENCE OF ANTITRUST MARKET POWER

The existence of discriminatory marketing arrangements such as 'over-priced' razor blades and 'under-priced' razors or 'over-priced' popcorn and 'under-priced' theater tickets or 'over-priced' service and 'under-priced' equipment in the *Kodak* case do not imply the presence of market power. All that is necessary for such practices to exist is that each individual firm's product have some unique features. For example, when Kodak entered the market in 1975 its product possessed some unique features such as its particular superior document feed device.[37] Another unique product feature is a firm's brand name or reputation. Once companies produce products that are somewhat distinguishable from their competitors' products, they face a downward sloping demand and, hence, have the ability to price discriminate. Competing firms do not have the ability to arbitrage the discriminatory arrangement because they cannot produce an identical product.

It is not surprising that Kodak did not provide a price discrimination explanation for its tie given the confusion that exists on the issue of whether the existence of price discrimination is evidence of market power. For example, Areeda and Turner claim that price discrimination provides 'direct evidence' of market power.[38] And even Scalia's *Kodak* dissent incorrectly asserts that Kodak's assumed absence of market power in equipment implies an inability to price discriminate, claiming that the 'opportunity to engage in price discrimination is unavailable to a manufacturer — like Kodak — that lacks power at the interbrand level.[39]

However, market power is not necessary for a firm to successfully engage in discriminatory pricing. All that is necessary is that the firm face a negatively sloped demand for its products, as all firms selling unique products do. Although such a negatively sloped demand and ability to price discriminate would not exist under the assumptions of perfect competition, it must be distinguished from the negatively sloped demand and ability to price discriminate that is present because a firm possesses a large share of the market. An example would be Alcoa's discriminatory pricing of aluminum depending on how the buyer planned to use the aluminum (for example, Alcoa charged high prices for aluminum used in airframe manufacture than for aluminum used in cable wire manufacture) when Alcoa essentially controlled all aluminum production.[40]

One must determine why a firm has a negatively sloped demand to determine whether a firm possesses market power. If a firm has a negatively sloped demand solely because it is producing one of many unique products with particular features that some consumers find valuable, this is different from a case where the firm has a negatively sloped demand because it possesses a large market share.[41]

The idea that a negatively sloped demand and the ability to engage in profitable price discrimination implies the possession of antitrust market power is based on a fundamental misconception of the nature of antitrust market power, a misconception grounded on the economic model of perfect competition. It is a misconception that is, unfortunately, accepted by many economists. For example, Carlton and Perloff in their leading industrial organization text assert: 'Whenever a firm can influence the price it receives for its product, the firm is said to have monopoly (sometimes called market power).'[42] Under the definition of market power, I, for example, would possess market power in the sale of economic consulting services. Although I compete with thousands of other suppliers of economic consulting services and have a trivial market share, if I increase my price a small amount, the demand for my services will not vanish. I face a negatively sloped demand curve, primarily due to my reputation from past experience with particular buyers and to the fact that I may have particular talents that are especially well-suited to specific tasks.

Carlton and Perloff recognize that this economic definition of market power is not useful because it implies that every firm in the economy, except possibly the wheat farmers of the economics principles textbook, has some market power. They attempt to solve this problem with their definition of market power by claiming that the existence of market power is a matter of degree and that one should define the degree of market power possessed by a firm by the amount by which the firm's demand deviates from a perfectly elastic demand curve. However, this commonly accepted economic idea that a firm's elasticity of demand can be used to define the degree of monopoly present in any situation is likely to lead to the wrong answer. For example, I may have more market power under this criteria than, say, General Motors. The definition confuses an individual firm's pricing discretion with a firm's market power.

Many relatively small firms operating in highly competitive industries engage in the type of discriminatory marketing practices described above. But these firms do not have significant market power. For example, studies of elasticities of demand for many of the branded products sold in supermarkets, such as particular brands of orange juice, coffee, beer and other products, find the majority of estimated own elasticities between 2.5 and 5, implying prices that are between 25 percent and 67 percent greater than marginal cost.[43] The sellers of these products also frequently employ coupons and other discriminatory marketing devices. It is incredible that these firms, that have small market shares, earn modest rates of return, and operate in highly competitive industries against vigorous competitors under conditions where potential entry is a real threat, possess any significant market power. Although these firms producing branded products are not 'price-takers' facing perfectly elastic demand curves, no court would conclude that the firms possess market power. Because the brand names or particular features of the products are important to various degrees to alternative consumers, the firms face negatively sloped demand curves and, therefore, the ability to price discriminate.

Only by using the economist's definition of market power can we infer the existence of market power from the presence of price discrimination. However, one would not want to infer from the pervasive examples of price discrimination in the real world that market power in any relevant policy sense also is pervasive. Certainly we would not want to declare all discriminatory marketing arrangements to be illegal exercises of market power because they would not exist in a perfectly competitive world. This would imply a level of detailed regulation that would be both economically inefficient and inconsistent with existing law.

All that the pervasiveness of price discrimination means is that most firms in the marketplace possess some 'individual pricing discretion' in the sense that they possess the ability to influence their own prices. However, instead of defining the degree of antitrust market power possessed by a firm in terms of the firm's *own* elasticity of demand, it is more useful to define a firm's antitrust market power in terms of whether changes in the firm's prices have any significant effect on *market* quantities and prices. Although a firm has the ability to influence its own prices, this does not imply the ability to influence market prices. For example, although a small breakfast cereal manufacturer may have a negatively sloped demand for its product, it may have essentially no power to restrict the aggregate supply or to increase the market price of breakfast cereal and, hence, have no real market power.[44].

Defining a firm's market power by the firm's ability to influence *market* conditions, rather than focusing on the firm's own elasticity of demand, is consistent with how monopoly or market power is used in antitrust case law.[45] The definition is certainly consistent with the authoritative judicial definition of market power set forth in *Cellophane* cases as 'the power to control prices or exclude competition.'[46] Landes and Posner (1981) mistakenly believe that 'the power to control prices' is referring to the economic definition of market power, i.e., to a firm's own elasticity of demand. However, they do not address the ambiguity present in the *Cellophane* and other similar judicial definitions of market power. Does 'the power to control prices' refer to a firm's ability to control its own prices or to a firm's ability to control market prices? Contrary to the Landes and Posner analysis, this ambiguity is clearly resolved in *Cellophane* against the technical economic definition and in favor of the market impact definition. In particular, the Court concluded, despite substantial evidence that Dupont could control its own prices at which it sold cellophane, that Dupont did not have market power.[47]

When more generally considering the case of firms which have the power to control their own prices because they sell nonstandardized products, the Court in *Cellophane* states:

> [O]ne can theorize that we have monopolistic competition in every nonstandardized commodity with each manufacturer having power over the price and production of his own product. However, this power that, let us say, automobile or soft-drink manufacturers have over their trademarked products is not the power that makes an illegal monopoly. Illegal power must be appraised in terms of the competitive market for the product.[48]

The overwhelming majority of other antitrust cases that define market power so that one can distinguish between whether the Court is referring to a firm's ability to affect its own prices or referring to a firm's ability to impact the market, clearly define market power in the latter sense of the ability of a firm to influence market outcomes. Very few cases explicitly adopt the technical economic (own elasticity) definition of market power. Judge Posner, perhaps knowing too much economics, is the only jurist who consistently attempts to use such an economic definition. For example, in *Olympia Equipment Leasing v Western Union* he defines market power as 'the power to raise prices without losing so much business that the price increase is unprofitable'.[49] This definition unambiguously defines market power in terms of a firm's own price elasticity. Judge Posner cites as support for his definition of market power a decision by Judge Easterbrook in *Ball Memorial Hospital, Inc. v Mutual Hospital Inc.*[50] However, Judge Easterbrook defines market power in *Ball Memorial Hospital* as 'the ability to cut back the market's total output and so raise price', a clear reference to the alternative, more useful and legally relevant ability to influence the market definition of market power.[51]

VII. PERFECT COMPETITION IS AN INAPPROPRIATE POLICY STANDARD

A major problem in using the economic definition of market power, i.e. own elasticity of demand, as the standard by which to measure antitrust market power is that it leads economists to label every real world deviation from the perfectly competitive model that results in a less than perfectly elastic demand, such as the conditions that produce discriminatory marketing arrangements as 'market imperfections'. The implication that then appears to follow is that these 'imperfections' require fixing. However, labeling something an imperfection merely indicates that there is a discrepancy between actual conditions and an artificial assumption of the economists' model of perfect competition. They are not imperfections in any relevant policy sense.

The economists' perfectly competitive model is merely an abstract construct. It is a useful abstract construct because it provides us with useful categories to analyze the basic economic forces or causal relationships at work in many situations and with accurate predictions in many cases. However, as is the case for all abstract theoretical constructs, the perfectly competitive model is unlikely to be a useful device to analyze all questions. Analogously, although the frictionless model in physics is extremely useful, the existence of friction is not an imperfection. And when deciding how to build a bridge one should employ a model that modifies the simplifying assumption of zero friction.

Similarly, the *Kodak* Court in rejecting Kodak's description of the competitive forces at work in the copier marketplace advocated use of a more complex model that more closely mirrored market realities than the perfectly competitive model. In particular, the Court believed it was necessary to modify the simplifying assumption of zero consumer information costs. However, the Court did not claim that this necessary modification implied that there was something anti-competitive in Kodak's behavior. One must clearly distinguish between rejection of a specific model as an accurate or useful description of reality and the use of deviations from the specific model as a policy standard. Deviations of real world conditions from the assumptions of the perfectly competitive model are pervasive throughout the economy. All that such deviations suggest is that it may be necessary to use a more realistic model to explain some phenomenon. It does not imply that these deviations are in any way anti-competitive or inefficient. The Court did not draw this implication, but unfortunately many economists do.

Some economists would want to use the government's antitrust enforcement budget to minimize the gaps between price and marginal cost, weighted by output, across the economy. However, this would imply that the government would, for example, be attacking supermarket coupons and other discriminatory marketing devices. Do we really think the antitrust laws should be concerned about, for example, fully anticipated 'high' popcorn prices in movie theaters or high after-dinner coffee prices in restaurants? Distinct from the infeasibility of carrying out such a policy, the policy would not be attacking the monopolistic problems isolated by the antitrust laws or the problems that should be of concern to society. Using the perfectly competitive model as a justification to attack such phenomenon would be analogous to pouring grease over a roadway when building a bridge to get as close as we can to the frictionless model of physics.

Perhaps the most extreme example of 'grease pouring' in aftermarket analysis is the alleged aftermarket inefficiency analyzed by Borenstein, MacKie-Mason and Netz (1994, 1995). As discussed above in connection with case 1 where consumers were assumed to be fully informed about aftermarket prices, Borenstein, MacKie-Mason and Netz believe that high aftermarket prices exist because of the inability of informed consumers to write contracts that fixed aftermarket prices. Therefore, they claim that manufacturers will increase aftermarket prices after consumers become locked in and consumers anticipating this aftermarket price increase demand initial offsetting decreases in equipment prices. As was noted above, this is an extremely unlikely explanation for the high aftermarket prices we observe in the real world. Transactors do not find it necessary to rely completely on written contracts, but instead commonly use unwritten reputational sanctions to prevent firms from acting contrary to a contractual understanding. Moreover, it would be fairly easy for consumers to more closely control aftermarket prices in many of the cases of high aftermarket prices and we do not see consumers even attempting to write such contracts. However, even if the Borenstein, MacKie-Mason and Netz incomplete contract explanation for high aftermarket prices were correct, their claim that this is an inefficient result, in spite of the fact that consumers pay a competitive package price, is not correct.

The supposed inefficiency isolated by Borenstein, MacKie-Mason and Netz from the fact that consumers pay high aftermarket service prices and low equipment prices in their model is that this leads consumers to substitute away from aftermarket service and towards equipment, a distortion that manifests itself primarily by consumers over-economizing on aftermarket service and prematurely replacing equipment. As noted above, the Supreme Court in *Kodak* is unconcerned about such relative price distortions as long as consumers pay a competitive package price. The Court is rightly unconcerned about such distortions because a competitive package price implies that there is competition in the initial equipment market. Therefore, the Court can be assured that any competitive pricing arrangements that are truly inefficient will be eliminated by the competitive process.

The market does not eliminate the alleged inefficiency of aftermarket overpricing and equipment underpricing isolated by Borenstein, MacKie-Mason and Netz because of an assumed inability of transactors to make contractual or reputational commitments. However, even accepting this abitrary assumption, their alleged inefficiency exists solely in the context of their specific unrealistic model. In particular, the Borenstein, MacKie-Mason and Netz model makes the counterfactual assumption that there are constant returns to scale in the production of equipment, ignoring the high fixed costs (including R&D expenditures) that are generally present in equipment production. Therefore, their model ignores by assumption an "inefficiency" that is reduced when equipment prices are lowered, namely that equipment is generally sold at a price greater than marginal cost. When aftermarket service prices are raised and equipment prices lowered, this offsetting efficiency gain from equipment prices moving closer to marginal cost must be included in the Borenstein, MacKie-Mason and Netz calculus, but it is not. In particular, Borenstein, MacKie-Mason and Netz do not consider the reduction of inefficiency associated with the fact that high equipment prices and low aftermarket prices would deter some low intensity consumers (such as households) from purchasing the equipment. These consumers benefit when equipment prices fall and move closer to marginal cost as a consequence of the rise in the price of aftermarket services. Borenstein, MacKie-Mason and Netz can ignore this factor only by making an artificial constant returns to scale assumption.

If equipment manufacturers were forced by regulation to abandon their aftermarket service tie (and any alternative method by which they similarly could price discriminate), and to reduce their aftermarket service prices, this necessarily would be accompanied by an increase in the price of equipment. (No regulatory limits have been placed on the manufacturer's control over the average package price it can charge customers. If equipment prices did not increase, this would imply that package prices would decrease to all customers, which we know would not be profit maximizing.) As a result, only some customers would gain from a regulatory change that controlled aftermarket service prices, while other customers would lose. In particular, high intensity, high service quality users would gain and low intensity, low service quality users would lose. For example, in the case of home copiers and computer printers, if manufacturers were prohibited from overpricing aftermarket service or parts such as toner cartridges and are thereby forced to raise equipment prices, low intensity users would lose by being priced out of the market. Discriminatory marketing does not necessarily involve the exploitation of uninformed customers that the Court claims is the case in *Kodak*. It is the small (relatively less informed) customers that are receiving the *best* deal with discriminatory pricing facilitated by high aftermarket prices. Borenstein, MacKie-Mason and Netz ignore the fundamental pro-competitive effect of high aftermarket prices — that many more individuals are likely to get low-priced equipment (such as copiers) in their homes and businesses.[52]

More important than the question of which customers gain and which lose if a discriminatory marketing practice is prohibited is the question of whether antitrust policy should be concerned with controlling discriminatory marketing practices adopted by competitive firms. It is absurd to believe that the type of deviaiton from the perfectly competitive solution isolated by Borenstein, MacKie-Mason and Netz are what the antitrust laws are designed to protect consumers against. In general, if such inefficiencies were large, we would expect transactors to use improved contractual arrangements and increased reputational capital to minimize them. As opposed to cases such as a horizontal conspiracy or a horizontal merger between competitors, here it is in the consumers' and manufacturer's joint interest to attempt to solve this supposed aftermarket 'monopoly' problem. A competitive manufacturer earns no more by taking advantage of locked in consumers since it is offset by initial equipment price decreases, but a manufacturer could expect its demand to increase dramatically and to earn additional profit (in the transitional period before other companies follow) if it figures out a solution to the failure to control aftermarket prices problem. For example, the manufacturer and consumer may find it in their joint interest to specify fixed long-term aftermarket prices, or to use a long-term warranty, or to have the manufacturer guarantee a second source supplier of aftermarket services. Although these contractual solutions are likely to be imperfect, if the distortion analyzed by Borenstein, MacKie-Mason and Netz were significant, competitors would make substantial efforts to design and use the best type of contractual guarantee possible. That we do not see transactors adopting these contractual arrangements suggests that the inefficiencies are not large or possibly non-existent.[53]

What can the antitrust laws do to improve these competitive contracting efforts? There is no reason to believe that the Antitrust Division, for example, can assure a second source supply more effectively than private action. More generally, this type of government regulation would not have anything to do with the desired goals of the antitrust laws. In particular, the Court in *Kodak* clearly was not intending the antitrust laws be expanded to alleviate the supposed inefficiencies isolated by Borenstein, MacKie-Mason and Netz. The Court is not concerned when relative prices in a total package, such as the pricing of after-dinner coffee, are set at the 'wrong' level. Antitrust law does not require us to micro-regulate the economy so as to eliminate all deviations from the perfectly competitive model. Instead, antitrust should be concerned with the degree of competition present when contractual arrangements are formed between consenting transactors, not with whether the particular terms competitively chosen by individual transactors are 'inefficient' based upon some abstract standard of perfect competition. To believe otherwise would imply a level of detailed government planning that is inconsistent with the fundamental goals of antitrust, which is to set ground rules that permit the competitive market process to operate.

The competitive contracting process does not entirely eliminate price discrimination because high intensity customers that are paying relatively high prices place a relatively high value on the particular features of the specific manufacturer's product and competing manufacturers cannot supply a perfect substitute. This does not mean that the negatively sloped demand created by such product features that permit price discrimination is anti-competitive. In fact, creation of such features is exactly what we want to encourage. The competitive process — whereby firms attempt to shift up their demand by creating differentiated products that are sold at higher price-cost margins — produces value for consumers. The fact that a firm faces a negatively sloped demand for the product created by this competitive process does not imply that the firm has created a monopoly. It merely implies that the firm can collect less than the consumer value it has created if it must sell the product at a single price. (The gain to the firm is related to how much it can push up its demand at various outputs. Steepness, that is, that fact that the firm's demand does not increase the same amount at all outputs is not of any value to the firm.) This dynamic competitive process by which firms attempt to shift their demand up involves the spending of money on research, product development, and distribution and marketing activities, all of which produce value for consumers. Therefore, the marketing innovations designed by firms, including the discriminatory marketing arrangements by which firms attempt to collect more of the added consumer value they have created should be encouraged because it leads firms to devote more resources to the product-improving competitive process.

Posner's (1976) contrary argument, that price discrimination is inefficient because it increases the return to a monopolist and thereby increases the wasteful expenditures made by firms to obtain a monopoly, mistakenly identifies the existence of a negatively sloped demand and hence the ability to price discriminate with the existence of a monopoly — a confusion that once again can be attributed to the use of the perfectly competitive model as the standard of monopoly. It is necessary to look at the source of a firm's negatively sloped demand and the rents it may be earning. In particular, one must distinguish between expenditures made by a firm to obtain a monopoly on a pre-existing asset (for example, an asset created by governmental decree such as taxi cab franchise) and expenditures made by a firm to create a more valuable product the demand for which is negatively sloped. It is true that resources devoted to establishing property rights on a pre-existing asset, such as resources devoted to bribing government officials for an exclusive right to operate taxicabs within a municipality, is merely redistributive wasteful rent dissipation. However, investments devoted to creating property rights on new valuable assets that do not have their source in governmental action is not merely redistributive but highly productive and should be encouraged — even if it leads to negatively sloped demands and price discrimination.

VIII. CONCLUSION

It is clear that Kodak priced service for its high-speed copier and micrographic equipment at relatively high prices, creating an opportunity for ISOs to enter. In attempting to answer the question of why Kodak found it profitable to price service in this way, it is important to recognize that overpricing of service implies the corresponding underpricing of equipment. This is not solely because many of Kodak's customers were large sophisticated business firms who explicitly considered full life-cycle pricing before making their purchasing decisions and demanded offsetting equipment price discounts, as was argued by Kodak and rejected by the Court. It is also because equipment manufacturers are knowledgeable about likely aftermarket prices and will compete with one another in supplying offsetting equipment price discounts. As a result, equipment price discounts will be received by consumers even when they are uninformed about the aftermarket or are forced by government purchasing regulations to ignore anything other than equipment prices in making their purchase decisions. When the equipment market is competitive, all consumers, whether informed or not, obtain the full benefits of competition and pay competitive package prices.

The only case where consumers pay a supracompetitive package price is when a manufacturer charges a higher aftermarket service price than was anticipated at the initial point of contracting. This can occur if consumers attempt to control aftermarket prices with contractual and reputational mechanisms (and therefore equipment prices will not be fully adjusted downward for the maximum possible later increase in aftermarket service prices determined by switching costs) and then an unexpected change in market conditions makes it profitable for the manufacturer to hold up its existing locked-in consumers by raising aftermarket service prices the maximum amount. Only in this case of unanticipated changes in market conditions that override contractual and reputational protections will consumers end up paying supracompetitive package prices.

Although such a hold-up is what is discussed by the Court in *Kodak*, Kodak's high aftermarket service prices are unlikely to be explained in these terms. While some evidence is consistent with a hold-up, namely the fact that Kodak made a parts availability policy change, the overwhelming force of the evidence is inconsistent with a hold-up explanation. There appears to have been no fundamental change in market conditions, as for example occurred in *Systemcare v. Wang*,[54] and Kodak made every effort to make the change prospective. Moreover, there does not appear to have been any bump up in package prices nor any decrease in Kodak's demand. Kodak was merely trying to formalize and enforce their long-established pricing arrangements. It is for this reason that on remand the ISO plaintiffs largely dropped the hold-up element of their claim. The ISOs emphasized not the *change* in Kodak's parts policy, as the Supreme Court did, but Kodak's parts policy itself, claiming that it was an illegal refusal to deal which resulted in the monopolization of the market for aftermarket service for Kodak machines.[55]

To defend against this monopolization claim, it would have been useful for Kodak to have supplied a reasonable business rationale for their pricing arrangement. As opposed to Kodak's quality assurance and free-riding justifications, which were summarily rejected by the Court, a price discrimination explanation is fully consistent with the facts. However, given the confusion that exists on whether price discrimination is evidence of market power, it is not surprising that Kodak did not present such an explanation for the overpricing of service and the de facto tie of service to parts. Nevertheless, discriminatory marketing arrangements are pervasive throughout the economy and exist in highly competitive industries. Such arrangements survive under competition because every manufacturer's product is unique. Taking advantage of such uniqueness in pricing one's product is not anti-competitive, but actually encourages the investments in product features and company reputations that consumers value. Moreover, such pricing arrangements generally benefit low intensity consumers (such as households) who would not otherwise purchase the product.

It is true that discriminatory marketing arrangements would not exist under perfect competition. However, antitrust law, including the law of *Kodak*, does not label all deviations from the perfectly competitive model as antitrust market power. Kodak presumably could have rented its machine to customers and included a direct charge related to intensity of use as an element of the rental price without any legal problem. This would have been similar to the mileage fee pricing used by car rental firms or to the percentage of sales royalty rate pricing used by franchisors. Although these examples of competitively determined discriminatory marketing arrangements would not exist under perfect competition, only economists who use the perfectly competitive model as a policy standard would suggest that they be prohibited.

NOTES

1. 112 S.Ct. 2072 (1992).
2. *Kodak*, 1989-1 Trade Cos. (CCH) at 60,213.
3. *Kodak*, 903 F.2d 612, 617 (9th Cir. 1990).
4. *Kodak*, 112 S.Ct. at 2082.
5. In addition to making its theoretical package price argument, Kodak argued as a factual matter that many of its customers considered aftermarket costs when making their initial purchase decision. See Wall (1992) at 5.
6. This conclusion is consistent with the economic literature that has developed over the past two decades on the potential for firms to hold up locked-in buyers. See, for example, Klein, Crawford and Alchian (1978); Williamson (1979) and Farrell and Shapiro (1989).
7. While a theater ticket is not a complex durable good of the type usually covered by lock-in analysis, the economic forces at work are identical to what is involved in the pricing of aftermarket services for a complex durable good. Although the term lock-in has an ominous connotation, it merely refers to the cost to the consumer of switching to another product once an initial purchase has been made. In the case of a movie theater ticket, the ticket probably has little resale value after it is purchased by a consumer. Moreover, even in the unlikely event that a theater owner would refund the ticket purchase price to a consumer after the consumer discovered high popcorn prices inside the theater, the consumer still would have the nonsalvageable investments associated with time costs, babysitting costs, travel costs, etc. that would make switching costly. Therefore, while a theater ticket does not represent a very large investment, a consumer can be said to be 'locked-in' after a ticket is purchased.
8. *Kodak*, 112 S.Ct. at 2092.
9. *Mozart Co. v. Mercedes-Benz of North America*, 833 F.2d 1342 (9th Cir. 1987).
10. *Id* at 1346-1347.
11. Similar reasoning can be found in *Grappone, Inc. v. Subaru of New England, Inc.*, 858 F.2d 792, 798 (1st Cir. 1988); *A.K. Root Co. v. Computer/Dynamics, Inc.*, 806 F.2d 673, 676 (6th Cir. 1986); *Will v. Comprehensive Accounting Corp.*, 776 F.2d 665, 673 n 4 (7th Cir. 1985); *General Business Systems v. North American Phillips Corp.*, 699 F.2d 965, 977 (9th Cir. 1983); and *Tominaga v. Shepard*, 682 F.Supp. 1489, 1495 (CD Cal. 1988). Some tying decisions are inconsistent with this reasoning. For example, *Metrix Warehouse, Inc. v. Daimler-Benz Aktiengesellschaft*, 828 F.2d 1033 (4th Cir. 1987), concerns the same business practice challenged in *Mozart*, but reaches a contrary result. However, *Metrix Warehouse* ignores the question of Mercedes' market power and concentrates solely on the validity of Mercedes' business justification for the parts tie.

    Mercedes' business justification, namely that a tie is used to assure that consumers receive high quality repair service, potentially makes sense in the Mercedes context. This is because absent a tie consumers would not know the source of the replacement parts used by Mercedes dealers in their cars. However, such an explanation does not make sense in the Kodak context, where consumers obviously knew when they were purchasing non-Kodak service from ISOs. Rather than using a tie to prevent consumer deception, Kodak attempted to justify its policy on the basis that consumers were incapable of judging service quality for themselves and would incorrectly blame the Kodak equipment for problems that were caused by "improper diagnosis, maintenance or repair by an ISO". *Kodak*, 112 S.Ct. at 2091 (quoting Brief for Petitioner at 6-7).
12. Salop (1992) at 16.
13. 112 S.Ct. at 2090 (citing *Jefferson Parish Hospital District No. 2 v. Hyde*, 466 U.S. 2 (1984)).
14. *Kodak* 112 S.Ct. at 2086.
15. See Joskow (1988) for a summary of the empirical literature on the different types of long-term contracts used by transactors to avoid hold-up problems.
16. See, for example, Klein (1996).
17. Klein (1996).
18. This is the analytical framework outlined by the Court in *Kodak*, 112 S.Ct. at 2087.
19. Klein (1996).
20. Klein, Crawford and Alchian (1978).
21. *Systemcare v. Wang*, 787 F.Supp. 179 (D. Colo. 1992). A similar analysis also may explain *Virtual Maintenance, Inc. v. Prime Computer, Inc.*, 1993-2 Trade Cos. ¶ 70, 446 (6th Cir. 1993), amended and withdrawing 995 F.2d 1324 (6th Cir. 1993) after the Supreme Court remanded and directed the Sixth Circuit to reconsider its prior opinion, 957 F.2d 1318 (6th Cir. 1992), in light of *Kodak*, 113 S.Ct. 314 (1992). Prime Computer argued that it could not take advantage of locked-in buyers by tying the purchase of hardware maintenance to its software support and software upgrades because of competition for new equipment sales. However, Prime Computer has since liquidated its equipment manufacturing operations and reorganized itself under the name Computervision.
22. Fox (1994) believes that the fact that successful ISOs were driven out of business, taken by itself, may have been what motivated the Court and that the Court used the economic concepts of lock-ins and aftermarket hold-ups merely as a way to reach what it considered to be the just or fair result of protecting small business firms and their customers.
23. Kodak entered with other competing manufacturers after Xerox was forced (pursuant to an FTC decree) to begin licensing its patents to all entrants at nominal cost. See Bresnahan (1985) and Xerox Corp., 86 F.T.C. 364, 373-79 (1975).
24. Festa (1993).
25. Hence the ISOs were in a sense 'free riding' on Kodak's pricing arrangement, but not (as Kodak claimed in its Brief) on Kodak's capital and R&D investments. The Court correctly rejected Kodak's free riding argument because Kodak did not pre-

sent any reason why it could not collect for its investments by fully pricing its equipment and parts, i.e., Kodak presented no rationale for underpricing equipment and overpricing service as elements of its competitive package price.

26. ISOs previously had obtained parts from customers who purchased parts from Kodak and then resold them to ISOs, from brokers who purchased parts from Kodak or who stripped used machines for parts, from used equipment purchased by ISOs themselves, and (as claimed by the plaintiff ISOs) from Kodak directly. See Festa (1993) at 627, n. 31.
27. Justice Blackmun notes that while 'service prices have risen from Kodak customers ... there is no evidence or assertion that Kodak equipment sales have dropped'. *Kodak*, 112 S.Ct. at 2085. Justice Blackmun states that 'Kodak never has asserted that it prices its equipment or parts subcompetitively and recoups its profits through service. Instead, it claims that it prices its equipment comparably to its competitors ...' *Id.* Justice Blackmun fails to understand (and Kodak apparently made no effort to clarify) that both of these propositions are true if all manufacturers in the industry are 'under-pricing' their equipment and 'over-pricing' their service. Justice Scalia in his dissent confusingly attempts to answer Justice Blackmun's argument by claiming that 'Gaps in the availability and quality of consumer information pervade real world markets' and create 'zones within which otherwise competitive suppliers may overprice their products without losing appreciable market share'. *Kodak*, 112 S.Ct. 2097-98.
28. See Klein (1980). Craswell (1982) agrees that contract law and consumer protection regulations rather than antitrust law should handle hold-ups.
29. Note 21 *supra*.
30. Areeda and Hovenkamp (1993) ¶ 1709.2 at 1195-96 believe that *Kodak* only deals with the definition of market power in tying cases. Arthur (1994), on the other hand, believes it is difficult to limit the *Kodak* reasoning to tying cases.
31. Arthur (1994) distinguishes between 'structural' and 'non-structural' market power with a hold-up asserted to be non-structural market power because price is set above cost not due to industry structural characteristics, such as the company's market share or barriers to entry, but merely because of deviations from the perfectly competitive model, in particular the absence of perfect consumer information. While I am generally sympathetic with this distinction and with Arthur's policy recommendation that only structural market power should be of concern to the antitrust laws, it fundamentally begs the question of the relevant product market. In particular, he does not discuss but merely assumes that, for example, one landlord's building is not a market. An outline of an answer to this question based upon defining generic and firm-specific elements of all products is discussed in Klein (1993).
32. This is referred to in the economics literature as third-degree price discrimination. See Pigou (1920).
33. Although in all these examples some buyers pay a higher price relative to marginal cost than other buyers, these examples of economic price discrimination do not violate the Robinson-Patman law because in some cases the products are not 'commodities', in other cases because the products are not considered of 'like grade and quality', and in all the cases because there is no primary-line or secondary-line competitive injury.
34. Justice Scalia's *Kodak* dissent incorrectly assumes, on the contrary, that parts and service are demanded in fixed proportions. 112 S.Ct. at 2097 n.2.
35. See, for example, Warren-Boulten (1974) for a discussion of the economics of tie-ins in the face of variable proportions.
36. Self-service customers were a small enough share of total sales (perhaps five percent) so that this effect alone was probably insufficient to prevent Kodak from maintaining its package pricing by increasing parts prices and decreasing service prices after the entry of competing service suppliers. On the contrary, in *Digidyne Corp. v. Data General Corp.*, 734 F.2d 1336 (9th Cir. 1984), which involved a tie by Data General of its hardware to its operating system after the entry of emulators that sold competing hardware, Data General had a significant number of customers (perhaps 40 percent) that purchased only hardware. Therefore, Data General could not profitably increase the price of its operating system while simultaneously decreasing the price of the hardware in response to emulator entry because it would have placed Data General's hardware price significantly below the profit-maximizing level on hardware only sales and had a large effect on its profit. See Klein (1993), n. 32 and n. 46.
37. Bresnahan (1985) at 17-18. The Court recognized that Kodak's copiers were distinct. *Kodak*, 112 S.Ct. at 2077.
38. Areeda and Turner (1978) Vol II, ¶ 514 at 342.
39. *Kodak*, 112 S.Ct. at 2099.
40. U.S. v. Aluminum Co. of America 148 F. 2d 416 (1945).
41. The importance of the source of rents in determining whether a firm has market power is emphasized by Hay (1992), who uses the example of a successful restaurant to illustrate a competitive firm with a negatively sloped demand. It is also emphasized by Fisher (1991) who claims that the term monopoly should be used only in cases where a negatively sloped demand is created artificially from collusion, legally restricted entry, or predation.
42. Carlton and Perloff (1989) at 97.
43. Telser (1972) at 274-306.
44. There remains the question of defining a relevant product market (see n. 31 *supra*). *Changes* in own elasticity may be the appropriate standard to judge the effect of a horizontal merger of, for example, two breakfast cereal manufacturers, and in some circumstances this will imply relatively narrow relevant product markets as defined in the Guidelines. (Department of Justice and Federal Trade Commission Horizontal Merger Guidelines, 57 Fed. Reg. 41,552 (1992).) However, this does not imply

that the level of own elasticity is the appropriate standard to judge whether an individual firm possesses market power. Once again, it is the source of the level or change in the elasticity of demand that is key.

45. A more complete discussion of the relevant antitrust case law can be found in Klein (1993).
46. *United States v E. I. Dupont de Nemours & Co.*, 351 US 377, 391 (1956).
47. Note I am concerned here with clarifying the Court's definition of market power, not with whether the Court's conclusion regarding the absence of such power in the particular case was correct.
48. *United States v E. I Dupont de Nemours & Co.*, 351 US 377, 393 (1956) (citation omitted).
49. 797 F.2d 370, 373 (7th Cir 1986).
50. 784 F.2d 1325, 1335 (7th Cir 1986).
51. Posner's definition does not necessarily lead to incorrect conclusions because a firm with a highly elastic demand does lack the ability to influence the market. A highly elastic demand is a sufficient (but not a necessary) condition for the absence of market power.
52. It is surprising that they ignored this effect since the result, along with the general, fairly broad conditions for increased social efficiency associated with discriminatory marketing which encourages new users, is outlined in an article co-authored by Mackie-Mason. See Hausman and MacKie-Mason (1988).
53. Shapiro (1995) presents a model where the type of distortion isolated by Borenstein, MacKie-Mason and Netz is unlikely to be large relative to the pure monopoly-type overcharge the antitrust laws are designed to protect against.
54. Note 21 *supra*.
55. *Kodak*, DCN Calif, No. C87 1686 AWT, 9/18/95.

REFERENCES

P. Areeda and D. Turner (1978). *Antitrust Law* New York: Little, Brown.

P. Areeda and H. Hovenkamp (1993). *Antitrust Law*, Supp. 1993, New York: Little, Brown.

T. C. Arthur (1994). The costly quest for perfect competition: Kodak and nonstructural market power. *New York Univ. Law Rev.* **69**, 1.

S. Borenstein, J. K. MacKie-Mason and J. S. Netz (1994). Market power in proprietary aftermarkets. Unpublished manuscript.

S. Borenstein, J. K. MacKie-Mason and J. S. Netz (1995). Antitrust policy in aftermarkets. *Antitrust L. J.* **63**, 455.

T. F. Bresnahan (1985). Post-entry competition in the plain paper copier market. *Am. Econ. Rev.* **75**, 15.

D. W. Carlton and J. M. Perloff (1989). *Modern Industrial Organization,* New York: Scott, Foresman/Little, Brown.

R. Craswell (1982). Tying requirements in competitive markets: The consumer protection issues. *BU L. Rev.* **62**, 661.

J. Farrell and C. Shapiro (1989). Optimal contracts with lock-in. *Amer. Econ. Rev.* **79**, 51.

L. T. Festa III (1993). Comment, Eastman Kodak Co. v. Image Technical Services Inc.: The decline and fall of the Chicago empire? *Notre Dame L. Rev.* **68**, 619.

F. M. Fisher (1991). Diagnosing monopoly. *Industrial Organization, Economics and the Law: Collected Papers of Franklin M. Fisher* (John Monz, ed.).

E. Fox (1994). *Eastman Kodak Company v. Image Technical Services, Inc.* — Information failure as soul or hook? *Antitrust L. J.* **62**, 759.

J. A. Hausman and J. K. MacKie-Mason (1988). Price discrimination and patent policy. *Rand Journal* **19**, 253.

G. H. Hay (1992). Market power in antitrust. *Antitrust Law J.* **60**, 807.

P. L. Joskow (1988). Asset specificity and the structure of vertical relationships: Empirical evidence. *J. L., Econ. & Org.* **4**, 95.

B. Klein (1980). The borderlines of law and economic theory: Transaction cost determinants of 'unfair' contractual arrangements. *Am. Econ. Rev.* **70**, 356.

B. Klein (1993). Market power in antitrust: Economic analysis after *Kodak. Supreme Court Economic Review* **3**, 43.

B. Klein (1996). Why "hold-ups" occur: The "self-enforcing range" of contractual relationships. *Economic Inquiry*, forthcoming, October 1996.

B. Klein, R. Crawford and A. A. Alchian (1978). Vertical integration, appropriable rents and the competitive contracting process. *J. L. & Econ.* **21**, 297.

B. Klein and K. Leffler (1981). The role of market forces in assuring contractual performance. *J. Pol. Econ.* **89**, 615.

W. M. Landes and R. A. Posner (1981). Market power in antitrust cases. *Harv. L. Rev.* **94**, 937, 939.

T. Muris (1981). Opportunistic behavior and the law of contracts. *Minn. L. Rev.* **65**, 521.

A. C. Pigou (1920). *Economics of Welfare*. London: Macmillan.

R. A. Posner (1976). *The Robinson–Patman Act: Federal Regulation of Price Differences*, American Enterprise Institute.

S. C. Salop (1992). Kodak as post-Chicago law and economics. Unpublished manuscript, presented at the ALI-ABA Course, *New Directions in Antitrust Law*, 21–22 January 1993.

C. Shapiro (1995). Aftermarkets and consumer welfare: Making sense of *Kodak. Antitrust L. J.* **63**, 483.

L. G. Telser (1972). *Competition, Collusion and Game Theory* New York: Macmillan.

D. M. Wall (1992). Kodak: A personal perspective. *Antitrust*, Fall/Winter 1992.

F. Warren-Boulton (1974). Vertical control with variable proportions. *J. Pol. Econ.* **82**, 783.

O. Williamson (1979). Transaction cost economics: The governance of contractual relations. *J. L. & Econ.* **22**, 233.

6
The Role of Economics in Defining Antitrust Injury and Standing

Roger D. Blair

Department of Economics, University of Florida, FLA, USA

and

William H. Page

Mississippi College School of Law, MS, USA

INTRODUCTION

Section 4 of the Clayton Act provides that 'any person who shall be injured in his business or property by reason of anything forbidden in the antitrust laws may sue therefore ... and shall recover threefold the damages by him sustained'. This language appears to provide a private right of action to literally anyone who has been injured by an antitrust violation. But the Supreme Court has created important limitations on the private damage remedy in order to assure that it furthers the purposes of the antitrust laws. First, the antitrust injury doctrine requires that the plaintiff's injury flow from the anticompetitive consequences of the antitrust violation.[1] In addition, antitrust standing rules further limit recovery to the most efficient plaintiffs among those who have suffered antitrust injury.[2] Together, the doctrines can make the treble damage remedy a rough approximation of an optimal deterrent penalty (Page, 1985). In this paper, we discuss the economic analysis involved in the application of these doctrines in specific antitrust settings and in specific antitrust cases.

Economics has undeniably influenced the development of substantive antitrust rules, particularly in the last quarter-century. But there are numerous institutional obstacles to a comprehensive reshaping of substantive law to meet the criterion of economic efficiency. (Page, 8, 1995) Consequently, the Supreme Court has used economic analysis most explicitly in the application of subsidiary decisional rules, including antitrust injury. As a relatively new doctrine, antitrust injury is less burdened by the weight of precedent; it permits courts to limit the anticompetitive consequences of certain (misguided) antitrust rules, without explicitly overruling decades of caselaw.

In the course of private antitrust litigation, an economic expert is often called upon to address the issue of antitrust injury. As we shall see, absent a demonstration of antitrust injury the plaintiff will not prevail. To aid in understanding how an economist can confront the antitrust injury requirement, we begin with an explanation of the antitrust injury standard enunciated in *Brunswick*. We then identify the indicia of anticompetitive effects: usually noncompetitive prices and outputs. Along the way, we examine the need for factual evidence and the role of economic inference. Building on this foundation, we analyze a variety of horizontal and vertical restraints for their anticompetitive effects — if any — and the potential for antitrust injury. When judicial reasoning is available, we point to specific cases to illustrate how one may proceed in cases dealing with a particular antitrust problem.

BRUNSWICK AND ANTITRUST INJURY

In *Brunswick Corp. v. Pueblo Bowl-O-Mat* (1977), the Supreme Court held that a private plaintiff must establish *antitrust* injury, not simply (as a superficial reading of the Clayton Act might suggest) any economic injury factually related to an antitrust violation. Consequently, a careful review of the facts and arguments of *Brunswick* is crucial to understanding the origin and development of the antitrust injury doctrine.

In the late 1950s, the popularity of bowling soared and with it the fortunes of Brunswick, which was one of the two largest manufacturers of bowling equipment. As new bowling centers opened, Brunswick's sales of lanes, pinsetters, and ancillary equipment increased rapidly. In the early 1960s, however, the bubble burst and sales returned to their former level, and Brunswick experienced considerable difficulty getting paid by the distressed bowling centers. Having made most of its sales on secured credit, Brunswick began repossessing the equipment. Given the decline in demand for bowling as a recreational activity, Brunswick's efforts to sell the repossessed equipment were largely unsuccessful. Since Brunswick had borrowed some $250 million to finance its credit sales, this caused severe financial difficulties for them. In an effort to minimize its losses, Brunswick decided to acquire and operate the failing bowling centers. Over a seven-year period, Brunswick acquired 222 bowling centers and operated 168 of them; the rest were disposed of or closed. In the USA, Brunswick became the largest operator of bowling centers in a highly fragmented market with a 2% market share.

Pueblo Bowl-O-Mat sued Brunswick on the theory that Brunswick's acquisitions violated Section 7 of the Clayton Act, which prohibits mergers that *may* substantially lessen competition. Because of the prophylactic character of Section 7, it was not necessary to prove that any anticompetitive results had actually transpired, only that they probably would. Pueblo argued that Brunswick was a giant in a land of pygmies and, as a result, had the financial ability to engage in predatory behavior and drive its smaller rivals out of business. The jury bought this theory and found that the acquisitions violated Section 7. When the case reached the Supreme Court, Brunswick had decided not to contest liability and to focus its efforts on the damage issue.

Pueblo had an interesting theory of injury and damages: but for Brunswick's unlawful acquisitions, the financially distressed bowling centers would have failed, and Pueblo's sales and profits would have been higher. Thus, Pueblo was in a worse financial position than it would have been absent Brunswick's violation of Section 7 and, therefore, it was entitled to recover its lost profits. Pueblo thus complained that Brunswick's acquisitions preserved existing competition and thereby deprived Pueblo of increased profits. The Court held, however, that it would have been inimical to the purposes of the antitrust laws to award damages for such an injury. The Court pointed out that if Pueblo 'were injured, it was not "by reason of anything forbidden in the antitrust laws": while [Pueblo's] loss occurred "by reason of" the unlawful acquisition, it did not occur "by reason of" that which made the acquisition unlawful' (*Brunswick*, 1978 at 488). In other words, it was true that the merger caused Pueblo's injury because the merger enhanced competition by not permitting a Pueblo rival to fail. What made the merger unlawful, however, was the *potential* for predatory behavior on Brunswick's part. But this had nothing to do with Pueblo's reduced profits.

The Court then went on to explain the burden of a private plaintiff in an antitrust suit:

> Plaintiffs must prove *antitrust* injury, which is to say injury of the type the antitrust laws were intended to prevent and that flows from that which makes defendant's acts unlawful. The injury should reflect the anticompetitive effect either of the violation or of anticompetitive acts made possible by the violation. It should, in short, be 'the type of loss that the claimed violations ... would be likely to cause' (*Brunswick*, 1978 at 489).

Thus, the test for antitrust injury is essentially economic. A private plaintiff must identify the economic rationale for a business practice's illegality under the antitrust laws and show that its harm flows from whatever it is that makes the practice unlawful. One approach to the question is to ask first what welfare loss or inefficiency justifies prohibiting the practice, then compare that inefficiency with the plaintiff's alleged harm. If, as in *Brunswick*, the plaintiff's harm bears no proportional relationship to an inefficiency, then it is not antitrust injury; if, however, the size of the harm the plaintiff alleges is directly proportional to the size of the welfare loss, then the harm may have the necessary causal relation to the inefficiency to constitute antitrust injury.[3] As we shall see, this is a simple exercise in some circumstances, but can be elusive in others.

VIOLATIONS WITH CLEAR ANTITRUST INJURY

There are instances in which it is relatively straightforward to identify the anticompetitive aspect of a business practice and the resultant injuries. Foremost among these are horizontal agreements on price among sellers or buyers. We shall examine these in turn.

Collusion Among Sellers

Horizontal price fixing is *per se* illegal under Section 1 of the Sherman Act, which generally forbids collusive restraints of trade. The economic rationale for this rule can be seen in Fig. 1. Absent horizontal collusion, competition will lead to a price and output of P_1 and Q_1, respectively. If the sellers collude on price and output in an effort to maximize their profits, they will behave as a multi-plant monopolist, restricting output to Q_2 and raising price to P_2. This causes some dislocations and rearrangement of consumer and producer surplus.[4] First, there is a deadweight social welfare loss equal to the area of triangle bce. This welfare loss is the usual concern that economists have with noncompetitive pricing. As an economic matter, we usually ignore the conversion of consumer surplus as a transfer within society; it is a distributional matter with minor — if any — allocative significance.[5] Private plaintiffs, however, are concerned about the conversion of area P_2bdP_1 from consumer surplus to cartel profit.[6] The profit is also relevant as a policy matter because it provides the incentive to restrict output; consequently, it must be taken into account in framing the deterrent penalty.[7]

Direct purchasers from cartels have long been

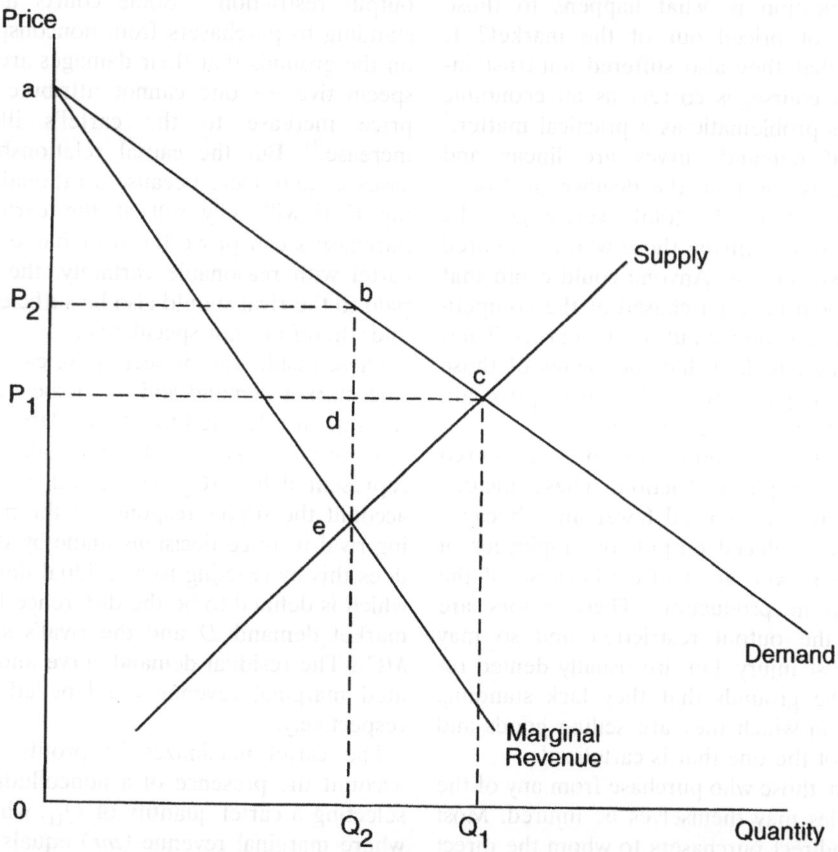

Figure 1.

entitled to recover any overcharge they pay as damages (*Chattanooga Foundry*, 1906). Such an overcharge constitutes antitrust injury. It is consistent with the Supreme Court's prescription in *Brunswick* in that it reflects the anticompetitive effect of the price fixing conspiracy and is the type of injury the antitrust laws were intended to prevent. When rivals agree on a price above the competitive level, it is clear that they must also agree on output in order to make the new price stick. Thus, the former rivals are agreeing not to increase output or cut prices, i.e., not to compete. The elevated price, therefore, is the anticompetitive consequence of the business practice and not the result of any inefficiency that can be attributed to the direct purchasers. Moreover, the size of the overcharge is directly proportional (within a rational range of output) to the amount of the output restriction: the more successful the conspirators are in reducing output, the larger will be the overcharge.

In Fig. 1, we see that output fell from Q_1 to Q_2. A natural question is, what happens to those buyers who got priced out of the market? It would seem that they also suffered antitrust injury. This, of course, is correct as an economic matter, but is problematic as a practical matter.[8] In theory, if demand curves are linear and marginal cost is constant, the deadweight loss is equal to one-half of the total overcharge. The difficulty lies in identifying those who are injured by the deadweight loss. Anyone could claim that he or she would have purchased at the competitive price, but was priced out of the market. Thus, courts are likely to find that the claims of those who refused to purchase at the cartel price are *speculative* (Blair and Page, 1995).

There are, of course, others who may be injured by a cartel's output restriction. These include suppliers of inputs, who sell fewer units because of the cartel's reduced output, or employees of cartel members who are laid off because of the cartel's drop in production. These actors are harmed by the output restriction and so may suffer antitrust injury, but are usually denied recovery on the grounds that they lack standing. The market in which they are selling goods and services is not the one that is cartelized.

In addition, those who purchase from any of the injured parties may themselves be injured. Most obviously, indirect purchasers to whom the direct purchasers pass on the overcharge may suffer a greater harm than the direct purchasers. Nevertheless, following the *Illinois Brick* (1977) decision, they are denied standing because of the difficulties associated with apportioning the overcharge among the various parties in the chain of distribution.[9] Because those difficulties create an unacceptable risk of duplicative recovery, the law assigns the full right to recover to the direct purchaser.

Finally, suppose that a cartel must share the market with a rival that is not a member of the cartel. The cartel creates a price umbrella over the rival firm, who takes the cartel's price as given. In this circumstance, the rival firm benefits from the cartel, and so (of course) suffers no injury. Consumers however, must pay an overcharge to both the cartel and to the noncolluding rival. Certainly, the overcharge paid to cartel members is antitrust injury. Less obviously, the overcharge paid to the noncolluding rival is also antitrust injury in a suit against the conspirators. The overcharge is clearly caused by the cartel's output restriction.[10] Some courts have denied standing to purchasers from nonconspiring rivals on the grounds that their damages are inherently speculative — one cannot attribute the rivals' price increase to the cartel's illegal price increase.[11] But the causal relationship in such cases is quite clear because a rational noncolluding rival will only sell at the cartel price. If purchasers can prove the overcharge paid to the cartel with reasonable certainty, the overcharge paid to the rival should also be sufficiently certain and, therefore, not speculative.

These results can be seen more clearly in Fig. 2. The market demand and the associated marginal revenue are denoted by D and MR, respectively. The supply curve of the noncolluding rival is represented by MC_2. The cartel must take into account the supply response of the noncooperating rival to price decisions made by the cartel. It does this by reacting to a residual demand curve, which is defined to be the difference between the market demand D and the rival's supply curve MC_2. The residual demand curve and the associated marginal revenue are labelled d and mr, respectively.

The cartel maximizes its profits (taking into account the presence of a noncolluding rival) by selecting a cartel quantity of Q_{11}, which is found where marginal revenue (mr) equals the cartel's marginal cost (MC_1). The price (P_1) corresponds

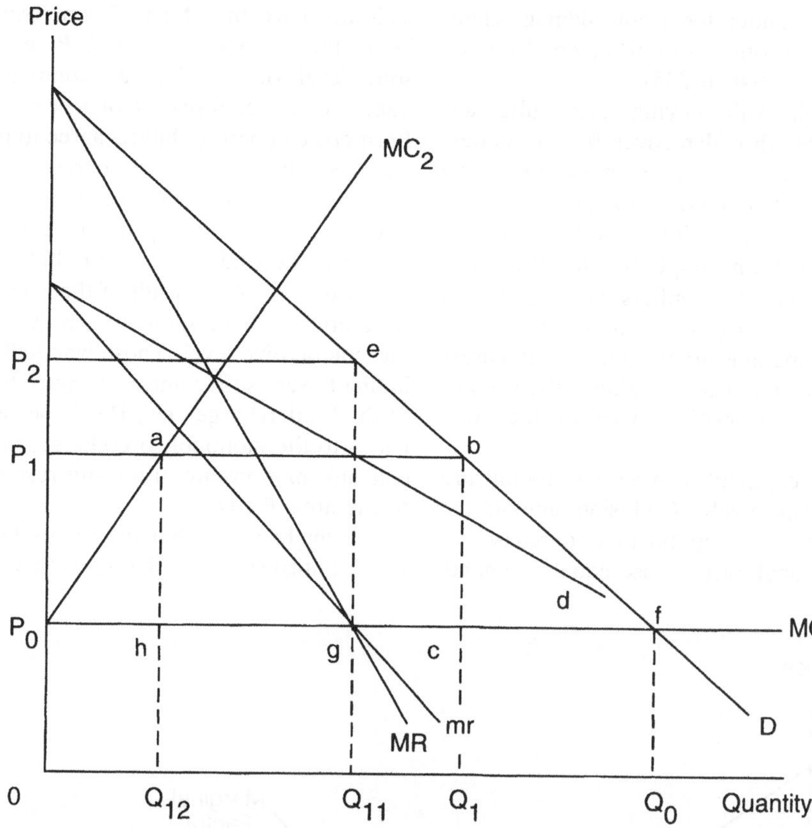

Figure 2.

to Q_{11} on the residual demand. At that price, the noncolluding rival will produce Q_{12} in order to maximize its profits. As a result, the total quantity produced and sold at P_1 will be Q_1, which is the sum of Q_{11} and Q_{12}.

Compared to a competitive price, which would be P_0, consumers are overcharged by $(P_1 - P_0)Q_1$. Of this amount, $(P_1 - P_0)Q_{11}$ is paid to members of the cartel and $(P_1 - P_0)Q_{12}$ is paid to the noncolluding rival. Note that the noncolluding rival does not earn any monopoly profit. It does, however, enjoy a rent equal to area P_1aP_0, the amount by which the price paid by purchasers exceeds its cost. Consumers should be permitted to recover both amounts from the cartel. Although the overcharge is in some sense an indirect consequence of the cartel, it is a sufficiently determinate consequence of the cartel's own overcharge to justify standing.

Thus, whether a price fixing conspiracy among sellers involves everyone or only a dominant group, this business practice leads to overcharges that constitute antitrust injury. The same can be said for business practices that are economically equivalent, e.g., collusive market division. As we will see, much the same can be said for collusive agreements among buyers.

Collusion Among Buyers

When buyers collude to depress the price that they must pay, they behave as a monopsonist and, therefore, we speak of collusive monopsony.[12] If there had been any doubt about the antitrust treatment of collusion among buyers, it was dispelled in *Mandeville Island Farms* (1948). In that case, sugar refiners in northern California agreed among themselves to adopt a pricing formula that resulted in uniform prices for sugar beets. The purpose and effect of the scheme was to reduce the average price paid to sugar beet farmers below the competitive level. The Court held that the agreement was *per se* illegal, 'even though the price-fixing was by purchasers and the persons specially injured under the treble damage claim are sellers, not customers or consumers' (*Mandeville Island Farms*, 1948 at 235).

Those who sell to the buying cartel suffer antitrust injury and should recover for the undercharge. As we saw above, suppliers of inputs who sell in a competitive market to members of a cartel that is, in turn, selling to others at fixed prices may suffer harm simply because the cartel needs fewer inputs. But suppliers who are paid an undercharge are selling in a cartellized market, and so are comparable to the direct purchasers from a seller's cartel. They constitute the class of plaintiffs in the best position to sue for the violation.

In Fig. 3, the competitive price and output are P_1 and Q_1, respectively. Collusion among the buyers leads them to depress their purchases to Q_2 where marginal factor cost equals demand. This will have the effect of depressing the price below the competitive level of P_1 to the monopsony level of P_2. The anticompetitive consequences of collusive monopsony are clear. Formerly competitive buyers agree to restrict their purchases in an effort to depress the price that they will pay below the competitive level. Each buyer has an individual profit motive to expand its purchases beyond its fair share, but each refrains from doing so. As a result of their agreement not to compete as buyers, the price is depressed below the competitive level. Those who sell to the colluding buyers suffer antitrust injury to the extent of the 'undercharge', i.e., P_1-P_2 per unit.[13] Analogous to the monopoly overcharge, the victims of collusive monopsony suffer antitrust injury equal to the area P_1cdP_2.

One might argue that the sellers have not suffered antitrust injury because their only com-

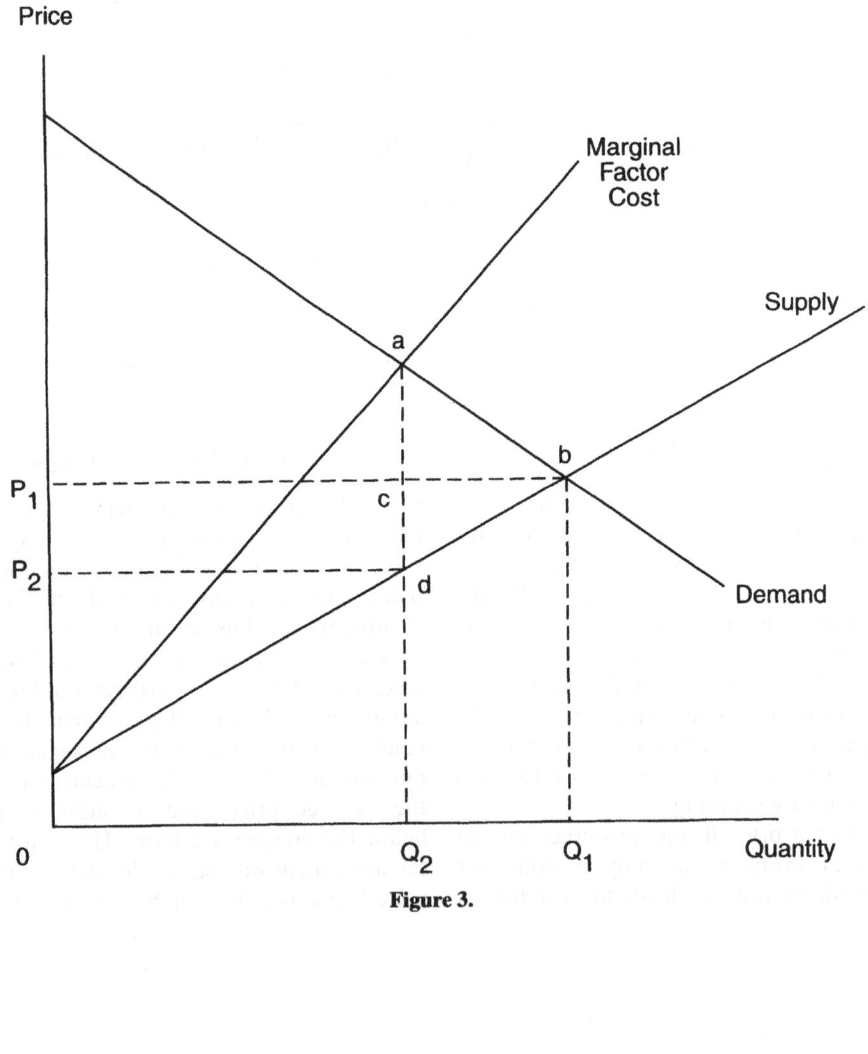

Figure 3.

plaint is that they were unable to raise price. Ordinarily, the antitrust laws are unconcerned with a seller's inability to raise price just as the Supreme Court was not concerned about Pueblo's reduced profit. But colluding buyers agree to refrain from competing in their purchases from the victims. The anticompetitive consequence of this agreement is the reduction of price below the competitive level, which creates a deadweight welfare loss that mirrors the welfare loss from sellers' cartels. The undercharge is proportional to the deadweight loss and constitutes antitrust injury.

Collusion in price — whether by sellers or by buyers — imposes a readily identifiable efficiency loss and corresponding antitrust injury. These are the easy cases because what makes the practice illegal is the cause of just about any conceivable injury. There are, however, some troublesome cases where antitrust violations can occur without any antitrust injury. We turn to these next.

VIOLATIONS WITHOUT ANTITRUST INJURY

There are times, as in *Brunswick*, when the antitrust precedents indicate that a violation has occurred, but no antitrust injury can be found. In *Cargill, Inc. v. Monfort, Inc.* (1986 at 116), for example, the Supreme Court held that when a merger increases productive efficiency, the resulting harm to competitors is not antitrust injury. Increasing the effectiveness of a competitor, like preserving competition, does not cause competitors an 'injury of the type the antitrust laws were intended to prevent'.

The phenomenon of the 'efficient offense' is not limited to statutes like Section 7 of the Clayton Act, under which mergers that merely threaten to reduce competition are illegal. Any *per se* rule necessarily implies that, at least in some instances, a violation of the rule will cause no injury to *competition*. In such cases, the violation may harm *competitors*, but not impose any antitrust injury. The *per se* prohibition on vertically imposed *maximum* resale prices offers an example. The imposition of *maximum* resale prices is a violation of Section 1 of the Sherman Act according to *Albrecht* (1968), but this vertical price restraint typically inflicts no *antitrust* injury.[14]

A brief review of *Albrecht* will put the economic analysis in perspective. The Herald Company, which published the *Globe-Democrat*, a St Louis morning newspaper, awarded exclusive territories to its carriers thereby creating a series of local monopolies. The carriers purchased a newspaper at wholesale prices from the publisher and resold them at retail by providing home delivery service to their subscribers. The Herald Company advertised a home delivered price and insisted that its carriers honor that price under threat of termination. Albrecht was a carrier who decided to charge his customers more than the advertised price. In response to Albrecht's price increase, the publisher hired a third party to solicit subscriptions from Albrecht's customers at the low advertised price. It also designated a replacement carrier who took over the route with the understanding that the publisher would tolerate no unauthorized price increases and that he might lose the route if Albrecht reduced his price to the publisher's prescribed level. During the ensuing squabble, Albrecht sued the Herald Company, which, in turn, gave him 60 days' notice to sell his route. Although the lower courts found no restraints of trade, the Supreme Court reversed and ruled for Albrecht.

In its ruling, the Supreme Court unambiguously condemned maximum resale price fixing:

> ...schemes to fix maximum prices, by substituting the perhaps erroneous judgment of a seller for the forces of the competitive market may severely intrude upon the ability of buyers to compete and survive in that market (*Albrecht*, 1968 at 152).

The Court went on to explain how it reached this conclusion:

> Maximum prices may be fixed too low for the dealer to furnish services essential to the value which goods have for the consumer or to furnish services and conveniences which consumers desire and for which they are willing to pay. Maximum price fixing may channel distribution through a few large or specifically advantaged dealers who otherwise would be subject to significant nonprice competition. Moreover, if the actual price charged under a maximum price scheme is nearly always the

> fixed maximum price ... the scheme tends to acquire all the attributes of an arrangement fixing minimum prices (*Albrecht*, 1968 at 152–153).

Thus, the Court found that fixing maximum resale prices was illegal *per se* under Section 1 of the Sherman Act.

In every case of maximum resale price fixing, there is an element of successive monopoly, which reveals the problem with the *Albrecht* rule as a substantive matter. For purposes of identifying antitrust injury, consider Fig. 4. The retail demand and the associated marginal revenue are represented by D and MR, respectively. The marginal cost of performing the retail distribution function is denoted by MC_D while the marginal cost of production is MC_P. Under conditions of successive monopoly, the derived demand facing the producer is $d = MR - MC_D$ and mr is the corresponding marginal revenue. Absent maximum resale price fixing, the producer will maximize its profits by producing Q_1 and selling it to the distributor at a price of p_1, thereby earning profits of $(p_1 - MC_P)Q_1$. The distributor will maximize its profits by marking up the product to P_1 and selling Q_1, thereby earning a profit of $(P_1 - p_1 - MC_D)Q_1$, which is clearly positive.

The producer can improve its lot by imposing a maximum resale price equal to P_2. The result will be a doubling of its profits to $(p_1 - MC_P)Q_2$. This, of course, provides the producer with an ample incentive to restrain the pricing freedom of its distributors. This vertically imposed restraint prevents the distributor from exercising its local monopoly power. In effect, the restraint is a substitute for competitive market forces at the distribution level. The reason why the producer wants to promote a competitive solution at this stage is not because of an abiding concern for consumer welfare. Rather, it is because such a solution

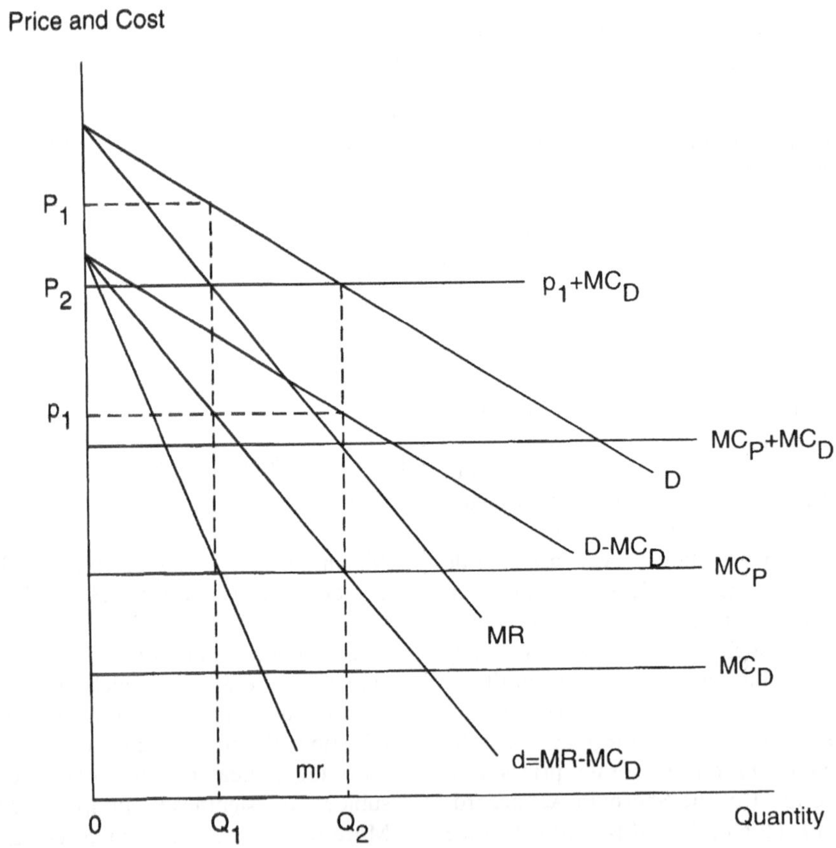

Figure 4.

enhances the producer's profits. Nonetheless, the effect on consumer welfare is also positive as consumer surplus expands considerably. The distributor will sell Q_2 at the constrained price of P_2 and thereby earn a competitive return.

Fixing maximum resale prices may harm some potential plaintiffs, but it is difficult to see how it could result in antitrust injury. In *Atlantic Richfield Co. v. USA Petroleum* (1990), the plaintiff gasoline retailers claimed that ARCO had imposed maximum resale prices on its own retailers in violation of the *per se* rule of *Albrecht*, thereby reducing the retail market price and damaging the plaintiffs. The Court found that the plaintiffs had suffered no antitrust injury, even though the plaintiffs may have been injured by a *per se* violation of Section 1. Any injury to the plaintiff was from lower, non-predatory prices. But '[w]hen a firm, or even a group of firms adhering to a vertical agreement, lowers prices but maintains them above predatory levels, the business lost by rivals cannot be viewed as an "anticompetitive" consequence of the claimed violation' (*Atlantic Richfield*, 1990 at 337). Indeed, a 'firm complaining about harm it suffers from nonpredatory price competition "is really claiming that it [is] unable to raise prices"'.[15] The Court added that, '[l]ow prices benefit consumers regardless of how these prices are set, and so long as they are above predatory levels, they do not threaten competition'.[16]

Atlantic Richfield left open the question of whether the distributor who is subject to maximum price fixing suffers antitrust injury. In our example, the distributor has been injured in fact because it no longer earns monopoly profits of $(P_1 - p_1 - MC_D)Q_1$. But the loss of monopoly profit is not antitrust injury. Price to consumers falls from P_1 to P_2, output expands from Q_1 to Q_2, and consumer surplus expands. Thus, the distributor's injury does not flow from any anticompetitive consequence of maximum resale price fixing.[17] Consequently, the distributor cannot have suffered antitrust injury. Nevertheless, then-Judge Breyer held in one of his last First Circuit decisions that the distributor may suffer antitrust injury if the agreement 'inhibited [the dealer] from selling to those potential ... customers who would have preferred higher quality service, even if that meant somewhat higher ... prices'.[18] But Judge Breyer cautioned that 'insofar as Caribe's claim of "lost profits" refers to "losses" that occurred because the agreement prevented Caribe from raising prices above the competitive level, it is at least arguable that no "antitrust injury" occurred' (*Caribe BMW*, 1994 at 753–754).

The cases in which antitrust violations may be found without any antitrust injury fall into two overlapping groups. First, there are cases in which no *actual* anticompetitive result need be shown to establish the substantive offense. Second, we have cases in which the substantive antitrust rule prohibits conduct that never causes anticompetitive harm. The *Albrecht* rule is a good example, with continuing vitality according to Justice Breyer. As a consequence, the economist can play a crucial role in analyzing any alleged injury for its anticompetitive genesis or lack thereof. There are other cases in which the existence of antitrust injury is problematic. We turn to these now.

VIOLATIONS WITH PROBLEMATIC ANTITRUST INJURY

When a producer forbids the resale of its product below a specified *minimum* price, it engages in resale price maintenance (RPM). Since the *Dr Miles* decision in 1911, RPM has been a *per se* violation of the antitrust laws. Three explanations for this business practice have been offered (Telser, 1960). First, the distributors may want to collude horizontally but recognize that the incentive to cheat will be irresistible. Accordingly, they try to get the manufacturer to impose and police their horizontal agreement. Second, the manufacturers may want to collude but also recognize the urge to cheat. They agree to implement an RPM scheme to reduce the incentive to cheat by removing the ability to shade price. Finally, a manufacturer may impose RPM to induce its distributors to provide product-specific services without fear of free riding by discounters. If RPM is motivated by a distributor cartel or by a manufacturer cartel, the consequences for determining antitrust injury are precisely the same as those described above and that analysis applies. If, however, RPM is motivated by the producer's conviction that product-specific services are necessary and that free riding may undermine their provision, the identification and measurement of antitrust injury becomes problematic. Most private

RPM suits are brought by distributors. Some of them have been terminated because they refused to adhere to the mandated minimum price and some of them have been coerced into acquiescing due to fear of termination. In these situations, the distributors may have suffered antitrust injury to some extent, but the measurement of damages may be too complicated for private suits.

In *Isaksen* (1987), the plaintiff was a coerced dealer who unwillingly acquiesced to the supplier's minimum price demands. From time to time, Isaksen would sell at reduced prices and earn substantially more profit while doing so. His damage model compared the profits while adhering to the minimum price with those when not adhering to the minimum price. Judge Posner correctly pointed out that the higher profits during periods of nonadherence could be attributed at least in part to the fact that other dealers were adhering to the minimum price. This, of course, meant that Isaksen was free riding on the efforts of the other dealers and enjoyed a price advantage because the other dealers maintained their prices. The portion of the lost profit that was attributable to taking a free ride on other dealers was not a form of antitrust injury (*Isaksen*, 1988 at 1164–1165). This raises an obvious question of whether a private plaintiff can separate out the damages — if any — that do not flow from taking a free ride.

Although Judge Posner conceded that a complaining distributor may have suffered antitrust injury, demonstrating anticompetitive consequences is problematic (Blair and Fesmire, 1994). As it turns out, a simple price test will not work. The whole point of RPM is to raise price, so, of course, one will observe higher prices. The producer hopes that price will rise to reflect the added value that the product-specific services foster, which should result in an increase in quantity demanded at the higher price. Unfortunately, the output test that this suggests is not dispositive.

The difficulty with an output test can be seen with the aid of Fig. 5. Without the provision of product-specific services, the demand and supply are D_1 and S_1, respectively. The resulting equilibrium yields a price of P_1 and a quantity of Q_1. Consumer surplus equals the area bfP_1 and producer surplus is equal to the area P_1fd. When the manufacturer imposes RPM on its distributors two things happen: the distributors' profit margins increase and their ability to compete on price is limited. From the manufacturer's perspective, this yields the desired result: the distributors must compete by providing more services and this, in turn, causes the demand curve to shift. Exactly what happens to social welfare depends upon the nature of the shift in demand.

First, suppose that there is a parallel shift in demand from D_1 to D_2. Since the enhanced level of product-specific services are costly, supply will shift from S_1 to S_2. At the new equilibrium, price has risen from P_1 to P_2 and quantity has also increased from Q_1 to Q_2. Social welfare also increased because consumer surplus increases from bfP_1 to aeP_2 while producer surplus increases from P_1fd to P_2ec. There are no losers in this scenario. In this instance, RPM is not anticompetitive and, therefore, there can be no antitrust injury.[19]

A number of critics, such as Comanor (1985), have correctly pointed out that the results described above depend upon the assumed parallel shift in demand. But such a shift implies that all consumers value the product-specific services equally. The infra-marginal customers, i.e., those who are already willing to pay more than P_1, may be willing to pay P_2 even though they place little or no value on the RPM-induced increase in product-specific services. If this is true, RPM may achieve the manufacturer's intended result, but lead to a decrease in social welfare. For example, suppose that the RPM-induced increase in product-specific services causes D_1 to rotate to D_3. For purposes of comparison, we have drawn this so the post-RPM equilibrium — P_2 and Q_2 — is the same as in the case of the parallel shift in demand. The increase in producer surplus is the same: P_1fd rises to P_2ec. Consumer surplus, however, declines from bfP_1 to beP_2. If the loss in consumer surplus exceeds the gain in producer surplus, social welfare will decline. In this instance, RPM can be termed anticompetitive and one can begin a search for antitrust injury.

As a practical matter, the empirical economic evidence is apt to show only that RPM led to both a price increase and a quantity increase. These results alone do not inform us about the consequences for social welfare: an RPM-induced increase in price and output is consistent with either an increase or a decrease in social welfare.

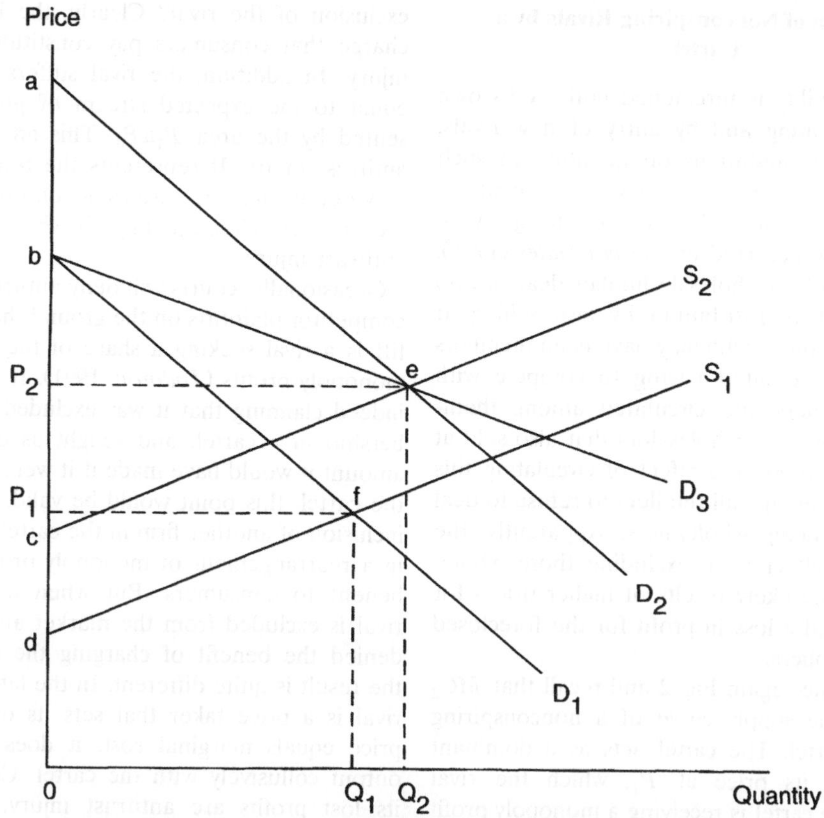

Figure 5.

In principle, we can measure our welfare triangles and resolve the matter. In practice, however, this will usually not be possible due to data limitations. Consequently, proving the existence of antitrust injury is problematic.

VIOLATIONS WITH MULTIPLE ANTITRUST INJURIES

To this point, we have centered our attention on the claims of a single class of plaintiff that alleges that it suffered antitrust injury. There are, however, cases in which more than one group may claim injury. Anticompetitive exclusionary practices may lead to multiple plaintiff classes.

Most antitrust violations inflict injury on many different groups. For example, a horizontal price fixing agreement has adverse consequences for customers, input suppliers, producers of complements, buyers of substitutes, and so on. Antitrust standing rules seek to limit recovery to those best situated to bring suit. There are times, however, when an antitrust violation may involve more than one plaintiff with standing. This result is particularly likely when the defendants are engaged in exclusionary practices that harm competitors and increase the offenders' market power.

Of course, as *Brunswick* and *Cargill* recognize, all competition excludes competitors. The mere fact that a rival has lost profits as a result of its competitors' conduct does not imply that the harm to rivals is antitrust injury; the harm to rivals must reflect an output restriction, not an increase in output.[20] In this section, we discuss two circumstances in which this kind of injury may occur. In the first, the offenders seek to reinforce a cartel by excluding nonconspiring rivals. In the second, the offenders are not members of a cartel, but seek to exclude lower-cost rivals.

Exclusion of Nonconspiring Rivals by a Cartel

A cartel's stability is threatened both by its own members' cheating and by entry of new rivals, who ignore its limitations on quantity. In such circumstances, the rival may try to shore up its position by excluding the nonconspiring rivals. This may have occurred in *Eastern States* (1914). That case involved wholesale lumber dealers who engaged in dual distribution by also selling at retail. The retailers, who may have been members of a cartel,[21] resented having to compete with these wholesalers and circulated among themselves a list of those wholesalers that also sold at retail. The purpose and effect of circulating this list was to encourage all retailers to refuse to deal with the offending wholesalers. Apparently, the scheme was effective in excluding those wholesalers, with the likely results of higher prices for consumers and a loss in profit for the foreclosed group of suppliers.

Consider once again Fig. 2 and recall that MC_2 represents the supply curve of a nonconspiring rival of a cartel. The cartel acts as a dominant firm, setting its price at P_1, which the rival matches. The cartel is receiving a monopoly profit equal to $(P_1 - P_0)Q_{11}$, while the rival is receiving a rent equal to area $P_1 a P_0$. The deadweight welfare loss in this equilibrium is area bcf. Now suppose that the cartel is able to exclude the rival from the market. The rival will now act as a pure monopolist, setting its output at the point at which the market marginal revenue (MR) intersects the cartel marginal cost, MC_1. Thus, the market output would decline by the amount of the rival's output, from Q_1 to Q_{11}. This output results in a price of P_2, and a monopoly profit to the cartel of $(P_2 - P_0)Q_{11}$.

Compared with the competitive price P_0 and output Q_0, the new equilibrium creates a deadweight welfare loss of egf. This deadweight loss clearly exceeds the welfare loss before the rival was excluded by the area ebcg. The net welfare loss attributable to the exclusion of the rival is actually less than this, because the less efficient rival's excess production costs of P_0ah would be saved. Nevertheless, the exclusion of the less efficient rival clearly increases social costs.

Who suffers antitrust injury as a result of the exclusion of the rival? Clearly, the larger overcharge that consumers pay constitutes antitrust injury. In addition, the rival suffers lost profits equal to the expected stream of profits, represented by the area $P_1 a P_0$. This amount is also antitrust injury. It represents the returns on the very output that the cartel's action excluded from the market. Consequently, it should represent antitrust injury.

Occasionally, courts will deny antitrust injury to competitor plaintiffs on the ground that the plaintiff is a rival seeking a share of the defendants' monopoly profits (*Todorov*, 1991). If a rival were indeed claiming that it was excluded from membership in a cartel, and sought as damages the amount it would have made if it were admitted to the cartel, this point would be valid. Clearly, the inclusion of another firm in the cartel only results in a rearrangement of monopoly profits, with no benefit to consumers. But when a competitive rival is excluded from the market and is thereby denied the benefit of charging the cartel price, the result is quite different. In the latter case, the rival is a price taker that sets its output where price equals marginal cost; it does not restrict output collusively with the cartel. Consequently, its lost profits are antitrust injury. This result would hold even if the excluded rival were a former member of the cartel, but had begun cheating and was excluded from the market by the remaining cartel members as a penalty.[22]

Exclusion of Rivals by Otherwise Competitive Firms

In some instances, firms may seek to exclude rivals, simply to reduce output in the market, even if the boycotting firms are not fixing prices among themselves. In *Fashion Originators Guild* (1941), for example, members of the Guild produced high-fashion dresses at considerable cost, only to find themselves competing with so-called style pirates, who simply copied the Guild's designs. Unfortunately for Guild members, there was neither patent nor copyright protection available. As a means of self-protection, the Guild organized an elaborate boycott, in which the stores that carried the Guild's dresses agreed not to sell those of the style pirates. There was no evidence that the Guild was fixing prices or programming production. Nevertheless, the court properly found the boycott unlawful.

This problem can be examined more generally with the aid of Fig. 6. Industry supply and demand yield an equilibrium at a price of P_1 and a quantity of Q_1. The industry supply is the horizontal sum of the supply curves of group A and of group B. Suppose that the firms in group A are successful in excluding group B from the industry. The new equilibrium price and output, which are P_2 and Q_2, respectively, are determined by the intersection of industry demand and the supply curve of group A. It is apparent that price has risen from P_1 to P_2 while quantity has fallen from Q_1 to Q_2. For consumers, the effect is the same as for a horizontal agreement on price. Thus, those who continue to buy at the higher price have suffered antitrust injury and their damage claim will be equal to the overcharge: $(P_2 - P_1)Q_2$.

The foreclosed producers in group B have also suffered due to their exclusion. In particular, they have lost the profit that they would have earned in the industry of their choice because they must reallocate their investments to other — presumably less profitable endeavors. This loss is represented by area abP_1 in Fig. 6. Since this loss flows directly from the anticompetitive exclusion of these would-be suppliers and since this loss is not duplicative of the claims by consumers, the foreclosed firms should have standing to sue. Their loss would clearly be antitrust injury as it flows from the anticompetitive consequences of the unlawful behavior of the defendants.

An examination of Fig. 6 reveals that the claims of overcharged customers and foreclosed rivals

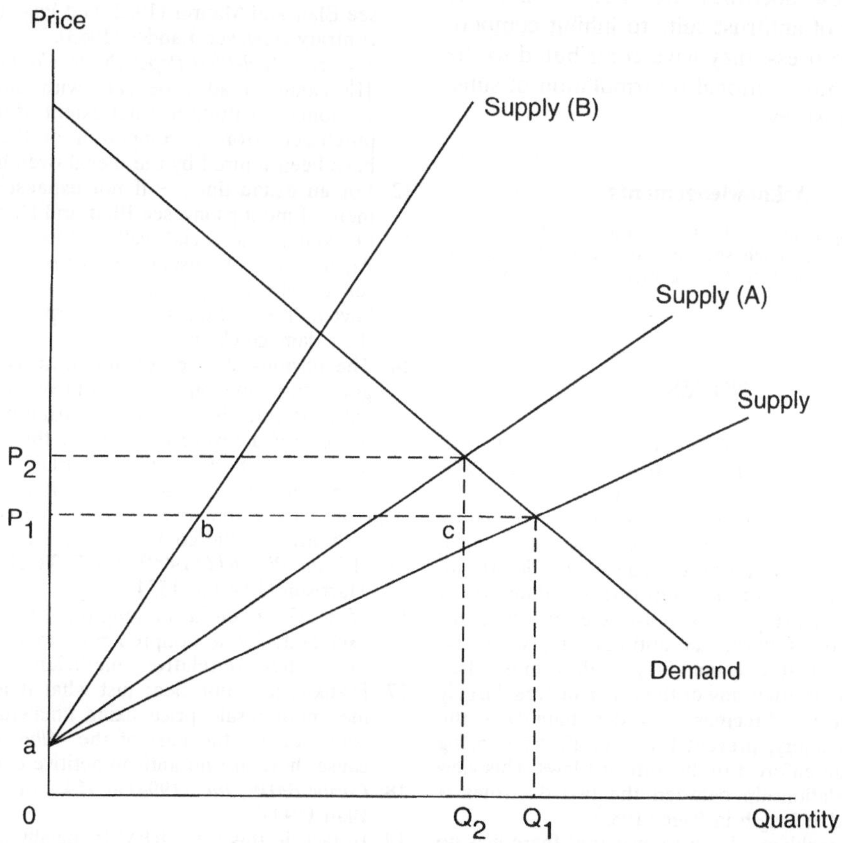

Figure 6.

are not duplicative. In cases of this sort (anticompetitive exclusion or foreclosure), there are two plaintiff classes that may legitimately claim that they have experienced antitrust injury. In these instances, there may be multiple claims.

CONCLUSION

While the substantive rules of antitrust still reflect a range of social and economic values, the antitrust injury and standing doctrines rest almost exclusively on economic analysis. The fact that an antitrust violation has occurred does not tell us whether an injured firm should be permitted to sue. Our analysis has revealed that identifying antitrust injury for most violations requires rigorous economic analysis. Although the courts have not always applied the antitrust injury and standing doctrines correctly, on balance, they have employed these doctrines effectively to limit the perverse use of antitrust suits to inhibit competition. In the process, they have contributed to the gradual and more rational reformulation of substantive antitrust law.

Acknowledgements

The authors appreciate the financial support of their respective institutions. Although she must be held blameless for what follows, we appreciate the constructive advice of Amanda K. Esquibel.

NOTES

1. *Brunswick Corp.* (1977). For antitrust law and economics treatments of antitrust injury, see Page (1980) and Blair and Harrison (1989).
2. *Cargill, Inc.* (1986) at 110, footnote 5. *Balaklaw* (1994) at 798. footnote 9: Over time, courts have developed a two-pronged analysis to determine whether a plaintiff has antitrust standing. As a necessary first step, courts must determine whether the plaintiff suffered an antitrust injury. If the answer to that question is yes, they must then determine whether any of the other factors, largely relating to the directness and identifiability of the plaintiff's injury, prevent the plaintiff from being an efficient enforcer of the antitrust laws. This view of the relationship between the two doctrines is developed at length in Page (1985).
3. Pueblo's problem, of course, was that there was no *actual* inefficiency as the grounds for holding the merger illegal were purely prophylactic.
4. We employ the traditional approximation to consumer surplus and rely upon Willig (1976) for justification.
5. Posner (1975) points out that these profits provide an incentive for the socially unproductive activity of trying to become a monopolist. To this extent, the profit also represents an allocative problem.
6. Strictly speaking, the cartel profit will be area P_2bdP_1 minus area dce, but the overcharged buyers do not care about the reduction in producer surplus (area dce).
7. See Landes (1983), which advocates a penalty equal to the net harm imposed on others. Although such a penalty would achieve deterrence, it may not be operational.
8. *Montreal Trading* (1981 at 867–868), held that if the plaintiff does not buy a product because the defendants limit production as part of a price fixing conspiracy, the plaintiff cannot recover damages, unless it can prove a 'regular course of dealing' with the defendant.
9. For an economic analysis, see Landes and Posner (1979). For a contrasting view, see Harris and Sullivan (1979).
10. For a more complete presentation of the economics, see Blair and Maurer (1982) and Page (1990). For a contrary view, see Landes (1983).
11. See, e.g., *Mid-West Paper Prods. Co.* (1979 at 583): '[I]t cannot readily be said with any degree of economic certitude to what extent, if indeed at all, purchasers from a competitor of the price-fixers have been injured by the illegal overcharge'.
12. For an exhausting — if not exhaustive — treatment of monopsony, see Blair and Harrison (1993).
13. Of course, the social welfare loss is triangle abd. Again, this is the usual concern of economists, but sellers who are priced out of the market would have a difficult time shedding a *speculative* label on their damage claims.
14. The obvious absence of any antitrust injury casts grave suspicion on the wisdom of the substantive antitrust rule that prohibits maximum resale price fixing. For a severe criticism of the *Albrecht* rule on social welfare grounds, see Blair and Kaserman (1981) and McChesney (1986). Blair and Fesmire (1987) argue that the *Albrecht* rule is inconsistent with any credible goal of antitrust policy.
15. *Atlantic Richfield* (1990) at 337–38, citing Blair and Harrison (1989) at 1554.
16. *Id.* at 339. Even in the long run, '[r]ivals cannot be excluded...by a nonpredatory maximum scheme unless they are relatively inefficient'. *Id.* at 338 n.7.
17. Frankly, it is not clear just what it is that makes maximum resale price fixing unlawful other than confusion on the part of the *Albrecht* Court because there are no anticompetitive consequences.
18. *Caribe BMW, Inc.* (1994) at 754. For a critique, see Blair (1995).
19. In fact, in this case, RPM is socially beneficial and the *per se* rule of illegality appears to be both misguided and socially harmful.

20. See also *Car Carriers, Inc.* (1984) at 1109:

    Losing business to a competitor is an inevitable consequence of the economic system that the Sherman Act was designed to protect; some enterprises will prevail and others will not, but it is the function of Section 1 to compensate the unfortunate only when their demise is accompanied by a generalized injury to the market.

21. Posner and Easterbrook (1981) suggest this interpretation.
22. *Hammes* (1994) held that a complaint stated antitrust injury if it were interpreted to allege that the plaintiff:

    wanted to compete by underselling the other dealers, thus weakening or breaking the cartel, and that it was ejected from the advertising pool in order to prevent it from, or punish it for, doing this. Losses inflicted by a cartel in retaliation for an attempt by one member to compete with the others are certainly compensable under the antitrust laws...for otherwise an effective deterrent to successful cartelization would be eliminated.

    (citations omitted).

REFERENCES

Albrecht v. Herald Company, 390 US 145 (1968).

P. Areeda (1976). Antitrust violations without damage recoveries. *Harvard Law Review*, **89**, 1127–39.

Atlantic Richfield Co. v. USA Petroleum, 495 US 328 (1990).

Balaklaw v. Lovell, 14F. 3d 793 (2d. Cir. 1994).

R. D. Blair, (1995). The Ghost of *Albrecht*: *Caribe BMW Inc. v. Bayerische Motoren Werke Aktiengesellbschaft*. *Antitrust Bulletin*, **40**, Spring, 205–25.

R. D. Blair and J. M. Fesmire (1986). Maximum price fixing and the goals of antitrust. *Syracuse Law Review*, **37**, June, 43–77.

R. D. Blair and J. M. Fesmire (1994). The resale price maintenance policy dilemma. *Southern Economic Journal*, **60**, April, 1043–7.

R. D. Blair and J. L. Harrison (1989). Rethinking antitrust injury. *Vanderbilt Law Review*, **42** November, 1539–73.

R. D. Blair and J. L. Harrison (1991). Antitrust policy and monopsony. *Cornell Law Review*, **76**, January, 297–340.

R. D. Blair and J. L. Harrison (1993). *Monopsony: Antitrust Law and Economics*, Princeton NJ: Princeton University Press.

R. D. Blair and D. L. Kaserman (1981). The *Albrecht* rule and consumer welfare: an economic analysis. *University of Florida Law Review*, **33**, Summer, 461–84.

R. D. Blair and G. L. Lang (1991). *Albrecht* after *ARCO*: maximum resale price fixing moves toward the rule of reason. *Vanderbilt Law Review*, **44**, October, 1007–39.

R. D. Blair and V. G. Maurer (1982). Umbrella pricing and antitrust standing: an economic analysis. *Utah Law Review*, **1982**, 763–96.

R. D. Blair and W. H. Page (1995). Speculative antitrust damages. *Washington Law Review*, **70**, April, 423–63.

Brunswick Corp. v. Pueblo Bowl O Mat, Inc., 429 US 477 (1977).

Car Carriers, Inc. v. Ford Motor Co., 745 F.2d 1101 (7th Cir. 1984), *cert. denied*, 470 US 1054 (1985).

Cargill, Inc. v. Monfort, Inc., 479 US 104 (1986).

Caribe BMW, Inc. v. Bayerische Motoren Werke, A.G., 19 F.3d 745, 754 (1st Cir. 1994).

Chattanooga Foundry & Pipe Works v. Atlanta, 203 US 390, 396 (1906).

W. B. Comanor (1985). Vertical price-fixing, vertical market restrictions, and the new antitrust policy. *Harvard Law Review*, **98**, March 983–1002.

Dr. Miles Medical Co. v. John D. Park & Sons Co., 220 US 373 (1911).

Eastern States Retail Dealer's Assoc. v. United States, 234 US 600 (1914).

F. H. Easterbrook (1985). Detrebling antitrust damages. *Journal of Law & Economics*, **28**, May, 445–68.

F. H. Easterbrook (1987). Allocating antitrust decision-making tasks. *Georgetown Law Journal*, **76**, 305–25.

Fashion Originators' Guild of America v. FTC, 312 US 457 (1941).

Hammes v. AAMCO Transmissions, 33 F.3d 774, 783 (7th Cir. 1994).

R. Y. Harris and L. A. Sullivan (1979). Passing on the monopoly overcharge: a comprehensive policy analysis. *University of Pennsylvania Law Review*, **128**, December, 269–360.

Illinois Brick Co. v. Illinois, 431 US 720, 737-38 (1977).

Isaksen v. Vermont Castings, Inc., 825 F. 2d 1158 (7th Cir. 1987), *cert. denied*, 108 S. Ct. 1728 (1988).

W. M. Landes (1983). Optimal sanctions for antitrust violations. *University of Chicago Law Review*, **50**, Spring, 652–78.

W. M. Landes and R. A. Posner (1979). Should indirect purchasers have standing to sue under the antitrust laws? An economic analysis of the rule of *Illinois Brick*, *University of Chicago Law Review*, **46**, Spring, 602–35.

Mandeville Island Farms v. American Crystal Sugar Co., 334 US 219 (1948).

F. S. McChesney (1986). Successive monopoly and maximum-price fixing: the case of newspapers. Unpublished manuscript, November.

Mid-West Paper Prods. Co. v. Continental Group, Inc.,

596 F.2d 573, 583-87 (3d Cir. 1979).
Montreal Trading v. AMAX, Inc., 661 F.2d 864, 867-68 (10th Cir. 1981), *cet. denied*, 455 US 1001 (1982).
W. H. Page (1980). Antitrust damages and economic efficiency: an approach to antitrust injury. *University of Chicago Law Review*, **47**, Spring, 467–504.
W. H. Page (1985). The scope of liability for antitrust violations. *Stanford Law Review*, **37**, July, 1445–1512.
W. H. Page (1989). The Chicago School and the evolution of antitrust: characterization, antitrust injury, and evidentiary sufficiency. *Virginia Law Review*, **75**, October, 1221–1308.
W. H. Page (1990). Optimal antitrust penalties and competitors' injury. *Michigan Law Review*, **88**, June, 2151–66.
W. H. Page (1995). Legal realism and the shaping of modern antitrust. *Emory Law Journal*, **44**, 1●.
R. A. Posner (1975). The social cost of monopoly and regulation. *Journal of Political Economy*, **83**, August, 807–27.
R. A. Posner and F. H. Easterbrook (1981). *Antitrust: Cases, Economic Notes and Other Materials*, 2nd edition, St Paul, MN: West Publishing.
L. Telser (1960). Why should manufacturers want fair trade? *Journal of Law & Economics*, **3**, October, 86–105.
Todorov v. DCH Healthcare Authority, 921 F.2d 1438, 1453-54 (11th Cir. 1991).
R. Willig (1976). Consumer's surplus without apology. *American Economic Review*, **66**, September, 589–97.

7
Breakfast at the Federal Trade Commission

William F. Shughart II

University of Mississippi, University, MS, USA

Robert D. Tollison

George Mason University, Fairfax, VA, USA

and

Eileen C. Reed

Robert Nathan and Associates, Washington, DC, USA

INTRODUCTION

Defining the relevant market is the first and in many respects the most important question in antitrust analysis. In most antitrust cases, the outcome falls neatly from the resolution of the market-definition issue. Depending on how the market is defined, a company is or is not a monopolist, or a merger is or is not approved by the antitrust authorities. Despite its importance, however, economists have not been of much practical help in establishing consistently reliable empirical criteria for determining what degree of substitutability among goods, distance, and time delineates a market for legal purposes. As a consequence, relevant markets are determined in a mostly *ad hoc* fashion in antitrust investigations.

Such an approach to market definition is clearly unsatisfactory as a matter of public policy. The narrow 'markets' that are found relevant for antitrust purposes are used to enjoin mergers and to forestall the use of certain business practices that might otherwise have led to real economic efficiencies. Antitrust policy thus becomes 'a kind of economic engineering project' (Neale and Goyder, 1980, p. 441).

In this paper, we tackle the market definition problem by going back to the basics of the theory of consumer behavior. Although our focus is on the delineation of product markets, the technique we employ can easily be extended to geographic-market definition. Using readily available data on income, own price, and the prices of related goods, we estimate an ordinary demand function for a product that was recently the subject of a celebrated antitrust investigation, ready-to-eat (RTE) breakfast cereal. While government investigators assigned to the case construed the market narrowly to include only RTE cereal, our results suggest that many foods compete for a place on the consumer's breakfast plate. In particular, we find statistically significant relationships between the sales of RTE cereals and the prices of such related goods as bread, fruit, coffee, and food eaten away from home (which includes all of the foregoing items as well as beef, pork, eggs, pastries, and so on). These results imply a broader market definition than the one found relevant for antitrust purposes, and suggest that the Federal Trade Commission was quite correct in dismissing the case against the cereal companies 'with prejudice'.

The paper is organized as follows. In the next section, we discuss the market definition problem in theory, and as it has been applied in practice. The empirical model and results are presented in the third section. The final section contains some conclusions.

THE MARKET-DEFINITION PROBLEM

Price is the ideal datum for measuring the extent of the market because it is the variable by which competition is most directly expressed and by which responses to competitive inroads are most directly made. Complex information about changing demand and supply conditions is transmitted through price.

Profit opportunities are revealed by widening price–cost margins, and rivals, moving to take advantage of transitional quasi-rents, will drive price and profit back to normal levels. Hence, Marshall (1930, p. 235) and, more recently, Stigler (1966, p. 85) offer the celebrated dicta that a market is defined by 'the tendency for the same price to be paid for the same thing at the same time in all parts of the market'. In making this point, however, both Marshall and Stigler were referring to the conditions for equilibrium in a perfectly competitive market, with all the necessary simplifying assumptions, including homogeneous goods, perfect information, and zero transaction costs. While free of theoretical ambiguity, this definition is difficult to apply in practice because of the real-world complications of product differentiation, imperfect information, indivisibilities in production and consumption, positive transactions costs, and so on.

Economists have not neglected the complexities of the real world, however. As early as Jevons (1871, p. 137), there was an awareness that price differences 'for the same kind of article' can 'arise from extraneous circumstances, such as the defective credit of the purchasers, their imperfect knowledge of the market, and so on'. The work of Chamberlain (1962), Robinson (1969), and Kaldor (1934) explored the competitive significance of such imperfections and the 'gaps in the chain of substitutes' that would identify distinct market boundaries. Indeed, Kaldor (1934) recognized that defining a market is not an all-or-nothing proposition, but rather a matter of degree:

> Different producers are not selling either 'identical' or 'different' products, but 'more or less different' products—the demand confronting them being neither completely sensitive nor completely unsensitive to the prices charged by other producers.

In short, the concept of elasticity is crucial in giving meaning to the concept of a market. Own-price effects measure the extent to which a firm can raise the price of its product without experiencing a decline in total revenue, and cross-price effects measure the extent to which changes in the prices of related goods affect the sales of the good in question. *Both* concepts of elasticity are important to consider in defining the relevant market for antitrust analysis. However, as Posner (1976, p. 125) notes, antitrust has failed to incorporate such principles 'because we lack confidence in our ability to measure elasticities, or perhaps because we do not think of adopting so explicitly economic an approach . . . '.

Instead, reliance has been placed on other indicia of market boundaries, such as the Elzinga-Hogarty (1973, 1978) test, which uses data on shipments to delineate geographic markets and, more recently, the simple pairwise price regressions proposed by Horowitz (1981). Observations on a single variable are not enough, however. Indeed, price alone can be misleading because in actual markets it 'may be tossed hither and thither like a shuttle-cock, as one side or the other gets the better of the "haggling and bargaining" (Marshall, 1930, p. 333). What is required is a *ceteris paribus* experiment, which holds constant the factors economic theory suggests have influence on the market process.

The consequences of ignoring this simple point are well known. 'Markets' found relevant for antitrust purposes in case after case would provide a nearly endless source of amusement if it were forgotten that mergers have been blocked and divestitures have been ordered on the basis of these market definitions. Posner (1976, p. 130), for example, singled out *Alcoa*, where the Court placed insulated copper and insulated aluminium wire in separate markets despite the fact that the two are readily substitutable in production; *Continental Can*, where metal cans and glass jars were found to be in the same market, but plastic containers were excluded; and *Pabst*, where 'in a fit of nonsense' the mere existence of transportation costs was sufficient to establish distinct regional markets for beer.[1] Similarly, Fisher (1979, p. 17) reports that in challenging Nestlé's acquisition of Stouffer, the Federal Trade Commission claimed that 'high-priced, nonethnic, frozen entrées' comprised the relevant product market. The list could go on.

On 1 September 1981, a Federal Trade Commission Administrative Law Judge issued his initial decision on the complaint brought in April 1972 charging the major US cereal producers with violating Section 5 of the FTC Act.[2] While denying the complaint, which charged the respondents with sharing a monopoly of RTE cereal by, among other practices, preempting entry through brand proliferation, Judge Berman adopted *in toto* the alleged relevant product market definition. Ready-to-eat cereals were described as 'food products made from barley, corn, oats, rice or wheat and various combinations of such grains which are flaked, granulated, puffed, shredded or processed in other ways. RTE cereals are eaten primarily as a breakfast food requiring no cooking or heating preparation by the consumer' (Initial Decision, p. 1).

The ALJ's finding was controlled by the standards set out in *Brown Shoe*, which quite correctly assert that 'the outer boundaries of a product market are determined by the reasonable interchangeability of use or the cross-elasticity of demand between the product itself and substitutes for it'.[3] However, the Court went on to say that within a market so delineated there may exist well-defined submarkets which are relevant for antitrust purposes. These submarkets 'may be determined by examining such practical indicia as industry or public recognition of the sub-market as a separate economic entity, the product's peculiar characteristics and uses, unique production facilities, distinct customers, distinct prices, sensitivity to price changes, and specialized vendors'.[4] Based upon these criteria, Judge Berman decided not only that RTE cereals comprised a product market distinct from such other breakfast foods as hot cereal, toaster pastries, instant breakfast drinks, and bacon and eggs, but that the RTE cereal market itself consisted of 15 different 'segments' (Initial Decision, pp. 36–59).[5] To illustrate, a bacon-and-egg breakfast was found not to fall within the relevant product market in part because these foods are 'materially higher in price than a bowl of cereal and milk to the extent of there being dollar differentials', require refrigeration, must be cooked prior to being eaten, and 'are not "produced" with manufacturing equipment' (Initial Decision, pp. 42–3).

Although following the spirit of *Brown Shoe*, the product market definition employed in the 'cereal' case clearly has no correspondence with reality. Moreover, as we have discussed above, such a narrowly construed market is not a mere aberration from the normal course of reasoning in the application of economics to law, but rather typifies market definition in practice. It is no excuse that documents discovered in the investigation referred to an 'RTE cereal market' (Initial Decision, p. 38) or that one of the respondents wanted its instant breakfast drink product shelved in grocery stores not with RTE cereals, but 'in the "Coffee, Tea, and Cocoa" department' (Initial Decision, p. 40). Markets are not made by internal company documents or by the adoption of a particular selling technique—they are defined in large part by the responsiveness of consumers to a change in relative price.[6] If, in response to an increase in the price of RTE cereal, consumers at the margin are willing and able to shift some of their cereal purchases to one or more related goods, then questions about 'market power' in cereal are irrelevant. We consider this basic issue in the following section.

EMPIRICAL MODEL AND RESULTS

Total US sales of ready-to-eat breakfast cereal averaged in the order of 170 million pounds per month over a recent four-year period. In this section, we seek to define the 'market' in which consumers purchase this food product. To do so, we estimate an ordinary demand function for RTE cereal using commonly accessible data sources. Our methodology demonstrates the feasibility of defining relevant markets for antitrust purposes empirically, guided only by the most basic of economic principles.

Economic theory suggests that the demand for any good is a function of its own price, the prices of related goods, income, and consumer preferences. We therefore specified a regression equation of the following general form:[7]

$$\begin{aligned} Q_t = {} & b_0 + b_1P_t + b_2WBP_t + b_3GFP_t + b_4CP_t \\ & + b_5FAWAY_t + b_6FLFPR_t + b_7ADV_t \\ & + b_8PCY_t + b_9MAY81 + b_{10}T_t + e_t \end{aligned}$$

where

Q_t = RTE cereal sales in pounds during period t
P_t = price per pound of RTE cereal
WBP_t = price per pound of white bread
GFP_t = price per pound of grapefruit
CP_t = average price per pound of 100% ground roast coffee
$FAWAY_t$ = US city average consumer price index for food eaten away from home (1967 = 100)
$FLFPR_t$ = female labor force participation rate
ADV_t = print and television advertising expenditures by RTE cereal producers
PCY_t = US income per capita in 1972 dollars
$MAY18$ = 1 for the month of May 1981, and zero otherwise
T_t = a linear time trend
e_t = regression error term.

The theory of consumer behavior provides straightforward predictions about the signs of the regression coefficients to be estimated. In particular, an increase in own price should, other things equal, lead to a decrease in the quantity of RTE cereal sold, and the estimated coefficient on *PCY* will be positive or negative according as RTE cereal is a normal or inferior good.

Our market-definition test centers on the signs and levels of statistical significance associated with the estimated coefficients on the remaining right-hand side variables. Toast, fruit, and coffee may be either gross substitutes or complements for RTE cereal, and *FAWAY* and *FLFPR* are alternative proxies for the opportunity cost of eating breakfast at home. (In a traditional family setting, as the opportunity cost of the wife's nonmarket time rises, a situation revealed by her decision to become a labor force participant, we expect households to substitute in favor of foods which require less preparation.) Moreover, as stressed earlier, *FAWAY* embodies various potential substitute breakfast foods for RTE cereal, including pork, beef, eggs and pastries. If RTE cereal indeed properly belongs in its own product market, then changes in the prices of related goods will have little or no effect on its sales. On the other hand, if the relevant product market is broader, then the estimated coefficients on the prices of substitutes will be positive, suggesting that RTE cereal is only one of many foods competing for a place on consumers' breakfast plates. Thus, statistically significant coefficients on the prices of white bread, grapefruit, coffee, and food eaten out, or on the labor force participation rate of females, will provide evidence against the narrow product market definition adopted by the FTC.

In addition, we included observations on monthly cereal advertising expenditures, *ADV*, in some of our regression specifications. This variable, which includes spending on print and television advertising for RTE products falling into the adult and all-family cereal categories, was entered with a one-month lag.[8] The dummy variable, *MAY81*, denotes an outlying observation in the cereal volume data series, and the linear time trend controls for factors affecting cereal sales not otherwise accounted for by our model.[9]

The observations on RTE cereal sales were obtained from Selling Areas-Marketing, Inc. (SAMI), and cover the months from January 1980 through October 1984.[10] They pertain to ready-to-eat cereals consumed primarily by adults, a category that excludes most of the presweetened and artificially flavored cereal brands.[11] Except for the cereal price data, which were taken from National Purchase Diary (NPD) and which take into account the effect of the many coupons used as incentives on the transaction price of cereals, observations on the remaining variables were obtained from standard sources.[12] All nominal values were converted to constant 1967 dollars with an appropriate price index (i.e., adult cereal price was divided by the US city average price of cereals and bakery products, and the price of bread, grapefruit, and coffee, as well as advertising expenditures, were deflated by the consumer price index).

The cereal demand equation was estimated by two-stage least squares. This involved, first, regressing cereal price on all exogenous variables in the system, including a supply variable. For the latter, we used an index of wholesale grain prices.[13] The predicted price values were then used as an explanatory variable in the demand equation. Using two-stage least squares accounts for the fact that observed cereal price and quantity are determined jointly by demand and supply conditions, and assures that the estimated coefficients in the demand equation are indeed demand parameters. The results are reported in Table 1.[14]

The results reported in Table 1 are strongly suggestive of a broad market definition which encompasses more than just RTE cereal. In particular, there is substantial evidence that the sales of adult

Table 1. Dependent variable: Adult Cereal Sales, by Months, January 1980–July 1984

Intercept	−428657	−200807	−543716	−158925
Own Price	−110794	−76524·0	−19397·7	−80394·4
	(−1·68)[c]	(−2·01)[b]	(−1·68)[c]	(−2·12)[b]
Bread Price	−278808	−234983	−72643·5	−167787
	(−1·41)	(−1·16)	(−0·38)	(−0·81)
Fruit Price	90255·0	73850·4	70063·8	60083·3
	(3·48)[a]	(2·75)[a]	(2·79)[a]	(2·12)[a]
Coffee Price	84827·4	27740·4	86470·5	24176·9
	(4·30)[a]	(3·52)[a]	(4·85)[a]	(2·95)[a]
Food Out	2004·3		2193·8	
	(3·07)[a]		(3·67)[a]	
FLFPR		6890·0		6160·5
		(2·84)[a]		(2·51)[a]
ADV(−1)			1·6636	0·9555
			(2·57)[b]	(1·39)
PCY	−4·1250	−5·7153	−10·0796	−9·1763
	(−0·50)	(−0·63)	(−1·33)	(−0·99)
MAY81	−14027·3	−16106·9	−15733·2	−17224·5
	(−4·16)[a]	(−4·78)[a]	(−4·54)[a]	(−5·03)[a]
T	−2006·4	−114·35	−2168·3	−72·937
	(−2·87)[a]	(−0·65)	(−3·42)[a]	(−0·41)
$\hat{\rho}$	0·10	0·20		0·20
R^2	0·616	0·621	0·647	0·638
D–W	2·11	2·36	1·80	2·23
F	9·01	9·21	9·16	8·62

t-statistics in parentheses. $\hat{\rho}$ is the estimated first-order autocorrelation coefficient. [a]Significant at the 1% level. [b]Significant at the 5% level. [c]Significant at the 10% level.

RTE cereal are sensitive to changes in its own price and the prices of a variety of other breakfast foods. The estimates suggest that fruit, coffee, and food eaten out (which includes a variety of cereal substitutes) are substitutes for RTE cereal, that white bread is a complement, and that increases in both female labor force participation and advertising expenditures shift consumer purchases in favor of RTE cereal. Overall, the regression specifications in Table 1 explain between 62% and 65% of the variation in adult cereal sales over a four and one-half year period.

Using the estimated coefficients reported in Table 1, we calculated the various price and income elasticities at the data means. As stressed earlier, both own- and cross-price effects are relevant to the market-definition issue. On the one hand, the own-price elasticity traces out small movements along the demand schedule holding all other demand determinants constant. On the other hand, given a particular own price, the cross-price elasticities show how demand shifts in response to changes in the prices of related goods. All such factors must be taken into account when evaluating the 'power over price' for producers of the good in question.

The responsiveness of monthly adult cereal sales to *ceteris paribus* changes in the independent variables are shown in Table 2. For example, our conversative estimate of own-price elasticity suggests that a 1% increase in adult cereal price causes a 0.10% decrease in quantity sold. This translates into a sales reduction of 87100 pounds per month. Similarly, a 1% increase in the average price per pound of ground roast coffee leads to an increase in cereal sales of 0.09% (78400 pounds). RTE cereal sales are most responsive to changes in the opportunity cost of eating breakfast at home. Other things equal, a 1% decline in either the average price of food eaten out or the labor force participation rate of females causes cereal sales to fall on the order of 4–7%

We interpret the relatively low own-price demand elasticities displayed in Table 2 as evidence that RTE cereal was sold at a competitive price over the time period covered by our sample. That is, because a monopolist would never operate in the inelastic region of his demand schedule, 'a finding that demand is *in*elastic at the current market price is rather good evidence that the sellers are not colluding—at least, not effectively' (Posner, 1976, p.57; emphasis in original). Taken together with the estimated cross-price elasticities, this result suggests that the ability of the cereal industry as a whole to raise price is severely constrained. That is, although the market demand schedule for RTE cereal is relatively steep in the relevant price range, its position in price-quantity space depends very much on the prices of a variety of other goods.

As a final check on these results, we tested whether or not two important substitutes (coffee and grapefruit) are properly included in the relevant product market for RTE cereal using the notion of instantaneous causality developed by Uri and Rifkin (1985) in extending the methodology of Horowitz (1981).[15] In brief, this technique involves estimating

$$D_t = \alpha + (D_0 - \alpha)\lambda^t$$

where $D_t = P_{ht} - P_{it}$ is the price difference between candidate products h and i during period t, D_0 is the price difference in period zero, representing the initial condition, and α and λ are the parameters to be

Table 2. Estimated Effects on Adult Cereal Sales, by Months, January 1980–July 1984

		Percent		Thousand pounds[b]		
Variable	Mean[a]	Low	High	Low	High	Significance
Own Price	\$0·47	−0·10	−0·60	−87·1	−522·9	5%
Bread Price	\$0·19	−0·16	−0·61	−139·4	−531·6	n.s.[c]
Fruit Price	\$0·13	0·09	0·13	78·4	113·3	1%
Coffee Price	\$0·96	0·27	0·95	235·3	827·9	1%
Food Out	300·55	6·91	7·57	6021·9	6597·1	1%
FLFPR	52·51	3·71	4·15	3233·2	3616·6	1%
ADV(−1)	\$5685·54	0·06	0·11	52·3	95·9	5%[d]
PCY	\$4607·60	−0·22	−0·53	−191·7	−461·9	n.s.[c]

[a]Prices in 1967 dollars, per capita income in 1972 dollars.
[b]Mean monthly adult cereal sales = 87147300 pounds.
[c]Denotes not significant.
[d]Low estimate not significantly different from zero.

estimated. If the two candidate products belong in the same market, one would obtain $\hat{\alpha} = 0$ and $|\hat{\lambda}| < 1$.

Factors that might cause spurious correlation between the prices of the candidate products can be removed by prewhitening the price series. In our data set, stationarity was achieved with the third differencing of the cereal–coffee price pair, D3CC, and with second differencing of the cereal–grapefruit price pair, D2CG. (Similar results were obtained when we prewhitened the individual price series before taking their difference.)

Estimates of α and λ can be obtained most readily by fitting a first-order autoregressive model to the differenced price series—$\hat{\alpha}$ is then the estimated constant term, and $\hat{\lambda}$ is the estimated autoregressive parameter. The results we obtained are as follows (t-statistics in parentheses):

$$\text{D3CC} = \underset{(0.08)}{0.0001} - \underset{(-3.18)}{0.3974}\,\text{AR}(1), \quad R^2 = 0.16$$

$$\text{D2CG} = \underset{(-0.34)}{-0.0008} + \underset{(1.14)}{0.1530}\,\text{AR}(1), \quad R^2 = 0.02$$

In both cases, we cannot reject the null hypotheses that $\hat{\alpha} = 0$ and $\hat{\lambda} < 1$. This offers further evidence that both coffee and grapefruit belong in the same relevant product market that includes RTE cereal.

In sum, our empirical estimates are fairly conclusive on the market definition question. RTE cereal appears to compete with other foods for a place on the breakfast table. There is no 'cereal market' as such.

CONCLUSIONS

We have shown that basic economic principles can be applied fruitfully for the purpose of defining relevant markets in antitrust proceedings. Specifically, using data readily available in standard government sources or easily obtainable through information requests to the respondent(s), we estimated an ordinary demand function for a broad segment of ready-to-eat breakfast cereal. The results, which showed statistically significant relationships between these RTE cereal sales and the prices of several substitute goods, implied a broader product market definition than the one adopted during the protracted antitrust investigation of the industry.

Our findings that RTE cereal belongs within a broader product market which encompasses a variety of breakfast foods becomes obvious when the sales of this product are placed in context. The roughly 170 million pounds of all RTE cereals sold per month translate into only 155 ounces (or 120 1.3-ounce servings) per person per year for the 210 million US consumers over the age of five. This figure pales in comparison with the 4.0 billion dozen eggs and over 1 billion pounds of sliced bacon sold in 1983.[16] Moreover, an estimated 2 million breakfasts are eaten away from home each day.[17] And we still have not accounted for the volumes consumed of pastry and doughnuts, other fruit, yogurt, hot cereal, instant breakfast drinks, or pancakes.

Acknowledgements

We benefitted from comments by James Buchanan and James C. Miller III. The usual caveat applies.

NOTES

1. *US v. Aluminum Co. of America*, 377 US 271 (1964); *US v. Continental Can Co.*, 378 US 441 (1964); and *US v. Pabst Brewing Co.*, 384 US 546 (1966).
2. *In the Matter of Kellogg Company et al.*, Docket No. 8883, Initial Decision, 1 September 1981. Hereafter cited as 'Initial Decision'. The Commission subsequently denied complaint counsel's appeal from the ALJ's findings, dismissing the complaint with prejudice.
3. *Brown Shoe Co. v. United States*, 370 US 294 (1962), p. 325. *Brown Shoe* essentially held that the standards laid down in *US v. El du Pont de Nemours & Co.*, 351 US 377 (1956), the 'cellophane' monopolization case, were applicable to merger cases, but only for the determination of the outer boundaries of a market. Hence, the origin of the 'submarket' approach. See Posner (1976, pp. 127–30), and Landes and Posner (1981, pp. 960–63).
4. *Ibid.*
5. The lines of demarcation between segments were drawn so as to create the following categories within the RTE cereal market: corn flakes; wheat flakes; Rice Krispies, OK's, Alpha-Bits and Cheerios; nutritional cereals; variety packages; raisin brans; whole bran; 40% brans; shredded wheat; presweets; presweetened, shaped oat cereals; chocolate flavored cereals; fruit flavored cereals; Rally and Life; and Sugar Smacks and Sugar Crisp.
6. Substitutability on the supply side is also important.
7. Use of a linear specification assumes that the elasticities and cross-elasticities remain constant throughout the sample period. This assumption is not overly restrictive, however, because the items included account for a small share of the typical consumer's

budget. Significant shifts in sensitivity to price changes are therefore unlikely.

8. The industrial organization literature typically focuses only on the relationship between advertising expenditures and profits. By including this variable in the demand equation, we implicitly treat advertising as a selling technique which attempts to make consumers aware of available opportunities (see e.g. Kirzner, 1973, p. 157). The advertising data include spending by all major US RTE cereal producers, over 90% of which is for television advertising. Only three cereal brands show up in the advertising numbers, but not in our volume series. These are Kellogg's Frosted Flakes and Rice Krispies, and General Mills's Cheerios.
9. Cereal sales during May 1981 were inexplicably lower by 5–7 million pounds per month.
10. Selling Areas-Marketing, Inc., *Brand Trend Reports*, Fiscal January 1980–October 1984. The following cereal brands were included:
Kellogg's: Concentrate, Most, Product 19, Smart Start for Women, Special K, All Bran, Bran Buds, Ex Fiber All Bran, Fruitful Bran, 40% Bran Flakes, Cracklin Bran, Rice & Bran, Country Morning Natural Cereal (all flavors), Apple Raisin Crisp, Nutri-Grain (all flavors), Pep, Raisin Squares, Shredded Wheat, Corn Flakes, Crispix, Graham Crackos, Honey & Nut Corn Flakes, Mini Wheats (all flavors), Puffa Puffa Rice, Raisin Bran, Raisin Bran Low Sodium, Raisins Rice & Rye;
General Mills, Inc.: Buc Wheats, Total (all flavors), Bran Plus, Fruit & Bran Wheaties, Fiber One, Bran Muffin Crisp, Nature Valley Granola (all flavors), Cinnamon Nut Cheerios, Crispy Wheats 'N Raisins, Nature Valley Raisin & Bran, Wheaties;
Post: Fortified Oat Flakes, Grape-Nuts, Raisin Grape-Nuts, 40% Bran Flakes, Fruit & Fibre (all flavors), C W Post (all flavors), Grape-Nuts Flakes, Country Crisp, Honey Nut Crunch Raisin Bran, Raisin Bran, Toasties;
Quaker: Corn Bran, 100% Natural Cereal (all flavors), Puffed Rice, Puffed Wheat, Shredded Wheat, Life Original, Life Raisin;
Ralston: Bran Chex, Honey Bran, 40% Bran Flakes, Chex (all flavors), Sun Flakes, Tasteeos (all flavors);
Nabisco: 100% Bran, Team Flakes, Total Shredded Wheat, Regular Shredded Wheat, Spoon Size Shredded Wheat, Toasted Wheat and Raisins; and
Heartland: Natural Cereal (all flavors), Granola Puffs (all flavors).
11. In our data set, total RTE cereal volumes are broken down into three subcategories: adult, children's, and all-family cereal. We chose to report the results obtained using cereal volume data for cereal consumed primarily by adults because it was the most stable of the series. In particular, the monthly observations on the excluded cereal brand volumes do not appear consistent with expected seasonal fluctuations or with any rational inventory policy. Moreover, our definition of the dependent variable takes account of recent survey evidence, which suggests that over the past five years many adults have continued to consume certain of the all-family RTE cereal brands they ate as children or young adults, blurring somewhat the distinction between adult and all-family cereals.
12. National Purchase Diary, *Household Reports*, January 1980–July 1984. The white bread, grapefruit, and coffee price data are US city average retail prices, and are published by the Bureau of Labor Statistics in the monthly news release, 'Consumer Prices: Energy and Food'. The consumer price index and its components were obtained from the *CPI Detailed Report*, and the observations on female labor force participation rates are reported in the BLS news release, 'Employment Situation'. Finally, the *Survey of Current Business* contains the per-capita income data.
13. Producer price index for commodity code 012, grains, as published by the Bureau of Labor Statistics. The index is an aggregate of wholesale prices for five different types of wheat, barley, corn, oats, and rye.
14. The reported results cover the period ending July 1984 because observations on all of the independent variables were not yet available for later months.
15. The technique is not appropriate either for the index variable *FAWAY*, or the variable measured in percentage terms, *FLFRR*. For a further extension and application of the instantaneous causality approach, see Stigler and Sherwin (1985).
16. Retail egg sales and bacon volumes were obtained from the US Department of Agriculture and the United Egg Producers.
17. Derived from information in Telberg (1985) and the report on McDonald's contained in Standard and Poor's *Corporation Records* (1984, p. 1477).

REFERENCES

E. H. Chamberlain (1962). *The Theory of Monopolistic Competition*, (8th edition) Cambridge, Mass: Harvard University Press.

K. G. Elzinga and T. F. Hogarty (1973). The problem of geographic market delineation in antimerger suits. *Antitrust Bulletin*, **18**, Spring, 45–81.

K. G. Elzinga and T. F. Hogarty (1978). The problem of geographic market delineation revisited: the case of coal. *Antitrust Bulletin*, **23**, Spring, 1–16.

F. M. Fisher (1979). Diagnosing monopoly. *Ouarterly Review of Economics and Business*, **19**, Summer, 7–33.

I. Horowitz (1981). Market definition in antitrust analysis: a regression-based approach. *Southern Economic Journal*, **48**, July, 1–16.

W. S. Jevons (1871). *The Theory of Political Economy*, reprint (Baltimore: Penguin Books, 1970).

N. Kaldor (1934). Mrs. Robinson's 'Economics of Imperfect Competition'. *Economica*, N.S. 1, August, 335–41.

I. Kirzner (1973). *Competition and Entrepreneurship*, Chicago: University of Chicago Press.

W. M. Landes and R. A. Posner (1981). Market power in antitrust cases. *Harvard Law Review*, **94**, March, 937–96.

A. Marshall (1930). *Principles of Economics* (8th edition), New York: Macmillan.

National Purchase Diary (various issues). *Household Reports*.

A. D. Neale and D. G. Goyder (1980). *The Antitrust Laws of the USA, A Study of Competition Enforced by Law* (3rd edition), Cambridge: Cambridge University Press.

R. S. Pindyck and D. L. Rubinfeld (1981). *Econometric Models and Economic Forecasts* (2nd edition), New York: McGraw-Hill.

R. A. Posner (1976). *Antitrust Law, An Economic Perspective*, Chicago: University of Chicago Press.

J. Robinson (1969). *The Economics of Imperfect Competition* (2nd edition), New York: St Martin's Press.

Selling Areas-Marketing, Inc. (various issues). *Brand Trend Reports.*

Standard and Poor's Inc. (1984). *Corporation Records*, Sec. 2, Vol. 45, No. 22, New York: Standard and Poor's.

G. J. Stigler (1966). *The Theory of Price* (3rd edition), New York: Macmillan.

G. J. Stigler and R. A. Sherwin (1985). The extent of the market. *Journal of Law and Economics*, **28**, October, 555–85.

R. Telberg (1985). Breakfast market war accelerates. *National Restaurant News*, **19**, No. 8, 18 February, 1, F3.

US Department of Commerce, Bureau of the Census (1967). *The X-11 Variant of the Census Method II Seasonal Adjustment Program*, Washington, DC: USGPO.

US Department of Commerce, Bureau of the Census (1985). *Survey of Current Business*, Washington, DC: USGPO, July.

US Department of Labor, Bureau of Labor Statistics (various issues). *CPI Detailed Report*, Washington, DC: USGPO.

US Department of Labor, Bureau of Labor Statistics (various issues). Monthly News Release, Consumer prices: energy and food. Washington, DC: Bureau of Labor Statistics.

US Department of Labor, Bureau of Labor Statistics (various issues). News Release, Employment situation. Washington, DC: Bureau of Labor Statistics.

US Department of Labor, Bureau of Labor Statistics (various issues). *Supplement to Producer Prices and Price Indexes*, Washington, DC: USGPO.

N. D. Uri and E. J. Rifkin (1985). Geographic markets, causality and railroad deregulation. *Review of Economics and Statistics*, **67**, August, 422–8.

8

Econometric Market Delineation

David T. Scheffman and Pablo T. Spiller

Owen Graduate School of Management, Vanderbilt University, Nashville, USA and Haas School of Business, University of California, Berkeley, USA

INTRODUCTION

In recent years it has become increasingly common in antitrust analysis to use econometric methods in market delineation. The FTC and DOJ Antitrust Division have generated a demand for such analyses, with agency economists pioneering econometric analyses in connection with the review of mergers. The methodology has then branched out into the usual variety of agency and private antitrust cases. This paper discusses the methodology of econometric delineation and provides as an empirical example econometric estimates of demand for margarine and butter.

MARKET DELINEATION AND THE DOJ / FTC MERGER GUIDELINES

The 1982 DOJ Merger Guidelines and its revisions in 1984 and 1992 set out a new economics-based paradigm for market delineation for mergers based directly in an assessment of potential market power. The now well-known 'hypothetical cartel' test defines a relevant market as a group of products and an area in which a hypothetical cartel could profitably raise price 'a small but significant non-transitory amount'. Analytically, this paradigm can be described as finding the relevant group of products and an area in which the demand facing the members of the hypothetical cartel for their products in that area is sufficiently inelastic that the costs of the hypothetical cartel would make it profitable to raise price to anticompetitive levels.[1] With a sufficient quantity of quality data on purchases, prices, and demand and cost shifters, this approach to market definition can be implemented on the basis of historical data via econometric estimation of the demand relationship faced by the hypothetical cartel.

HISTORY OF THE ECONOMETRIC APPROACH

In a paper not directly related to the Guidelines, Baker and Bresnahan (1985) put forward an approach for estimating the demand facing an individual firm. In a paper based directly on the Guidelines, Scheffman and Spiller (1987) developed an analysis of *residual demand* applied to the Guidelines' market definition methodology and showed how Guidelines markets could be estimated econometrically. Although the Scheffman and Spiller analysis and empirical estimates were based on homogeneous product markets, as discussed in that paper, the basic technique can clearly be used in delineating markets with heterogeneous products. In a series of papers Froeb and Werden (1991, 1992) and Scheffman (1992) further explained the econometric approach to market delineation and discussed some of the problems and pitfalls in the technique. Finally, Hausman, Leonard and Zona (1992, 1994) proposed some new techniques for econometric analysis of market delineation and the assessment of the impact of a merger on market power in differentiated product industries.

ISSUES OF ECONOMETRIC SPECIFICATION

Overview

Let firms $i = 1, \ldots, n$ be producers of widgets, a homogeneous product, and assume that all these widgets producers are at the same location. Denote the actual or potential customers of these producers for plausible variations of relevant prices as $j = 1, \ldots, m$. Then the demand facing the widget producers, in aggregate, can be expressed as

$$q_w = D(p_w, \mathbf{p}_s, \mathbf{d}) \quad (1)$$

where this function is the aggregate demand of purchasers $j = 1.,,, m$, $\mathbf{p}_s$, is a vector of prices of competing/substitute products,[2] and $\mathbf{d}$ is a vector of other prices and other variables affecting this group of customer's demand for these producers' widgets. Assuming that $\mathbf{p}_s$ and $\mathbf{d}$ are exogenous (uncorrelated with the errors in the relationship), this is a standard demand estimation problem that requires cost instruments for consistent estimation.

This ordinary (Marshallian) demand relationship and the costs of the hypothetical cartel, at first pass, directly provide an answer to the hypothetical cartel test. However, the answer may not be definitive since there may be interactions between p_w and $\mathbf{p}_s$.

Residual Demand

If the w and s producers are engaged in oligopolistic competition, there will be an interrelationship between p_w and $\mathbf{p}_s$ that will affect the responsiveness of widget purchases from the hypothetical cartel to the price of widgets. Even in competitive (non-oligopoly) markets, there can be a relationship between p_w and $\mathbf{p}_s$. For example, an increase in price of the core producers' widgets may lead to substitution by customers to other widget producers or substitute products. Then, if these other producers have upward-sloping supply curves, the increase in the core widget producers' price would result in increases in the prices of alternative sources of widgets or of substitutes, making the actual price responsiveness smaller than would be measured by the ordinary demand relationship (see Scheffman and Spiller, 1987).

In theory, this can be dealt with via a reduced-form estimation in which the prices of alternative sources of widgets or substitutes are not included as independent variables. That is, there is a relationship between $\mathbf{p}_s$ and p_w:

$$\mathbf{p}_s = p_s(p_w, \mathbf{x}) \quad (2)$$

where $\mathbf{x}$ is a vector of other factors affecting p_s. This relationship can be substituted into the demand relationship for widgets, producing a reduced-form equation:[3]

$$q_w = D(p_w, \mathbf{x}, \mathbf{d}) \quad (3)$$

How $\mathbf{p}_s$ is treated in the estimation can be quite important in the empirical results. If some of the s products are in fairly inelastic supply, treating $\mathbf{p}_s$ as exogenous will produce a more elastic demand estimate than when taking into account the endogeneity of $\mathbf{p}_s$. On the other hand, if $\mathbf{p}_s$ is exogenous, then leaving it out in Eqn (3) is a misspecification that will bias the estimates of demand elasticity.

In the case of oligopolistic competition between the core widget producers and some of the other producers, an analysis analogous to Eqns (2) and (3) might permit residual demand estimation. In an oligopolistic market, the underlying structure of residual demand is complex, depending on oligopolistic interactions between the hypothetical cartel members themselves and between them and the producers of competing products who are not in the hypothetical cartel. Specifically, a stable structure of demand-interrelationship and a stable structure of oligopoly-interrelationships, both of which can be adequately captured in exogenous data, is required (see Froeb and Werden, 1991).

Heterogeneous Products

Thus far we have been assuming homogenous products. Differentiated products introduce an additional complexity. With differentiated products the demand relationship is a function of the vector of prices of the hypothetical cartel members

$$\mathbf{q}_w = D(\mathbf{p}_w, \mathbf{p}_s, d) \quad (4)$$

where $\mathbf{q}_w$ and $\mathbf{p}_w$ are vectors.

To directly implement the Guidelines, a market must be defined according to the Guidelines' methodology. To do this with differentiated products, products must be grouped into potential markets to which the hypothetical cartel test is applied. In carrying out the hypothetical cartel test, the nature of the hypothetical price increase must be specified. For example, do all prices increase by the same percentage, or do price increases vary by producer/product? Two general approaches have been taken. First, an *implicit* assumption of proportional price increases is made and the hypothetical cartel test is conducted using an industry-level estimate of demand, assuming that the proportional price change assumption is approximately valid historically. In simplest terms, this involves estimating industry-level demand for total 'units' of 'stuff' as a function of an index of prices along with other determinants of demand. This is a crude, *ad hoc* approach.

Alternatively, the structure of the consumer buying decision is imposed in the econometric estimation. Hopefully, the consumer choice is nested, in that a consumer decides whether or not to buy widgets, and then decides what particular brand/type of widgets to purchase. Below, we will demonstrate specifically how this can be done.

Baker and Bresnahan (1985) propose a methodology that dispenses with market definition when the antitrust issue is a merger of producers of substitute differentiated products. At the simplest level, residual demand elasticities are estimated for each party to the merger, taking the price of the other party as exogenous. Then, using the estimated cross-elasticities between the parties to the merger, a post-merger elasticity can be estimated. If the post-merger elasticity is considerably lower, the conclusion is that the merger creates significant market power. There are a number of very strong assumptions underlying this sort of analysis. In any event, this analysis does not lead to defined markets as required under the Guidelines.

The system of equations represented by Eqn (4) is usually estimated in a cross-section of markets, or for a given market over time. Such estimation may be inappropriate for several reasons. As we show below, under some very general representations, with differentiated products, such system of equations may be misspecified. In addition, the estimation of a set of equations *à-la* Eqn (4) is appropriate only under an important set of assumptions: first, the set of products available to customers is relatively small, second, all customers face the same choice set (that is, same products are available in all markets), third product quality is standardized (that is, the products mean the same) across markets. Although many grocery goods purchased in supermarkets may fit these assumptions, that need not be the case for all customers. For example, in the airline industry markets are characterized by origin–destination city pairs. The choice in each market is different. Furthermore, in some markets there are few options (just one), while in others the options are more than one thousand. Thus, unless a fairly simple aggregation is justified, equations like Eqn (4) are not appropriate for the airline industry. In those cases an approach that looks at products as a set of characteristics is more appropriate (for such an approach see, Berry, Carnall and Spiller, 1995).

Relationship Between Estimates and Market of Interest

It is important to keep in mind that a number of important aspects of the selling and purchasing modes and the purchase decision are buried in Eqns (1)–(4). For example, in the demand specification (1), p_w is the price paid by the customers — i.e. it is the delivered price — which includes channel costs and markups and delivery costs. One common, serious error in econometric market delineation exercises is to estimate residual demand from *downstream* data (e.g. supermarket sales of packaged products) and apply those estimates to make inferences about market definition and market power for upstream markets (e.g. packaged grocery goods manufacturing) without thinking through how the upstream residual demand is related to the downstream estimates.

It has become common, for example, to use estimates of the demand for consumer products based on scanner data from supermarket transactions to make inferences about product market delineation for grocery products *manufacturers*. As one illustration, in a merger of involving ready-to-eat cereals manufacturers, scanner data on retail sales of ready-to-eat products would be used to the estimate own-price elasticity of demand at the industry and product levels. Of course such estimates are of the *retail* demand for ready-to-eat cereals, not the demand facing manufacturers.

Simple economic models predict that upstream elasticities will be equal to or smaller than downstream elasticities, since a given percentage increase in price at wholesale would generally be expected to translate into a equal-or-lower percentage increase in price at retail.[4] But such a view of the relationship between downstream and upstream elasticities can be misleading. These models do not envisage sophisticated purchasing strategies. Supermarkets are sophisticated purchasers, using techniques such as 'forward buying'[5] and 'diverting'[6] and charging for shelf space via 'slotting allowances'. Consumers at retail must purchase at whatever the going price (although they may be able to inventory), but supermarkets have much more latitude to bargain. Although a major supermarket needs to have Kellogg's Corn Flakes on its shelves, the supermarket has considerable discretion as to how much shelf space to allocate to Kellogg's Corn Flakes *and* to Kellogg's products as a whole, including for new product introductions. Similarly, although a supermarket must offer ready-to-eat cereals, but, when faced with anticompetitive increases in *industry*-wide prices, the supermarkets has discretion as to how much shelf space to devote to ready-to-eat cereals, how much promotional activity for major brands versus its own private label, and discretion with respect to its purchases of other products produced by the ready-to-eat cereals producers.

Thus, a major supermarket's purchases are more realistically modeled as a component of a bargaining game rather than as a 'demand curve'. In this case it is easy to see that the 'demand' facing manufacturers may be considerably more elastic than the demand at retail.[7] Of course, a way around this problem is to model and estimate purchasing of the relevant products by supermarkets. However, this would require developing theoretical specifications based on bargaining games. In addition, in consumer goods industries it is generally very difficult to obtain manageable data that would be required to estimate purchasing at the wholesale level. Pricing data at wholesale is generally extremely messy because of the great variety and complexity of promotional deals[8] offered by manufacturers to retailers. Therefore, attention has continued to be focused on retail data, because of the availability of relatively high quality scanner data. However, there has been little research exploring the relationship between estimates based on retail data with inferences on wholesale elasticities.

WHAT IS KNOWN ABOUT DEMAND ELASTICITIES FOR PACKAGED CONSUMER PRODUCTS?

Over the past several years there have been a number of papers authored by economists and marketing researchers that present estimates of own-price elasticities of demand for branded products. The typical finding is a low estimated own-price elasticity, even at the specific branded product level. For example, a 1988 survey of 42 published studies containing 367 estimates of price elasticities for 220 different brands/markets, found that the average estimated own-price elasticity reported in these studies was (−)1.76 (Tellis, 1988). These estimates are *retail* elasticities. If you make the usual assumption that wholesale elasticities are smaller the retail elasticities, estimated wholesale price elasticities at the brand level are quite small. This is one of the conclusions drawn in a 1990 *Harvard Business Review* article that points out that, given what is known about the own-price elasticity of demand facing major branded products and their cost structures, the typical major brand is apparently charging a significantly lower price than its *apparent* market power would profitably permit (Jones, 1990).

Of course, this conclusion again is using estimates of demand elasticity at retail to make inferences about demand elasticities at wholesale. We view the evidence on brand price elasticities at retail to confirm our presumption that price elasticities at wholesale are considerably *larger* than at retail, because of sophisticated purchasing by supermarkets.

The fact that researchers generally find relatively low own-price elasticities despite presumably wide differences across markets and products in the state of competition (and market power) demands that the own-price elasticity of residual demand estimated in a particular context not be viewed in isolation. We believe that a reasonable *ad hoc* inference is that, absent other credible information to the contrary, an estimate of own-price elasticity of residual demand for a packaged consumer product that is larger than 1.76 is too large to infer a relevant market.

CURRENT TRENDS IN MARKET RESEARCH

Price-responsiveness models have been a long-standing topic of academic marketing researchers and economists. Recently, practice appears to have caught up and perhaps surpassed academic research. One of the hottest areas these days in marketing practices in companies is conducting studies of price responsiveness as inputs into pricing, marketing, and selling strategies and tactics. In the new product development process, for example, many companies are more closely following best practices, which specify that customer valuation and price sensitivity be built into the new product development process (so that products can be designed at a cost that will justify the realities of the market at introduction). For new and existing products many companies are undertaking price-responsiveness studies, generally conducted by outside consultants. There are two basic types of studies: survey or focus group research, and statistical analyses of historical purchase data or purchase data arising from experimental variation in prices and other variables.

Nielsen and IRI sell data services to grocery manufacturers, based on the two companies' supermarket and mass merchandiser cash register scanner data. These data are created from a sample of supermarkets/mass merchandisers that each company has in major metropolitan markets. These sample data are then grossed up to provide estimates of total sales in each major metropolitan market, and nationally. The basic data service provides estimates of unit and dollar sales by product/brand and SKU[9] nationally, and by major metropolitan market. Historically, grocery manufacturers purchased these data to track their sales and market share and store penetration. Store penetration is measured by 'All Commodity Volume' (ACV), which is the percentage of total sales of all products sold in the market represented by the stores that carry a given product. For example, if Kellogg's Corn Flakes has an ACV in a given weekly period in a given market of 91%, this means that the product is on the shelves of 91% of the 'stores', measured by percentage of total sales of all products in the market represented by the stores that carry Kellogg's Corn Flakes.

In recent years Nielsen and IRI have enlarged their data services to provide more detailed information, including information on advertising and promotional activities in each major market. There are variables indicating the extent that a product was featured in a supermarket newspaper advertisement in a given weekly period measured by ACV (measured by the percentage of total sales of all products that the advertising supermarket represents of total sales in the market). Supermarket display activities are similarly tracked. The two market research companies also provide customized data services, such as tracking sales in particular specific stores, which allows a grocery manufacturer to attempt to assess the impact of particular displays, promotional pricing, etc.

In recent years both Nielsen and IRI have been aggressively selling 'price elasticity' studies to their grocery manufacturer clients. Although based on scanner data, these price elasticity studies are quite different from those conducted by economists in market delineation exercises. Although the methodology is proprietary, the basic approach involves separating the data into 'promoted' and 'non-promoted' categories. For example, Kellogg's Corn Flakes is 'promoted' by a specific supermarket if the supermarket promoted the product (via advertisement, in-store display, etc.). Such promotional activity is almost always accompanied by a promoted price. Units sold and average price (measured by average revenue) are then analyzed statistically to attempt to determine the impact of promoted price on incremental volume. A typical study estimates incremental volume moved at various promoted prices.

As far as we can determine the basic methodology is approximately as follows. Over some time span of weekly observations and across a number of major metropolitan markets, the market share of Kellogg's Corn Flakes is calculated *within each price segment*. For example, for a price segment of \$0.95–1.05, the market share of the product is calculated for a market limited to supermarkets that have average shelf prices within that range. Suppose, for example, that this market share is 5%. Suppose further that the price segment \$0.80–0.90 brackets a common promoted price and that the market share of Kellogg's Corn Flakes (again, measured as share for the supermarkets that are selling the product in this price range) is 6%. From these two observations a 'price elasticity' can then be calculated, which would be about (−)2.0. In the typical price elasticity study, a 'price elasticity' would be calculated for each major promoted price segment.

Generally, these type of price elasticity studies are *not* significant inputs into the determination of a grocery manufacturer's wholesale prices. The studies, of course, focus on *retail* shelf prices and volume. Rather, the main purpose of these studies is to identify effective *retail* promotional tactics and to attempt to influence retailers to adopt these tactics through expenditures by the manufacturer on promotional activities. A conclusion of one of these price elasticity studies might be that a substantial amount of incremental volume is moved if the product is featured in an end-aisle display and promoted at a price 15¢ below the 'regular' price. The grocery manufacturer would then try to influence retailers to use such a promotional program through sales presentations and promotional expenditures.

ESTIMATION OF RESIDUAL DEMAND FOR MARGARINE AND BUTTER

In this section we use scanner data on margarine and butter products to clarify some of the preceding discussion.

Data

The data are Nielsen/IRI-type scanner data by major metropolitan markets by weekly periods for brands and SKUs of margarine and butter. These data are typical of scanner data available for econometric analyses of market delineation for packaged consumer products. We use price, quantity, and advertising information at the brand-city level. We employ the information on promotion as shifters in the demand (or share) equations as described above. Issues to be considered include whether butter and margarine are in the same antitrust market and the extent of cross-elasticity between different segments of margarine and with butter. First, we present results from estimating a margarine demand function imposing no restrictions. We then go on to show that such formulation may have some important misspecifications, and provide structural estimates based on certain assumptions about consumer purchasing decisions for margarine and butter.

Unrestricted Estimation

Our first estimates place no restrictions on the structure of the residual demand estimates. We estimate a margarine demand function of the following form:

$$marg_{tc} = \alpha_1 + \Sigma_{j=1,2}\,\alpha^*_{2j}\,price_{jtc} + \Sigma_{i=1,3}\,\beta^*_i\,adv_{ijtc} + \Sigma_{k=1,2}\,\gamma^*_j\,inc_{ktc} + \delta^*_j\,winter_t + \epsilon_{jtc} \quad (5)$$

where j represents margarine or butter, t the time period (week), and c the city. All variables (except the dummy for winter) are in natural logarithms. *Price* represents the average price paid for margarine or butter in the city, *adv* is a three-component vector of advertising variables for that particular city for margarine, *inc* is a two-component vector of income variables (disposable income and unemployment) for the city in question. Furthermore, all variables are differenced. Differencing eliminates, to a large extent, the problem of serial correlation and also deals with city-specific fixed effects.

Results

This demand estimation produces the following results. The own-price elasticity for margarine, although implausibly small (−1.78), is quite significant. The cross-elasticity with butter is very small (−0.16, and significant also). Advertising increases, and unemployment reduces the demand for margarine.

The results of this estimation suggest that the elasticity of demand facing all the margarine producers is relatively low, indicating that margarine is a relevant Guidelines market. However, as discussed above, the own-price elasticity is almost exactly the same as the average across studies of own-price elasticities, making us skeptical about the validity of the hypothetical cartel test for this level of elasticity. In any event, there are some important problems with such a regression. First, that regression does not take into account the fact that different brands may represent different things to customers. Indeed, the left-hand side variable is just the sum over quantities of margarine. Second, the demand system is *ad hoc*, with important aggregation assumptions implicitly imposed on the specification.

To test for the potential aggregation problems involved in this very simple model, we also estimated individual brand regressions of the same type as above. The results of these regressions revealed many inconsistencies. For example, some brands had non-significant own-price elasticities, and many brands had negative cross-elasticities with other brands, seemingly suggesting that margarine brands are complements rather than substitutes. We believe that the reason for these inconsistencies is the fact that the system of equations is not properly specified. In the next section we present an approach that is rooted in consumer theory, and that provides more consistent results.

Structural Estimation

The problems arising in our unrestricted estimates are common problems in estimations of demand systems, with roots in the *ad hoc* implicit aggregation imposed in the specification. An alternative approach is to impose a structure on the specification that is consistent with the structure of purchasing decisions. This has been a long-standing approach to demand estimation (see, for example, Deaton and Muellbauer, 1980). Hausman, Leonard and Zona (1992, 1994) apply this approach in an econometric analysis of the demand for beer at the brand level. This methodology is based on the 'multi-stage budgeting approach' (Gorman, 1971). The basic idea is that demand for differentiated goods can be estimated in a three-stage demand system, based on an assumption that consumers decide first whether they are going to purchase a product in a broad product category; consumers then decide which segment within the broad category that they will purchase a product; and, finally, consumers decide which specific product (brand/variety) to purchase. In this three-stage, nested process, the top level corresponds to the 'overall demand for the product category'. The econometric specification for this stage is real expenditures on the total product category as a function of a real price index for the product category, income, etc. The middle level of the demand system breaks down the overall product category by segments. The econometric specification of the middle level is an expenditure function equation where each segment real expenditure is regressed on segment real price indices and total real product category expenditures. The bottom level of the demand system is at the individual brand level. The econometric specification of the bottom level is share of brand i as a function of all real prices of brands in its segment and real segment expenditures.

The estimation procedure begins at the brand level. Following Deaton and Muellbauer (1980), the bottom-level equations are expenditure share equations of the following form:

$$w_{itc} = \alpha_1 + \Sigma_j \gamma_{ij} \log p_{jtc} + \beta_i \log\{x_{tc}/P_{tc}\} \quad (6)$$

where w_i represents the share of brand i in total margarine expenditure in time period t, city c, p_{jtc} is the (real) price of such brand in time period t in city c, x_{tc} is total expenditure on margarine in city c at time period t, and P_{tc} is a price index of margarine, which (eliminating the time and city subscripts) is defined as

$$P = \alpha_0 + \Sigma_k \alpha_k \log p_k + 1/2 \Sigma_j \Sigma_k \log p_k \log p_j \quad (7)$$

Deaton and Muellbauer (1980) call this an 'Almost Ideal Demand System' because 'the demand functions derived from it are first order approximations to any set of demand functions derived from utility-maximization behavior' (p. 315).

Equation (6) could be estimated by substituting Eqn (7) into Eqn (6) and using nonlinear estimation techniques. However, the usual approach is as follows. Deaton and Muelbauer show that P can be approximated by P^*, where P^* is given by

$$\log P^* = \sum_k w_k \log p_k \quad (8)$$

The substitution of P^* for P allows Eqn (6) to be estimated with linear estimation techniques.

Following the 'multi-stage budgeting approach' of Gorman (1971), these price indices are then used in the second level (margarine and butter) segment equations to define the real expenditures on each segment (x/P) and to construct the real price index for 'Fat' the broad product category composed of margarine and butter. Thus, the second-level equation is then given by

$$w_{itc} = \alpha_i \sum_j \gamma_{ij} \log p_{jtc} + \beta_i \log\{x_{tc}/P_{tc}\} \quad (9)$$

where i now represents margarine or butter rather than individual brands. Thus, w_{itc} reflects now the share of, say, margarine in total 'Fat' expenditure, p_{jtc} represents the price index for, say, margarine, x_{tc} represents the expenditure on fat, and P_{tc} the price index of fat derived in the similar fashion as the segment price indexes.

Finally, our top-level equation is the demand for 'Fat', as a function of its own price index, general macro-economic conditions in the city, weather (winter dummy) and advertising levels.[10]

Price elasticities at the brand, segment (margarine and butter), and Fat levels are then calculated. Two types of elasticities can be derived: conditional and unconditional. Conditional elasticities assume that the change in the price of a given brand will not affect overall demand for the segment. That is, we held x/P constant. Unconditional elasticities take into account that changing an individual price p will change P and hence will also change x, for example a decrease in the price of a given brand may increase overall demand. To ascertain the subsequent changes in x the estimates from the higher-level equation are then used to calculate unconditional elasticities.

Estimates

Methodology

The specification of the top-stage regression is log of real Fat expenditures regressed on real price of Fat, income, etc. The middle level of the demand system corresponds to segments of the overall Fat industry. A number of segments could be specified. For example, margarine brands are generally marketed and advertised as 'value', 'taste', or 'health' products, so a detailed segmentation by this categorization plus a category for butter could be used. Alternatively, we could use segments made up of branded margarine, private-label margarine, branded butter, and private-label butter.

We estimated two segmentations. First, we used no segmentation, i.e. we used a two-stage nesting assumption in which consumers choose first whether to purchase 'Fat' (butter or margarine), and then they choose which brand to purchase. The top-level regression is the demand for 'Fat'. The bottom-level regressions are shares of brands as a function of log of price and log of total real fat expenditure (total expenditure deflated by the real price of fat). The top-level regression results

Table 1. Middle-level and top-level regressions

Margarine, butter and fat equations Two-stage least squares estimators

Margarine Equation			Butter Equation	
	Estimate	Std error	Estimate	Std error
Constant	0.00	0.00	0.00	0.00
Marg. price	−2.34	0.64	−0.35	0.26
Butter price	−0.15	0.45	−3.78	0.20
Total fat	0.31	0.20	0.98	0.04

Fat equation

	Estimate	Std error
Constant	0.00	0.00
Fat price	−5.27	0.31
Winter	0.03	0.01
Fat display	0.01	0.01
Fat coupon	0.01	0.00
Fat maj. add.	0.07	0.00
Unemploy	−1.66	0.45
Income	1.47	1.17

Margarine and butter total elasticities

	Margarine	Butter
Margarine	−3.50	−4.00
Butter	−0.60	−5.30

Notes:
(1) All variables in logs.
(2) Elasticities can be read directly from price coefficients.
(3) Instruments: average of price in all other cities at that particular week.

Table 2. TWO-LEVEL ESTIMATION

Expenditure share regression coefficients

	B1	B2	B3	B4	B5	B6	PL	B7	B8	Brand	PL
							Marg		butter	butter	
B1	−0.096	0.000	0.002	0.013	0.016	0.002	0.011	−0.002	0.006	0.018	0.032
B2	−0.005	−0.152	0.010	0.014	0.014	0.001	0.006	0.016	0.016	0.032	0.047
B3	0.005	0.000	−0.088	0.006	0.007	0.007	0.008	0.010	0.007	0.008	0.030
B4	0.007	0.000	0.001	−0.053	0.007	0.000	0.005	0.001	0.003	0.017	0.013
B5	0.016	−0.002	0.005	0.008	−0.087	0.001	0.008	−0.003	0.007	0.011	0.035
B6	0.002	0.000	0.000	0.006	0.000	−0.031	0.000	0.001	0.001	0.005	0.017
PL marg	0.011	−0.005	0.001	0.001	0.012	0.000	−0.074	0.005	−0.006	0.001	0.064
B7	0.012	0.013	0.010	0.013	0.002	0.009	0.002	−0.127	0.013	0.024	0.030
B8	0.007	−0.001	−0.001	0.011	0.016	−0.001	0.005	−0.006	−0.130	0.053	0.046
Brand butter	0.017	0.018	0.018	0.016	0.024	0.004	0.020	0.014	0.027	−0.375	0.217
PL butter	0.027	0.027	0.022	0.023	0.037	0.007	0.033	0.016	0.034	0.133	−0.358
FAT	0.002	−0.042	−0.024	0.006	−0.003	−0.007	−0.009	−0.036	0.038	0.054	0.097

Conditional demand elasticities

	B1	B2	B3	B4	B5	B6	PL	B7	B8	Brand	PL
							marg		butter	butter	
B1	−2.489	0.000	0.021	0.478	0.163	0.091	0.137	−0.031	0.040	0.142	0.182
B2	−0.080	−2.388	0.114	0.503	0.144	0.052	0.083	0.213	0.114	0.255	0.272
B3	0.079	0.002	−1.974	0.206	0.078	0.363	0.097	0.138	0.052	0.061	0.170
B4	0.113	−0.002	0.012	−2.948	0.075	0.010	0.060	0.010	0.021	0.132	0.074
B5	0.252	−0.021	0.058	0.295	−1.902	0.072	0.098	−0.034	0.048	0.086	0.202
B6	0.027	−0.003	0.004	0.209	0.002	−2.647	−0.004	0.007	0.008	0.036	0.099
PL marg	0.171	−0.042	0.010	0.037	0.123	0.000	−1.956	0.069	−0.040	0.004	0.367
B7	0.179	0.119	0.113	0.457	0.018	0.477	0.030	−2.707	0.091	0.190	0.174
B8	0.114	−0.005	−0.009	0.389	0.166	−0.040	0.060	−0.077	−1.919	0.421	0.265
Brand butter	0.267	0.165	0.203	0.566	0.251	0.234	0.252	0.187	0.188	−3.974	1.245
PL butter	0.417	0.247	0.249	0.825	0.384	0.376	0.422	0.218	0.238	1.055	−3.053

Unconditional demand elasticities

	B1	B2	B3	B4	B5	B6	PL	B7	B8	Brand	PL
							Marg		butter	butter	
B1	−2.901	−0.146	−0.162	0.128	−0.100	−0.064	−0.100	−0.143	−0.327	−0.279	−0.281
B2	−1.341	−2.854	−1.147	−0.758	−1.117	−1.209	−1.178	−1.048	−1.147	−1.006	−0.989
B3	−0.497	−0.383	−2.410	−0.464	−0.471	−0.034	−0.415	−0.199	−0.641	−0.708	−0.658
B4	−0.062	−0.119	−0.120	−3.152	−0.092	−0.111	−0.096	−0.093	−0.190	−0.101	−0.178
B5	−0.362	−0.430	−0.406	−0.419	−2.486	−0.351	−0.447	−0.393	−0.690	−0.732	−0.680
B6	−0.093	−0.082	−0.087	0.070	−0.111	−2.730	−0.111	−0.063	−0.136	−0.124	−0.073
PL marg	−0.323	−0.372	−0.364	−0.538	−0.347	−0.341	−2.396	−0.220	−0.635	−0.655	−0.343
B7	6.333	−1.175	−1.279	1.192	−1.370	−2.212	−1.132	−2.986	−0.526	−0.418	−0.547
B8	2.961	−1.619	−1.600	0.117	−6.460	−1.521	−2.177	−1.472	−3.008	−0.651	−1.155
Brand butter	9.289	−1.890	−2.204	1.086	−8.758	−2.119	−3.729	−1.846	−0.762	−5.049	0.789
PL butter	14.754	−2.665	−2.931	1.692	−13.175	−3.081	−5.818	−2.470	−1.136	0.446	−4.658

are reported in Table 1. The bottom-level regression results and calculated elasticities are reported in Table 2.

In our second segmentation we used two segments: margarine and butter. The middle-level regressions are in the form of log segment expenditure regressed on log of segments real prices and log of total real fat expenditure (total expenditure deflated by the real price of fat). The results are reported in Table 1. The bottom level of the demand system corresponds to competition among brands within the margarine segment in a given segment. The bottom-level equation is in the form of share of brand i regressed on real log of prices of all brands in the segment and on log of real expenditures on margarine (nominal divided by the segment price index). We estimate all three levels, and as discussed above, by combining results from each we can derive unconditional demand elasticities, which are reported in Table 3.

As discussed above, in estimating these models two statistical problems must be dealt with: serial correlation and endogeneity. To solve both problems, as in Hausman *et al.* (1992), we take advantage of having time-series/cross-section data. To correct for serial correlation we took first differences. Besides dealing with serial correlation taking first differences gets rid of city-specific fixed effects. We performed tests of endogeneity at the brand, segment and fat levels. As would be expected, endogeneity does not seem to be an issue at the brand level. Since our observations are weekly, unexpected weekly demand shocks for a particular brand should not translate in supermarket shelf price adjustments at that brand level. On the other hand, segment and fat equations do show significant endogeneity problems, and those

Table 3. Three-stage estimation

Expenditure share regression coefficients

	B1	B2	B3	B4	B5	B6	PL marg	B7	B8
B1	−0.131	0.009	0.012	0.030	0.030	0.009	0.022	0.004	0.016
B2	0.013	−0.237	0.034	0.033	0.040	0.007	0.025	0.042	0.044
B3	0.017	0.010	−0.136	0.017	0.021	0.015	0.019	0.022	0.016
B4	0.016	0.004	0.008	−0.075	0.018	0.003	0.014	0.004	0.008
B5	0.032	0.005	0.015	0.023	−0.120	0.006	0.020	0.001	0.017
B6	0.007	0.005	0.004	0.013	0.007	−0.050	0.003	0.006	0.006
PL marg	0.026	0.005	0.013	0.015	0.031	0.006	−0.099	0.001	0.002
B7	0.028	0.035	0.032	0.028	0.013	0.023	0.012	−0.207	0.036
B8	0.030	0.021	0.017	0.032	0.047	0.006	0.021	0.006	−0.181
Marg	0.030	−0.034	−0.007	0.034	0.028	0.002	0.013	−0.037	−0.030
Shares in marg	0.086	0.154	0.140	0.041	0.149	0.029	0.103	0.107	0.190

Conditional demand elasticities

	B1	B2	B3	B4	B5	B6	PL Marg	B7	B8
B1	−2.511	0.057	0.084	0.725	0.204	0.294	0.216	0.033	0.083
B2	0.146	−2.536	0.245	0.807	0.267	0.248	0.238	0.388	0.232
B3	0.196	0.068	−1.975	0.409	0.139	0.504	0.183	0.204	0.087
B4	0.180	0.027	0.057	−2.834	0.121	0.109	0.134	0.041	0.042
B5	0.373	0.034	0.107	0.551	−1.804	0.220	0.194	0.010	0.091
B6	0.085	0.030	0.028	0.318	0.047	−2.727	0.025	0.054	0.030
PL marg	0.296	0.032	0.094	0.372	0.206	0.199	−1.957	0.011	0.011
B7	0.324	0.229	0.226	0.678	0.088	0.777	0.117	−2.930	0.192
B8	0.342	0.139	0.121	0.790	0.317	0.195	0.205	0.058	−1.952

Unconditional demand elasticities

	B1	B2	B3	B4	B5	B6	PL Marg	B7	B8
B1	−2.969	−0.283	−0.298	0.083	−0.237	−0.143	−0.236	−0.265	0.162
B2	−0.769	−3.081	−0.426	−0.368	−0.533	−0.514	−0.562	−0.170	0.368
B3	−0.548	−0.423	−2.616	−0.529	−0.518	−0.128	−0.464	−0.238	0.200
B4	−0.047	−0.123	−0.110	−3.177	−0.073	−0.085	−0.070	−0.101	0.077
B5	−0.378	−0.457	−0.445	−0.413	−2.606	−0.403	−0.454	−0.422	0.206
B6	−0.095	−0.087	−0.103	0.097	−0.106	−2.770	−0.128	−0.050	0.057
PL marg	−0.346	−0.384	−0.375	−0.442	−0.341	−0.329	−2.434	−0.343	0.112
B7	−0.326	−0.202	−0.242	−0.138	−0.492	0.209	−0.441	−3.213	0.287
B8	−0.796	−0.609	−0.720	−0.665	−0.678	−0.741	−0.773	−0.587	−1.738

were addressed using the approach in Hausman *et al.* (1992), where the instrument for each price is the average price at that period of time everywhere else in the nation. This is a valid instrument if demand shocks are not highly correlated across cities. This seems a reasonable assumption given that we are correcting for general macroeconomic conditions, and given that we difference the data.

Thus, for the middle-level and top-level regressions we used instrumental variable estimation, where we take advantage of the nature of the data. Since any endogeneity between price and quantity will be at the city level, the average price of a brand across cities other than city X should be an excellent instrument for the price of a brand in city X. That average price should not be statistically related to city-specific shocks in demand, and as a consequence, that instrument will be orthogonal to the demand error. The OLS and instrumental equation estimates for the middle and top levels differ significantly, implying the presence of endogeneity at those levels. Therefore, we report the instrumental variables estimates for those levels.

Estimation Results

The results of the estimations are reported in Tables 1–3 and the formulas for calculating the unconditional elasticities are provided in the Appendix.

(1) The demand for 'Fat' is highly elastic, with an estimated own-price elasticity of −5.3 (Table 1).
(2) Margarine and butter are highly elastic segments. The unconditional own elasticity of margarine is −3.5, while that of butter is −5.3 (Table 1). These are high elasticities, indicating that margarine is not a relevant market.
(3) The cross-elasticities between margarine and butter are negative, but not significant. However, it is quite implausible that this cross-elasticity is not negative and significant.[11] The reasons for this implausible result are unclear. If margarine and butter have good substitutes other than each other, then our specification is incorrect. The major uses of margarine and butter are as 'spreads' or baking ingredients. There are a number of alternatives to margarine and butter in these two uses. Thus, a proper model might need to include other products.
(4) The brand level estimates in the two-stage estimation (Table 2) produce elastic demands at the brand level. The conditional elasticities are calculated from the brand-level estimates keeping real Fat expenditures constant. The unconditional elasticities are the ordinary demand elasticities at the brand level.
(5) The estimated brand level own price elasticities appear to be biased downward. This conclusion arises from the fact that the total own-price elasticity for margarine is larger than *any* of the own-price elasticities of the individual brands. We conjecture that this bias arises because the price index used in the bottom-level (brand-level) regressions is an approximation to the true price index.
(6) The cross-elasticities between brands are generally negative. This is probably a result of having so many brands and, perhaps, from using only a simple two-stage model.
(7) The brand level estimates in the three-stage estimation (Table 3) produce somewhat more elastic demands at the brand level than the two-stage estimates. There is still a downward bias in these estimated elasticities. The cross-elasticities between margarine brands are still generally negative. However, cross-elasticities of margarine brands with butter are now large and positive.
(8) The similarity of results in the two- and three-stage estimates indicates that the nesting assumptions (choose Fat/then brand, or choose Fat/then segment/then brand) are not important. If margarine and butter were competitively distinct segments, it would be expected that the estimates of the two specifications would have been more different. Thus, the similarity of results are consistent with margarine and butter being in the same Guidelines market.

SUMMARY AND CONCLUSIONS

We have surveyed the techniques of econometric market delineation, discussed problems and pitfalls in these techniques, and provided an example illustrating the importance of a theoretically sound specification in generating meaningful results. These techniques are relatively new, and only a few econometric market-delineation exercises have been conducted.

One obvious are for considerable future attention is to reconcile these techniques with the techniques used by marketing researchers. It is discomforting to realize that although large consumer product companies have access to good data and statistical expertise and are undertaking price elasticity studies, what they are doing appears to bear little obvious relationship to the techniques antitrust researchers use in attempting to assess potential market power.

APPENDIX: DERIVATION OF FORMULAS FOR UNCONDITIONAL ELASTICITIES

Two-stage Model

Two equations: share equation and fat equation:

Definition of shares for each brand: $w_i = \dfrac{p_i q_i}{x}$

Share equation: $w_i = \alpha_0 \Sigma_i \alpha_i \ln(p_i) + \gamma \ln\left(\dfrac{x}{P}\right)$

Fat equation: $\ln\left(\dfrac{x}{P}\right) = \delta_0 + \delta_1 \ln(P)$

Definition of price index P: $\ln P = \Sigma_i w_i \ln(p_i)$

Derivative of w_i with respect to p_i:

$$\frac{\partial w_i}{\partial \ln(p_i)} = p_i \frac{\partial w_i}{\partial p_i} = p_i \frac{[p_i x(\partial q_i/\partial p_i) - p_i q_i \cdot (\partial x/\partial p_i) + x q_i]}{x^2}$$

$$= p_i \frac{p_i}{x}\frac{\partial q_i}{\partial p_i} - p_i \frac{q_i}{x}\frac{\partial x}{\partial p_i}\frac{p_i}{x} + w_i$$

$$= \frac{p_i q_i}{x}\left[\frac{p_i}{q_i}\frac{\partial q_i}{\partial p_i} - \frac{\partial x}{\partial p_i}\frac{p_i}{x} + 1\right]$$

$$= w_i[\epsilon^{q_i, p_i} - \epsilon^{x, p_i} + 1]$$

where ϵ means elasticity $\quad (A1)$

From the share equation:

$$\frac{\partial w_i}{\partial \ln(p_i)} = \alpha_i + \gamma \frac{\partial \ln(x/P)}{\partial \ln(p_i)}$$

$$= \alpha_i + \gamma \frac{\partial \ln(x/P)}{\partial \ln P}\frac{\partial \ln P}{\partial \ln(p_i)}$$

$$= \alpha_i + \gamma \delta_1 w_i \quad (A2)$$

So that we have:

$$w_i[\epsilon^{q_i, p_i} - \epsilon^{x, p_i} + 1] = \alpha_i + \gamma \delta_1 w_i \quad (A3)$$

Now

$$\epsilon^{x, p_i} = \frac{\partial \ln x}{\partial \ln P}\frac{\partial \ln P}{\partial \ln p_i}$$

but $\dfrac{\partial \ln x}{\partial \ln P} = (\delta_1 - 1)$ so that

$$\epsilon^{x, p_i} = (\delta_1 - 1) w_i \quad (A4)$$

Substituting Eqns (A4) into (A3) we obtain

$$\epsilon^{q_i p_i} = \frac{\alpha_i}{w_i} - w_i + \delta_1(\gamma + w_i) - 1 \quad (A5)$$

This is a negative number as long as $\delta_1 < 0$, $\gamma > 0$ and $\alpha_i < 0$.

Assuming that x/P remains constant (as in the conditional elasticities), the third term in Eqn (A5) is not taken into account.

Three-stage Model

Three-level equations:

Brand margarine shares: w_i: $w_i = \dfrac{p_i q_i}{x_m}$

Margarine share: w_m

Margarine expenditure: x_m

Margarine price index: $P_m = \Sigma_i p_i w_i$

Butter price index: P_b

Fat price index: $P = w_m P_m + (1 - w_m) P_m$

Equations and nomenclature:

$$w_i = \alpha_0 + \Sigma_j \alpha_{ij} \ln P_j + \gamma_i \ln\left(\frac{x_m}{P_m}\right)$$

$$\ln\left(\frac{x_m}{P_m}\right) = \delta_0 + \delta_1 \ln(P_m) + \delta_2 \ln(P_b) + \xi \ln\left(\frac{x}{P}\right)$$

$$\ln\left(\frac{x}{P}\right) = \eta_0 + \eta_1 \ln P \quad (A6)$$

Derivation:

From the definition of brand share:

$$\frac{\partial w_i}{\partial \ln p_i} = w_i[\epsilon^{q_i, p_i} - \epsilon^{x_m, p_i} + 1]$$

From the brand share equation:

$$\frac{\partial w_i}{\partial \ln p_i} = \alpha_{ii} + \gamma_i \delta_1 w_i + \gamma_i \xi \eta_1 w_m w_i$$

From the definition of ϵ^{x_m, p_i}:

$$\epsilon^{x_m, p_i} = (\delta_1 - 1) w_i + \xi \eta_1 w_m w_i$$

Substituting all in first equation and solving for ϵ^{q_i, p_i} we obtain

$$\epsilon^{q_i, p_i} = \frac{\alpha_{ii}}{w_i} - w_i + [\delta_1 + \eta_1 \xi w_m] \times (\gamma_i + w_i) - 1 \qquad (A7)$$

Observe that this is very similar to two-stage model equations, with only the added term $\eta_1 \xi w_m$ in the term in parentheses.

Cross-elasticities:

$$\epsilon^{q_i, p_j} = \frac{\alpha_{ij}}{w_i} - w_j + \delta_1 w_j \left(\frac{\gamma_i}{w_i} + 1 \right) + \eta_1 \xi w_m w_j \left(\frac{\gamma_i}{w_i} + 1 \right) \qquad (A8)$$

Observe that if $i = j$ we obtain that Eqn (A8) is the same as Eqn (A7).

NOTES

1. We ignore here the issue of the benchmark (competitive, etc.) against which the price increase is assessed.
2. For example, gadgets, which are a substitute for widgets, or widgets available from other locations.
3. This is the approach taken by Scheffman and Spiller (1987) in dealing with the price of gasoline outside the geographic area being estimated.
4. If retail prices are proportional to wholesale prices, retail and wholesale price elasticities are identical. If retail prices vary less than proportionately to wholesale prices, wholesale price elasticities are smaller than retail price elasticities.
5. Essentially, purchasing when the product is being promoted by the manufacturer for needs outside the sales period. For example, a very high percentage of annual dry pasta products are purchased by supermarkets during the two 'windows' during the year in which the major dry pasta manufacturers have 'sales'.
6. Acquiring product in one part of the county (or in other countries) where it was sold at wholesale at a low enough price that it pays to acquire it there and ship it to higher wholesale price areas. Some supermarkets and third parties operate a profitable line of business as 'diverters'.
7. For a theoretical model of purchasing strategies that has these features see Scheffman and Spiller (1982).
8. Various volume-based prices, annual cumulative incremental volume discounts, free goods, special payment terms, etc.
9. 'Stock-keeping unit' — for example, on size box of Kellogg's Corn Flakes is one SKU.
10. We differ here from Hausman *et al.* in that the top equation is not a national-level equation but rather a city-specific equation.
11. Of course, a statistically significant negative cross-elasticity would not necessarily imply that butter and margarine are in the same Guidelines market. This conclusion would depend on the size of the cross-elasticity relative to own-price elasticities.

REFERENCES

J. Baker and T. Bresnahan (1985). The gains from merger and collusion in product-differentiated industries, *Journal of Industrial Organization*, **33**, 427–44.

Berry, Carnal and Spiller (1995). Airline hubs: cost and demand considerations, Mimeo.

C. Blackorby *et al.* (1978). *Duality, Separability, and Functional Structure*, New York: American Elsevier.

A. Deaton and J. Muellbauer (1980). An almost ideal demand system, *American Economic Review*, **70**, 1981.

L. Froeb and G. Werden (1991). Residual demand estimation for market delineation: complications and limitations, *Review of Industrial Organization*, **6**, 33–48.

L. Froeb and G. Werden (1992). The reverse cellophane fallacy in market delineation, *Review of Industrial Organization*, **7**, 241–47.

W. Gorman (1971). Two stage budgeting, Mimeo.

J. Hausman (1994). Valuation of new goods under perfect and imperfect competition, MIT Economics Department Working Paper 94–21, June.

J. Hausman, G. Leonard and J. D. Zona (1992). A proposed method for analyzing competition among differentiated products, *Antitrust Law Journal*, **60**, 889–900.

J. Hausman, G. Leonard and J. D. Zona (1994). Competitive analysis with differentiated products, *Annales d'Economique et Statistique*, **34**, 159–80.

J. Hausman and W. Taylor (1981). Panel data and unobservable effects, *Econometrica*, **49**.

J. P. Jones (1990). The double jeopardy of sales promotions. *Standard Business Review*, **68**, No. 5, September–October.

D. Scheffman (1992). Measures of market power: uses and abuses, *Antitrust Law Journal*, **60**, No. 3, 901–19.

D. Scheffman and P. Spiller (1987). Geographic market definition under the *U.S. Department of Justice Merger Guidelines*, *Journal of Law and Economics*, **30**, No. 1, 123–48.

D. Scheffman and P. Spiller (1992). Buyer's strategies, entry barriers, and competition. *Economic Inquiry*, **30**, 418–36.

A. Tellis (1988). The price elasticity of selective demand: a meta-analysis of econometric models of sales. *Journal of Marketing Research*, **25**, November, 331–41.

U.S. Department of Justice and FTC Horizontal Merger Guidelines (1992), 2 April, reprinted in 4 Trade Reg. Rep. (CCH) ¶ 13, 104.

G. Werden (1992). The history of antitrust market delineation, *Marquette Law Review*, **76**, 123–215.

9

The Nuts and Bolts of Antitrust Analysis: some thoughts on how to develop the facts

David P. Kaplan

Capital Economics, Washington, DC, USA

Economic literature addressing theoretical issues related to industrial organization and antitrust is robust. Intelligent and thought-provoking discussions of market power, monopoly, oligopoly, conjectural interdependence, coordinated interaction, contestability, game theory, entry, opportunistic behavior with respect to an installed base, systems competition, and many other issues are numerous. A basic understanding of such literature is, of course, important to a proper consideration of the issues encountered by an economist when asked to analyze a particular set of market circumstances in a pending or possible lawsuit involving antitrust issues. Equally important, however, is a proper consideration of the specific market facts of the industry and business conduct under review. Indeed, an economists' opinion concerning a certain set of market circumstances without the proper factual support is of questionable value.

In a recent decision, the Supreme Court addressed the role of economic expert testimony in an antitrust matter. The case involved allegations of 'predatory price discrimination' on behalf of a particular firm and related issues of 'oligopolistic price coordination' and 'recoupment'. Plaintiff's theory was supported by economic expert testimony. When considering the weight to be given that testimony, the Court concluded that when an 'expert opinion is not supported by sufficient facts' or where 'indusputable record facts contradict or otherwise render the opinion unreasonable, it cannot support a jury's verdict'.[1] The Court concluded that 'expert testimony is useful as a guide to interpreting market facts, but it is not a substitute for them'.[2]

The remainder of this paper discusses the arguably mundane but critically important identification and collection of relevant market facts by an economist analyzing an antitrust issue. It also discusses how facts and related information can be used to evaluate issues such as market definition, entry, and the competitive implications of various business practices.

DATA COLLECTION AND ANALYSIS

The collection and analysis of data is an important part of the economist's job portfolio in the analysis of any antitrust matter. Important data can include information related to reserves, capacity, production, sales (in the units and dollars), market share, prices, costs, and margins. Relevant data can be obtained from many sources, including the firms associated with the particular matter, independent third-party entities, trade associations, trade press, independent consultants, survey information, or government sources (state and federal).

Sales and Market Share Data

Sales and market share data may be obtained from documents maintained by the company involved in the antitrust matter under review. These data may be maintained in strategic documents, marketing plans or other forms of contemporaneous business papers. Individual company data are, of course, ultimately based on transactional documents maintained by the company, including invoices and various financial documents. Industry-wide data (the relevant 'universe'), sales data for each relevant industry participant, and related market share information may be based on a number of sources, including information published by trade associations, trade press, government agencies, or estimates by industry consultants or company representatives, among others.

The quality and usefulness of all such data is dependent on the rigor involved in its collection. If industry sales data are obtained from a trade association, for example, it becomes important to understand whether all market participants are members of the trade association. If industry consultants publish similar data based on some form of formal or informal survey, an appreciation of how the survey is conducted (telephone versus written responses, any adjustments made to raw data, etc.) would be helpful. If sales and market share data are simply not available from any organized source, it may be necessary for informed business representatives to estimate the relevant industry data and great care is required in evaluating the utility of data generated in this fashion.

There are third parties that collect and sell market share data. For example, in the food industry, IRI and Nielsen collect sales data (measured in dollars, units, and volume equivalents) and market share data, in addition to price information. They also generate and provide statistics on various merchandising measures such as percent of product sold on 'deal' and other related information and provide data on issues such as the level of geographic coverage (so-called 'ACV') a particular brand or firm has achieved. Many of these statistics are based on the collection of data and related information obtained from 'scanners' located in retail establishments such as grocery stores (Von's, Kroger, etc.) or other retailers (drug stores, mass merchandisers, etc.). Data are generally available for individual products (including particular package sizes), individual firms, and entire industries. Data are provided on a weekly, monthly, or yearly basis and can be generated for individual store accounts, metropolitan areas, regional areas, or the entire United States.[3]

These data are a rich source of information and can be used for ascertaining market shares. Care is required when using such data, however, because they may not cover all sales outlets or all channels off distribution. Some firms may refuse to provide data to firms such as IRI or Nielsen or may not be asked to provide information because they are considered too small or they do not have the necessary scanner equipment. In a recent merger between two pet food companies, market share data obtained from Nielsen suggested that the merging firms had relatively significant shares of pet food sales. These data, however, primarily accounted for pet food sales through grocery stores and failed to account for all sales through various large mass merchandisers (Wal-Mart, K-Mart, Sam's), those made through the emerging channel of pet superstores, and those made through more traditional pet food stores. When all channels were taken into account, the relevant shares of the merging firms were substantially reduced.

Price Data

Like sales and market share data, price information can also be obtained from a number of sources. Price data may be obtained from the companies involved in the antitrust matter under review and take the form of list price sheets or transactional documents (invoices, etc.). In industries where transaction prices differ significantly from list prices, more detailed financial data would be necessary to approximate actual price levels. Price data can also be obtained from price surveys. For example, in a recent matter it was suggested that a particular segment of trade was denied access to supply in order to support supracompetitive price levels by other industry participants. A telephone survey, however, suggested that the alleged 'favored' class of trade actually charged lower prices than the allegedly excluded rivals. In another matter, data on sales of used construction equipment collected and published by a third party was useful in examining the level of price competition between new and used heavy machinery.

Price data may also be obtained from government sources. The International Commerce Commission's Annual Rail Waybill Sample provides detailed rail rate and shipment data for a stratified random sample of all rail shipments in a given year. The Federal Communications Commission provides consumer and producer price indexes for local, long-distance and international telephone service, local and long-distance traffic volumes, and local residential and business rates in 95 cities across the country.

Scanner data from firms such as IRI and Nielsen are another source of price information. In the recent merger of pet food producers referred to above, these data were used to demonstrate that the brands of the merging parties could not be considered next-best substitutes and that private-label or store-label pet food products were substantial competitors of branded products.[4] These data can also be used to test whether one type of category of products competes on a direct and substantial basis with a potential substitute.

For example, scanner data were used to test — by way of residual demand analysis — whether all carbonated soft drinks (CSDs) constituted a relevant market.[5] Scanner data were used for price and volume of carbonated soft drinks and relevant cost variables included factor prices specific to non-CSD production and distribution and factor prices common to CSD and non-CSD supply. To complete the residual demand experiment, several CSD-specific cost variables were included in the first stage regression but not in the residual demand for CSDs. The relevant variables used are identified in Table 1, and the results are reported in Table 2. From Table 2 it is evident that the regressors as a group explained a significant amount of the variation in the price of CSDs, the dependent variable, and that the coefficient for CSD volume is highly significant.[6] The residual demand elasticity estimated was −6.00. The large magnitude of the residual demand elasticity means that CSD suppliers as a group would have to restrict volume substantially to achieve a significant price increase.[7]

Price and volume data can also be used to evaluate entry issues and can be gathered from a number of different sources, in addition to firms such as IRI and Nielsen. When evaluating the

Table 1.

Direct demand factors	
USSUMDUM	A dichotomous seasonal variable for the United States. May through September is designated as summer.
ETOTALL	The monthly average of weekly earnings for all manufacturer workers in the United States. Source: Bureau of Labor Statistics.
Non-CSD and common cost factors	
WKBEARN	The US average weekly earnings of brewery workers. (Monthly) Source: Bureau of Labor Statistics.
WRGRDIST	The US average weekly earnings of grocery distribution workers. (Monthly) Source: Bureau of Labor Statistics.
PBEERCAN	The US Producer Price Index (PPI) for beer cans. (Monthly) Source: Bureau of Labor Statistics.
PFRJCAN	The US PPI for fruit juice cans. (Monthly) Source: Bureau of Labor Statistics.
FCOFFEE	The US futures price index for coffee beans. (Monthly) Source: George Gordon Paton & Co., Inc.
AAPPLES	The US futures price index for apples. (Monthly) Source: US Department of Agriculture.
PCANESUG	The US PPI for cane sugar. (Monthly) Source: Bureau of Labor Statistics.
CSD cost factors	
WCSDEARN	The US monthly average weekly earnings of CSD bottling workers. (Monthly) Source: Bureau of Labor Statistics.
PCSDCAN	The US PPI for CSD cans. (Monthly) Source: Bureau of Labor Statistics.
PKOLA	The US PPI for cola concentrate. (Monthly) Source: Bureau of Labor Statistic.

Table 2. Regression Coefficient Estimates All CSD Residual Demand.

Dependent Variable	Price Total US
Constant	10.503
	(4.98)
CSD volume	−0.166[a]
	(−8.24)
USSUMDUM	0.012
	(1.61)
ETOTALL	0.388
	(0.94)
WKBEARN	0.298[a]
	(3.02)
WGRDIST	−1.534[a]
	(−3.26)
PBEERCAN	−0.305
	(−1.61)
PCANESUG	0.263
	(1.04)
AAPPLES	−0.015
	(−1.11)
FCOFFEE	0.018
	(−1.02)
PFRJCAN	−0.302
	(−1.02)
rho	0.529
	(4.08)
Adj. R^2	0.89
Durbin–Watson stat	1.97
F-statistic	50.86

[a] Significant at the 1% level in a two-tailed test.

likely competitive outcome of a combination of firms producing and marketing replacement tires, for example, an issue was raised concerning whether subsequent to the merger, the leading marketers of replacement tires in the United States might be able to profitably raise prices. Using price data published by various countries around the world and volume data generated by a trade association in the United States, an analysis was prepared which suggested that fringe tire producers would substantially expand output if prices were raised above competitive levels.

To determine the magnitude of the fringe output expansion, the familiar residual demand elasticity formula was used in reverse to express fringe supply elasticity as a function of industry demand elasticity, residual demand elasticity, and fringe market share. Thus, statistical estimates were generated for overall US market demand and residual demand for the eight largest replacement tire manufacturers in the United States. The variables used in the estimation of market demand for replacement tires are contained in Table 3 and the results are presented in Table 4. The estimated own-price elasticity of demand was −0.82. For the estimation of residual demand for the leading tire firms, Producer Price Indices for tires were used and volume data were obtained from a trade association. Variables used in the residual demand equation are identified in Table 5, the sources of these variables in Table 6, and results in Table 7. The estimated residual demand elasticity was −4.81 and highly significant. Using these estimates and determining the share of the fringe suppliers (12%), the supply elasticity was calculated to be 27.3 and highly significant. This elasticity implied that in response to a 10% price increase, the competitive fringe would expand shipments to the United States by 273%, or 136.5% in response to a 5% price increase.[8]

Costs and Margin Information

Various sources also exist for cost, margin, and other financial data. Cost data can, of course, be obtained from various government (CPI, PPI, labor costs, etc.) and third-party sources. Company financial documents are also likely to contain relevant income statements and balance sheets containing a great amount of cost and other financial data. Such cost data can be compared to price information when analyzing allegations of below-cost pricing. Company financial data may also be available on a monthly basis and be sufficiently robust to allow for the examination of the relationship between various cost categories and output. Such analyses can be quite helpful when examining whether particular costs vary with output. Care should be taken with monthly financial documents, however, to ensure that reported data are reflective of actual transactions and not some function of accounting routine such as ‘booking’ costs or revenues in a particular month — although not actually expended or collected during that month — simply for budgeting or other reasons.

Company financial data can also be used to determine contribution or operating margins and be used to test, for example, whether particular price increases might be profitable depending on the associated level of volume losses. Such an analysis, based on margin data from company income statements, can prove useful in defining the scope of a product market. Specifically, the estimated variable contribution margin may allow for the measurement of the per-unit cost of restricting output, which is weighed against the price premium enjoyed on inframarginal units

Table 3. Variables Used in the Estimation of the Market Demand for Small Tires in the United States

USTIRES	Monthly RMA shipments of small tires in the United States plus monthly non-RMA imports
CPITIRE	Monthly consumer price index for small tires in the United States deflated by the all-item US consumer price index
Demand shifters	
MILES	Monthly number of vehicle miles driven in the United States
DISPOS	Monthly disposable income in the United States deflated by the all-item consumer price index
VEHICLES	Estimated number of vehicles in the United States that require new replacement tires based on their age and the percent of vehicles, given their age, that were originally fit with radial, non-radial or high-performance tires
Cost shifters[a]	
RUBBERP	Average monthly price of natural rubber quoted in pounds sterling — world price
WAGE	Average monthly wage of workers in the US tire and inner tube industries
ELECI	Average monthly retail price of electricity to industrial users in the United States
PPISYNR	US monthly producer price index for synthetic rubber
PPIWIRE	US monthly producer price index for steel wire
PPISTYB	US monthly producer price index for styrene butadiene
PPIPOLY	US monthly producer price index for polyester
TITAN	US monthly producer price index for titanium pigments
PPIADV	US monthly producer price index for newspaper advertising
JCBLK	Japan carbon black monthly price index
WJAPAN	Japan monthly earnings index
JWIRE	Japan steel wire monthly price index
JSYNR	Japan synthetic rubber monthly price index
JELEC	Japan electric power monthly price index
JPOLY	Japan polyester monthly price index
JTITAN	Japan titanium oxide monthly price index
JZINC	Japan zinc oxide monthly price index
KCBLK	Korea carbon black monthly price index
KWIREROD	Korea steel wire monthly price index
KSYNR	Korea synthetic rubber monthly price index
WKOREA	Korea monthly earnings index
KELEC	Korea electric power annual price index

Table 3. *(Continued)*

KPOLY	Korea polyester monthly price index
FSYNR	France synthetic rubber monthly price index
WFRANCE	France monthly earnings index
FELEC	France electric power monthly price index
EUROCBLK	Europe carbon black monthly price
WWGERMAN	West German monthly earnings index
GRAYON	West German rayon monthly price index
GDWIRE	West German drawn wire monthly price index

[a] All foreign input prices were converted to US dollars and then deflated by the all-item consumer price index. US input prices were deflated by the all-item consumer price index. All variables enter the regression in logarithmic form.

that results from an output reduction (which, of course, depends on demand elasticity).

In addition to being found in individual company financial documents, margin data can also be obtained from third parties where industry financial ratios are provided by four digit Standard Industrial Code. Similarly, the Federal Trade Commission publishes financial data for various industry categories ('food and kindred products', etc.). With all such accounting data, of course, great care should be taken when evaluating the results of any empirical exercise given the differences between how accountants and economists approach issues such as historical versus replacement costs and the treatment of intangible assets, among others.

BUSINESS DOCUMENTS

The concept of a paperless office has not yet found a home in the vast majority of American businesses. As a result, the files of a particular firm or set of firms are likely to contain a significant amount of material. Such documents can be an important source of information about individ-

Table 4
TSLS/Dependent Variable is *USTIRES*
SMPL range: 1982.01–1988.12
Number of observations: 84
Instrument list: *C MILES VEHICLES DISPOS RUBBERP JSYNR FSYNR KSYNR JZINC JTITAN JWIRE KWIREROD GDWIRE JCBLK EUROCBLK KCBLK WJAPAN WWGERMAN WFRANCE WKOREA JELEC FELEC KELEC JPOLY GRAYON KPOLY WAGE ELECI PPIPOLY PPISTYB PPIADV PPIWIRE PPISYNR TITAN*

Variable	Coefficient	Std Error	*T*-stat.	Two-Tail sig.
C	6.0037651	4.2355585	1.4174672	0.161
CPITIRE	−0.8233077	0.4233258	−1.9448561	0.056
MILES	0.9724860	0.0950643	10.229776	0.000
VEHICLES	0.1416914	0.3277852	0.4322690	0.667
DISPOS	−1.2198375	0.5913889	−2.0626654	0.043

R^2	0.713127	Mean of dependent var.	9.502513
Adjusted R^2	0.698602	SD of dependent var.	0.142316
SE of regression	0.078131	Sum of squared resid.	0.482255
Durbin–Watson stat.	1.830972	*F*-statistic	49.09576
Log likelihood	97.53333		

Table 5. Variables Used in the Estimation of the Residual Demand for Small Tires in the United States

DOMESTIC	Monthly RMA shipments of small tires in the United States
PPITIRE	Weighted average of the monthly producer price indices for passenger radial tires, passenger non-radial tires, and light truck non-radial tires, deflated by the all-item consumer price index. The weights are equal to the shares of passenger radial, passenger non-radial and light truck tire monthly RMA shipments in the United States
Demand shifters	
MILES	Monthly number of vehicle miles driven in the United States
DISPOS	Monthly disposable income in the United States deflated by the all-item consumer price index
VEHICLES	Estimated number of vehicles in the United States that require new replacement tires based on their age and the percent of vehicles, given their age, that were originally fit with radial, non-radial or high-performance tires
Foreign specific cost shifters and world cost shifters[a]	
RUBBERP	Average monthly price of natural rubber quoted in pounds sterling — world price
JSYNR	Japan synthetic rubber monthly price index
JWIRE	Japan steel wire monthly price index
JCBLK	Japan carbon black monthly price index
WJAPAN	Japan monthly earnings index
JELEC	Japan electric power monthly price index
JPOLY	Japan polyester monthly price index
JTITAN	Japan titanium oxide monthly price index
JZINC	Japan zinc oxide monthly price index
KCBLK	Korea carbon black monthly price index
WKOREA	Korea monthly earnings index
KELEC	Korea electric power annual price index
KPOLY	Korea polyester monthly price index
KSYNR	Korea synthetic rubber monthly price index
KWIREROD	Korea steel wire monthly price index
WFRANCE	France monthly earnings index
FELEC	France electric power monthly price index
FSYNR	France synthetic rubber monthly price index
EUROCBLK	Europe carbon black monthly price
WWGERMAN	West German monthly earnings index
GRAYON	West German rayon monthly price index
GDWIRE	West German drawn wire monthly price index

[a]All foreign input prices were converted to US dollars and then deflated by the all-item consumer price index. US input prices were deflated by the all-item consumer price index. All variables enter the regression in logarithmic form.

ual firms, an overall industry, or various forms of business practices. These documents may also contain market facts (number of firms, market share, entry conditions, price history, etc.).

Strategic Documents

Almost invariably, managers of American business create various 'strategic' or 'marketing' documents which provide some form of overview or summary of the current business climate, particular market facts, past developments, and likely future prospects. Such documents carry many labels including, not surprisingly, strategic plans, marketing plans, corporate planning documents, five-year plans, annual or periodic reviews, business reviews, and operating plans, among many others. Such documents are generally prepared on a regular basis (such as yearly) by company employees. However, similar documents may be prepared on a more irregular basis by third-party analysts, such as McKinsey or Boston Consulting Group.

These documents can reflect a rich set of useful market facts. They usually identify at least some of the firms marketing competitive products; contain some form of 'competitive profiles' discussing the perceived strengths and weaknesses of rivals; identify potentially new forms of competition (phone versus cable, etc.) or new competitors; discuss the attributes of particular products; include some estimate of current and past market shares; provide price histories and discuss pricing strategies; outline advertising and promotional campaigns; discuss recent entry and exit; make projections concerning future market conditions; discuss developments among buyers such as consolidations or changes in purchasing practices (such as efficient consumer response); provide financial information, including margin data; discuss research and development activities along

Table 6. Sources of Data

Variable	*Source*
CPITIRE	US Bureau of Labor Statistics
DISPOS	Survey of Current Business, US Department of Commerce
DOMESTIC	Rubber Manufacturers Association, RMA Industry Report #38
ELECI	Monthly Energy Review, US Department of Energy
EUROCBLK	Michelin
FELEC	Institut National de Statistique Etudes Economiques, Bulletin de Statistique (NAP#0601)
FSYNR	Institut National de Statistique Etudes Economiques, Bulletin de Statistique (NAP#1728)
GDWIRE	Deutsche Bundesbank
GRAYON	Deutsche Bundesbank
JCBLK	Bank of Japan, Price Indexes Annual
JELEC	Bank of Japan, Price Indexes Annual
JPOLY	Bank of Japan, Price Indexes Annual
JSYNR	Bank of Japan, Price Indexes Annual
JTITAN	Bank of Japan, Price Indexes Annual
JWIRE	Bank of Japan, Price Indexes Annual
JZINC	Bank of Japan, Price Indexes Annual
KCBLK	Bank of Korea (DSB1W3519303)
KELEC	Principal Economic Indicators, Bank of Korea
KPOLY	Bank of Korea (DSBQE3514202)
KSYNR	Bank of Korea (DSB1W3115)
KWIREROD	Bank of Korea (DSB1W3815404)
MILES	Traffic Volume Trends, Federal Highway Administration
PPIADV	US Bureau of Labor Statistics
PPIPOLY	US Bureau of Labor Statistics (PPU2824#8031)
PPISTYB	US Bureau of Labor Statistics (PPU2822#1)
PPISYNR	US Bureau of Labor Statistics (PPU2822)
PPITIRE	US Bureau of Labor Statistics (PPU3011#215, PPU3011#15, PPU3011#112)
PPIWIRE	US Bureau of Labor Statistics (PPU3315#5)
RUBBERP	Malaysian Rubber Research and Development Board, Malaysian Rubber Review
TITAN	US Bureau of Labor Statistics (PPU2816#1)
USTIRES	Rubber Manufacturers Association, RMA Industry Report #38, US Department of Commerce

Table 6. *(Continued)*

Variable	*Source*
VEHICLES	*Ward's Automotive Yearbook 1989* and *Modern Tire Dealer*
WAGE	US Bureau of Labor Statistics (EEU32301006)
WFRANCE	International Monetary Fund, International Financial Statistics
WJAPAN	International Monetary Fund, International Financial Statistics
WKOREA	International Monetary Fund, International Financial Statistics
WWGERMAN	International Monetary Fund, International Financial Statistics

The US all-item consumer price index is from the US Bureau of Labor Statistics. Foreign exchange rates for Japan, France, Korea and West Germany are from the International Monetary Fund, International Financial Statistics.

Table 7
TSLS//Dependent variable is *DOMESTIC*
SMPL range: 1982.01–1988.12
Number of observations: 84
Instrument list: *C MILES VEHICLES DISPOS RUBBERP JSYNR FSYNR KSYNR JTITAN JZINC JWIRE KWIREROD GDWIRE JCBLK EUROCBLK KCBLK WJAPAN WWGERMAN WFRANCE WKOREA JELEC FELEC KELEC JPOLY GRAYON KPOLY WAGE ELECI PPIPOLY PPISTYB PPIADV TITAN PPISYNR PPIWIRE*

Variable	Coefficient	Std error	*T*-stat.	Two-Tail sig.
C	31.283665	12.595332	2.4837506	0.016
PPITIRE	−4.8140270	1.9923011	−2.4163150	0.019
MILES	0.4126597	0.1919870	2.1494146	0.036
VEHICLES	−1.1422212	0.7300022	−1.5646818	0.123
DISPOS	−0.6376598	1.0818958	−0.5893911	0.558
RUBBERP	0.0675192	0.1307938	0.5162263	0.608
JSYNR	0.9868591	0.6238921	1.5817786	0.119
FSYNR	0.1631101	0.4010411	0.4067167	0.686
KSYNR	1.4279530	0.7095275	2.0125408	0.049
JTITAN	0.8153455	0.8213008	0.9927489	0.325
JZINC	0.4714635	0.2444418	1.9287351	0.059
JWIRE	0.7888060	1.2359993	0.6381929	0.526
KWIREROD	1.0497986	1.3053466	0.8042298	0.425
GDWIRE	−1.6664181	0.9506200	−1.7529802	0.085
JCBLK	−1.7991651	1.4240344	−1.2634281	0.212
EUROCBLK	−0.7187206	0.2903548	−2.4753186	0.016
KCBLK	−4.1729897	1.6242705	−2.5691470	0.013
WJAPAN	−1.0887034	0.7396709	−1.4718754	0.147
WWGERMAN	−1.8556588	0.9013323	−2.0587955	0.044
WFRANCE	−1.1116420	0.9117856	−1.2191923	0.228
WKOREA	0.0311734	0.0633057	0.4924262	0.624
JELEC	−0.5265313	0.3424274	−1.5376437	0.130
FELEC	−0.2809414	0.0572135	−4.9104078	0.000
KELEC	0.4280397	0.8962880	0.4775693	0.635
JPOLY	0.0403456	0.1937574	0.2082272	0.836
GRAYON	5.3704798	1.3282872	4.0431617	0.000
KPOLY	2.6504876	2.2803786	1.1623016	0.250

R^2	0.873411	Mean of dependent var.	9.423674
Adjusted R^2	0.815669	SD of dependent var.	0.150260
SE of regression	0.064512	Sum of squared resid.	0.237224
Durbin–Watson stat	2.283653	*F*-statistic	15.12600
Log likelihood	127.3309		

with upcoming technological changes and how such changes may effect competition; and on and on.

The importance of these documents to the investigating economist depends on a number of issues, including the quality of information found in the document (accuracy, reflective of current developments as opposed to 'old news', etc.), the reason the document was prepared (to reflect actual market activities, to facilitate debate concerning a particular issue, etc.), who may have prepared and reviewed the document (senior executives, lower-level employees, third-party consultants with little background in the relevant industry), and whether action was taken because of recommendations included in the document (recommended strategies carried out or rejected, etc.), among other considerations.

Absent a consideration of such issues, strategic and marketing documents can be misleading. For example, a set of marketing plans covering a span of five years each contained language suggesting that a particular firm was operating as a maverick with regard to market prices. A review of actual market data did not support this representation. An interview with the author of the marketing plan revealed that, in order to save time, the language in question was simply repeated on a yearly basis without any updated investigation of whether the described market activity was consistent with actual market experience. In another matter, a great deal of debate concerned a recommendation in a marketing plan that a particular firm should price below 'cost' as part of its market activities. Available data suggested that this particular recommendation was not acted on and further investigation uncovered that the relevant business decision maker rejected the recommendation and had communicated the rejection in a separate memorandum. Conversely, in another matter, it was suggested that senior management had rejected a certain description of current market conditions memorialized in a strategic plan. However, a copy of this plan was reviewed and approved by the firm's president as indicated by a checked 'box' on the document indicating review and approval.[9]

The relevance of particular language included in such documents must also be carefully considered. For example, the discovery of words such as 'dominant', 'market leader', and 'market leverage' in strategic or marketing documents can result in a great deal of churning and debate between litigants in an antitrust matter. However, to the investigating economist, language such as this may or may not have particular significance depending on a careful consideration of a larger set of relevant facts, including some understanding, if possible, of what the document's author actually intended to communicate by the use of such language. Similarly, language suggesting that one competitor 'knows' what another rival is likely to do in the future may simply reflect speculation or guesswork as opposed to actual knowledge.

On the other hand, strategic documents may be relevant when attempting to appreciate more fully the factors affecting price and output decisions, such as the identification of competitive firms, products, and emerging technological trends. They may also be quite informative when attempting to understand better how certain long-run considerations may affect short-run pricing decisions. When analyzing the relevance of systems competition related to a particular antitrust matter, for instance, business documents may indicate whether buyers are informed about long-run costing issues — parts and services — and how these costs may affect the economics of the initial purchase of related 'hardware'. Similarly, marketing documents or strategic plans may contain useful and informative discussions of which, if any, options are available to buyers and related switching costs when further investigating allegations of opportunistic behavior with regard to an installed base.

Management documents such as strategic and marketing plans may well be of value. However, as with all documents, the reviewing economist must be cautious concerning how the information in such documents is used in any substantive analysis.

Other Management-Related Documents

In addition to strategic marketing plans, other management-related documents may also be a source of relevant market information to the economist. Examples include board presentations, board minutes, and representations by business executives conducted during interviews and the like before the investment community. Of course, documents filed with regulatory officials such as annual reports, 10-Ks, and documents filed with respect to stock offerings (initial, secondary, etc.) may also be of value.

Other Marketing Documents

In addition to so-called high-level marketing plans, other marketing documents can be an important source of information to the investigating economist. One such document is a 'brand plan'. This is a marketing document that focuses on a specific brand, such as a particular brand of cheese (Kraft) or soap (Ivory) or some other consumer product. It likely contains some objective data concerning the brand (sales, prices, etc.), discusses particular competitive rivals and particular competitive strategies, and contains some detail concerning upcoming promotional activities.

These documents, along with others, may well be instructive as to which products may be considered 'close' substitutes in a highly differentiated industry and, as a result, be relevant to a consideration of product market definition or likely competitive effects associated with the merger of two brands (taking into consideration, of course, all the admonitions discussed above). For example, in a recent acquisition, plan after plan for a particular branded product failed to discuss or even identify as competitively relevant the acquisition target. These documents were consistent with other evidence (price analysis, usage studies, etc.) that suggested the two brands were not in direct and substantial competition.

Other internal marketing documents informative on issues related to market definition, both product and geographic, and competitive effects, would include those documents that relate to the determination of price. These documents are usually prepared by or for brand managers or other similar executives. Documents such as these may well discuss, for example, which particular brands are taken into account when price changes are considered or whether a particular firm in a geographic area is considered as having some influence over price in a different geographic area.

Documents such as 'call reports' or 'sales activity' reports can also be informative on market definition. These documents are generally prepared by sales representatives in the 'field' which call on customers and generally contain anecdotal information concerning which firms are particularly aggressive on price or adopting a new promotional program or are just providing some form of specialized competition. Related documents would include so-called 'meeting competition documents' that are prepared to justify certain price discounting activity for particular customers. Such documents will generally identify the reason the discount is being proposed, including the identification of which firm is offering the competitive price. Comparative advertising or promotional programs can also be informative on such issues.

Usage Studies and Switching Analyses

Another potentially useful set of internal corporate documents, particularly in consumer product industries, are documents and data related to consumer buying patterns. Various third-party vendors (including Nielsen and IRI) assemble large 'panels' of consumers and then track the buying patterns of these consumers on a continuous basis. These data sets — if properly prepared and maintained — can be a very useful set of facts when analyzing the level of competition between particular products. They would allow for an analysis of which products are being consumed at particular points in time or on particular occasions (and relative amounts). These data may also allow for the analysis of which products consumers may purchase if their first choice is unavailable. Such 'switching studies' can, not surprisingly, say something important about the competitive interaction of various products (properly taking into consideration, of course, relative prices).

In a recent merger analysis, for example, a series of switching studies were useful in identifying a set of products that interacted with a specific collection of similarly priced products and, conversely, much less with a group of much higher priced but physically similar products. In a similar matter, such documents were quite useful in supporting a finding of significant competitive interaction between branded and private-label or store-brand products.

Other Business Documents

The differing types of other business documents are almost infinite. Some particular documents which the investigating economist might collect include, for example, capital appropriation documents which are used to support investment decisions. These documents may be informative on issues such as determining costs associated with entry, the timing of new entry, and the motivation associated with the building or expansion of additional capacity. In merger matters, so-called 'offering memorandums' may be a source of information. These documents, which must be carefully considered given that they reflect attempts to sell assets, may include information on competitive rivals, price histories, and entry conditions. Documents used in an attempt to obtain debt financing from a lending institution may also contain useful information concerning competitive conditions in general and the particular strengths or weakness of a competitor, or future prospects for a firm or industry. Actual sales contracts and other transactional data (invoices, etc.) may also be relevant depending on the issues involved in a particular investigation.[10]

Electronic Transmissions

The emergence of electronic communication has opened up another area of possible useful information for the investigating economist. For example, certain documents prepared historically on a 'paper' basis may, in the future, be communicated by e-mail or certain data may be transmitted in this fashion. The increasing relevance of such documents is memorialized in the 'form' Second Request provided by the Federal Trade Commission and Department of Justice to the public. This document was prepared to provide guidance to firms that might become involved in a merger that required government investigation associated with possible competitive implications. It includes the following request for documents:

> The term 'documents' includes electronic correspondence and drafts of documents, copies of documents that are not identical duplicates of the originals, and copies of documents the originals of which are not in the possession, custody or control of the company. The term 'computer files' includes information stored in, or accessible through, computer or other information retrieval systems. Thus, the company should produce documents that exist in machine-readable form, including documents stored in personal computers, portable computers, workstations, minicomputers, mainframes, servers, backup disks and tapes, archive disks and tapes, and other forms of off-line storage, whether on or off company premises. Electronic mail messages should also be provided, even if only available on backup or archive tapes or disks.

The usefulness of many such electronic communications to the investigating economist depends on a number of issues, including who authored the communication, what was the intended message, and who received it, among many others.

Summary

As discussed above, an economist must be careful when evaluating the substantive significance of contemporary business documents. They are, nevertheless, a rich source of potentially useful market facts. Indeed, in certain circumstances, they can be critically important and even outcome determinative of at least certain issues. In a recent matter involving allegations of price fixing and market allocation among a group of firms, literally hundreds of documents memorialized meetings between the competitors and agreements reached to exclude competitive rivals. The message to the investigating economist: be careful when evaluating the implications of business documents, but do not overlook the obvious.

THE INTERVIEWING PROCESS

In addition to business documents, much can be learned from interviewing the relevant business representatives in an attempt to better appreciate a whole host of issues, including market definition, business strategies, entry conditions, and so forth. Such interviews are useful at almost all stages of the economist's investigation, including at the beginning (to better discipline the collection of relevant information), after documents have been reviewed (to better appreciate the contents of the documents), and after tentative conclusions have been reached (to engage in certain 'market reality' testing). Of course, the importance of information gained in these interviews must be considered in light of other relevant facts gathered during the investigation.

Other potential candidates for interviews include, among others, customers, competitors, distributors, retired employees, and other industry observers (consultants, brokers, etc.). In fact, depending on the industry in question, so-called third-party interviews may well be an extremely important source of information. For example, I have analyzed mergers in industries where the relevant products consisted of frozen soup sold to food service accounts and coated vegetables sold to eating establishments. In both matters available market facts were scarce. Industry consultants, however, were extremely helpful in identifying a list of competitive firms, explaining the nature of competitive interaction between firms and products, and testing the competitive implications of the proposed transactions.

Again, relying exclusively on the views of a particular third party can also be misleading. In a recent commercial dispute, an expert based her entire estimate of potential lost sales on an interview with a particular consultant. When that consultant was interviewed, however, it was discovered that he knew little about the market in general, was basically 'guessing' at the figures at issue, and could provide few details concerning the estimates he did provide.

OTHER SOURCES

There are a large number of other possible sources of relevant market information. For example, numerous articles in the trade press or technical journals may exist which discuss the industry at issue. Informative trade press involving products such as haircare products sold to professional salons, rice cakes, soybean processing, asphalt pavers, sponges, syringes, and rechargeable batteries, among many other examples, do exist. Such literature can be useful in identifying new competitors, new products, and new technologies. For instance, one publication does nothing but detail new product introductions on a monthly basis and has such information going back over a large number of years. Various books may also exist addressing the industry at issue.

Investment brokers (Value Line) generate reports on firms and industries that may be useful, as does Moody's and Standard & Poors. Trade associations may generate fact books and provide other sources of relevant information. Trade association libraries, in fact, can be a useful stop as may various 'think tanks' (Heritage, Brookings, etc.) Material generated in Congressional reviews can also be helpful, including reports and testimony. And, of course, various government agencies (state and federal) may produce not only data but a collection of reports and analyses that may be useful. In the health care field, states generally collect and make available to the public a great deal of information concerning the number of hospitals in operation, the number of beds in use at these hospitals, where the hospital draws patients from (relevant to geographic market definition), and the number of specific procedures performed at a particular hospital.[11]

Other relevant materials can include something as simple as a newspaper. In one matter, an individual claimed that certain 'unfair' competitive practices had denied him certain job opportunities. The local newspaper identified numerous such opportunities, however, and interviews confirmed that this individual could have successfully pursued many. For many consumer products, a trip to the grocery store or Wal-Mart can be quite informative in terms of identifying competitors and collecting price information. For other products, trade shows can be a useful source of market information.

DISCOVERY MATERIALS

Another important area to investigate are materials produced during discovery between the parties, if the matter is in active litigation. Possibly relevant materials include depositions, interrogatory responses, responses to requests for admissions, various pleadings (complaint, motions, etc.), and the documents produced by the parties. In addition, previous litigation may have generated certain facts that could be of use to the investigating economist.

CONCLUSION

In every antitrust matter, much of the significant time involved is in locating and reviewing the necessary facts. As indicated above, diligence is required at almost every step of this process. Once discovered, even more time can be involved in returning again and again to review the significance of the gathered facts. I trust that the thoughts expressed in this paper will provide some discipline to this process and at least serve as a beginning on where to look for the facts necessary to reach an informed opinion.

NOTES

1. Brooke Group Ltd v. Brown & Williamson Tobacco Corp., 113 S. Ct. 2578, 2598 (1993).
2. Id.
3. Many other firms market similar data. In the oil industry, for example, Lundberg offers price and volume data and NPD provides market share information. In the health care field, IMS markets various forms of data — including price data — for the sale of various products, including pharmaceuticals.
4. Three-stage least squares (35LS) or seemingly unrelated regression (SUR) analysis may be used to estimate a system of demand equations. See Greene (1993).
5. For a further discussion of competition in the car-

bonated soft drink industry, see Tollison, Kaplan and Higgins (1990).

6. CSD residual demand was also estimated with logged quantity as the dependent variable. This model fit equally well as the model in inverse form. With one exception, the regressor coefficients are statistically significant, and their signs are identical. In the direct specification, the seasonal dummy variable also has a statistically significant coefficient. The residual demand elasticity estimate was −4.78.
7. The residual demand model whose estimates are reported in Table 2 was specified in several alternative ways to include different explanatory factors. Various combinations of the variables reported in Table 1 and several other input price variables were alternatively included as regressors. The other variables include monthly Producer Price Indices for (1) high-fructose corn syrups; (2) beer bottles; (3) the monthly agriculture price of oranges; (4) the monthly auction price of tea; and (5) the average weekly earnings of beer distribution workers. The estimated residual demand elasticity ranged from −5.6 to −7.6 in these alternative specifications.
8. This analysis is part of a larger report prepared jointly with Richard Higgins.
9. Even this document was of questionable significance because many of the so-called facts contained in the document were inconsistent with other objective and undisputed information.
10. Something as simple as a checkbook or invoice can be informative. For example, in a matter involving allegations concerning diversion of product outside an exclusive distribution system and related questions of 'free riding', one party claimed it had not participated in certain product shipments at issue. A review of available checkbooks and related invoices, however, allowed for the recreation of the relevant purchase and sale activity which, upon review, clearly involved this particular firm.
11. State agencies may also retain bid documents submitted by firms bidding on state-related business that may be relevant when analyzing allegations of bid-rigging and market allocation between firms.

REFERENCES

W. H. Greene (1993). *Economic Analysis*, 2nd edn, Englewood Cliffs, NJ: Prentice Hall, pp. 486–510.

R. Tollison, D. P. Kaplan and R. Higgins (1990). *Concentration and Competition: Competition in the Carbonated Soft Drink Industry*, Boston, MA: Lexington Books.

10
Market Share and Market Power in Merger and Monopolization Cases

Duncan Cameron and Mark Glick

Capital Economics and University of Utah, USA

In light of the growing sophistication of the tools of industrial organization economics and reliance on the federal courts to resolve complicated competitive issues, it may be time for the courts to make greater use of economists in analyzing antitrust cases. While the costs of such an endeavor remain unexplored, we argue below that the benefits may be significant. In particular, we assert that the legal precedent requiring the courts to draw inferences about market power based primarily or exclusively on market shares and/or market concentration[1] can often be misleading. However, the only alternative to such judge-made bright-line rules is to utilize modern economic tools to undertake more extensive competitive analyses. The latter choice is essentially the course that the antitrust enforcement agencies are following. This article explores some of the arguments in favor of such an approach.

In the first section of this paper we explain how the essential legal elements of a monopolization claim under Section 2 of the Sherman Act[2] and an illegal merger under Section 7 of the Clayton Act[3] require that the courts draw strong inferences from market share information. We then explain in the second section how, under the 1992 Department of Justice and Federal Trade Commission Horizontal Merger Guidelines (the 'Merger Guidelines'),[4] more meaningful reliance is placed on a competitive effects inquiry which in practice relies heavily on economic analysis. Market share or concentration is used solely as a screening device to identify situations that warrant further analysis. The third section of this paper exposes the underlying economic justification for courts drawing competitive inferences from market share data. In this section we also show how the simple judicial treatment based on market share fails to distinguish among situations that differ significantly in terms of competitive outcomes. We conclude that the only viable avenue in which to improve judicial accuracy in antitrust cases is to expand the use of economic tools to undertake more extensive factually specific competitive effects analyses, as is done at the enforcement agencies. Revamping the present judicial tests is not a viable option.

MARKET SHARE AND MARKET POWER IN MERGER AND MONOPOLIZATION CASES

The federal courts have developed an analysis of mergers (Clayton Act Section 7) and monopolization (Sherman Act Section 2) that structurally connects market performance with market structure through inferences from market shares. In monopolization cases, for example, a two step process is employed.[5] In the first step, the court defines the products and firms that comprise the relevant product and geographic markets. If the defendant's market share is above some threshold (usually above 70%), then monopoly power is assumed.[6] Many courts have taken the position that a 50% market share is a 'prerequisite for a finding of monopoly.'[7] The second step examines whether any anticompetitive conduct exists. This is important to avoid the prosecution of companies who have garnered large market shares from 'superior product, business acumen, or historic accident'.[8] In merger cases under Section 7 of the Clayton Act the inquiry is similar. However, in a merger the issue is not the anticompetitive use of market power but rather the possibility that the merger enhances or entrenches market power. As a result of this difference, courts in merger cases have employed only a one-step test that relies on inferences drawn from post-merger market shares in the relevant market to infer the likelihood of future market power from the merger.[9] For example, in *United States v. Philadelphia National Bank*,[10] the Supreme Court held that a post-merger market share of 48.8% was sufficient in itself to establish prima facie illegality of the merger. That decision clearly established that post-merger market shares are to be judicially considered to be an accurate proxy for appraising the dangers of increasing market power through horizontal merger. Not only was the market share threshold for a finding of market power lower for merger cases than for monopolization cases, but in situations where a trend of increased concentration was identified, post-merger shares of as low as 7.5% have been declared illegal.[11] However, unlike monopolization cases, in merger cases the courts allow defendants a limited ability to rebut the presumption of market power derived from large market shares.[12] In any event, in both merger and monopolization cases, the courts have relied, nearly exclusively, on inferences of market power drawn from market shares in the relevant product and geographic markets.[13]

THE MERGER GUIDELINES

The Merger Guidelines promulgated by the Department of Justice and the Federal Trade Commission[14] take a much different approach to analyzing market power in merger cases than do the courts.[15] Market power is not presumed from market shares or market concentration. Under the Merger Guidelines, market concentration analysis (using the HHI) acts only as a screening device to filter out cases that require no further competitive analysis. No inference is made that large market shares, as reflected in concentration statistics, necessarily mean that market power exists. Instead, the real competitive analysis takes place using the elaborate 'competitive effects' section of the Merger Guidelines that assesses the probability that a merger will either result in anticompetitive coordinated (collusion) or unilateral effects in the future.[16] In practice, the enforcement agencies utilize the significant economic talent represented at the agencies to analyze the likely competitive impact of each merger taking account of the specific economic and factual environment of the industry.[17]

Indeed, one author of the Merger Guidelines has stated forthrightly that the Merger Guidelines, 'use of market delineation as the first step of a largely structural analysis was compelled by case law precedent', (see Werden 1993). Since the enforcement agencies' ultimate ability to prevent anticompetitive mergers is derived from its ability to win lawsuits in the federal courts, effective merger control requires that some significant role be reserved for a market definition and market share-based structural analysis.

Thus, the Merger Guidelines approach can be viewed as a compromise of sorts between court precedent and the preference of many economists that market delineation be relegated to a secondary status or even abandoned.[18] In fact, there are many situations in which market analysis is simply redundant of the more important competitive effects analysis. For example, a merger involving next best substitutes in a differentiated product market, in which competition is primarily 'localized', may not require precise market delineation and market share measurement for an analysis of market power. In such circumstances, the mandatory concentration calculation merely acts as an administrative screen.

COSTS OF DRAWING STRONG INFERENCES FROM MARKET SHARE

The question of whether courts should reduce their reliance on market share and concentration measures to infer market power in monopolization and merger cases is a difficult one. Market share analysis is simple and easy to administer. To abandon such reliance would require a much-expanded use of economic tools and reasoning in legal proceedings. Although a more thorough analysis would be costly, the current state of theoretical and empirical economics reveals that much inaccuracy can result from drawing strong conclusions from market concentration data. In the following sections we discuss the economic reasoning underlying the relationship between market share and market power, and illustrate how limited the relationship is.

Assumptions Underlying the Court's Analysis

A variety of models of economic behavior suggest a relationship between market share and market power. Consider three common types of models used in Industrial Organization: the dominant firm model, the collusive cartel model and non-cooperative oligopoly models (See Carlton and Perloff, 1990, Part 4).

The dominant firm in a market is a firm that can profitably raise price above competitive levels because output expansion by 'competitive fringe' firms is not sufficient to make the price increase unprofitable. In this model, the competitive fringe firms do not cooperate with the dominant firm, but nonetheless benefit from the increase in price. More formally, the elasticity of demand facing the dominant firm is directly related to the overall demand elasticity and the supply elasticity of the competitive fringe as follows:

$$\eta_{\mathrm{df}} = \frac{\eta}{S_{\mathrm{df}}} - \frac{1 - S_{\mathrm{df}}}{S_{\mathrm{df}}}\epsilon_{\mathrm{cf}} \tag{1}$$

where η_{df} and S_{df} are the demand elasticity facing the dominant firm and the market share of the dominant firm, η is the elasticity of demand facing the market, and ϵ_{cf} is the supply elasticity of the competitive fringe. The optimal markup of price over competitive price (equal to marginal cost) for the dominant firm is described by

$$\frac{P_{\mathrm{df}} - P_{\mathrm{c}}}{P_{\mathrm{df}}} = \frac{1}{\eta_{\mathrm{df}}} \tag{2}$$

Combining Eqns (1) and (2) yields the following expression relating markups over competitive prices to market elasticity of demand, market share of the dominant firm and supply elasticity of the competitive fringe:

$$\frac{P_{\mathrm{df}} - P_{\mathrm{c}}}{P_{\mathrm{df}}} = \left(\frac{\eta}{S_{\mathrm{df}}} - \frac{1 - S_{\mathrm{df}}}{S_{\mathrm{df}}}\epsilon_{\mathrm{cf}}\right)^{-1} \tag{3}$$

Equation (3) provides a direct relationship between market performance, in terms of markups, and market share. Higher market share of the dominant firm would, *ceteris paribus*, lead to a higher markup over competitive price levels.[19] However, it is also clear that another important determinant of market power of the dominant firm is the supply elasticity of the competitive fringe; high values of supply elasticity can eliminate market power of the dominant firm, whatever the dominant firm's share and the elasticity of demand for the product.

The importance of market share (or industry concentration) is also an element of models of collusive or coordinated cartel behavior. In such models, the costs of detecting and punishing cheating on a collusive agreement are presumed to increase as concentration falls.[20] Other important considerations involve the ability to reach an agreement that is mutually beneficial to the group, the efficiency of mechanisms to detect and punish cheating, and the legal treatment of collusion. Thus, in the standard models the more concentrated the industry the more likely, *ceteris paribus*, is anticompetitive collusive activity.

A relationship between market share and performance can be derived as well from non-cooperative models. Such models generally yield a relationship between concentration and pricing performance. For example, consider the general 'conjectural variation' representation of a firm's price–cost margin (percentage markup over marginal cost):

$$\frac{P - P_{\mathrm{c}}}{P} = \frac{1 + v_i}{\eta} S_i \tag{4}$$

where

$$v_i = \sum_{j \neq i} \frac{\partial q_j}{\partial q_i}$$

is firm i's conjectural variation; i.e. firm i's assessment of the output response of all other firms in the industry to a change in firm i's output.[21] Clearly, it can be gleaned from Eqn (4) that the value of v_i is of critical importance. Perfect competition corresponds to $v_i = -1$, in which case there would be no markup over marginal cost. The case where $v_i = 0$ corresponds to the Cournot assumption; that other firms will not respond to changes in output by firm i. As we shall see, the Cournot assumption plays a special role in antitrust analysis.

Market share enters into all of these standard models in such a way that, *ceteris paribus*, greater concentration will generally be associated with reduced market performance.[22] This is a basis for the courts' inferences about market performance derived from market structure. But in real-world situations in which courts must make decisions, the assumptions underlying these models are generally not applicable.

Even the simple models discussed above reveal that market share is, at best, only an imperfect proxy for market power. Other factors play critical roles. In collusive models, the ability and costs of detecting and punishing cheating and the gains from colluding will differ across industries. In dominant firm and oligopoly models, the ability and incentives of competing firms to react to price increases, either by entering or expanding output, are crucial to the outcome. Firms with high market shares may have little or no market power if price increases resulted in extensive entry or output expansion by competitors. Similarly, firms with small shares may have considerable market power when competitors are unable to respond to price increases.

The models discussed above are highly stylized. In such models, firms are assumed to compete only in the market in question, compete according to constant and highly restrictive assumptions regarding their reactions to competitors actions, etc. But even these highly stylized models of competitive interaction require that conclusions regarding market power derived from market concentration be treated with care.

Consider the well-known relationship between the HHI measure of concentration and industry sales weighted price–cost margins in the Cournot model of oligopoly. Weighting the optimal markup expression for an individual firm, given above, by that firm's sales share produces:

$$S_i \frac{P - P_c}{P} = \frac{S_i}{\eta} S_i = \frac{S_i^2}{\eta} \tag{5}$$

The above relationship, summed over all firms in the market, produces the HHI:

$$\sum_{i=1}^{n} S_i \frac{P - P_c}{P} = \sum_{i=1}^{n} \frac{S_i^2}{\eta} = \frac{\text{HHI}}{\eta} \tag{6}$$

This relationship is sometimes posited as a justification for the heavy reliance on a measure of concentration to summarize industry performance, where performance is measured by price–cost margins. Several problems immediately arise. First, although the Cournot assumption results in a neat relationship between price–cost margins and HHI, Cournot is only one of many possible assumptions regarding firm interaction.[23] Many, but not all, other models of oligopoly interaction also imply a relationship between performance and concentration. However, which model applies in a particular case is itself an important subject of analysis. Therefore, the Cournot assumption can be interpreted only as a convenient benchmark or starting point, but not a determination that firms are expected to interact in the Cournot manner. This interpretation supports the Merger Guidelines approach of using the HHI only as a screening device to identify situations in which further analysis should be pursued.

In addition, the relationship between performance and the HHI is parameterized by η, the elasticity of demand. This means that for every value of η there will exist a distinct relationship between performance and HHI. One of the most important achievements of the Merger Guidelines approach was to standardize questions of market power by using a 5% price increase test to define markets. That is, antitrust markets are constructed such that the elasticity of demand is roughly the same across markets. The result is that markets are defined so that HHI's will be comparable.[24] This simplification allows us to represent the relationship in a more familiar form:

$$\eta \sum_{i=1}^{n} S_i \frac{P - P_c}{P} = \text{HHI} \tag{7}$$

Finally, the above formulation assumes that the optimal output of firms is informed only by each firm's sales and costs in that market; i.e. each firm's incentive to raise price depends solely on profitability in the market in question. If this is not true, the simple relationship between the Eqn (7) HHI and performance, described above, will no longer hold.

The following section demonstrates the effect of relaxing the assumption that firms participate only in the market in question by deriving 'modified' HHIs that are comparable to the Eqn (7) HHI. The modifications required to produce a comparable market share-based analysis illustrates the potential errors associated with drawing inferences solely from market shares, as well as the type of other facts that must be considered.

Modifying the HHI to Account for Interrelated Markets

The relationship between the HHI and industry performance discussed above is derived from the individual firm's profit-maximization condition in which each firm competes only in the market in question and the individual firms play Cournot. We now allow the firms to also have interests in related markets, and derive modified HHIs that are comparable in the sense that like values of the HHI correspond to like price–cost margin performance in the candidate market. This exercise illustrates, in a few simple cases, the type of analysis that would be required if meaningful conclusions had to be drawn from market share data alone in such situations.

Complementary Products

Consider first the situation in which a producer of product X also is a producer of complementary product Y, and we are interested in drawing inferences about market power in the market for X. Complementarity means that increased sales of X also increase demand for Y, and vice versa. For example, a manufacturer of computer hardware and software finds that increased sales of hardware increase demand for software, and increased software sales increase demand for hardware.

A seller of both X and Y will realize less of a benefit (in terms of overall profitability) from an increase in the price of X than would a seller of only X. We can modify the standard HHI for an n firm industry to account for these altered incentives as follows:

$$\eta \sum_{i=1}^{n} \left(S_{xi} \frac{P_x - c'_x}{P_x} \right) = \mathrm{HHI} + \left(\frac{Y}{X} \frac{\partial P_y}{\partial P_x} \bigg|_{y=y_0} \right) \sum_{i=1}^{n} (S_{xi} S_{yi}) \tag{8}$$

where HHI represents the usual HHI for market X, X and Y are total industry sales of X and Y, S_{xi} and S_{yi} represent firm i's shares of total output of X and Y, respectively, and $\partial P_y/\partial P_x$ (quantity of Y held constant) measures the relative response of changes in the prices of X and Y elicited by a change in the quantity of X produced.

Equation (8) is the usual HHI plus the cross-product of complementary product selling firms' shares of sales of each of the complementary products weighted by the relative sizes of Y and X industries and an expression relating changes in product prices to changes in X output. Since an increase in X production reduces the price of X but increases demand for complement Y, the sign of the weighting factor is negative, and Eqn (8) is a reduction from the usual HHI. Equation (8) is a concentration measure where complementary goods are at issue that is comparable to the normal case in the sense that like values of the concentration measure (HHI) correspond to like values of performance (measured in terms of markups over cost).

Equation (8) illustrates a fundamental principle. Because increased sales of a product increase demand for its complements, a firm producing complementary products has more of an incentive to sell each complement that would a firm that did not participate in the sale of both products. Therefore, the comparable modified HHI for a market in which some firms also sell complementary products is *less* than the normal HHI to account for increased incentives to sell output.

Vertical Integration

Consider now a situation where firms produce both X and Y, and where X is used as an input in the production of Y. In this case, X and Y are vertically related, and a firm that produces both is said to be vertically integrated. A firm could be self-sufficient (produce X to use only in its own production of Y), be a net seller of X (produce more X than it uses internally), or be a net buyer of X (produce less X than it uses in production of Y). The significance for incentives is that a producer of X that also produces Y will consider how his or her production of X will affect the market price of Y. By producing more X, lower market prices for X are 'passed on', resulting in lower prices for Y. Also, the integrated firm will not necessarily recognize the market price for X as the relevant marginal cost of the input.

Assuming that the market for Y is competitive and that firms that produce X hold Cournot conjectures, we can derive the following modified HHI when all production of X is included in the market.[25]

$$\eta \sum_{i=1}^{n} \left(S_{xi} \frac{P_x - c'_x}{P_x} \right) = \text{HHI} - \left(1 - \frac{\partial P_y}{\partial P_x} \right) \sum_{i=1}^{n} (S_{xi} S_{yi}) \tag{9}$$

Thus the comparable HHI for a market with this type of vertically integrated firms is the usual HHI plus the cross-product of each firms shares in the upstream and downstream markets, weighted by the amount by which higher prices of X result in higher prices of Y, less 1.

Equation (9) illustrates a fundamental principle. Since the pass-on of higher (lower) X prices into higher (lower) Y prices is less than one, this means that the resulting HHI is *less* than the normal HHI. In general, vertically integrated firms have increased incentives to produce output (when markets are less than perfectly competitive) relative to non-integrated firms. Therefore, the HHI modified to capture this effect is reduced relative to the normal HHI.

The modified HHIs described in the above analysis produce concentration statistics in the complementary products or partially integrated producer settings that are comparable, in the sales weighted price–cost margins sense when firms play Cournot, to the standard case HHI. This exercise is meant to illustrate that the measurement of concentration, especially when used to draw important conclusions, is more than a perfunctory exercise based on historical sales if gross inaccuracies are to be avoided. Such examples illustrate that, in many situations where firms compete in more than one market, simple rules just will not suffice. Accordingly, direct analysis of competitive effects utilizing economic tools may be more economical than modifying the traditional market share rules to increase accuracy.

Derived Demands

Derived demand is another common situation in which the Courts' simple rules cannot even be used. Consider as an example the demand for televised professional football games. Television networks buy rights to televise games from the National Football League, and in turn sell rights to advertise during the televised games. Television networks are, in effect, reselling an audience of pro-football viewers to advertisers who value access to this audience, say sellers of beer and of power tools. In this sense, the demand for televised games is derived from the demand for audiences that in turn demand beer and power tools.

What is the relevant antitrust market? The antitrust market must include all the constraints on a profitable increase in the price of rights to televise games. Obviously, a threshold inquiry would be whether other sports, such as college football, would be viable substitutes to the network by attracting demographically similar audiences. However, identifying the next best substitute may not be obvious. Networks may find that the next most profitable substitute is non-sports programming that provides a different audience appealing to different advertisers. For example, networks may find the best alternate use of the time slot is showing soap operas, appealing to audiences that buy cosmetics. It seems odd to include college football and programming that appeals to cosmetics buyers in the same relevant market, but this set of alternatives may best capture the constraints on an exercise of market power by the National Football League. Construction of market 'shares' that meaningfully capture these competitive constraints is, at best, problematic.

The lesson is that market shares, as implemented by the courts, will have difficulty summarizing important competitive constraints. In the case of derived demand, delineation of a market, a 'necessary predicate' to antitrust analysis, and construction of meaningful shares from which to draw conclusions will be problematic. Since the Merger Guidelines approach uses market definition and market shares only as a 'screen' for further analysis, the agencies may get to the right result in spite of the market delineation detour. For example, assume that we determined that a monopolist of professional and college football would not find it profitable to raise prices by 5%, due to network substitution away from sports audience marketing to selling other types of audiences to advertisers. Accordingly, we can conclude that there should be no competitive concerns even though shares in a hypothetical market for professional and college football telecasts are high, and we have failed to delineate the full boundaries of a market in which professional and college football compete.

Differentiated Products

When products differ in their characteristics, and consumers differ in their preferences for these characteristics, some products will compete more closely than others. This situation poses serious challenges for market share-based analyses. First, it will be difficult to usefully discern the boundaries of the relevant market. As stated by the court analyzing competition among brands of ready-to-eat breakfast cereals, 'In a differentiated product market such as the [ready-to-eat] cereal market, the decision whether to include a product in the market is inevitably somewhat arbitrary, because not all products in a relevant market compete equally with all other products. In such a market, any market definition is likely to exclude some products that are reasonable substitutes for products that are included in the market.'[26]

Second, when competition is 'localized' due to differentiation, market shares may indicate little about the degree of competition among products. For example, consider a market for automobiles in which the two best-selling products are a minivan and a sports car. While the minivan appeals most strongly to practical buyers, the sports car appeals primarily to buyers not motivated by practical concerns. It is likely that the best-selling minivan competes most closely with other minivans, while the sports car competes primarily with other sports models. Therefore, the degree of competition between the two best-selling models would be limited; the best-selling minivan is primarily constrained by the price and features of other minivans (even if their market share is low), and similarly for sports models.

Professor Willig has shown that when consumer preferences are structured to satisfy Luce's Choice axiom[27] market shares can be reliable indicators of competitive interaction among brands, and market share analysis will yield useful results. This assumption essentially means that the probability that a consumer views a particular product as a next best substitute for any other product can be inferred solely from market share. However, as the example above makes clear, this assumption is very restrictive. As stated by Willig, 'The value in [the exercise] for present purposes is to carefully expose the substantive content of the underlying assumptions. We shall see that the assumptions are unlikely to be valid in many areas of application where specific information can be developed about product characteristics and about consumer preferences for them. For such applications, merger analysis that focuses exclusively on market shares is likely to go awry' (Willig, 1991).

Thus, in the common case of competition among differentiated products, market share analysis is unlikely to produce useful results. In such cases, the most useful analysis involves discerning the pattern and degree of substitution among products and characteristics using the tools of economic analysis.

CONCLUSION

On the issue of the usefulness of judicial rules drawing inferences about market power based on market shares, economic theory affirms in part and dissents in part. On the affirming side, a variety of economic models imply that greater concentration, *ceteris paribus*, will be associated with reduced performance. On the dissenting side, inspection of these models reveals that concentration is only one of many factors relevant to competitive performance. Thus, the judicially approved rules of thumb based on market shares are very crude tools for drawing inferences about market power. Improving the analysis requires an inquiry into a variety of economic factors; the variety of competitive interaction, the ability and incentives of firms to expand output, entry and exit conditions and the effect of firm's participation in related markets on their incentives to compete in the market in question. Thus, we conclude that judicial accuracy in antitrust cases requires greater use of economic tools to directly analyze the competitive effects of mergers and monopolization. This is the avenue the enforcement agencies are currently taking. The Courts may find that it is an example worth following.

NOTES

1. Market concentration refers to a summary of the distribution of sales shares among firms in the industry. The Herfindahl–Hirshmann Index (HHI)

is one such measure of concentration, and is used in the Merger Guidelines by the Department of Justice Antitrust Division and the Federal Trade Commission. The HHI is the sum of the squares of the individual firm's market shares. The HHI is sensitive to the number of firms in the market as well as the distribution of sales among firms.

2. 15 USC Section 2.
3. 15 USC Section 18.
4. 57 Fed. Reg., 41554-55 (September 10 1992).
5. See *United States v. Grinnell Corp.*, 384 US 563, 570 (1966) (the 'offense of monopoly power under Section 2 ... has two elements: (1) possession of monopoly power in the relevant market, and (2) the willful acquisition or maintenance of that power ...').
6. Illustrative Supreme Court cases include: *Otter Tail Power Co. v. United States*, 410 US 366 (1973) (91% market share); *International Boxing Club of New York, Inc. v. United States*, 358 US 242 (1959) (81% market share); *United States v. American Tobacco Co.*, 221 US 106 (1911) (86% market share); *United States v. United Shoe Machinery Corp.*, 347 US 521 (1954) (75% market share); *Standard Oil Co. v. United States*, 221 US 1 (1911) (90% market share); See also *Hiland Dairy Inc. v. Kroger Co.*, 402 F.2d 968, 974 n.6 (8th Cir. 1968) (collecting cases).
7. *Cliff Food Stores, Inc. v. Kroger, Inc.*, 417 F.2d 203, 207 n.2 (5th Cir. 1969).
8. 384 US at 571.
9. The Supreme Court has clearly said that the market definition procedure in merger and monopolization cases must be the same. *Id.*at 573.
10. 374 US 321 (1963).
11. See *United States v. Vons Grocery Co.*, 384 US 270 (1966).
12. See *United States v. General Dynamics Corp.*, 415 US 486 (1974) (market power presumption rebutted by depleting reserves); *United States v. Waste Management, Inc.*, 743 F.2d 476 (2nd Cir. 1984) (market power presumption rebutted by evidence of entry); *FTC v. Elders Grain, Inc.*, 868 F2d 901 (7th Cir. 1989) (market power presumption rebutted by evidence of sophisticated buyers.)
13. One exception is *Broadway Delivery Corp. v. United Parcel Serv.*, 651 F.2d 122, 128 (2nd Cir. 1981) ('the true significance of market share data can be determined only after careful analysis of the particular market').
14. 57 Fed. Reg., 41554-55 (September 10 1992).
15. Obviously, the Merger Guidelines are designed to analyze only mergers, and not monopolization cases.
16. See Denis (1992) (... 'it instructs both government enforcers and the merging firms to tell a story about why the merger will or will not have adverse effects').
17. The Department of Justice and the Federal Trade Commission together employ upwards of 100 economists.
18. E.g., see Fisher (1987) (market definition 'is an artificial construction created by antitrust litigation').
19. We are adopting the convention that performance is measured by the size of the percentage price distortion, or deviation, of the dominant firm's price from the competitive price.
20. See Stigler (1964); Aspremont and Gabszewicz (1986); and Jacquemin and Slade (1989). However, Andrew Dick finds that export cartels formed under the Webb–Pomerene Export Act of 1918 were more likely to successfully form in industries characterized by *low* concentration among sellers. Professor Dick explains that this seemingly anomalous result is consistent with a model in which cartels form to minimize transactions costs. See Dick (this issue pp. 203–216).
21. The term, v_i, is best thought of as a parameter measuring competitiveness of the industry. This heuristic interpretation sidesteps a fundamental flaw of the conjectural variation approach, which attempts to combine static concepts in a dynamic setting. See Shapiro (1989).
22. This is true where performance is measured by price–cost margins. However, price cost margins may not be good measures of industry performance. For example, industry output may be a better measure of total welfare. It can be shown that under some conditions price–cost margins, and industry concentration as measured by the HHI, can increase even as industry output increases. See Farrell and Shapiro (1990).
23. There are several desirable features of the Cournot model, despite its restrictive and unrealistic assumptions regarding behavior. First, Cournot is the prototype for the concept of Nash equilibrium. Second, because Cournot is a single-period Nash equilibrium, Cournot behavior is consistent with equilibrium behavior in a repeat game setting. Finally, it has been shown that some two-stage models of investment followed by competition in prices result in Cournot outcomes. See Kreps and Scheinkman (1983).
24. See Willig (1991). However, HHIs will not be strictly comparable across markets because competitive margins differ across industries and it will not generally be possible to define markets such that the optimal monopoly price increase is exactly 5%.
25. The market could have been defined to exclude internally used production of X. In that case, an analogous derivation of a modified HHI can be developed. See Cameron and Reiffen (forthcoming).
26. *New York v. Kraft General Foods Inc.*, Civ. 0811, United States District Court for the Southern District of New York, 1995 US Dist. LEXIS 2145, at 38.
27. A structure of random preferences is said to satisfy Luce's Choice Axiom if the ratio of the probabilities that i and j respectively are chosen from the

set of alternatives S is invariant to the membership of S. A convenient demand system with this property is the logit.

REFERENCES

Aspremont and Gabszewicz (1986). On the stability of collusion. In *New Developments in the Analysis of Market Structure* (edited by Stiglitz and Mathewson), Cambridge, MA: MIT Press.

Cameron and Reiffen (forthcoming). Merger analysis with captive capacity: a suggested approach. *Research in Law and Economics*.

Carlton and Perloff (1989). *Modern Industrial Organization*, New York: Scott, Foresman/Little, Brown.

Denis (1992). Practical approaches: an insider's look at the new horizontal merger guidelines. *Antitrust*, **6**, No. 3 Summer.

Farrell and Shapiro (1990). Horizontal mergers: an equilibrium analysis. *American Economic Review*, March.

Fisher (1987). Horizontal mergers: triage and treatment. *J. Econ. Perspectives*, **1**, 23, 27.

Jacquemin and Slade (1989). Cartels, collusion and horizontal merger. In *The Handbook of Industrial Organization* (edited by Schmalansee and Willig), Amsterdam: North-Holland.

Kreps and Scheinkmam (1983). Quantity pre commitment and Bertrand competition yield Cournot outcomes. *Bell Journal of Economics*, **14**, 326–37.

Shapiro (1989). Theories of oligopoly behavior. In *The Handbook of Industrial Organization* (edited by Schmalansee and Willig), Amsterdam: North-Holland.

Stigler (1986). A theory of oligopoly. *Journal of Political Economy*, **LXXII**, No. 1, February.

Werden (1993). Market delineation under the Merger Guidelines: a tenth anniversary retrospective. *Antitrust Bulletin*, **38**, 517, 521.

Willig (1991). Merger analysis, industrial organization theory and Merger Guidelines. *Brookings Papers on Economic Activity — Microeconomics*, 281–332.

11

Measuring Market Power When the Firm Has Power in the Input and Output Markets

Keith N. Hylton

Boston University School of Law, USA

and

Mark Lasser

Honigman, Miller, Schwartz and Cohn, Detroit, MI, USA

INTRODUCTION

We examine the problem of measuring market power when the firm has monopoly power in the output market and monopsony power in the input market—a case we refer to as 'dual-market' power. We show how the Lerner index, which measures the mark-up over marginal cost,[1] can be modified to reflect the firm's ability to set price above the competitive level.

The derivation of the Lerner index is straightforward—the sort of exercise an economics professor might give a first-year graduate student. However, the implications of the new index are broad. Moreover, the case of dual-market power seems as an empirical matter worthy of attention. Though the one-company mining town has been offered, traditionally, as the classic example of a monopsonized labor market (see Boal, 1995),[2] several empirical studies have suggested that monopsonies may exist in many labor markets (Katz and Krueger, 1992 (fast food); Sullivan, 1989 (nurses); Scully, 1974 (baseball players)). Further, if some workers skills are industry-specific, then the possibility arises that competition among employees within relevant labor markets will be imperfect. If this describes a broad range of industries, then the market power index derived here could provide some guidance to enforcement agencies.

The implications are as follows:

(1) If we define market power as *the power to set price above the competitive level*, then the standard Lerner index—and any assessment which fails to take input market power into account—may understate market power. Market power should be carefully assessed in cases in which competition is imperfect in both output and input markets.

(2) The sources of market power are diverse—all the factors giving rise to power in the output market (e.g. differentiation) have their analogues in the input market. Further, the nature of competition in an imperfectly competitive market influences the measure of market power. Since competition in both the output and input market matters, assessment of market power in imperfectly competitive markets can be quite complex.

(3) An aggregate market power index based on the new measure suggests that a simple comparison of pre- and post-merger Herfindahl–Hirschman Indexes overstates the increase in monopoly power that results from a merger of rival firms. An instantaneous power index based on the new measure suggests that the bias that results from using the standard Lerner index in a market in which price and output are determined intertemporally is smaller than suggested in the Pindyk (1985) analysis.

(4) The analysis suggests that, in the absence of an efficiency justification, extension of monopoly power through leverage is welfare-reducing. In other words, society should not be indifferent to the manner in which a monopolist exploits its monopoly power.

(5) Counterintuitive effects of price regulation, minimum wage laws, and unionization may be observed in the presence of dual-market power.

Putting a ceiling on output prices may lead to an increase in wages and expansion of employment. Putting a floor on wages may cause a reduction in output prices and expansion of output. Unionization of employees in an industry may lead to a reduction in output prices.

MEASURING MARKET POWER: THE 'DUAL-MARKET' CASE

Derivation of Market Power Index

In this section, we derive the Lerner index in the case in which the firm has monopoly power in the output market and monopsony power in the input market. Recall that when the firm has monopoly power in the output market (facing a competitive input market), the Lerner index is given by

$$L_1 = \frac{p - MC}{p} = \frac{1}{e_d} \tag{1}$$

where MC is the firm's marginal cost, p is the product price, and e_d is the elasticity of demand for the product produced by the firm.[3] It is generally understood that because marginal cost at the monopoly output level is smaller than if measured at the competitive output level, the Lerner index overstates the degree to which the monopolist's price exceeds the competitive level.

Assume the firm uses the production function $q = f(l)$, where q is output and l is the single input (labor). The demand curve is $p = p(q)$, and the labor supply curve is given by $w = w(l)$. Profit maximization implies the first-order condition:

$$\left[p + \left(\frac{dp}{dq}\right)q\right]\frac{df}{dl} = w + \left(\frac{dw}{dl}\right)l \tag{2}$$

or equivalently

$$p\left(1 - \frac{1}{e_d}\right)MP_l - w\left(1 + \frac{1}{e_1}\right) \tag{3}$$

where MP_l is the marginal product of labor evaluated at the firm's optimum output and e_d is the elasticity of labor supply. We can rewrite the first-order condition as

$$p\left(1 - \frac{1}{e_d}\right) = MC'\left(1 + \frac{1}{e_l}\right) \tag{4}$$

where $MC' = w/MP_l$. If the firm did not have monopsony power (e_l approaches infinity), Eqn (4) would be the standard marginal-revenue-equals-marginal-cost condition, where MC' would be equal to the firm's marginal cost at the profit maximizing level of output (see e.g. Intriligator, 1971).[4] We will use MC' to approximate the firm's marginal cost at the profit-maximizing output level under the assumption the firm does not have monopsony power. This is an approximation, of course, because if the firm did not have monopsony power its output would be larger than the level suggested by Eqn (4). However, if the marginal cost curve is relatively flat between the monopoly-no-monopsony and monopoly-plus-monopsony output levels, this approximation will be close.[4]

Rearranging Eqn (4), it is easy to show that an alternative measure of market power can be expressed as follows:

$$L_2 = \frac{p - MC'}{p} = \frac{(e_d + e_l)}{e_d(e_l + 1)} \tag{5}$$

We focus on L_2 as the relevant measure of market power. Although the firm's marginal cost is given by the right-hand side of Eqn (4), that would be an inappropriate measure of the potential of a competitive market. For in a competitive market, the firm would have neither monopoly nor monopsony power. Thus, although L_2 is not a measure of percentage mark-up over marginal cost, it is appropriate to consider it a measure of percentage mark-up over the competitive price.

As e_l approaches infinity, L_2 approaches the standard measure $1/e_d$. As e_d approaches infinity, L_2 approaches $1/(e_1 + 1) > 0$; thus, because of the firm's power in the input market, the percentage mark-up over the competitive price remains positive even though e_d is infinite.

As long as e_d and e_l are positive, $1/e_d < (e_d + e_l)/[e_d(e_l + 1)] < 1$ and $1/(e_l + 1) < (e_d + e_l)/[e_d(e_1 + 1)]$. Thus, the percentage mark-up over the competitive price is greater for the firm with dual-market power than for the firm with power in only the output market or the firm with power in only the input market.

Suppose a firm has market power in both the output and input markets. When would an increase in input market power have the greatest impact on the firm's ability to set price above the competitive level? This is equivalent, of course, to asking when consideration of dual-market power is most likely to substantially alter a market power assessment based on the output market alone. Differentiating L_2 with respect to e_l, we have $\partial L_2/\partial e_1 = (1 - e_d)/[e_d(e_i + 1)^2]$, which is negative, given that the point-elasticity of demand is greater than one at the firm's optimum. Let e_d approach infinity, so that the firm becomes weaker in the output market. Then in the limit $\partial L_2/\partial e_i = -1(e_i + 1)^2$, which is greater than $(1 - e_d)/[e_d(e_l + 1)^2]$ (given, again, that the point elasticity of demand is greater than one at the firm's optimum. This implies that the firm's ability to set price above the competitive level is enhanced most, by a slight increase in input market power, when the firm is weak in the output market. In other words, the 'power gradient' in the input market declines as the firm gains power in the output market. It is easy to show that the power gradient in the output market declines as the firm gains power in the input market. *Thus, consideration of dual-market power is most likely to substantially alter an assessment of market power based solely on the output market when the firm is relatively weak in the output market.*

Determinants of Power

Here, following Landes and Posner (1981) (and Encaoua and Jacquemin, 1980), we examine the determinants of market power in the dual-market power setting, and provide a simple numerical illustration of the importance of dual-market power. Table 1 shows the six variables that are used below to assess a firm's monopoly and monopsony power.

Table 1

e_{dm}	Market elasticity of demand for the product
e_{si}	Elasticity of supply of competing or fringe firms
M	Dominant seller's market share
e_{sm}	Market elasticity of supply for the input market
e_f	Elasticity of demand of fringe buyers for inputs
S	Dominant buyer's market share
e_{di}	Elasticity of demand for the product of the dominant seller

Landes and Posner (1981) show that

$$\frac{1}{e_{di}} = \frac{M}{[e_{dm} + e_{si}(1 - M)]} \tag{6}$$

The relationship is important because it shows that market power is a function of market share, demand-side substitution, and supply-side substitution. Further, as Landes and Posner note, the relationship suggests that the particular market chosen should not greatly affect the assessment of the firm's power. The reason is as follows. Consider the choice between two markets, one narrow, the other broad. In the narrow market, the firm's market share will seem large. However, because the market is narrow, demand-side substitution will be greater, implying a larger elasticity of market demand. Similarly, there will be more opportunities for producers of substitutes to compete in the narrow market, so supply-side substitution will be greater implying a larger elasticity of fringe supply. Thus, if one chooses a narrow market, the large market share measure will be offset by large elasticity measures. Conversely, if one chooses a broad market, the narrow market share measure will be offset to some extent by small elasticity measures.

Blair and Harrison (1992) derive a formula, similar to that of Landes and Posner, that can be applied to the input market:

$$\frac{1}{e_{li}} = \frac{S}{[e_{sm} - e_f(1 - S)]} \tag{7}$$

Below, we present the results of a simple numerical simulation of the L_2 index. The simulation assumes the following: (1) $e_{si} = 0$, (2) $e_f = 0$, (3) $[e_{dm} + e_{si}(1 - M)] > M$ (or, in this case, $e_{dm} > M$). Note that the third assumption follows from the fact that a monopolist will always produce where the elasticity of demand for his product exceeds one.

In Table 2, we consider three cases; low, medium, and high monopoly power. The L_2 index is calculated under these assumptions. The table shows that the level of monopsony power a firm possesses in each of these cases significantly alters a firm's dual market power measure. For example, in the 'low monopoly power, high buying power' case we see that the firm's mark-up over the competitive price is 68%. This suggests that a researcher could vastly understate a firm's effective market power by focusing solely on the output market.

Table 2. The Effect of Input Power on Overall Market Power

	No buying power	Low buying power $S = 0.1; e_{sm} = 2$	High buying power $S = 0.9; e_{sm} = 0.5$
Low monopoly $M = 0.2; e_{dm} = 2$	0.1	0.14	0.68
Medium monopoly $M = 0.5; e_{dm} = 1.5$	0.33	0.37	0.76
High monopoly $M = 0.9; e_{dm} = 1$	0.9	0.905	0.96

Note that as we move in the direction of greater power in one market, the greatest increases in effective market power are observed in those cases in which the firm starts with little power in its relevant markets. Consider the case in which the firm has low power in both the input and output markets. If we increase the firm's power in the input market slightly, Table 2 indicates that L_2 increases substantially. The move from 'low monopoly, no buying power' to 'low monopoly, low buying power' in Table 2 results in a 40% increase in the firm's mark-up over the competitive price. The increase from 'low monopoly, no buying power' to 'low monopoly, high buying power' is close to 600%. The market power gradient is substantially lower if we start with a firm with high monopoly power and no input market power, and consider the increase in effective power that is registered as we assume the firm gains additional market power in the input market.

Oligopolistic Interdependence

Following Ordover, Sykes, and Willig (1982), it is straightforward to extend the market power measure to the case in which firms anticipate the actions of rivals. Suppose there are two firms, so that price is now determined by $p = p(q_1, q_2)$. Wage is determined by $w = w(l_1, l_2)$. Let total quantity be $q = q_1 + q_2$, and let total labor be $l = l_1 + l_2$. Assume prices are affected by changes in total quantity only, so that $\partial p/\partial q_1 = \partial p \partial q_2 = \partial p/\partial q$, and $\partial w/\partial l_1 - \partial w/\partial l_2 = \partial w/\partial l$. The marginal revenue resulting from an expansion of output by firm 1 is

$$p\left[1 - \left(\frac{1}{e_{d1}}\right)(1 + k_1)\right] \tag{8}$$

where $1/e_{d1} = -(\partial p/\partial q_1)q_1$, and where k_1 is the familiar conjectural variation of the Cournot duopoly model. Alternatively Eqn (6) can be expressed as

$$p\left[1 - \left(\frac{1}{e_d}\right)(1 + k_1)(m_1)\right] \tag{9}$$

where $m_1 = q_1/q$. The marginal factor cost of an additional unit of l is given by

$$w\left[1 + \left(\frac{1}{e_{l1}}\right)(1 + h_1)\right] \tag{10}$$

where h_1 is the conjectural variation in the input market

$$w\left[1 + \left(\frac{1}{e_l}\right)(1 + h_1)s_1\right] \tag{11}$$

where $s_1 = l_1/l$. It follows that the new Lerner index is

$$L_3 = \frac{[e_{l1}(1 + k_1) + e_{d1}(1 + h_1)]}{[e_{d1}(e_{l1} + 1 + h_1)]} \tag{12}$$

Alternatively, the index can be expressed as

$$L_3 = \frac{\left[\frac{e_i}{s_1}(1 + k_1) + \frac{e_d}{m_1}(1 + h_1)\right]}{\left[\frac{e_d}{m_1}\left(\frac{e_i}{s_1} + 1 + h_1\right)\right]} \tag{13}$$

We will focus on expression (10), since it is simpler. Note that if $k_1 = h_1 = 0$ (firm's act independently, or Cournot–Nash competition), this simplifies to L_2. If $h_1 = -1$ (and $-1 < k_1 < 1$) the firm anticipates that its reductions in hiring in the labor market will be offset by expansions by the competing firm (aggressive competition). In this case, L_3 simplifies to $(1 + k_1)/e_{d1}$, which is the Ordover, Sykes, and Willig formula. Thus, if the firm anticipates aggressive competition in the input market, then even though the number of rivals in the input market is small, its power to raise price above the competitive level will be the same as that of a firm that has monopoly power in the output market and hires labor in a perfectly competitive labor market. Obviously, if $h_1 = k_1 = -1$, the mark-up over the competitive price is zero, which implies the firm has effectively no market power.

If $k_1 = -1$ and $-1 < h_1 < -1$, so that the firm anticipates aggressive competition only in the output market, the index becomes $(1 + h_1)/(e_{l1} + 1 + h_1)$. Thus, even though the firm anticipates aggressive competition in the output market, its mark-up over the competitive price remains positive. In the extreme case in which it anticipates aggressive competition in the output market and perfect parallelism in the input market ($h_1 = 1$), the mark up over the competitive price is $2/(e_{l1} + 2)$, so that as the point-elasticity of labor supply (to firm 1) approaches zero, the firm's mark up over competitive price approaches 100%.

If $h_1 = k_1 = 1$ (pure parallelism), the ratio of L_3 to L_2 is $2(e_{l1} + 1)/(e_{l1} + 2)$, so that as labor supply elasticity measured at the firm's output increases, the extent to which L_2 understates the firm's effective monopoly power approaches 100%.

Table 3, which shows the Lerner index under different assumptions on the competitive interaction, summarizes this discussion. As you move toward the right in any row, or toward the bottom of any column, the power to raise price above the competitive level increases.

Aggregation Issues

Previous analyses have noted that the standard Lerner index fails in some respects to capture the impact of monopoly pricing on consumers, and have suggested methods of aggregating the index across firms (Encaoua and Jacquemin, 1980) or across time periods (Pindyck, 1985). In this section, we consider the implications of the new index for the aggregation results of these studies.

1. Oligopoly Under the assumption of Cournot–Nash competition, Encaoua and Jacquemin show that a weighted sum of the Lerner index for each firm, using market share as weights, can be expressed as

$$L_a = \sum_{i=1}^{N} m_i\left(\frac{1}{e_{di}}\right) = \sum_{i=1}^{N} m_i\left(\frac{m_i}{e_d}\right) \tag{14}$$

or equivalently

$$L_a = \left(\sum_{i=1}^{N} m_i^2\right)\left(\frac{1}{e_d}\right) \tag{15}$$

Note that $\sum m_i^2$ is the Herfindahl-Hirschman Index (HHI) of concentration. Thus L_a, which is an aggregate measure of monopoly power, is the product of the HHI and Lerner indexes. Using the new market power index, L_2, the across-firm aggregation index can be expressed as follows:

$$L_{a2} = \frac{1}{e_d}\sum_{i=1}^{N} m_i^2 \frac{\left(\dfrac{e_d}{m_i} + \dfrac{e_l}{s_i}\right)}{\left(\dfrac{e_l}{s_i} + 1\right)} \tag{16}$$

The relationship between L_{a2} and L_a can be summarized by the following two propositions.

Table 3

		Output market		
		$k_1 = -1$	$-1 < k_1 < 1$	$k_1 = 1$
Input market	$h_1 = -1$	0	$\dfrac{1 + k_1}{e_{d1}}$	$\dfrac{2}{e_{d1}}$
	$-1 < h_1 < 1$	$\dfrac{(1 + h_1)}{(e_{l1} + 1 + h_1)}$	$\dfrac{e_{l1}(1 + k_1) + e_{d1}(1 + h_1)}{e_{d1}(e_{l1} + 1 + h_1)}$	$\dfrac{2e_{l1} + e_{d1}(1 + h_1)}{e_{d1}(e_{l1}(e_{l1} + 1 + h_1)}$
	$h_1 = 1$	$\dfrac{2}{(2 + e_{l1})}$	$\dfrac{e_{l1}(1 + k_1) + 2e_{d1}}{e_{d1}(2 + e_{l1})}$	$\dfrac{2(e_{l1} + e_{d1})}{e_{d1}(2 + e_{l1})}$

Proposition 1: $L_{a2} > L_a$.

Proof: The difference between the two indices can be expressed as

$$L_a - L_{a2} = \frac{1}{e_d} \sum_{i=1}^{N} \left\{ m_i^2 \left[1 - \frac{\left(\frac{e_d}{m_i} + \frac{e_l}{s_i} \right)}{\left(\frac{e_l}{s_i} + 1 \right)} \right] \right\} \tag{17}$$

Thus, it is sufficient to demonstrate that $e_d/m_i > 1$ for each i. This holds because $e_d/m_i = e_{di} > 1$ in the monopoly pricing equilibrium. □

Proposition 2: As the number of firms declines as a result of mergers, L_{a2} increases more slowly than does L_a.

Proof: To capture the effects of mergers on market shares, let each m_i be a nonincreasing function of N and strictly decreasing in N for at least one m_i. Differentiating L_{a2} and L_a with respect to N, it is straightforward to show that both indices decline as N increases. However, the effect of a change in m_i is smaller in the expression of L_{a2} because it is multiplied by the term $(e_d/m_i + e_l/s_i)/(e_l/s_i + 1)$, which is less than 1 in equilibrium. In addition, the term $(e_d/m_i + e_l/s_i)/(e_l/s_i + 1)$ increases as N increases, further dampening the effect of an increase in N on L_{a2}. □

Consider the special case in which market shares are equal, so that $m_1 = m_2 = \cdots = 1/N$, and $s_1 = s_2 = \cdots = 1/N$, the aggregation index is

$$\left(\frac{1}{N} \right) \left(\frac{e_d + e_l}{\left(e_l + \frac{1}{N} \right) e_d} \right) \tag{18}$$

which, like the index derived by Encaoua and Jacquemin, can be described as the product of the Herfindahl–Hirschman and Lerner indexes.

2. Variation over Time Periods Pindyck (1985) makes the important point that in a multiple period setting, the standard Lerner index is inappropriate as a measure of monopoly power. For example, in the case of a monopolist exploiting an exhaustible resource, the standard Lerner index incorrectly measures monopoly power because it relies on an inappropriate measure of marginal cost. Pindyck proposes a measure based on 'full marginal cost', which includes a measure of marginal 'user cost', which is 'the sum of discounted future costs or benefits that result from current production decisions' (Pindyck, 1985, p. 197). For example, in the case of an exhaustible resource, the user cost is the per-period marginal rental cost of the stock the monopolist exploits.

In the case of an exhaustible resource, Pindyck shows user cost is positive, so that the standard Lerner index, by failing to take user cost into account, overstates monopoly power. However, in the case in which costs fall over time (learning curve effect), user cost is negative, which implies that the standard Lerner index overstates monopoly power.

Following Pindyck, let $\lambda_{c,m}(t)$ be the measure of user cost. The subscripts denote the fact that user cost is measured under the assumption that the firm is a price taker, and evaluated at the monopoly output level. $\lambda_{c,m}(t)$ is positive in the exhaustible resource case, and negative in the learning curve example. Pindyck's instantaneous Lerner index can be expressed as

$$L^*(t) = 1 - \left(\frac{e_d - 1}{e_d} \right) \left(\frac{1 + \lambda_{c,m}(t)}{MC} \right) \tag{19}$$

In this model, the instantaneous Lerner index is

$$L^*(t) = 1 - \left(\frac{e_l(e_d - 1)}{e_d(e_l + 1)} \right) \left(\frac{1 + \lambda_{c,m}(t)}{MC} \right) \tag{20}$$

As Eqn (18) demonstrates, consideration of dual-market power dampens the impact of user costs on the instantaneous measure of market power. The intuition for this should be clear in the case of an exhaustible resource. Inclusion of user cost implies a reduction in the firm's market power measure. Inclusion of dual-market power offsets this reduction to some extent. Hence, the bias that results from using the standard Lerner measure, L_1, rather than the instantaneous measure is not as severe in the dual-market power setting.

IMPLICATIONS

Antitrust Law

The results presented here have implications for antitrust law and the practices of enforcement agencies. We consider those implications here.

1. Sherman Act It has been clear for some time that collusive monopsonies violate section 1 of the Sherman Act.[5] This is true, regardless of the market shares possessed by the defendants.

The interesting question suggested by this analysis is whether section 2 doctrine gives appropriate consideration to the dual market power problem—i.e. of simultaneous monopolization and monopsonization. The case law is scant, but the little that is there suggests that it does not. In *Beef Industry v. Iowa Beef Processors*,[6] sellers of feed cattle brought monopsonization and monopolization claims against beef packers, alleging that the defendants conspired to depress cattle prices. Although the facts indicated that four major packers shared the meat packing market, the court dismissed the monopsonization claim on the ground that a cartel among packers would probably be too unstable for the packers to have monopsony power.[7]

The implication of this analysis is that dual-market power may allow the firm to earn monopoly projects even though it would not be deemed a monopolist on the basis of the traditional examination of market share and other factors (e.g. demand-side substitution). To require proof of monopoly power or monopsony power under traditional criteria, in these cases, would result in instances in which a defendant that had effectively attained monopoly power was immune from suit under section 2 because its market shares were too small in the relevant input and output markets. The analysis here suggests that some relaxation of the traditional criteria for determining monopoly power seems appropriate in this case.

2. Merger Guidelines The most obvious set of implications are for the market power measurement algorithm set forth in the 1992 Department of Justice and Federal Trade Commission Horizontal Merger Guidelines. The Guidelines do note that monopsony power is an important consideration, and that the agency's measurement algorithm should be applied in an analogous manner to measure monopsony power.[8] The Guidelines also note the importance of demand- and supply-side substitution possibilities in assessing a firm's market power. However, the Guidelines do not adequately consider the problem of modifying a market power assessment to take dual-market power into account.

One approach to taking power in both input and output markets into account would be to use the aggregation index proposed by Encaoua and Jacquemin, L_a. Suppose, for example, that one is examining the market power implications of a merger. If one examines both input and output markets using the L_a index, this would essentially involve comparing Herfindahl–Hirschman Indices (HHIs) for both markets. However, the new index, L_{a2}, indicates that a comparison of HHIs would be inappropriate. Because of the enhancement effect of simultaneous power in both markets, a comparison of HHIs would understate market power. A better approach would rely on calculating the pre- and post-merger levels of L_{a2}. Numerical thresholds would have to be developed for this new measure.

Consider an industry in which there are ten firms with equal shares. Suppose each firm merges with one another, producing an industry with five firms, again with equal shares. The Encaoua and Jacquemin index pre-merger is $L_a(10) = 1/10e_d$, where $1/10$ is the HHI. Post-merger the Encaoua and Jacquemin index is $L_a = 1/5e_d$, where $1/5$ is the HHI. The ratio of the pre- and post-merger measures is 2, which is the same as the ratio of the pre- and post-merger HHIs. However, pre-merger, $L_{a2}(10) = (e_d + e_l)/(10e_d + 1)e_d$ and post-merger $L_{a2}(5) = (e_d + e_l)/(5e_d + 1)e_d$. The ratio of pre- and post-merger power indices ranges between 1 and 2 in this case, reaching 2 only in the limiting case in which labor supply is infinitely elastic. This suggests that comparison of pre- and post-merger HHIs overstates the increase in monopoly power resulting from a merger when firms have simultaneous power in both input and output markets.

3. Standing Employees are generally denied standing except in the cases where the employee's job is a 'commercial enterprise'[9] or when the employee's firm and its rivals are colluding with respect to wages.[10] The analysis of this paper suggests that input market power should be taken into account in an analysis of standing.

The reason is as follows. Suppose a firm that already has monopsony power gains monopoly power in its output market. Then the acquisition of monopoly power will result in a downward shift in the monopolist's labor demand curve (compared to the demand curve under competition), which implies a reduction in employment and the equilibrium wage. Compare this to the case in which the firm faces a competitive labor market. In this case, acquisition of monopoly power in the output market will result, again, in a downward shift in the demand for labor, which will reduce total employment in the industry. However, the downward demand shift will not affect the equilibrium wage, given the assumption that the employer is a price-taker in the labor market. This comparison suggests that the employees of a monopsonist, or a firm with monopsony power, have a substantially higher likelihood of suffering an injury (specifically, decline in wages) as the result of the firm's acquisition of monopoly power.[11] The argument applies generally to all input providers who claim to have been injured as the result of a purchaser's acquisition of monopoly or monopsony power.

4. Boycott Doctrine In *Northwest Wholesale Stationers v. Pacific Stationery & Printing Co.*, 472 US 283 (1985), the Supreme Court held that *per se* analysis applies to a boycotting consortium only when the consortium has market power or exclusive access to an essential facility. The market power threshold works as a filter that excludes *per se* claims when the likelihood of public harm, resulting from an increase in market price and reduction in total quantity, is small. However, consideration of dual-market power suggests that there may be instances in which the consortium has a relatively small share of the relevant output market, but the consortium as a whole has monopsony power in the input market. In this instance, public harm may indeed result from the consortium's exclusion of a rival. The harm may result if exclusion of the rival facilitates collusion in the input market.

5. Leveraging Monopoly Power The new Lerner index, L_2, has implications for the 'leverage' debate in the antitrust literature (Kaplow, 1985). A firm leverages its monopoly power when it uses its monopoly power in one market to gain a competitive advantage in a separate market. The Supreme Court held in *United States v. Griffith*, 334 US 100 (1948), that leveraging is a form of abuse of monopoly power that could result in a finding of a violation of the Sherman Act. Some antitrust commentators, however, have argued that society should be indifferent as to the various contractual arrangements a monopolist may choose in order to increase its power (Bowman, 1957).

The new Lerner index suggests that a firm with market power may have an incentive to leverage its market power in order to increase its ability to set price above the competitive level. This would be profitable to the firm if it could structure an arrangement in which it forgoes full exploitation of its monopoly power in one market in order to gain monopoly power in a separate market. Consider the case in which the firm forgoes full exploitation in the input market in exchange for additional market power in the output market. Since this is equivalent to accepting an increase in the elasticity of supply in the input market in exchange for a reduction in the elasticity of demand in the output market, one could use L_2 to see when such an exchange would be profitable to the firm. It is straightforward to show that the firm would exchange a small increase in the elasticity of supply of labor for a small reduction in the elasticity of demand for its output when:[12]

$$-e_d(1 - e_d) < (1 + e_l)e_l \tag{21}$$

The question whether society should be indifferent to this type of exchange is also answered by this analysis. If leveraging market power really does permit the firm to increase the mark-up over the competitive price, then it necessarily follows that society's welfare is reduced.

Price Regulation

The foregoing analysis has implications for the effects of price regulation. First, consider minimum wage laws. Suppose the firm has monopsony power in the labor market and monopsony power in the labor market. It is well known that in the case of monopsony, a minimum wage, set at the appropriate level, could enhance efficiency. Taking output market power into account suggests an additional way in which a minimum wage statute could enhance efficiency; by reducing the marginal factor cost of labor (at the firm's optimum output level), the statute would lead to a reduction in the monopolist's price, enhancing the welfare of the monopolist's consumers.

Second, consider direct regulation of the monopolist/monopsonist's output price. If the regulated output price exceeds $p(1 - 1/e_d)$ (evaluated at the firm's optimum), the marginal revenue of the monopolist *increases*, leading the firm to expand hiring in its monopsonized labor market.

Of course, it would be difficult for a government to find the right wage floor or price ceiling to bring about the results just described. If the costs of error and of encouraging rent-seeking legislation were brought into this analysis, these suggestions of the possible benefits of price regulation would have to be weighed against substantial costs.

CONCLUSION

We have provided a measure of market power when the firm has monopoly power in the output market and monopsony power in the input market. The derivation of the measure is quite simple. The main contribution of the new measure is its implication that the measure of market power is enhanced substantially by considering power in both input and output markets. The enhancement effect is greatest when the firm's market power is relatively low in either the input market alone or the output market alone.

NOTES

1. See Lerner (1934) for the original presentation.
2. We should note that Boal (1995) examines the one-company mining town case and rejects the monopsony power hypothesis.
3. Since the firm is a monopolist, it makes no difference whether we refer to this as the elasticity of demand for the firm's product or the market elasticity of demand. It is well known that the index actually overstates the extent to which price exceeds the competitive level, because the firm's marginal cost, evaluated at the monopoly output level, will be below marginal cost evaluated at the competitive output level (see e.g. Landes and Posner, 1981, p. 941).
4. And even if the marginal cost curve is not relatively flat in this range, the use of MC' would only slightly exaggerate the overstatement of monopoly power already associated with the Lerner index.
5. *Mandeville Island Farms v. American Crystal Sugar Co.*, 334 US 219 (1948).
6. *In re Beef Industry Litigation*, 907 F.2d 510, 516 (5th Cir. 1990).
7. *Beef Processors*, at 515.
8. Horizontal Merger Guidelines, Issued by the US Department of Justice and the Federal Trade Commission, 2 April 1992, Section O.1.
9. See e.g. *Reibert v. Atlantic Richfield Co.*, 471 F.2d 727, 728 (10th Cir. 1973).
10. *Radovich v. NFL*, 352 US 445, 446 (1957); *Wilson v. Ringsby Truck Lines*, 320 F. Supp. 699 (D. Colo. 1970).
11. In theory, the employees who lose their jobs as the result of the demand shift should also have standing. Their injury is a direct result of their previous employer's monopolization. However, courts generally deny standing to these plaintiffs, on the theory that their injury is too remote or indirect to merit standing under the Sherman Act, see e.g. *Sharp v. United Airlines*, 967 F. 2d 404, 405–6 (10th Cir. 1992).
12. Differentiating L_2 with respect to e_l yields Eqn (8). Differentiating L_2 with respect to e_d yields $-e_e(e_l+1)/[e_d^2(e_l+1)^2]$. $|\partial L_2/\partial e_l| < |\partial L_2/\partial e_d|$ when the condition in Eqn (20) holds.

REFERENCES

R. D. Blair and J. L. Harrison (1992). Cooperative buying, monopsony power, and antitrust policy. *Nw. U. L. Rev.*, **86**, 331.

W. M. Boal (1995). Testing for employer monopsony in turn-of-the-century coal mining. *RAND J. Econ*, **26**, 519, Autumn.

W. S. Bowman, Jr (1957). Tying arrangements and the leverage problem. *Yale L. J.*, **67**, 19.

D. Encaoua and A. Jacquemin (1980). Degree of monopoly, indices of concentration and threat of entry. *International Economic Review*, **21**, 87–105, February.

M. D. Intriligator (1971). *Mathematical Optimization and Economic Theory*, Englewood Cliffs, NJ: Prentice Hall.

L. Kaplow (1985). Extension of monopoly power through leverage. *Columbia L. Rev.*, **85**, 515.

L. F. Katz and A. B. Krueger (1992). The effects of minimum wage on the fast-food industry. *Indus. and Labor. Relations Review*, **46**, 6–21.

W. M. Landes and R. A. Posner (1981). Market power in antitrust cases. *Harvard L. Rev.*, **94**, 937.

A. P. Lerner (1934). The concept of monopoly, and the measurement of monopoly power. *Rev. Econ. Stud.*, **1**, 157.

J. A. Ordover, A. O. Sykes, and R. D. Willig (1982). Market power with interfirm rivalry. *Harv. L. Rev.*, **95**, 1857.

R. S. Pindyck (1985). The measurement of monopoly power in dynamic markets. *J. Law and Economics*, **28**, April, 193–222.

G. W. Scully (1974). Pay and performance in major league baseball. *American Econ. Review*, **64**, 915–30.

D. Sullivan (1989). Monopsony power in the market for nurses. *Journal of Law & Economics*, **32**, S135–78.

12

The Demsetz Postulate and the Welfare Effects of Mergers in Differentiated Products Industries

Luke M. Froeb

Owen Graduate School of Management, Vanderbilt University, USA

Timothy J. Tardiff

National Economic Research Associates, Cambridge, Massachusetts, USA

and

Gregory J. Werden

Antitrust Division, US Department of Justice, USA

This paper examines the welfare effects of mergers in industries characterized by the 'Demsetz Postulate', which holds that larger firms grew because of cost and product advantages over rivals. In such industries, mergers may enhance welfare because they induce shifts in production from small- or medium-sized merging firms, to larger *non-merging* firms, which have lower costs and produce superior products. Although this result is quite general, it is demonstrated in the context of Bertrand competition and logit demand. In addition, simulations of mergers among Japanese long-distance carriers predict that mergers not involving the dominant carrier would enhance welfare. The simulations are based on a demand parameter estimated from the results of a survey of Japanese residential customers.

INTRODUCTION

The conventional view (see American Bar Association, 1986, pp. 225–27; Williamson, 1968) has been that the potential efficiencies from horizontal mergers stem from the realization of economies of scale and from the transfer of superior technology, managerial skill, or other resources from one merging firm to the other. We consider a different source of efficiency—the shifting of output among firms in the industry, that results from a merger. Efficiencies from this source arise in industries characterized by what we will term the 'Demsetz Postulate'.

The Demsetz Postulate was put forward two decades ago in the long-running debate about the relationship between industrial concentration and economic welfare. Demsetz (1973) and Peltzman (1977) suggested that the direction of causality may run not just from concentration to welfare. Rather, some firms may become large, and thereby generate concentration, because they hit upon production techniques or product designs that are both superior to those of rivals and also firm-specific to some degree, so rivals cannot completely copy them. The reason some firms do better than others may be that their managers have superior insight, or that they are just lucky.[1]

We address the efficiency effects of mergers in industries that evolved along the lines Demsetz suggested. We posit a static, noncooperative, price-setting oligopoly with differentiated products.[2] Our focus is on logit demand, but the basic results do not depend on that assumption. Since the model is static, it cannot incorporate Demsetz's view of industry evolution; instead, it incorporates the Demsetz Postulate as an equilibrium relationship. The greater a firm's market share in the pre-merger equilibrium, the lower is its marginal cost and the greater is the average intensity of consumer preference for its product. Larger firms are also more profitable than smaller ones, as Demsetz found empirically to be the case.

We analyze the price and welfare effects of mergers under two different assumptions concerning the relationship between mergers and the superiority of larger firms. One assumption is that a firm's marginal-cost advantage is shared with a merger partner. The alternative assumption is that marginal costs are unaffected by merger.[3] Under the latter assumption, mergers always raise prices, but they may still enhance total welfare. That occurs when the welfare gain from shifting output to lower-cost firms with more-preferred products outweighs the welfare loss from higher prices and reduced industry output.[4] Under the former assumption, mergers are even more likely to enhance total welfare, because there may be substantial additional cost savings, and the merged firm may even reduce the price of one of its products.

Welfare gains can arise because a merger causes a shift in production from merging to nonmerging firms. If small or medium-sized firms merge, there is a shift in production to larger firms, which have lower costs and more preferred products, and total welfare may increase as a result. Welfare gains also can arise because a merger causes a shift in production from one merging firm to the other. The merger of a large firm with a smaller firm causes a shift in production from the smaller merging firm to the larger, which has lower costs and more preferred products, and total welfare may increase as a result.

For an industry consisting of firms of roughly the same size, there is so little potential for gain by shifting production that all mergers lessen welfare—even those in relatively unconcentrated industries.[5] For an industry with considerable asymmetry of firm sizes and efficiencies, however, there is a significant potential for gain by shifting production. Considerable asymmetry of firms sizes is likely to entail substantial concentration; thus, mergers in concentrated industries are much more likely to enhance welfare than mergers in unconcentrated industries.

Similar effects arise in Cournot models with homogeneous products (see generally Farrell and Shapiro, 1990; McAfee and Williams, 1992; Werden, 1991b). The literature on Cournot models, however, has not focused on shift of production from the merging firms to nonmerging firms as we do. Moreover, a differentiated-products model better reflects the Demsetz Postulate for several reasons. First, differentiated products are essential to capture asymmetries in consumer preference for the products of the individual firms. Second, Cournot models cannot be said to reflect the implications of the Demsetz Postulate for merger policy with either of the cost assumptions generally made in the literature on mergers in Cournot industries. One common assumption is constant marginal cost, but as Perry and Porter (1985) explain, that makes mergers meaningless in a model with a homogeneous product. The other common assumption is linear marginal cost with firms distinguished strictly on the basis of capital stock. However, the size of a firm's capital stock can easily be imitated, so it cannot be a source of firm superiority consistent with the Demsetz Postulate (see Werden, 1991b, p. 1003). A differentiated products model also has other advantages, including that mergers are privately profitable (see Deneckere and Davidson, 1985).

To explore the practical relevance of the foregoing points, we simulate mergers among existing long-distance carriers in Japan, assuming that demand is characterized by a logit model.[6] We choose a logit specification for three reasons: (1) we rely on estimate of a key demand parameter that was made in the context of a logit model;[7] (2) the logit model has been embraced by antitrust policy makers;[8] and (3) the logit model permits a very parsimonious parameterization.

With the logit model, an industry can be completely characterized by four primitives: two readily observed features of the premerger equilibrium—prices and market shares; and two readily estimated demand parameters—one reflecting the aggregate industry elasticity of demand, and one reflecting the cross-elasticities of demand within the industry. The critically important, firm-specific demand and cost parameters are neither easy to observe nor easy to estimate directly, but they can be inferred from the primitives of the model. This inference relies on the assumption that observed prices and market shares are consistent both with logit demand and with noncooperative equilibrium. Thus, before simulating the effects of the Japanese long-distance mergers, we calibrate the model by inferring firm-specific demand and cost parameters from the observed market shares and average prices.

Under both cost assumptions, the simulations predict that all the possible (two-firm) mergers involving the one very large Japanese long-distance carrier would lessen total welfare. All the possible (two-firm) mergers not involving the one very large carrier would enhance total welfare. We also predict the effects of the mergers assuming that the industry is first transformed by equal-access rules, as the US industry was. This transformation reduces the degree of both product and cost asymmetry and thereby tends to make the mergers worse in welfare terms, even though concentration is reduced.

LOGIT OLIGOPOLY[9]

A logit demand system generally is motivated by a random utility model in which consumers make a discrete choice among a set, C, of n alternatives, selecting the alternative yielding the greatest utility. We consider a version of the model that specifies the indirect utility of consumer i associated with the choice of product j as

$$U_{ij} = \alpha_j - \beta p_j + e_{ij} \tag{1}$$

The price coefficient, β, is assumed to be constant for all consumers and products, and all generally perceived quality differences among products are summarized by the α_j's, which can be constants or linear functions of product characteristics. The disturbance term, e_{ij}, represents an individual-specific component of utility that is uncorrelated with price, p_j. If the e_{ij}'s are independently and identically distributed according to the extreme value distribution, the choice probabilities have the familiar logistic form (see McFadden, 1974, pp. 110–12):

$$\pi_j = \exp(\alpha_j - \beta p_j) / \sum_{k \epsilon C} \exp(a_k - \beta p_k) \tag{2}$$

For our purposes, it is more convenient to express the model in traditional antitrust terms. We define product n to reflect the choice of 'none of the above', i.e. to be the outside good, and we assume $p_n \equiv 0$ to make the utility of the outside good a constant. The vector of the remaining prices is denoted $\mathbf{p}$, and the unweighted average pre-merger price for the inside goods is denoted $\bar{p}$. The choice probability for an 'inside good' (i.e. one other than the outside good), conditional on the choice being an inside good, is termed its 'share' and denoted s_j.

Adopting the convention of expressing the own-price elasticity as a positive number, the own-price and cross-price elasticities of demand for particular inside goods, ϵ_j and ϵ_{jk}, are

$$\epsilon_j = \beta p_j (1 - \pi_j) = [\beta \bar{p}(1 - s_j) + \epsilon s_j] p_j / \bar{p} \tag{3}$$

$$\epsilon_{jk} = \beta p_k \pi_k = s_k(\beta \bar{p} - \epsilon) p_k / \bar{p} \tag{4}$$

There is also an implied (positive) 'aggregate elasticity of demand for the inside goods', specifically

$$\epsilon \equiv -[\partial \pi_I(\lambda p)/\partial \lambda][\bar{p}/\pi_I(\mathbf{p})] = \beta \bar{p} \pi_n \tag{5}$$

where $\pi_I(p) \equiv 1 - \pi_n(p)$ is the sum of the choice probabilities for the inside goods, λ is a scalar, and the derivative is evaluated at $\lambda = 1$.

The primitives of the model, which completely characterize an industry, are shares and prices, both of which can be observed, and the parameters, ϵ and β, both of which can be estimated. Roughly speaking, β is the cross-elasticity of demand parameter, controlling the substitutabilities among the inside goods; and ϵ is the aggregate elasticity of demand parameter, controlling the substitutability between the inside goods and the outside good.

Differences among the α_j's are all that matter, and they are unaffected by the arbitrary choice of one of them. Thus, α_n is set equal to an arbitrary constant, and the α_j's for the inside goods are calculated by taking the logs of the ratios of π_j to π_n, substituting, and rearranging. It is easy to show that

$$\alpha_j = \alpha_n + \beta p_j + \ln s_j + \ln(\beta \bar{p}/\epsilon - 1) \tag{6}$$

To complete the model, we assume: each product is initially sold by a single firm; each firm has constant marginal cost, c_j; and there are no fixed costs. We assume that the equilibrium is Nash in prices both pre- and post-merger. We also assume that economies of scale and scope cannot be realized through merger. Finally, we assume that product characteristics other than price are fixed, so that a merger cannot result in any strategic effects other than those involving price. In particular, mergers cannot lead to entry, or to product repositioning by established firms.

Given these assumptions, each of the first-order conditions for profit maximization,

$$p_j - c_j = 1/\beta(1 - \pi_j) = \bar{p}[\beta \bar{p}(1 - s_j) + \epsilon s_j]^{-1} \tag{7}$$

can be solved uniquely, albeit numerically, for the implied value of c_j.[10] With all the demand and cost parameters, it is straightforward to calculate the effects of a merger on prices and shares by solving the post-merger first-order conditions for profit maximization. Anderson and Palma (1992) and Anderson *et al.* (1992, pp. 264–66) have proved the existence and uniqueness of the equilibrium.

In logit models, the welfare effect of a change in any argument of the utility function is calculated as the compensating variation necessary to restore consumers to the original level of utility. Based on the work of Small and Rosen (1981), the change in consumer welfare brought about by changing prices from p^0 to p^1 is given by

$$\left[\ln \sum_j \exp(\alpha_j - \beta p_j^1) - \ln \sum_j \exp(\alpha_j - \beta p_j^0)\right] \beta^{-1} \tag{8}$$

Setting α_n arbitrarily does not affect this measure,[11] but it does preclude the calculation of the total consumer welfare pre- or post-merger. For comparison purposes, we express consumer welfare and total welfare loss (consumer welfare loss minus the increase in industry profits) as a percentage of pre-merger total revenue for inside goods.

Werden and Froeb (1994) analyze mergers in the context of this model, under the assumption that marginal costs are unaffected by merger. They show that a merger causes all firms to increase price, but firms do so in a highly asymmetric fashion. Consequently, a merger leads to a reallocation of output. There is a reallocation of output from the merging firms to the nonmerging firms, because the nonmerging firms raise price less than the merged firm raises the weighted average of its two prices. If the shares of the merged firm's products differ pre-merger, there is a shift in output from the product with the smaller pre-merger share to the product with the larger pre-merger share, because the merged firm raises the price of the former product more than the price of the latter. Either of these effects can cause a merger to produce a net increase in welfare, but that is far more likely with the former. The reason is primarily that a welfare gain from the latter effect requires that the merger involve a large firm, but mergers involving a large firm raise prices more than mergers involving only smaller firms.

A net increase in welfare arises, however, only if there is substantial asymmetry in the industry due to one or a few firms having a substantial advantage over the others, and this is reasonably likely under the Demsetz Postulate. Thus, mergers are more likely to enhance welfare in highly concentrated industries than in unconcentrated industries.[12]

CALCULATED PRICE AND WELFARE EFFECTS OF JAPANESE LONG-DISTANCE-CARRIER MERGERS

The Japanese telecommunications industry resembles in important ways that in the United States before the break-up of AT&T.[13] Nippon Telegraph and Telephone (NTT) is the dominant long-distance carrier, with over 85% of the residential business, and it is the only carrier offering 'dial-1' service. It is also the dominant provider of local service. In parts of the country, three fairly recent entrants also offer residential long-distance service: Daini-Denden Inc. (DDI), Japan Telecom Co. (Telecom), and Teleway Japan Corp. (Teleway).

To calculate the effects of mergers among the Japanese residential long-distance carriers, we need values for the four primitives. NTT's pre-merger price is scaled to equal one and the other carrier's prices scaled to equal 0.9. This price differential is consistent with our information but unimportant.[14] The scaling does not affect the calculations, because β is estimated using the scaled prices, and only $\beta\bar{p}$ matters. Nambu *et al.* (1989, p. 159) estimate the aggregate elasticity of demand to be between 0.61 and 0.63, so we take ϵ to be 0.62.

Pre-merger market shares[15] and the estimate of β are based on a door-to-door survey, conducted by a Japanese survey research firm, of 500 residential customers living in or near three large Japanese cities. Respondents were asked to rank their choices of long-distance carriers. The alternatives differed with respect to price, carrier, and three other variables: length of time required to get new service, measured in weeks (Delay); a dummy variable equal to 1 if the carrier is vertically integrated into local service (Local); and a dummy variable equal to 1 if the carrier has 'dial-1' service (Dial-1).

The use of survey data to estimate β offers two important advantages over the use of data on observed choices. First, price variation specified in surveys is necessarily exogenous, so there is no need to resort to instrumental variables to cope with simultaneous equations bias. Second, the use of surveys avoids the need to extrapolate outside the range of observations, since surveys are designed to

Table 1. Estimated Logit Model

Variable	NTT	DDI	Telecom	Delay	Local	Dial-1	Price	Choice-2	Choice-3
Coefficient	0.923	0.361	0.250	− 0.228	1.330	0.409	9.557	0.685	0.466
Standard error	0.155	0.186	0.145	0.079	0.024	0.142	0.937	0.074	0.074
t-statistic	5.97	1.94	1.73	− 2.88	6.52	2.88	10.20	9.29	6.29

explore choice under conditions, particularly relative prices, outside the range of observations (but within the range of what may arise as a result of mergers).

We use the survey data to estimate an ordered-logit model (see Beggs *et al.*, 1981).[16] The ordered-logit model uses not just information on first choices, but rather the complete ranking of alternatives. A linear combination of the variables other than price constitutes the α_j in the estimated model. The estimated coefficients and their standard errors are reported in Table 1. The three carrier variables reflect the degree of preference of these carriers over the fourth, Teleway. Choice-2 and Choice-3 are decision-weight variables that assign relative importance to lower-ranked choices and correct for heteroskedasticity arising from greater uncertainty about lower-ranked choices (see Hausman and Ruud, 1987). The price coefficient, which we use as the value of β, is 9.56.

Table 2 presents the predicted price and welfare effects for all possible mergers among the carriers, assuming that marginal costs are unaffected by mergers. It employs the following notation:

$\Delta p_j \equiv$ the percentage price increase for firm j

$\Delta p_{Ind} \equiv$ the share-weighted average percentage price increase for the industry

$\Delta CW \equiv$ change in consumer welfare a percentage of pre-merger revenue

$\Delta W \equiv$ change in total welfare as a percentage of pre-merger revenue.

A striking feature of these results is the substantial asymmetry of the price increases between the two merging firms and between the merging and non-merging firms. For the mergers involving NTT, its merger partner increases price more than 10 times as much as NTT, and as much as 289 times. The nonmerging firms increase price by a fraction of the amount that NTT does, and by less than 1% as much in several cases.

Mergers involving NTT reduce total welfare, while mergers not involving NTT enhance total welfare, if only slightly. Mergers not involving NTT enhance total welfare because NTT's very large share implies that it has both lower costs than its rivals and a more preferred product,[17] so the substitution to NTT induced by mergers among its rivals yields a significant welfare gain. As noted above, shifts in production within the merging firms are less likely to cause mergers to enhance welfare than are shifts in production between the merging and nonmerging firms. Thus, it is not surprising that mergers involving NTT lessen total welfare even though they result in an efficient reallocation of production between NTT and its merger partner.

We also consider the possibility that the cost advantages of large firms can be extended through merger. Table 3 presents the calculated price and welfare effects of the mergers under that assumption. A comparison of Table 2 with Table 3 indicates that changing the cost assumption has two principal effects. The price increases by the smaller of the two merging firms are much smaller when the cost advantages of a large firm are extended through merger, and the welfare losses associated with mergers involving NTT are substantially lower. The cost assumption can affect the sign of the net

Table 2. Calculated Price and Welfare Effects of Possible Mergers Assuming that Mergers Do Not Affect Marginal Costs

Merger	Δp_{NTT}	Δp_{DDI}	$\Delta p_{Telecom}$	$\Delta p_{Teleway}$	Δp_{Ind}	ΔCW	ΔW
NTT–DDI	4.87	53.34	0.30	0.03	5.21	− 5.487	− 0.897
NTT–Telecom	2.10	0.24	50.81	0.01	2.16	− 2.365	− 0.323
NTT–Teleway	0.17	0.02	0.01	49.11	0.17	− 0.197	− 0.024
DDI–Telecom	0.33	0.53	1.08	0.00	0.40	− 0.368	0.026
DDI–Teleway	0.03	0.05	0.00	1.04	0.04	− 0.033	0.035
Telecom–Teleway	0.01	0.00	0.04	0.49	0.01	− 0.016	0.017

Table 3. Calculated Price and Welfare Effects of Possible Mergers Assuming the Cost Advantages of Large Firms Can Be Extended Through Merger

Merger	Δp_{NTT}	Δp_{DDI}	$\Delta p_{Telecom}$	$\Delta p_{Teleway}$	Δp_{Ind}	ΔCW	ΔW
NTT–DDI	5.19	16.88	0.30	0.03	5.46	– 5.426	– 0.497
NTT–Telecom	2.25	0.24	13.61	0.01	2.27	– 2.332	– 0.127
NTT–Teleway	0.19	0.02	0.01	11.32	0.19	– 0.193	– 0.006
DDI–Telecom	0.25	0.54	0.54	0.00	0.31	– 0.282	0.041
DDI–Teleway	0.02	0.05	0.00	0.05	0.02	– 0.018	0.005
Telecom–Teleway	0.01	0.00	0.05	0.05	0.01	– 0.009	0.002

welfare effects of a merger, but that is not the case here. The mergers generally have slightly more positive welfare effects under the assumption that cost advantages can be extended through merger, but the reverse can be true, and it is for the DDI–Telecom merger. There is no general tendency for industry average price to increase more under one cost assumption or the other.

Finally, we can consider the impact of changes in the characteristics of the nondominant carriers, specifically the impact of equal access, which places the smaller carriers on a par with NTT in terms of Delay and Dial-1. Pre-merger prices and market shares cannot be observed in this case, but rather must be predicted using the estimated logit model. Equal access directly reduces NTT's perceived product superiority. Consequently, the market shares of the nondominant carriers increase somewhat at the expense of NTT, and this reduces NTT's implied cost advantage. With NTT having less product and cost superiority, the merger tends to have more adverse welfare effects, as is shown in Table 4.[18] This is the case even though concentration is lower.

CONCLUSIONS

The efficiency effects of mergers are many and complicated, particularly with differentiated products and asymmetric firms. Even in a static model, mergers have the prospect of enhancing total welfare for a variety of reasons. One reason to which little attention has been paid is that mergers in asymmetric industries cause asymmetric price effects and therefore shifts in production. It is plausible that the merger of small or medium-sized merging firms will enhance total welfare because it causes a reallocation of production to a much larger and more nonmerging firm, with lower costs and a more preferred product. Indeed, simulations of Japanese long-distance mergers indicate that such would be the case.

This potential for mergers to enhance welfare in this way arises from substantial differences in firm efficiencies, which lead to substantial differences in market shares. Thus, the potential for mergers to enhance efficiency arises from high market concentration. This result does not depend a great deal on the particular demand assumption we have made. The most important force driving the results is that larger firms have larger margins, and that is the case quite generally in noncooperative oligopoly models.

To the extent that merger policy remains essentially structural, it should recognize that high market concentration may not merit greater restraints on the mergers of smaller firms. A superior way in which to incorporate our insights, however, would be to replace or supplement structural merger policy with simulations of mergers in differentiated products in the context of an oligopoly model and a particular demand system. In this way, it becomes a simple matter to assess a variety of efficiency effects. It is easy to incorporate possible fixed or marginal cost reductions into the calculations and explicitly compute the Williamsonian welfare tradeoff.

Table 4. Calculated Price and Welfare Effects of Possible Mergers Assuming Equal Access

Merger	Δp_{NTT}	Δp_{DDI}	$\Delta p_{Telecom}$	$\Delta p_{Teleway}$	Δp_{Ind}	ΔCW	ΔW
NTT–DDI	5.41	42.17	0.44	0.04	5.43	– 6.171	– 1.237
NTT–Telecom	2.36	0.35	39.78	0.01	2.30	– 2.702	– 0.439
NTT–Teleway	0.20	0.03	0.01	38.15	0.19	– 0.225	– 0.033
DDI–Telecom	0.48	0.73	1.47	0.00	0.58	– 0.553	0.044
DDI–Teleway	0.04	0.06	0.00	1.40	0.05	– 0.049	0.004
Telecom–Teleway	0.02	0.00	0.06	0.66	0.03	– 0.024	0.002

AUTHORS' NOTE

The views expressed herein are not purported to represent those of the US Department of Justice.

NOTES

1. Demsetz sought to explain existing levels of concentration as the consequence of a process of industry evolution—the result of greater success by more efficient firms. His purpose was to argue that the observed positive association between profits and concentration did not justify strict limits on mergers or deconcentration of markets. Demsetz' critique of the concentration–profits studies was one of many. For a host of reasons, there is now a consensus that those studies do not justify a restrictive merger policy. See Werden (1991a, pp. 15–17).
2. All firms in such a model have market power in the sense that their demand curves are not infinitely elastic, and all firms exercise that power in the sense that they charge prices in excess of marginal cost. On the other hand, industry returns need not be supracompetitive, as the model considers neither fixed costs nor risk.
3. The latter assumption is more plausible in many, but certainly not all, cases. Marginal costs may differ solely because of differences in product designs and therefore may not be affected by merger. In the short term, the merged firm may also have no alternative to using the separate production facilities of the two merging firms.
4. A superior firm's advantage in intensity of consumer preference could be extended through merger as well, but that seems less likely. Moreover, we see no sensible and non-arbitrary way in which to model such effects.
5. Thus, symmetric models, such as those of Deneckere and Davidson (1985) and Levy and Reitzes (1992), are incapable of producing the effects on which we focus and are otherwise of limited interest because they are symmetric.
6. A similar analysis could be done under alternative specifications for demand, such as probit, almost ideal demand systems used by Hausman *et al.* (1994), and much more complex, multi-attribute differentiation models used by Berry (1994) and Berry *et al.* (1995).
7. The data from which this parameter estimate was derived were generated through a survey, which has several important advantages discussed below.
8. The 1992 Merger Guidelines use the logit model as the base case for the analysis of mergers in differentiated products industries. The logit model is a base case in the sense that the merging firms are neither especially close in product space nor especially far apart. See US Department of Justice and Federal Trade Commission (1992, § 2.21) and compare with Willig (1991, pp. 299–304).
9. The material in this section is treated more extensively in Werden and Froeb (1994).
10. For certain parameter values, negative marginal cost is implied by Eqn (7) if a firm's share is sufficiently great. Negative marginal costs would cause mergers to have unrealistic welfare effects, so we assume throughout that all shares are small enough that all marginal costs are positive. With all product prices equal to one, as we generally assume, avoiding negative marginal costs requires argmax $\{s_j\} < (\beta - 1)/(\beta - \epsilon)$, and there can be a negative marginal cost only if demand is inelastic.
11. This is easily shown. Increasing any α_j by $\Delta\alpha_j$, while holding the choice probabilities constant, increases all the others by the same amount. By totally differentiating Eqn (8), it can be verified that increasing all the α_j by the same amount leaves the value of Eqn (8) unchanged.
12. The results are somewhat different under the assumption that a firm can share its cost advantage with a merger partner. Merger of different-sized firms then reduces the marginal cost of the lower-share, higher-cost firm. This greatly reduces the price increase for that product, and may even lead to a price decrease for it. The combination of greater cost savings and lower price increases makes it more likely that mergers will yield a net increase in welfare. Consequently, high concentration is not so important for mergers to enhance welfare.
13. This description relies on Nambu *et al.* (1989).
14. Holding shares, β, ϵ, and $\bar{p}$ constant, while changing individual prices, forces offsetting changes in the c_j's and the α_j's that maintain the pre-merger price-marginal cost margins and differences among the $(\alpha_j - \beta p_j)$'s. With the α_j's changing in this way, the post-merger first-order conditions are satisfied by the same mark-ups and shares for any set of relative pre-merger prices, and pre-merger prices do not affect the welfare change calculations. Pre-merger relative prices do matter, however, if mergers are assumed to reduce the marginal cost of the higher-cost merging firms to a level dependent on the marginal cost of the lower-cost merging firm.
15. The shares we use are: NTT—86.5%, DDI—8.8%, Telecom—4.3%, and Teleway—0.4%.
16. The estimation was done by NERA as part of a proprietary study. Whether the logit model fits the data can be examined through an explicit test of the assumption from which the model can be derived—Independence of Irrelevant Alternatives (IIA). The IIA assumption implies that, when the price of one product is increased, consumers substitute to others in proportion to the relative shares of those products. The IIA assumption can be tested in several ways (see Hausman and McFadden, 1984; Ben-Akiva and Lerman 1985, pp. 183–94). We did so by re-estimating the model using data on choices not involving NTT. The coefficients were very close to those reported (the price coefficient was a bit lower), but the estimation was sufficiently precise so that two sets of coefficients were significantly different ($\chi^2 = 18.6$, d.f. $= 6$). Re-estimation with a nest around the nondominant carriers yielded inclusive values so close to 1 as to make no practical difference in the simulations.

17. With pre-merger prices being fairly close, the implied α_j's are fairly close, but the implied marginal cost of the nondominant carriers are at least 73% greater then NTT's implied marginal cost.
18. It is necessary to make an additional assumption to do these simulations, because ϵ has not been estimated at the equal-access equilibrium. Table 4 reflects the assumption that the same value of ϵ applies in the new equilibrium. This is probably a very good approximation, although there should be a slight change in the equilibrium demand elasticity premerger, since more equal access changes the prices and quantities premerger. An alternative assumption is that the ϵ in equal-access-equilibrium is that implied by the equal-access-equilibrium prices and shares through Eqn (5). That turns out to be 0.36, which seems implausibly low. Using this estimate, however, does not alter the sign of any of the welfare effects of the mergers, but the welfare effects of the mergers are more favorable.

REFERENCES

American Bar Association (1986). *Horizontal Mergers: Law and Policy*, Section of Antitrust Law, Monograph 12.

S. P. Anderson and A. de Palma (1992). Multiproduct firms: a nested logit approach. *Journal of Industrial Economics*, **40** (3), September, 261–76.

S. P. Anderson, A. de Palma and J-F. Thisse (1992). *Discrete Choice Theory of Product Differentiation*, Cambridge, Mass.: MIT Press.

S. Beggs, S. Cardell and J. Hausman (1981). Assessing the potential demand for electric cars. *Journal of Econometrics*, **17** (1), September, 1–19.

M. Ben-Akiva and S. R. Lerman (1985). *Discrete Choice Analysis*, Cambridge, Mass.: MIT Press.

S. T. Berry (1994). Estimating discrete choice models of product differentiation. *Rand Journal of Economics*, **25** (2), Summer, 242–62.

S. T. Berry, J. Levinsohn and A. Pakes (1995). Automobile prices in market equilibrium. *Econometrics*, **63** (4), July, 841–90.

H. Demsetz (1973). Industry structure, market rivalry, and public policy. *Journal of Law and Economics*, **16** (1), April, 1–9.

R. Deneckere and C. Davidson (1985). Incentives to form coalitions with Bertrand competition. *Rand Journal of Economics*, **16** (4), Winter, 473–86.

J. Farrell and C. Shapiro (1990). Horizontal mergers: an equilibrium analysis. *American Economic Review*, **80** (1), March, 107–26.

J. A. Hausman, G. Leonard and J. D. Zona (1994). Merger analysis with differentiated products. *Annales d'Economique et Statistique*, **34** (2), April–June, 159–80.

J. A. Hausman and D. McFadden (1984). Specification tests for the multinomial logit model. *Econometrica* **52** (5), September, 1219–40.

J. A. Hausman and P. A. Ruud (1987). Specifying and testing econometric models for rank-ordered data. *Journal of Econometrics, 34* (1/2), January/February, 83–109.

D. T. Levy and J. D. Reitzes (1987). Anticompetitive effects of mergers in markets with localized competition. *Journal of Law, Economics, & Organization*, **8** (2), April, 427–40.

R. P. McAfee and M. A. Williams (1992). Horizontal mergers and antitrust policy. *Journal of Industrial Economics*, **40** (2), June, 181–87.

D. McFadden (1974). Conditional logit analysis of qualitative choice behavior. In *Frontiers in Econometrics* (edited by P. Zarembka), New York: Academic Press, 105–42.

T. Nambu, K. Suzuki and T. Honda (1989). Deregulation in Japan. In *Changing the Rules: Technological Change, International Competition, and Regulation in Communication* (edited by R.W. Crandall and K. Flamm), Washington, DC: Brookings Institution.

S. Peltzman (1977). The gains and losses from industrial concentration. *Journal of Law and Economics*, **20** (2), October, 229–63.

M. K. Perry and R. H. Porter (1985). Oligopoly and the incentive for horizontal merger. *American Economic Review* **75** (1), March, 219–27.

K. A. Small and H. Rosen (1981). Applied welfare economics with discrete choice models. *Econometrica*, **49** (1), January, 105–30.

US Department of Justice and Federal Trade Commission (1992). Horizontal Merger Guidelines, 2 April, reprinted in 4 Trade Reg. Rep. (CCH) ¶ 13,104.

G. J. Werden (1991a). A review of the empirical and experimental literature on the relationship between market structure and performance. Economic Analysis Group Discussion Paper 91–3, 8 May.

G. J. Werden (1991b). Horizontal mergers: comment. *American Economic Review*, **81** (4), September, 1002–06.

G. J. Werden and L. M. Froeb (1994). The effects of mergers in differentiated products industries: logit demand and structural merger policy. *Journal of Law, Economics, & Organization*, **10** (2), October, 407–26.

O. E. Williamson (1968). Economies as an antitrust defense: the welfare tradeoffs. *American Economic Review*, **58** (1), March, 18–36.

R. D. Willig (1991). Merger analysis, industrial organization theory, and merger guidelines. *Brookings Papers on Economic Activity, Microeconomics*, 281–332.

13
Monopoly and the Problem of the Economists

William F. Shughart II

The University of Mississippi, MS, USA

By any measure economists have played increasingly prominent roles in antitrust policy making, at least since the early 1970s. Indeed, the approach to the analysis of public policy toward business pioneered by Chicago school economists dominates the academic literature nowadays. According to the Chicago school's adherents, their insistence that antitrust be examined through the lens of price theory should have produced discernably 'better' (read pro-consumer) laws and 'better' law enforcement. This chapter contends that economists have in fact not had a positive influence on antitrust policy, but have instead actively contributed to its use as a way of subverting competitive market forces.

Economists have their glories, but I do not believe that the body of American antitrust law is one of them (Stigler, 1982, p. 7).

INTRODUCTION

At the start of his presidential address to the American Economic Association in 1981, the late George Stigler (1982) jokingly observed that, had he instead been invited to speak before the American Monopolists' Association, the title of his lecture would have been 'Monopoly and the Problem of the Economists'. He then went on to survey the available evidence concerning the impact economists have had on the course of antitrust policy in the United States. Stigler's conclusion is summarized nicely by this article's epigram: he found little reason to commend the profession for its contributions to the theory and practice of antitrust.

Stigler's tale of the economists and the problem of monopoly echoes Winston Churchill's colorful description of Russia as a 'riddle wrapped in a mystery inside an enigma'. The riddle is the profession's inexplicable change of heart toward antitrust, a nearly unanimous reversal of opinion that occurred some time during the early part of this century. As Stigler (1982, p. 3) put it so aptly, 'a careful student of the history of economics would have searched long and hard, on the unseasonably cool day of July 2 of 1890, the day the Sherman Act was signed by President Harrison, for any economist who had ever recommended the policy of actively combatting collusion or monopolization in the economy at large'.

Lurid accounts of the evils wrought by bloated 'robber barons' aside, the majority of the economists of the late nineteenth century were in fact opposed to the Sherman Act (Gordon, 1963; DiLorenzo and High, 1988). Their opposition was based on the widely held belief that the trust movement was a natural and mostly unobjectionable response to the rising forces of competition triggered by America's industrial revolution. The trusts assembled by John D. Rockefeller, Andrew Carnegie, and their fellow capitalists facilitated the exploitation of the new economies of scale and scope that made large-scale enterprises profitable. Any harm consumers may have suffered from price-fixing agreements or other abuses, which surely did occur, was more than offset by the benefits of increased price stability and the cost advantages of large-scale production. Although no economists were called upon to testify before Congress during the hearings held on Senator John Sherman's bill, the published opinions of economists overwhelmingly 'seemed to reject the idea that competition was declining, or showed no fear of decline' (Gordon, 1963, p. 166).

Contrary viewpoints were certainly expressed. The socialist Richard T. Ely, a founder of the American Economic Association, for instance, thought that the trust movement had brought great distress to the working class. Ely endorsed proposals limiting the use of child labor and restricting the number of hours adults could be required to work each day. He even went so far as to call for government ownership of industry to cure these perceived social ills. But Ely, too, opposed the Sherman Act, stating that 'the so-called trusts are not a bad thing, unless business on a large scale is a bad thing. On the contrary, when they come about as the result of free development, they are a good thing, and it is a bad thing to attempt to break them up' (Ely, 1887, p. 265; 1900, p. 162).

At least two well-known economists, Henry Carter Adams and Allyn Young, came out strongly in favor of an antitrust policy that would dismantle the great 'monopolies'. By and large, though, the economists of the 1880s saw no need for antitrust legislation (DiLorenzo and High, 1988, p. 429); they were in fact downright hostile to it (Stigler, 1982, p. 3).

The economics profession's opposition to an antitrust policy had reversed almost completely by the middle of this century's second decade. By the late 1970s, 85% of the economists surveyed by Kearl *et al.* (1979) agreed or agreed provisionally with the statement that the 'antitrust laws should be enforced vigorously to reduce monopoly power from its current level'.[1] Shortly before his death, even George Stigler was firmly in the camp of antitrust's supporters. Antitrust, he said, 'is a public interest law in the same sense in which ... having private property, enforcement of contracts, and suppression of crime are public interest phenomena ... I like the Sherman Act' (Hazlett, 1984, p. 46).

The mystery is that the reversal of opinion was grounded not in the principles of positive economics, but apparently sprang full grown like Athena from the head of Zeus: 'It would be gratifying to me if I could report that our profession's changing view was based upon the systematic study by economists of the effects of the policy, in short, that hard evidence carried the day. Unfortunately, there have been no persuasive studies of the effects of the Sherman and Clayton Acts throughout this century' (Stigler, 1982, p. 5).

The continuing enigma is why the profession's majority, especially those members of it identified with the 'Chicago school', steadfastly cling to the belief that antitrust's failures, which became evident almost immediately and have persisted for more than a century, can be explained chiefly on the basis of ignorance of economics among the lawyers, judges, and bureaucrats charged with the responsibility of enforcing the law. If only they were better equipped with the economist's toolkit and way of thinking, so the conventional Chicago school wisdom goes, public policy makers would do a much better job distinguishing competition from monopoly, thereby finally fulfilling the Sherman Act's promise as the bulwark of freely functioning markets.

Antitrust economists are prescribers (e.g. Dick, this issue). They develop elegant mathematical models with the avowed purpose of helping the Justice Department's Antitrust Division and the Federal Trade Commission identify and attack sources of allocative inefficiency in the economy so as to enhance consumer welfare. Yet many of these same economists would not be caught dead making similar recommendations to the Interstate Commerce Commission or to the now-defunct Civil Aeronautics Board. More than 30 years of research in the economic theory of regulation pioneered by George Stigler (1971) has produced evidence that, almost without exception, public regulation of price and entry has harmed consumers by reducing competition and raising prices.[2]

Economists also found that regulation has frequently been acquired by the regulated industry and has been designed and operated primarily for its benefit (Stigler, 1971, p. 3): 'Consumers never asked for an Interstate Commerce Commission to prevent new truckers from entering the business. Nor had consumers been heard from when the federal government set up milk marketing boards to restrict the supply of milk and drive up the price. The main players were truckers and milk producers, who wanted to limit competition' (Henderson, 1995, p. 62).

In short, interest-group politics, not economics, is now widely seen to be the driving force behind more traditional forms of public regulation of industry. The majority of economists would therefore not waste their time building and fine tuning models of optimal pricing mired in a regulatory nirvana where regulators maximize a non-existent social-welfare function. Why is it that the ghost of Pigou uniquely haunts the literature of antitrust (McCormick, 1984, p. 26)? Are antitrust economists simply naive?

The burden of this paper is to suggest that far from contributing to improved antitrust enforcement, economists have for reasons of self-interest actively aided and abetted the public law enforcement bureaus and private plaintiffs in using the Sherman, Clayton, and FTC Acts to subvert competitive market forces. It does so, first, by summarizing the literature attempting to explain antitrust law enforcement decisions available to George Stigler on the occasion of his presidential address. This is followed by a review of the subsequent contributions to this same literature which, being grounded in public-choice principles, has produced fairly strong evidence that politics shapes antitrust processes in much the same way it does more traditional forms of regulation. The paper then presents some data suggesting that economists' puzzling support for antitrust is at least in part explained by self-interest: Employment opportunities for economists in the private sector seem to be positively correlated with 'exotic' antitrust theories.

WHAT DID GEORGE STIGLER KNOW AND WHEN DID HE KNOW IT?

At the time George Stigler gave his presidential address, few attempts had been made to measure the impact of economists or economic theory on antitrust policy making. One relevant study was his own early effort to gauge the overall effects of the antitrust laws on the basis of broad-brush comparisons of concentration ratios, merger activity, and price-fixing conspiracies in selected US and UK industries (Stigler, 1966). He reported evidence that the Sherman Act had had modestly salutary effects, but characterized the findings as 'meager'.

Stigler also have available to him, but failed to cite, a series of important contributions to the literature that explored the antitrust law enforcement process more systematically. In the first of these studies, Long, Schramm and Tollison (1973) compared the actual distribution of antitrust cases across industries with the pattern that would be consistent with a public-spirited law enforcement agency selecting cases to prosecute on the basis of their potential net social benefit. Their approach was to regress the number of cases instituted against firms in particular industries on various industry-specific welfare-loss measures.

The Long–Schramm–Tollison model performed best in explaining case-bringing activities when industry size, measured by sales, was used as a proxy for welfare loss. Overall, though, the empirical evidence failed to support the hypothesis that the Antitrust Division's behavior was grounded in a benefit–cost model. Specifically, the results suggested that 'the composite measures of the potential benefits from antitrust action — the welfare-loss triangle or [the triangle] together with excess profits — appear to play a minor role in explaining antitrust activity' (Long, Schramm and Tollison, 1973, p. 361).

Subsequent comments on the Long–Schramm–Tollison study reported additional evidence that the law enforcement activities of the antitrust bureaucracy do not follow a public-interest 'model'.[3] Peter Asch (1975) estimated similar regression specifications for the Antitrust Division and the Federal Trade Commission separately. He concluded from the coefficient estimates that 'case-bringing activity cannot be characterized as predominantly "rational" or predominantly "random"' (Asch, 1975, pp. 580–81).

Exploiting a data set significantly less aggregated than that used by the other researchers, John Siegfried (1975) produced evidence that more antitrust cases were brought in industries exhibiting *greater* excess profits and *lower* welfare losses. These findings suggested that the antitrust agencies target successful firms whose profits are based on efficient resource use, not market power. But when Siegfried refined his model to include improved measures of industry profitability, its explanatory power plummeted, coefficient estimates switched signs, and their standard errors ballooned. Siegfried (1975, p. 573) ended by saying that 'economic variables have little influence on the Antitrust Division'.

By the late 1970s, then, economists had stumbled upon their own Holmesian mystery of the dog in the night: no support for the public-interest 'model' of antitrust policy making has been found. No one at the time had an explanation for the dog's failure to bark. There were, however, some hints that the modern architect of the economic theory of regulation (Stigler, 1971) could have put to better use. One of these was Suzanne Weaver's (1977) study of the Justice Department's

Antitrust Division. Based on personal interviews conducted during 1971 with staff members, private attorneys, and other observers of the antitrust law enforcement process, she sought to answer the question, 'Why does the division choose to bring any particular case?' (Weaver, 1977, p. 66).

According to her, events during the early 1950s, including the passage of the Celler–Kefauver Act and the indictment of the leading electrical equipment manufacturers for price fixing, 'made antitrust expertise a more valuable commodity to the business community and to the law firms serving it'. Due to the increased demand for such expertise, 'experience in the Antitrust Division became newly valuable to a young lawyer who wanted eventually to work in private practice'. And the specific experience wanted was trial experience in the federal courts (Weaver, 1977, pp. 38–40).

Weaver's study thus suggested that, at the margin, the goal of getting to trial may dominate the economic merits of a particular case in the Antitrust Division's decision to prosecute. A companion study of the incentive structure faced by the Federal Trade Commission's attorneys published three years later reached similar conclusions. Robert Katzmann (1980) also observed that the ultimate career goal of most members of the FTC's legal staff is a job with a prestigous private law firm. Such ambitions mean that the commission's senior managers will tend to avoid complex 'structural matters and industry wide cases [that] threaten the morale of the staff because they often involve years of tedious research before they reach the trial stage'. Instead, bureau directors will support 'the opening of a number of easily prosecuted matters, which may have little value to the consumer, ... in an effort to satisfy the staff's perceived needs' (Katzmann, 1980, p. 83).[4]

Katzmann's main point is that one cannot explain the FTC's case selection process on the basis of market characteristics economists customarily associate with allocative inefficiency. The decision to prosecute is instead dominated by factors internal to the FTC bureaucracy — staff career objectives, the availability of law enforcement resources, the need to produce 'output' visible to congressional oversight committees, and so on.

A subsequent study of the FTC likewise identified internal organizational conflicts, staff incentives, and external constraints as important determinants of antitrust case selection decisions (Clarkson and Muris, 1981). For instance, a bureaucratic explanation is given for the commission's change of strategy in the early 1970s that devoted more resources to wide-ranging investigations of highly concentrated industries. It was apparently hoped that this reallocation of the commission's law enforcement resources would yield a number of highly visible monopolization cases which would both help reduce frictions between FTC lawyers and economists, who were at loggerheads over enforcing a law (the Robinson–Patman Act amendment to Clayton Act Section 2) 'that requires business decision makers to consult their attorneys before making price moves' (Scherer, 1980, p. 81), and provide staff members with the human-capital-building experience of a more legally complex and intellectually challenging caseload. Clarkson and Muris (1981, pp. 303–4) also attribute the FTC's reluctance to institute price-fixing cases to the desire on the part of the commission's attorneys to differentiate themselves in the post-government job market from their Antitrust Division counterparts.

Taken as a group, the three studies of organizational behavior summarized above point to the conclusion that the antitrust cases instituted by the public law enforcement agencies are not selected on the basis of their potential net benefits to society. The bureau managers and employees of the Antitrust Division and the Federal Trade Commission instead use the discretion available to them to launch investigations and pursue cases that help advance their own interests (by raising their expected lifetime earnings) rather than those of consumers.

In sum, the evidence available to George Stigler at the time of his presidential address to the American Economic Association provided little reason for thinking that the antitrust law enforcement agencies choose cases to prosecute on the basis of their potential net social benefit.[5] And to the extent that this evidence suggested that the antitrust laws were not being used to attack sources of allocative inefficiency in the economy, there were substantial doubts that antitrust policy was guided by a public-interest model or that economists had had much influence on it.

But what was the cause of these failures? To members of the Chicago school, who insist that the organization of industry be studied 'through the lens of price theory' (Posner, 1979, p. 127), the answer is simple ignorance. Given proper instruction in economic principles, policy makers, the private antitrust bar, and the judiciary will all apply the laws to better effect. Are there grounds for such optimism?

WHAT DO ANTITRUST ECONOMISTS DO?

Antitrust's partisans, at least those residing intellectually in Hyde Park, maintain that 'better' antitrust policy will automatically follow an expanded role for economists in the law enforcement process and a greater appreciation for economics by the lawyers and judges who try antitrust cases. As the prior discussion shows, however, this superficially appealing proposition seems to be inconsistent with the facts.

Economists can, perhaps, claim a few minor victories: Very few Robinson–Patman price discrimination complaints are issued nowadays and the Supreme Court has said several times recently that it believes predatory pricing to be a rare event.[6] But the era of job growth for antitrust economists coincided with the launching of a number of clumsy, old-fashioned structural antitrust investigations based on novel, untested theories of 'shared monopoly' and predatory 'brand proliferation'.[7] The Justice Department began its quixotic pursuit of IBM and AT&T at about the same time.[8] *Exxon* dragged on for ten years, employing the energies of over 200 FTC lawyers and economists, and ended up producing little more than tens of thousands of pages of microfilmed oil company documents and reams of internal commission memoranda. Except for AT&T, which was settled by an agreement that created an oligopoly in long-distance telephone service and arguably impeded the development of competition in local telephone markets, the other cases met similar fates.

Economists working for the antitrust bureaus invented the idea of 'raising rivals' costs', which contends that firms can take actions unilaterally in input markets to provide themselves with competitive advantages in output markets, expressly to undermine the Chicago school's effective critique of predatory pricing.[9] As discussed in the next section, antitrust economists have also been accessories both before and after the fact in tilting merger policy further in the direction of protecting competitors rather than consumers. More recently, they have used the theory of games almost exclusively to build exotic models of anticompetitive behavior with little empirical content (Peltzman, 1991).[10] It is, in short, far from clear that 'better' economics makes 'better' antitrust policy.

It might be better to ask why it was ever expected to. In a geographically based representative democracy, politicians and policy makers receive almost no payoff from taking vague positions on behalf of the 'public interest' (Buchanan and Tullock, 1962; McCormick and Tollison, 1981). Instead, the logic of collective action (Olson, 1965) suggests that well-organized pressure groups will tend to dominate the political process, obtaining benefits for themselves at the expense of unorganized taxpayers and consumers.

Like all government agencies, the antitrust bureaus must produce visible output to satisfy their congressional sponsors (Lindsay, 1976). Investigations, complaints, consent orders, and litigation are the meat and bread of the Antitrust Division and the Federal Trade Commission. The careers of the economists employed by these agencies accordingly progress not on soundness and impartiality of their analyses of the theories and facts on which antitrust matters are based, but rather on their proficiency in 'working with' the lawyers to whom they are assigned. Economists who consistently oppose moving forward with antitrust actions do not prosper in this environment.

Antitrust provides numerous employment opportunities for economists in the private sector as well. They serve as expert witnesses for defendants in antitrust cases, they obtain post-government positions in academia, and they have recently found new sources of remuneration from spreading the antitrust gospel to the newly independent republics of Eastern Europe, to Taiwan, which adopted its first antitrust law just a few years ago, and even to Mongolia, which sought advice on writing its own Robinson–Patman Act.

Both more than economists' personal self-interest in an active antitrust policy, the bottom line is that antitrust is no different than other forms of government intervention into the private economy. Insofar as they provide the means of short-circuiting competitive market forces, the

Sherman, Clayton, and FTC Acts are the domestic equivalents of tariffs, quotas, and 'voluntary' export restraints in international trade. In the realm of antitrust, as in all other public policies toward business, it is the interplay between the demanders of protectionism — the firms who seek shelter from the Schumpeterian 'perennial gale' of 'creative destruction' — and the legislative suppliers of such protection that determine policy outcomes.

The dominance of politics in antitrust processes has never been more conspicuous than in the Justice Department's unprecedented decision to open its own investigation of Microsoft Corporation after the FTC had, on tied votes, twice failed to issue a complaint against America's leading producer of computer software. The Justice Department's intervention occurred only after several telephone calls from Capitol Hill to Anne Bingaman, the Assistant Attorney General for Antitrust. As the *Wall Street Journal* reported,

> because Ms. Bingaman's request for FTC documents followed prodding by two senators, her action 'does appear to have taken on a bit of the political aspect,' [former Assistant Attorney General for Antitrust] Mr. [Charles] Rule said.
>
> But if it's political, it's also bipartisan. Sen. Howard Metzenbaun (D., Ohio), chairman of the Senate Judiciary Committee's antitrust subcommittee, and Sen. Orrin Hatch, the ranking Republican on the full committee, both have urged Ms. Bingaman to examine the Microsoft case (Davidson, 1993, p. B8).

The *Journal* did not report, though other publications did, that the headquarters of two of Mircosoft's major competitors, Novell and Wordperfect, Inc., which at the time were independent but subsequently merged, are both located in Utah, whose voters sent Orrin Hatch to the US Senate (McChesney and Shughart, 1995, p. 344).

Just as Stacy Koon and his fellow Los Angeles police officers were going to be found guilty of using excessive force in the beating of Rodney King, no matter how many trials were required for that verdict to be reached, so Microsoft will be pursued until its competitors are satisfied. Economists and economic theory will only play supporting roles in this drama.

DO ECONOMISTS MATTER?

Whether or not economists' influence on antitrust policy making has grown over time, there are certainly more of them. The data series collected by George Stigler (1982, p. 10) and updated by me in Table 1 show the number of economists employed by the Justice Department's Antitrust Division and the FTC essentially doubling by the late 1980s. Although there has been some modest retrenchment since then, especially so at the commission, if numbers count economists certainly play much more prominent roles in the public antitrust agencies nowadays.

Notable periods of job growth for economists in the public antitrust bureaus followed passage of the Celler–Kefauver Act in 1950, which closed section 7's 'asset loophole', thereby strengthening the government's hand in merger law enforcement,[11] and the Hart–Scott–Rodino Antitrust Improvement Act of 1976, which established a pre-merger notification process requiring prospective merger partners to obtain the approval of either the Antitrust Division or the FTC before consummating their transaction.[12] Although information on the number of antitrust economists working in the private sector is harder to come by,[13] the data shown in Table 2 suggest that employment opportunities there are considerably more volatile. They also lend credibility to Stigler's (1982, p. 7) conjecture that the number of economists engaged in private antitrust consulting may 'possibly [be] twenty times as large' as the number employed in the public sector. While employment data were supplied by only one private consultancy, there are dozens of these firms, including Capital Economics, Charles River Associates, Economists, Inc., MiCRA, and NERA (National Economic Research Associates).

Perhaps one of the most interesting conclusions that can be drawn from the data in Table 2 is that economists' job opportunities in the private sector seem to be positively correlated with 'exotic' antitrust theories. If the information supplied by one firm is at all representative of general trends, the number of economists and support staff employed by private consultancies dropped precipitously during the Reagan era. This is noteworthy because the number of investigations and cases underway at the two public antitrust agencies

Table 1. Economists in the Antitrust Agencies, 1913–93

Year	Justice Department	FTC
1913	N/A	N/A
1923	N/A	30
1930	N/A	44
1951	N/A	18
1955	N/A	26
1971	N/A	47
1972	21	53
1973	26	56
1974	24	66
1975	36	67
1976	43	73
1977	40	73
1978	44	81
1979	45	78
1980	45	80
1981	38	92
1982	41	84
1983	43	84
1984	43	77
1985	46	80
1986	44	78
1987	39	74[a]
1988	39	72
1989	36	67
1990	44	66
1991	45	70
1992	47	70
1993	44	70

Sources: 1913–81: Stigler (1982, p. 10). 1982–93: The Justice Department data were supplied by Thomas D. King of the Antitrust Division; the FTC data were supplied by Malcolm B. Coate of the Bureau of Economics.

[a] Beginning in 1987, the FTC data are based on an internal employment series that includes economists working in the Office of the Director of the Bureau of Economics. The Office of the Director currently comprises the director, three area directors, and one assistant. In the past, up to six economists have been employed there.

remained fairly constant throughout the 1980s (Shughart, 1989). But the focus of the FTC's and the Antitrust Division's law enforcement activities shifted away from 'shared monopoly' and other imaginative legal theories having little economic foundation toward 'bread-and-butter' antitrust (Tollison, 1983) — horizontal mergers, price-fixing conspiracies, and similarly traditional antitrust matters. The activist antitrust agenda of the 1990s, with its renewed emphasis on resale price maintenance and other vertical restraints of trade have been good to antitrust economists.[14]

What impact have these additional law enforcement powers and additional numbers of economists had on the course of merger policy? There is evidence, at least for the horizontal mergers and acquisitions proposed between 1963 and 1978, that the transactions challenged by the Antitrust Division and the FTC under Clayton Act Section 7 would not, on average, have lessened competition or tended to create monopolies in the relevant lines of business or sections of the country (Eckbo, 1983; Stillman, 1983). It is conceivable, however, that the failures of government antimerger policy during this period can be explained by the fact that the information necessary for assessing the competitive effects of proposed mergers was not available to the antitrust authorities prior to implementation of the pre-merger notification process in 1978 and, moreover, that

Table 2. Economists and Support Staff in One Private Consultancy, 1980–94

Year	Economists	Support and Clerical
1980	109	61
1981	59[a]	32[a]
1982	48	40
1983	37	33
1984	40	33
1985	40	33
1986	42	35
1987	33	34
1988	52	36
1989	52	41
1990	70	49
1991	80	52
1992	83	58
1993	77	47
1994	94	41

Source: Private correspondence.
[a]1980–81 change due to an unusually large number of case settlements.

the inability of the law enforcement agencies to block mergers prior to their consummation made it more difficult to achieve effective relief against transactions subsequently determined to be unlawful.[15]

The hypothesis that the Hart–Scott–Rodino Act has improved merger case selection has been tested. Using capital market data from 82 horizontal mergers challenged by the Antitrust Division or the FTC between January 1963 and December 1981 (17 of which challenges occurred after the pre-merger notification rules went into effect), Eckbo and Wier (1985) asked whether the public law enforcement agencies' newfound authority had enhanced their ability to identify and challenge transactions likely to substantially lessen competition. The evidence suggested no such improvement. Indeed, the competitors of the prospective merger partners seemed to have benefitted most from pre-merger notification:

> While it is possible that the government's merger policy has deterred some anticompetitive mergers, the results indicate that it has also protected rival producers from facing increased competition due to efficient mergers. The additional enforcement powers granted under the HSR Act apparently have not led the agencies to pick cases better (Eckbo and Wier, 1985, p. 121).

More law enforcement authority and more economists have failed to produce outcomes consistent with antitrust's avowed public-interest goals. If economics does not seem to have much influence on antitrust, politics is an obvious alternative. Writing in 1969, Richard Posner advanced a pork-barrel hypothesis with respect to the FTC. Posner (1969) charged that the commission was significantly impaired in carrying out its mission of promoting competitive markets by its dependence on Congress. He emphasized the obvious fact that in a geographically based representative democracy each member of the legislature is obligated to protect and further the provincial interests of the citizens of the jurisdiction who have elected him. More specifically, 'the welfare of his constituents may depend disproportionately on a few key industries. The promotion of the industries becomes one of his important duties as a representative of the district'.

In addition, because oversight responsibilities regarding the commission's budget and its political appointees are vested in the hands of the members of certain key committees and subcommittees of the Congress, a legislator holding such a position will have a 'a great deal of power to advance the interests of businesses located in his district however unimportant the interests may be from a national perspective'. Posner contended that a major reason FTC investigations seldom seem to be in the public's interest is that many of them are initiated 'at the behest of corporations, trade associations, and trade unions whose motivation is at best to shift the costs of private litigation to the taxpayer and at worst to harass competitors'.[16]

Posner's pork-barrel hypothesis was tested in an important study of the FTC's case-bringing activities from 1961 through 1979. After identifying the committees and subcommittees of the House and Senate having proximate jurisdiction over the FTC, Roger Faith, Donald Leavens, and Robert Tollison (1982) tallied the number of antitrust actions instituted against firms headquartered in the districts and states of sitting committee members that were *dismissed* relative to the total number of actions brought against these firms. They then tested whether this ratio was significantly different from the ratio of dismissals to total complaints issued against firms not so represented.

Comparisons were made for each of two subperiods, 1961–9 and 1970–9, to see whether congressional influences on antitrust actions were affected by major reform measures implemented at the FTC following the release in 1969 of two reports highly critical of the commission's case selection policies and administrative procedures (ABA, 1969; Cox *et al.*, 1969). The empirical results suggested that FTC complaints issued against firms headquartered in the jurisdictions represented by the relevant committee members — particularly so in the case of companies headquartered in the districts of key House subcommittee members — were more likely to be dismissed than complaints involving firms headquartered elsewhere. Moreover, there was no evidence of any lessening of the role played by politics in FTC decision making between the two subperiods studied: 'If anything, the pork-barrel relationship between Congress and the commission became statistically stronger during the reform period of the 1970s' (Faith, Leavens and Tollison, 1982, p. 342).

More recent evidence suggests that economists' opinions are taken into account in decisions to prosecute, but that their recommendations are of lesser importance than either legal or political considerations. Coate, Higgins and McChesney (1990) examined the information gathered by the FTC in response to all 'second requests' issued under the authority of the Hart–Scott–Rodino Act between 14 June 1982 and 1 January 1987. The resulting sample consisted of 70 commission decisions. In 27 of the cases, the FTC issued a complaint alleging that the transaction violated Clayton Act Section 7; the proposed merger was allowed to proceed in the other 43 cases.

A regression model designed to explain the commission's decision whether to challenge a merger or not included variables measuring the extent of agreement between the staff attorneys and economists working on the case as to the transaction's likely competitive effects — its impact on market concentration and the probability of collusion, based on their independent judgments concerning the existence of barriers to entry into the relevant market. The model also included measures of the intensity of the political pressure, if any, exerted on the commission regarding the proposed merger. Possible congressional influence was proxied by two explanatory variables — the number of *Wall Street Journal* articles devoted to the merger published prior to the FTC's decision and the number of times commission officials were called to testify before congressional committees during the 12-month time interval centered on the date the FTC issued its second request.

All these variables had statistically significant effects on the commission's decision to prosecute. In particular, mergers were more likely to be challenged the more highly concentrated the industry was prior to the merger (i.e., the more narrowly the relevant market boundaries were drawn), the higher the barriers to entry were thought to be, and the more the merger was perceived to raise the benefits or lower the costs of collusion among the remaining firms. Although these results are consistent with an economic approach to merger law enforcement, *when the FTC's lawyers and economists disagreed on the competitive issues, the commission typically sided with its legal staff*. Moreover, greater political pressure — more news coverage and more summonses to appear before congressional committees — increased the probability that the FTC would vote to oppose the merger.

Based on this evidence, it appears that

> there is a constellation of identifiable interests who benefit from the FTC's stopping mergers.

> Politicians, their organized constituents opposed to mergers, and agency attorneys apparently are among the principal beneficiaries ... [T]his combination of personal interests creates an upward bias in the way the Merger Guidelines are applied, resulting in a greater propensity to challenge mergers in the marginal case (Coate, Higgins and McChesney, 1990, p. 23–24).[17]

The minimal influence of economists on antitrust processes is further exposed by evidence from the United Kingdom. Weir (1992) investigated how the British Monopolies and Mergers Commission dealt with transactions referred to it between 1974 and 1990. To his apparent surprise, various economic indicators associated with a proposed merger's likely competitive impact (e.g., its estimated effects on prices and costs) carried little, if any, weight in the commission's decision to challenge it. The only variable that consistently seemed to increase the probability of a merger challenge was whether or not the merger bid was contested by the target firm. Politics trumps economics.

There is no shortage of anecdotes to bolster the econometric evidence of significant political influences on antitrust enforcement. According to an anonymous source, one reason that Australia's Trade Practices Commission (TPC) launches so many investigations that ultimately go nowhere is that such actions raise the profile of the TPC and, in particular, that of its current chairman, Alan Fels. The basis of this explanation is contained in remarks by Australia's Prime Minister who, in a recent cabinet meeting, dismissed the TPC's chairman as a 'nymphomaniac for publicity' (Ramsey, 1995).[18]

CONCLUSIONS

By the close of the Sherman Act's first century, *no* evidence had been produced by antitrust's partisans that the law enforcement activities of the Department of Justice's Antitrust Division or the Federal Trade Commission had systematically provided benefits to consumers by promoting open market conditions. Indeed, scholars taking a positive approach to the study of the subject have uniformly found that antitrust follows the same interest-group principles that have been shown to be robust in explaining more traditional forms of public regulation (Shughart and Tollison, 1985; McChesney and Shughart, 1995). This research suggests that economists have failed to produce 'better' antitrust policies because the public's interest carries little weight in the objective function being maximized by antitrust's law enforcers.

Economists have important roles to play in developing and testing positive models that expose the political forces that shape antitrust. But there is a dark side to antitrust economics as well. It is that economists

> do have some control over legislative agenda. That is, they can generate public policy alternatives of which legislators are previously unaware. Then, legislators combine these alternatives with all other alternatives before them and rank these alternatives with respect to their political productivity and the probability of passage. Legislators then turn to academics for a second contribution: argument and evidence in support of their preferred alternatives and against those they do not prefer (Aranson, 1990, p. 285–6).

One can charitably conclude that 'this interpretation of the role of academics — and their information — in the political regulatory process at best casts that role as transitory, and sometimes even epiphenomenal' (Aranson, 1990, p. 286). On the other hand, the 'essential facilities doctrine' and the doctrine of 'unilateral action' may just be the most recent examples of the shopworn ideas antitrust economists periodically reinvent in order to support plaintiffs' pleas for protection from the forces of unfettered market competition.

Acknowledgements

I thank Willie Shughart for help with mythological metaphors and Fred McChesney for inviting me to contribute to this special issue. Any remaining errors are my own.

NOTES

1. Frey *et al.* (1984) find comparable percentages of European economists responding positively to this

statement. In the most recent such study, however, Alston *et al.* (1992) report that only 62% of the economists they surveyed agreed or agreed provisionally with the need for more vigorous antitrust law enforcement.

2. Representative contributions to this literature are collected in Stigler (1988).
3. Aranson (1990, p. 259) argues that proponents of government intervention to correct so-called market failures do not in fact have a model that conforms with conventional scientific standards: 'The essential problem with the public interest theory of regulation is that its form is conditionally normative, and not necessarily positive (explanatory and predictive).'
4. As Posner (1969, p. 86) had put it earlier, 'the principal attraction of Commission service to lawyers who wish to use it as a steppingstone to private practice lies in the opportunities it affords to gain trial experience... It is the experience of trying cases, *the more the better*, not the social payoff from the litigation, that improves the professional skills and earning prospects of FTC lawyers' (emphasis added).
5. Stigler also had available to him an extensive literature employing a case-study approach to assess the effects of antitrust law enforcement. The verdict of this literature, it is fair to say, is that many more 'bad' than 'good' cases have been brought. In evaluating one of the merger law's leading precedents, for example, John Peterman (1975a, p. 143) concludes that 'neither the government nor the Courts seemed able to distinguished between competition and monopolizing'. Even when the law has conceivably struck at anticompetitive acts and practices, the relief granted to the plaintiff is frequently ineffective (Elzinga, 1969). In summing up his detailed study of the FTC's lengthy prosecution of the Brown Shoe Company, Peterman (1975b, p. 393) ends up by saying that, at best, 'nothing was accomplished by bringing this case'. A representative sample of these case studies is summarized in Rubin (1995).
6. See, for instance, *Matsushita Electrical Industrial Co. v. Zenith Radio Corp.*, 475 US 574 (1986); *Cargill, Inc. v. Montfort of Colorado, Inc.*, 479 US 104 (1986); and *Brooke Group Ltd. v. Brown & Williamson Tobacco Corp.*, 113 S. Ct. 2578 (1993).
7. *In re Kellogg Co. et al.*, FTC dkt. no. 8833; and *In re Exxon Corp. et al.*, FTC dkt. no. 8934.
8. *U.S. v. International Business Machines* Corp., 69 Civ. 100 (1969); and *U.S. v. American Telephone & Telegraph Co.*, 74 Civ. 2974 (1968).
9. Steven Salop and David Scheffman, both of whom held high positions in the Federal Trade Commission's Bureau of Economics, first advanced the theory of raising rivals' cost at the 1982 meetings of the American Economic Association (Salop and Scheffman, 1983). A critical summary of the ensuing literature, with applications of the theory of three well-known cases, is contained in Coate and Kleit (1994). McGee (1958) still represents the most cogent statement of the Chicago school's position on predatory pricing.
10. 'Consider one small example: the earlier literature of predatory competition had the predator cut prices in the vicinity of the prey and raise prices elsewhere to recoup the loss. Today it would be embarrassing to encounter this argument in professional discourse' (Stigler, 1982, p. 9). However, dressed up appropriately in game theory clothing, antitrust economists routinely and unabashedly make this same argument nowadays in proving the existence of Nash subgame perfect noncooperative equilibria in models with asymmetric information and N players (no entry allowed).
11. As enacted in 1914, the original language of Clayton Act Section 7 condemned only those anticompetitive mergers effectuated by the purchase of 'the whole or any part of the stock or other share capital of another corporation engaged also in commerce'. Mergers effectuated by the purchase of physical assets where held by the courts to be beyond Section 7's reach. The Celler–Kefauver Act of 1950 added language explicitly prohibiting the acquisition of another firm's assets if the effect of the acquisition was to 'substantially lessen competition or tend to create a monopoly'. See Ekelund, McDonald and Tollison (1995) for theory and evidence suggesting that the original asset 'loophole', which remained open for nearly 40 years, was not a simple legislative error.
12. Although the merger partners must notify both the Antitrust Division and the FTC simultaneously of their intention to merge, one agency grants jurisdiction over the proposed transaction to the other through a clearance process worked out in the wake of the Supreme Court's decision in *Federal Trade Commission v. Cement Institute et al.*, 333 US 683 (1948). This decision allowed the commission to attack under Section 5 of the FTC Act business practices that would also be unlawful under the Sherman Act. The impact of this so-called liaison agreement on antitrust budgets and law enforcement activity is explored in Higgins, Shughart and Tollison (1987).
13. Even though promised anonymity, only one of the major private consulting firms heavily engaged in antitrust litigation responded to my request for information on the number of economists and support staff in their employ. Such are the weaknesses of survey data.
14. For instance, one of the first acts of Anne Bingaman, President Clinton's Assistant Attorney General for Antitrust, was to rescind the 1985 Vertical Restraints Guidelines. See Bingaman (1994).
15. Additional empirical support for Elzinga's (1969) conclusion that the remedies imposed in Section 7 cases have not placed significant constraints on the behavior of the parties involved is contained in

Ellert (1976) and Rogowsky (1986, 1987). The evidence that the antitrust penalties are often ineffective has an important implication for the efficacy of antitrust policy (Shughart and Tollison, 1987). One of the key prongs of the case for an activist antitrust law enforcement policy is that charges brought successfully against one firm can deter many other firms from committing similar law violations — that, in George Stigler's (1950, p. 32) felicitous phrase, 'the ghost of Senator Sherman is an *ex officio* member of the board of directors of every large company'. Research pointing to the ineffectiveness of the relief granted in antitrust proceedings weakens the support for bringing antitrust cases in the first place.

'Ineffectiveness' in this context should not, of course, be taken to mean that firms accused of merger law violations do not bear any costs. Indeed, McWilliams, Turk and Zardkoohi (1993) provide evidence that the reduction in stockholder wealth that follows in the wake of a government merger challenge goes far beyond that borne by the owners of the firms targeted by the antitrust complaint. The values of *all* mergers — including uncontested mergers — ongoing at the time an unfavorable Supreme Court ruling is announced appear to be affected adversely.

16. The political influences on antitrust policy making are explored more fully in Shughart and Tollison (1985), Shughart (1990), and McChesney and Shughart (1995). Also see Baumol and Ordover (1985), who provide numerous examples of firms using the antitrust laws to gain competitive advantages over their rivals.
17. Also see Coate and McChesney (1992, p. 291–2), who conclude that while 'rumors that economists were actually taking part in antitrust enforcement decisions' during the 1980s seem to have some basis in fact — 'both economist and attorney evaluations of [merger] guidelines factors appear to have an impact' on decisions to prosecute — nevertheless 'at the margin, attorneys seem to have more influence at the Commission if one accepts the econometric' results. Moreover, models that include political variables explain a greater proportion of FTC decisions to challenge mergers than models that contain only economic variables.
18. According to my source, the TPC's current chairman is the odds-on favorite to be named the first head of the Australian Competition and Consumer Commission, a new agency to be created by merging the TPC with the Prices Surveillance Authority. Additional anecdotes are contained in McChesney and Shughart (1995, p. 341–4).

REFERENCES

R. M. Alston, J. R. Kearl and M. B. Vaughn (1992). Is there a consensus among economists in the 1990's? *American Economic Review Papers and Proceedings*, **82**, May, 203–9.

American Bar Association (ABA) (1969). *Report of the American Bar Association Commission to Study the Federal Trade Commission*, Chicago: ABA.

P. H. Aranson (1990). Theories of economic regulation: From clarity to confusion. *Journal of Law and Politics*, **6**, Winter, 247–86.

P. Asch (1975). The determinants and effects of antitrust policy. *Journal of Law and Economics*, **18**, October, 575–81.

W. J. Baumol and J. A. Ordover (1985). Use of antitrust to subvert competition. *Journal of Law and Economics*, **28**, May, 247–65.

A. K. Bingaman (1994). Antitrust policy for the 21st century. Remarks before the Antitrust Section of the American Bar Association, 17 November.

J. M. Buchanan and G. Tullock (1962). *The Calculus of Consent: Logical Foundations of Constitutional Democracy*, Ann Arbor, MI: University of Michigan Press.

K. W. Clarkson and T. J. Muris (eds) (1981). *The Federal Trade Commission since 1970: Economic Regulation and Bureaucratic Behavior*, Cambridge: Cambridge University Press.

M. B. Coate, R. S. Higgins, and F. S. McChesney (1990). Bureaucracy and politics in FTC merger challenges. *Journal of Law and Economics* **33**, October, 463–82.

M. B. Coate and A. N. Kleit (1994). Exclusion, collusion, or confusion? The underpinnings of raising rivals' costs. In *Research in Law and Economics*, Vol. 16 (edited by R. O. Zerbe, Jr), Greenwich, CT: JAI Press, pp. 73–93.

M. B. Coate and F. S. McChesney (1992). Empirical evidence on FTC enforcement of the merger guidelines. *Economic Inquiry*, **30**, April, 277–93.

E. F. Cox, R. C. Fellmeth, and J. E. Schultz (1969). *The Nader Report on the Federal Trade Commission*, New York: Richard W. Baron Publishers.

J. Davidson (1993). U.S. considers a second probe of Microsoft. *Wall Street Journal*, 2 August, p. B8.

T. J. DiLorenzo and J. C. High (1988). Antitrust and competition, historically considered. *Economic Inquiry*, **26**, July, 423–35.

B. E. Eckbo (1983). Horizontal mergers, collusion, and stockholder wealth. *Journal of Financial Economics*, **11**, 241–73.

B. E. Eckbo and P. Wier (1985). Antimerger policy under the Hart–Scott–Rodino Act: A reexamination of the market power hypothesis. *Journal of Law and Economics*, **28**, April, 119–49.

R. B. Ekelund, Jr, M. J. McDonald and R. D. Tollison (1995). Business restraints and the Clayton Act of 1914: Public- or private-interest legislation? In *The Causes and Consequences of Antitrust: The Public-Choice Perspective* (edited by F. S. McChesney and W. F. Shughart II), Chicago: The University of Chicago Press, pp. 271–86.

J. C. Ellert (1976). Mergers, antitrust law enforcement,

and stockholder returns. *Journal of Finance,* **31**, 715–32.
R. T. Ely (1887). The future of corporations. *Harper's*, July.
R. T. Ely (1900). *Monopolies and Trusts*, New York: Macmillan.
K. G. Elzinga (1969). The antimerger law: Pyrrhic victories. *Journal of Law and Economics*, **12**, April, 43–78.
R. L. Faith, D. R. Leavens, and R. D. Tollison (1982). Antitrust pork barrel. *Journal of Law and Economics*, **15**, October, 329–42.
B. S. Frey, W. M. Pommerehne, F. Schneider and G. Gilbert (1984). Consensus and dissension among economists: An empirical inquiry. *American Economic Review,* **74**, December, 986–94.
S. D. Gordon (1963). Attitudes toward trusts prior to the Sherman Act. *Southern Economic Journal*, **30**, October, 156–67.
T. W. Hazlett (1984). Interview with George Stigler. *Reason,* January, 4–48.
D. R. Henderson (1995). Antitrust busters. *Reason,* August/September, 62–64.
R. S. Higgins, W. F. Shughart II, and R. D. Tollison (1987). Dual enforcement of the antitrust laws. In *Public Choice and Regulation: A View from inside the Federal Trade Commission* (edited by R. J. Mackay, J. C. Miller III and B. Yandle), Stanford, CA: Hoover Institution Press, pp. 154–80.
R. A. Katzmann (1980). *Regulatory Bureaucracy: The Federal Trade Commission and Antitrust Policy*, Cambridge, MA: MIT Press.
J. R. Kearl, C. L. Pope, G. C. Whiting and L. T. Wimmer (1979). A confusion of economists? *American Economic Review Papers and Proceedings*, **69**, May, 28–37.
C. M. Lindsay (1976). A theory of government enterprise. *Journal of Political Economy*, **84**, October, 1061–77.
W. F. Long, R. Schramm and R. D. Tollison (1973). The economic determinants of antitrust activity. *Journal of Law and Economics*, **16**, October, 351–64.
F. S. McChesney and W. F. Shughart II (eds) (1995). *The Causes and Consequences of Antitrust: The Public-Choice Perspective,* Chicago: The University of Chicago Press.
R. E. McCormick (1984). The strategic use of regulation: A review of the literature. In *The Political Economy of Regulation: Private Interests in the Regulatory Process* (edited by R. A. Rogowsky and B. Yandle), Washington, DC: Federal Trade Commission, pp. 13–32.
R. E. McCormick and R. D. Tollison (1981). *Politicians, Legislation, and the Economy: An Inquiry into the Interest-Group Theory of Government*, Boston, MA: Martinus Nijhoff.
J. S. McGee (1958). Predatory price cutting: The Standard Oil (N.J.) case. *Journal of Law and Economics*, **1**, April, 137–69.
A. McWilliams, T. A. Turk and A. Zardkoohi (1993). Antitrust policy and mergers: The wealth effect of Supreme Court decisions. *Economic Inquiry*, **31**, October, 517–33.
M. Olson (1965). *The Logic of Collective action: Public goods and the theory of groups*, Cambridge, MA: Harvard University Press.
S. Peltzman (1991). The Handbook of Industrial Organization: A review article. *Journal of Political Economy*, **91**, February, 201–17.
J. L. Peterman (1975a). The Brown Shoe case. *Journal of Law and Economics*, **18**, April, 81–146.
J. L. Peterman (1975b). The Federal Trade Commission v. Brown Shoe Company. *Journal of Law and Economics*, **18**, October, 361–419.
R. A. Posner (1969). The Federal Trade Commission. *University of Chicago Law Review*, **37**, Autumn, 47–89.
R. A. Posner (1979). The Chicago school of antitrust analysis. *University of Pennsylvania Law Review*, **127**, April, 925–48.
A. Ramsey (1995). Keating sings to his mates' tune. *Sydney Morning Herald*, 29 April, 33.
R. A. Rogowsky (1986). The economic effectiveness of section 7 relief. *Antitrust Bulletin*, **31**, Spring, 187–233.
R. A. Rogowsky (1987). The pyrrhic victories of section 7: A political economy approach. In *Public Choice and Regulation: A View from inside the Federal Trade Commission* (edited by R. J. Mackay, J. C. Miller III and B. Yandle), Stanford, CA: Hoover Institution Press, pp. 220–39.
P. H. Rubin (1995). What do economists think about antitrust? A random walk down Pennsylvania Avenue. In *The Causes and Consequences of Antitrust: The Public-Choice Perspective* (edited by F. S. McChesney and W. F. Shughart II), Chicago: The University of Chicago Press, pp. 33–61.
S. C. Salop and D. T. Scheffman (1983). Raising rivals' costs. *American Economic Review Papers and Proceedings*, **73**, May, 267–71.
F. M. Scherer (1980). *Industrial Market Structure and Economic Performance*, 2nd edn, Boston, MA: Houghton-Mifflin.
W. F. Shughart II (1989). Antitrust policy in the Reagan administration: Pyrrhic victories? In *Regulation and the Reagan Era: Politics, Bureaucracy and the Public Interest* (edited by R. E. Meiners and B. Yandle), New York: Holmes & Meier, pp. 89–103.
W. F. Shughart II (1990). *Antitrust Policy and Interest-Group Politics*, New York: Quorum Books.
W. F. Shughart II and R. D. Tollison (1985). The positive economics of antitrust policy: A survey article. *International Review of Law and Economics*, **5**, 39–57.
W. F. Shughart II and R. D. Tollison (1987). Antitrust recidivism in Federal Trade Commission data: 1914–1982. In *Public Choice and Regulation: A View from inside the Federal Trade Commission* (edited by R. J. Mackay, J. C. Miller III and B. Yandle), Stanford, CA: Hoover Institution Press, pp. 255–80.
J. Siegfried (1975). The determinants of antitrust activity. *Journal of Law and Economics*, **18**, October, 559–74.

G. J. Stigler (1950). Monopoly and oligopoly by merger. *American Economic Review*, **40**, May, 23–34.
G. J. Stigler (1966). The economic effects of the antitrust laws. *Journal of Law and Economics*, **9**, October, 225–58.
G. J. Stigler (1971). The theory of economic regulation. *Bell Journal of Economics and Management Science*, **2**, Spring, 3–21.
G. J. Stigler (1982). The economists and the problem of monopoly. *American Economic Review Papers and Proceedings*, **72**, May, 1–11.
G. J. Stigler (ed.) (1988). *Chicago Studies in Political Economy*, Chicago: The University of Chicago Press.
R. Stillman (1983). Examining anti-trust policy towards horizontal mergers. *Journal of Financial Economics* **11**, 225–40.
R. D. Tollison (1983). Antitrust in the Reagan administration: A report from the belly of the beast. *International Journal of Industrial Organization*, **1**, 211–21.
S. Weaver (1977). *The Decision to Prosecute: Organization and Public Policy in the Antitrust Division*, Cambridge MA: MIT Press.
C. Weir (1992). Monopolies and Mergers Commission, merger reports and the public interest: A probit analysis. *Applied Economics*, **22**, January, 27–34.

Index

Printed and bound by CPI Group (UK) Ltd, Croydon, CR0 4YY
16/09/2026
14963385-0005